CODING FOR KIDS 5 BOOKS IN 1

CODING FOR KIDS IN C++

Table of Contents

Book 2: Coding for Kids in Javascript

Book 3: Coding for Teens in Javascript

Book 5: Coding for Teens in Python

Disclaimer

While the author has taken the utmost effort to ensure the accuracy of the written content, all readers are advised to follow the information mentioned herein at their own risk. The author cannot be held responsible for any personal or commercial damage caused by the information. All readers are encouraged to seek professional advice when needed.

Free Gift

We do want you to succeed in coding. To ensure your success, we are giving you a free list of projects that you can work on once you are completed with this book.

https://coding.gr8.com/

Introduction

What is Programming

Programming is the art of writing a computer program. A computer program is a set of instructions that a machine can comprehend to perform a certain task. Computer programming is how humans communicate with machines.

Computers are pretty good at following the instructions we give them.

A program is just simply a list of steps that should be followed to achieve a goal. It is just like a recipe, to prepare your favorite dish you just need to follow the instructions on the recipe.

The only issue is that computers do not speak English as we do, they speak their own language. This computer language is known as machine language.

There is a part on the computer called the interpreter, which interprets our instructions to machine language so that the computer is able to understand the instructions we are giving it. This interpreter is also known as a **compiler.**

A compiler is the interface between the programming language and the machine. A programming language is a very simple language to learn and there are numerous programming languages out there. We are only going to learn C++ in this book.

As you know, spoken languages usually have grammar. Grammar is a way of arranging words in a language to make sense to others who speak that language. Programming languages have grammar as well, which we call ***syntax***.

In order for the compiler to understand you, you have to use the proper syntax or else it will cause an error. We will at first spend a lot of time learning the syntax of our programming language.

In summary, we write a program using a programming language. The programming languages communicates with the compiler. The compiler translates the language to machine language and then runs the program. The computer reads our instructions and does what we have told it to do.

Your first programming language is usually the toughest to learn but after learning it, it becomes easier to learn other languages.

Why C++

You can do a lot after learning C++. You can make games, use the Arduino board to make cool projects or even program planes if you are allowed to do that. The only limit you have is your imagination.

The main benefit of C++ is that it is very portable between operating systems and compilers. This means that the same code can be used in Windows, Linux, Opera etc.

C++ has a large community support with developer forums, online tutorials, Facebook community groups, which is very significant for beginner programmers. It's much easier to learn as you can ask other people in the community if you get stuck.

C++ is also very scalable and flexible in multiple environments. This means that it can be used by beginner programmers and advanced professionals for different purposes. It can also be used to code games, applications, software and apps.

C++ is wildly used in graphics and is now used in emerging technologies like image processing, pattern recognition and in embedded systems like location tracing.

C++ is more efficient at using computer memory, so it saves space on your hard drive.

Why Learn Programming

Programming at its core is not really about writing code but thinking of ways to solve problems. You get to learn and appreciate that there are different ways to tackle a problem and sometimes one way is better than the other. You also learn that breaking a big problem into small parts makes your work easier.

It is also about learning how to collaborate with others. People usually assume that programmers work by themselves to solve problems, but programmers act as a team most of the time. We like sharing what we have built with others, and this enables us to learn from one another there by advancing each other's skills.

In addition, programming teaches you to never give up easily, because your programs will never work out the first time you write them. You will get errors from time to time but as a programmer you don't let them bring you down. You pick yourself up when you fall and try again.

Finally, you feel comfortable in this digital world where computers run almost everything. To you it will not be magic as you know how to use computers to do your tasks.

At the end of the day even if you don't become a programmer, you will be able to know how computers can help you out in your work and gain all these skills.

Setting Up the Workspace

In order to write code, you need at least a text editor and a compiler.

A text editor is just a program that enables you to write and save code as a file.

Files usually have extensions to their file names to indicate the kind of file it is. When writing
C++ files, the files will have the extension .cpp , example main.cpp

We are going to use an application known as Code::Blocks to write, compile and run our programs. Code::Blocks is what is known as an IDE , integrated development environment.

An IDE has everything you need to write, compile and run a program in one place.

Below is a picture of the layout of the Code::Blocks IDE

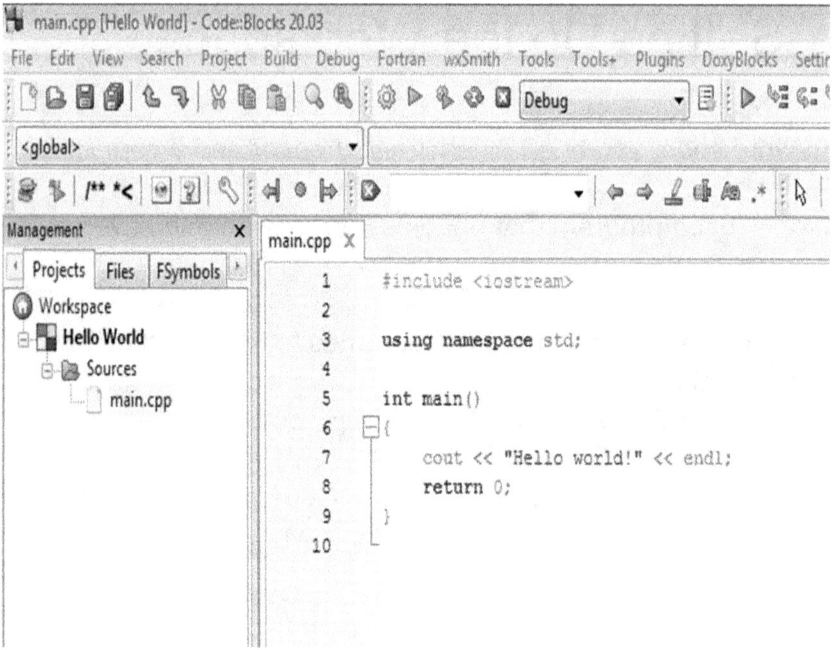
main.cpp [Hello World] - Code::Blocks 20.03
File Edit View Search Project Build Debug Fortran wxSmith Tools Tools+ Plugins DoxyBlocks
Debug
<global>
Management
Projects Files FSymbols
Workspace
Hello World
Sources
main.cpp
main.cpp
#include <iostream>
using namespace std;
int main()
{
cout << "Hello world!" << endl;
return 0;
}

Downloading and Installing Code::Blocks

You will need:

1. A laptop/ Desktop
2. Internet Connection
3. Web browser such as Chrome, Windows Edge or Firefox

Go to this website and download the Code::Blocks application: https://www.fosshub.com/Code-Blocks.html?dwl=codeblocks-20.03mingw-setup.exe

Just copy and paste the link to the browser

Note: please ensure that you download the file named Code Blocks Windows 64 bit (including compiler).

This version includes the compiler which we need

After that just install the application and open it when done:

You can head over to the Code::Blocks website at the following link: https://www.codeblocks.org/ to learn more about it. It also includes user manual and links to download the IDE for other operating systems

Hello World in C++

The first program that all programmers write when learning a new programming language is known as Hello World.

It is just basically writing a program that displays the words 'Hello World' to the screen. Since we are programmers now, we say that we are *printing* the words 'Hello World' to the screen.

I will be giving out code examples, and you will have to type the examples in the Code::Blocks and click on the build and run button to compile and execute the code in order to see the results.

Creating A Project in Code::Blocks

In order to run code in Code::Blocks we have to first create a project. So first of all we need to open up Code::Blocks.

To create a project, click on **File > New > Project**

In the pop-up window select **Console application** and click on the button **Go**

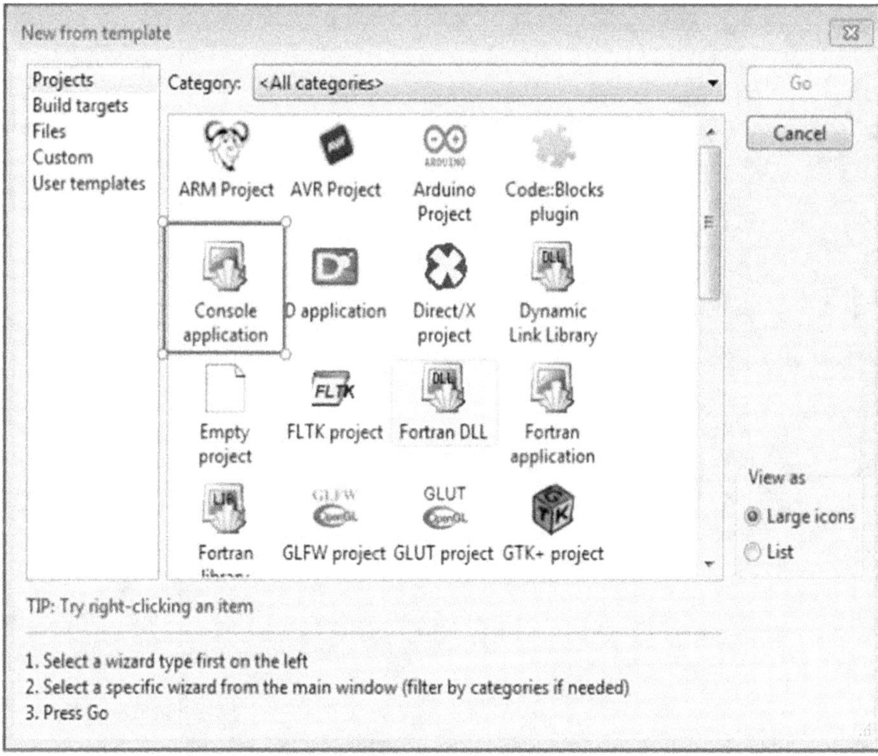

Ensure you select **C++** in this window
Click **Next** on the information window

Give the Project a title, for now it is **Hello World**. Select which folder it will be saved at.

Ensure that you have **GNU GCC Compiler** selected as the compiler and click on **Finish.**

Now on the left-hand side, under Hello World, click on the **+** icon next to the **Sources folder** to reveal the **main.cpp** file. Double click on it to display the file on the editor window on the right-hand side.

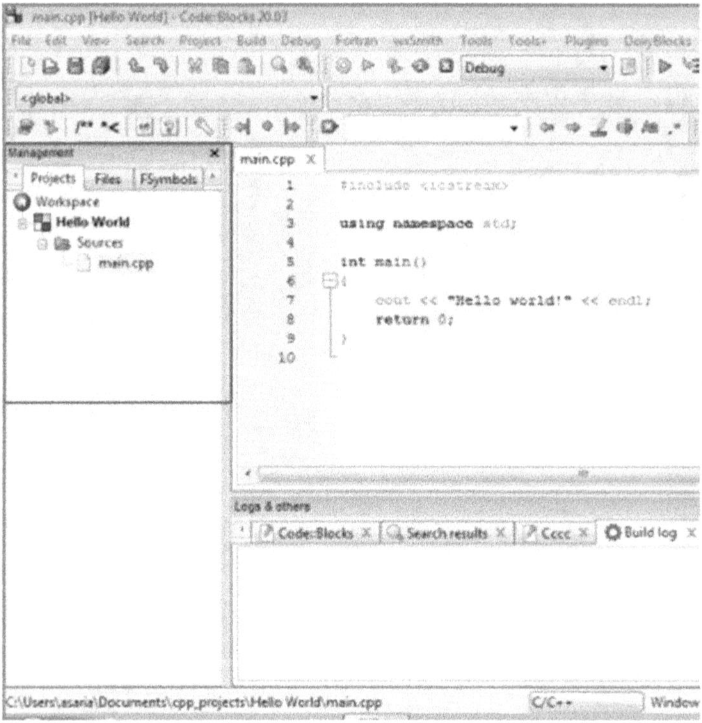

The code in the editor looks like the example below

Code

```
#include <iostream>
 using namespace std;

int main()
{

     cout << "Hello World" << endl;

     return 0;
```

```
}
```

I am pretty sure that the above code looks overwhelming when you first see it. But we are going to understand what it all means by the end of a few chapters. For now hang in there as I try to explain the main part of this program.
The trick with programming is to persevere as things get easier the more you learn.

Let's first run the code.

Running the code

To run the code, we have to compile it first.

In Code::Blocks, we use the term *build* instead of compile. This is because a project usually consists of multiple C++ files and we call the process of compiling all of them building.

There are three buttons on top of the editor that enable us to build and run our project.

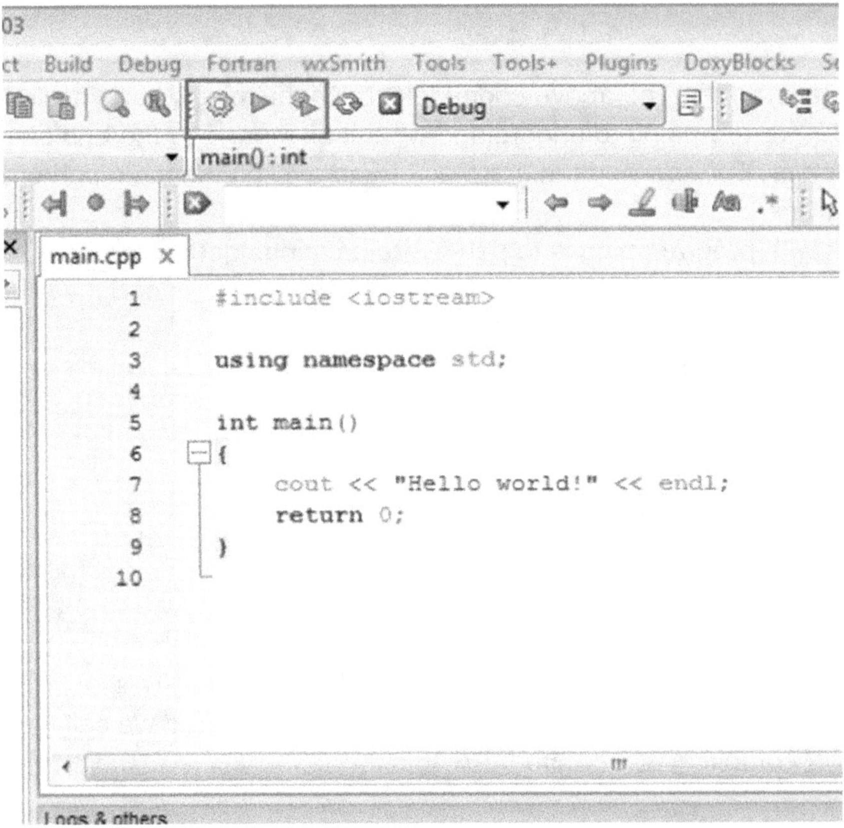

The yellow gear button enables you to build the project, the green play button enables you to run the build project, while the third, which is a combination of the gear and play button, enables you to build and run the project. Click on the combination of the two to execute the project.

A pop-up window will appear with the words 'Hello World' as shown below.

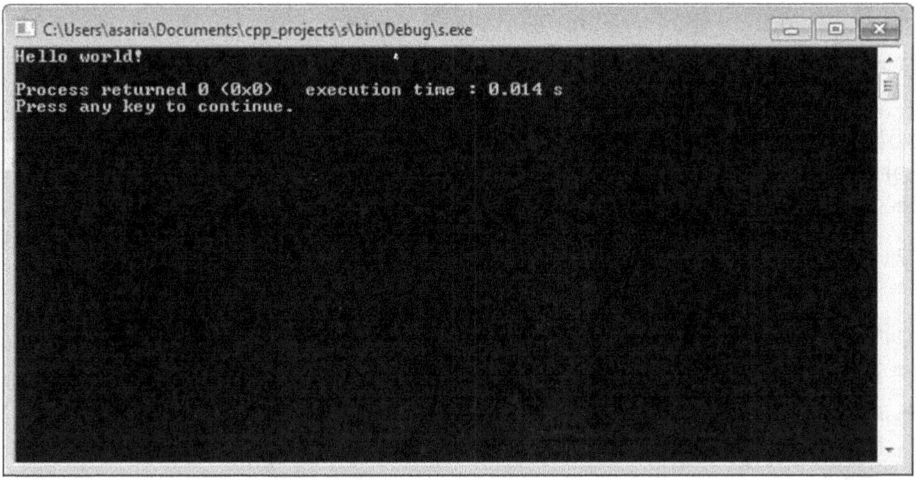

This is what is known as the **console** or **terminal**. The console shows the output in C++. Just close the window to get rid of it.

NOTE: make sure that you save you file before building and running it, this can be done by pressing **Control-s (Ctrl+s)** after every change

Explanation of the code

The main line in this program, is the line:

```
cout << “Hello World” << endl;
```

First of all, notice that the line ends with a semicolon (;), this is very important as it indicates the end of this instruction.

cout is just the programmer way of calling a screen, you can think of it as the short form of console output.

The symbols **<<** just mean display the things after me on the screen

'Hello World' is the text that we want to display on the screen. Notice that it is surrounded by double quotes. The double quotes are part of the syntax and are very important.

We call text surrounded by double quotes a ***string.***

The next << symbol over means, add what's after me to the text 'Hello world'. In programming we call this **concatenation** that is adding two strings together

endl, means add a newline, a newline is just like pressing enter while typing something on the computer, it takes you to a next line below the current text

As you can see when writing programs, we do not just write it in plain English, we follow some specific rules known as the *syntax* of the language.

Exercise

1. Change the text so that the program prints out your name, build and run the code.

2. Write the line of code **cout << “Hello World”;** two times and see what is printed on the console. How is that different from writing **cout << 'Hello World' << endl;** two times

3. Create a new project and give it any name you like and store it in a different folder location.
    a. For this new project click the run icon and notice what happens
    b. For this new project click the build gear icon then the run icon individually and note what happens.

Variables

In this chapter I will first take you through the main parts of the computer that are important in programming.

The main part of the computer is known as the processor. This is what actually reads your code and does what you instructed.

In addition, there is a storage area known as **RAM**, which stands for **Random Access Memory**. This is where everything you need is stored, even your program is stored here.

You can think of it as a bunch of shelves with boxes where you can store things. In addition, these boxes are of different sizes and type. Hence you can determine what you can store in them.

In addition, we can label these boxes so that we can refer to the name later easily.

Variable Assignment

A variable is a name given to a value that is stored in memory.

A variable name is also known as an **identifier.**

You can think of a variable as a box where we place our value in, and a variable name as a label we place on the box.

There is also a thing called data type assigned to each box. A data type is a type of information that is stored in a box. That means that the particular variable can store only a particular type of data. Examples of data types include strings, numbers, booleans etc.

Below is an example of a variable assignment. We write it in Code::Blocks in a new project called variables, save the file by pressing **Control-S** then build and run.

Example code

main.cpp

```
#include <iostream>
  using namespace std;

  int main() {

      int radius = 20;
      cout << radius << endl;
        radius = 40;
      cout << radius << endl;
      return 0;
  }
```

Above we have declared a variable of the name *radius* of data type int, meaning integer and initialized it to the value 20.

int is what we call the **data type**. Using the box analogy a data type determines the type of the box to store our value. The value which we store is 20. The variable name is called ***radius***, which means the label on the box is radius.

The value of the variable can change throughout the program as long as it is of the same data type. In the above program, we change the value to 40.

This is acceptable as 40 is an int (integer) data type.

Data types

Below is a list of data types available and the kind and range of values they represent. Each data type has an example associated with it.

int

The data type **int** stands for integer. An integer is a whole number, meaning that it cannot have a decimal to it. Examples of integers are 1,0,45,768,23343 etc.

Example: int radius = 2;

long

The data type **long** is also a whole number, but the numbers used can be a lot bigger than int. long variables can hold up to 20 digits, while in variables can only hold 10 digits.
For example, below, **x**, **y** and **result** are long variables that can hold numbers up to 20 digits.

main.cpp

```
#include<iostream>
using namespace std;

int main(){
        long x = 9988891919;
        long y = 3465829;
        long result = x * y;
        cout << result;
        return 0;
}
```

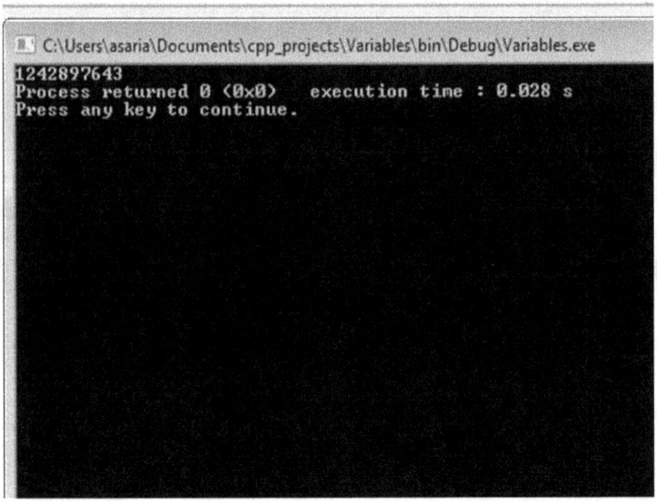
C:\Users\asaria\Documents\cpp_projects\Variables\bin\Debug\Variables.exe
1242897643
Process returned 0 (0x0)   execution time : 0.028 s
Press any key to continue.

float

Represent numbers with decimals places. See example below. pi is a float variable with a value of 3.142 and areaofcircle is another float variable.

main.cpp

```
#include<iostream>
using namespace std;

int main(){
    float pi = 3.142;
    int radius = 3;
    float areaOfCircle = pi * radius * radius;
    cout << areaOfCircle;
    return 0;
}
```

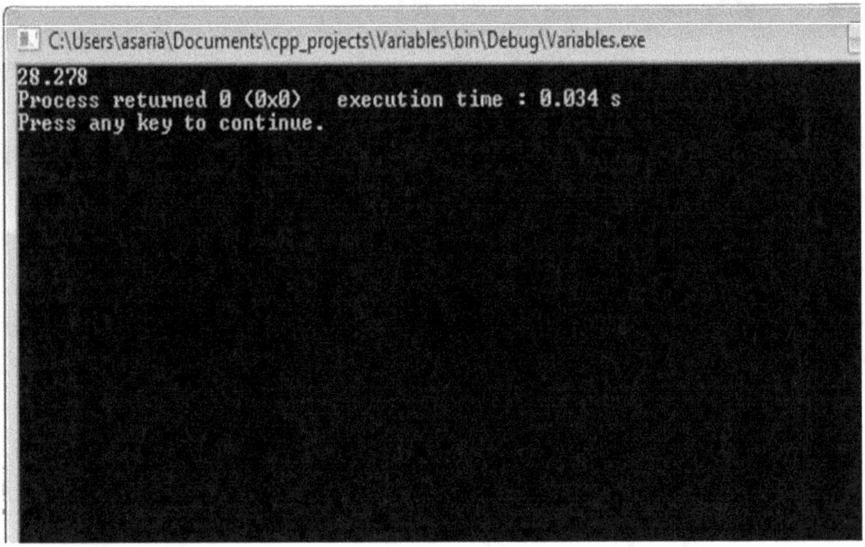
C:\Users\asaria\Documents\cpp_projects\Variables\bin\Debug\Variables.exe
28.278
Process returned 0 (0x0)   execution time : 0.034 s
Press any key to continue.

double

A double variable can hold numbers that contain decimals places with higher precision and can hold more decimal places (up to 15 decimal places).

In below example, acceleration, mass and force are three double variables that can each hold numbers that contain up to 15 decimal places.

main.cpp

```
#include<iostream>
using namespace std;

int main(){
    double acceleration = 9.98;
    double mass = 30.03;
    double force = acceleration * mass;
    cout << force;
    return 0;
}
```

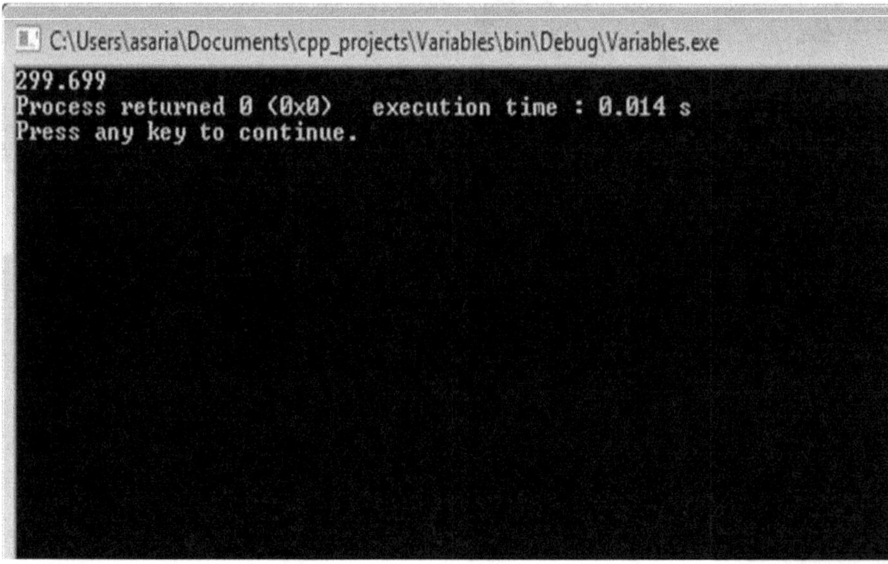
C:\Users\asaria\Documents\cpp_projects\Variables\bin\Debug\Variables.exe
299.699
Process returned 0 (0x0)   execution time : 0.014 s
Press any key to continue.

bool

It stands for boolean.
It can only hold two values, the value **true** or **false**.
The boolean variable is used for conditionals.
In the example below, two boolean variables **isHungry** and **isSleepy** are declared.
If **isHungry** is true, the program prints **“I am hungry”** on the screen.
If **isSleepy** is true, the program prints **“I am sleepy”** on the screen.

main.cpp

```
#include<iostream>
using namespace std;

int main(){
    bool isHungry = true;
    bool isSleepy = false;
    if(isHungry){
        cout << "I am hungry" << endl;
    }
    if(isSleepy){
        cout << "I am sleepy" << endl;
    }

    isSleepy = true;
    if(isSleepy){
        cout << "I am going to bed" << endl;
    }

    return 0;
}
```

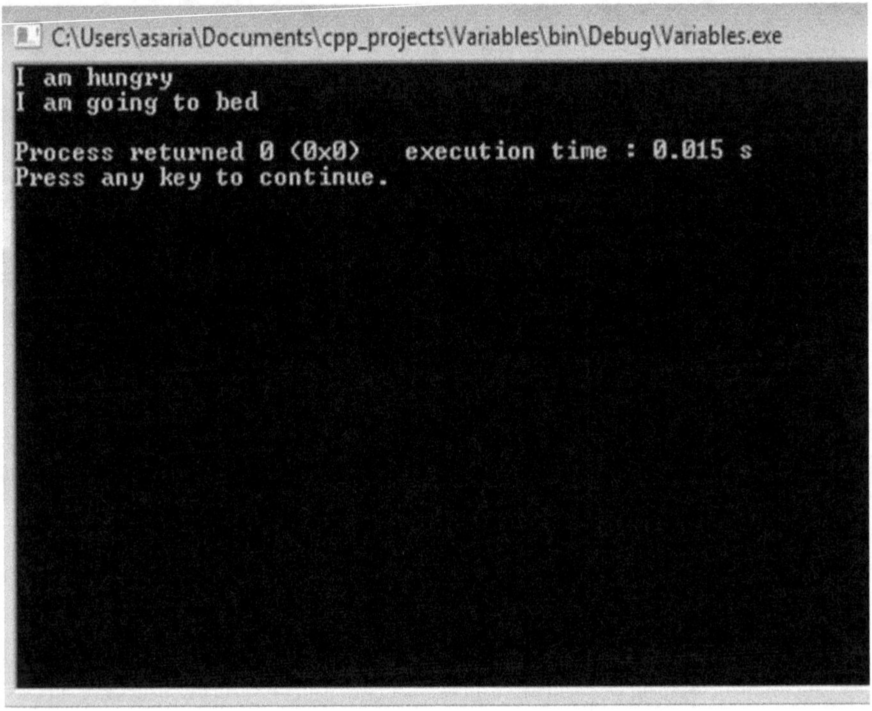
C:\Users\asaria\Documents\cpp_projects\Variables\bin\Debug\Variables.exe
I am hungry
I am going to bed
Process returned 0 (0x0)   execution time : 0.015 s
Press any key to continue.

char

char stands for character. char is a variable that can hold only one value. The value is a string of length 1. In below example, **excellent** is a char variable that holds the grade of a student in Mathematics.

main.cpp

```
#include<iostream>
using namespace std;

int main(){
    char excellent = 'A';
    cout << "Congratulations you got an " << excellent << " in maths" << endl;
    return 0;
}
```

C:\Users\asaria\Documents\cpp_projects\Variables\bin\Debug\Variables.exe

```
Congratulations you got an A in maths

Process returned 0 (0x0)   execution time : 0.015 s
Press any key to continue.
```

string

A string is a variable used to store text. It can hold a string of any length. In the below example, **yourName** is a variable that holds the value **"Catherine"**.

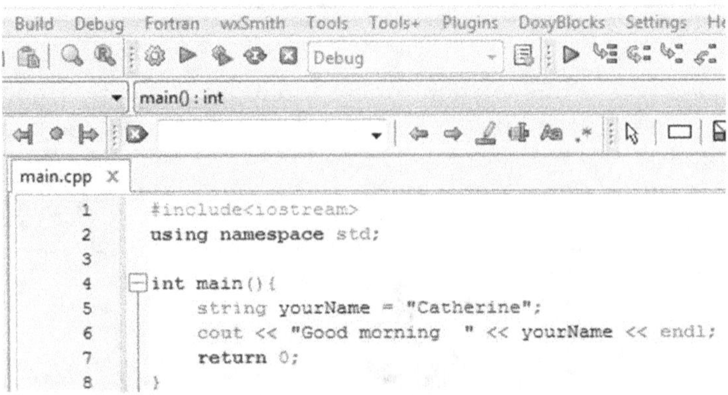

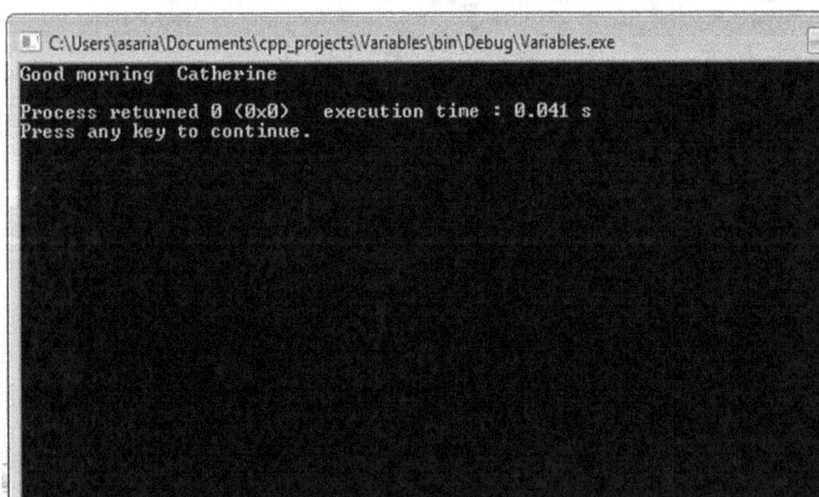

Variable names

A C++ variable name must start with either a letter or an underscore and all the rest of the characters must be letters, digits or an underscore.

Examples of valid variable names are:

```
x
x1
x_1_abc
RATE
bigBonus_
```

Examples of invalid variable names:

```
 12
3x
%change data
-1 PROG.CPP
```

The first three, 12 3x %change, are not allowed because they do not start with a letter or an underscore.

C++ is also case sensitive, meaning that the following are three distinct variable names:

```
Rate
RATE
Rate
```

Camel Case

Camel case is a programming practice where multiple words are written without spaces and the first letter of each word is capitalized (except for the first word)

The word *end of car* would become: endOfCar
Camel case is a commonly used programming practice to name variables.

Keywords

Keywords are names that cannot be used as variable names as they are reserved for programming language syntax.

If you use them as variable names the compiler will throw errors, or you might end up changing the basic functionality of some basic function.

Examples of keywords include the basic data types, such as int, bool and the rest, and names such as struct and class.

Comments

Sometimes we want to explain our code so that others can understand what we did. In the future that information will help us remember what we did as we go through the code.

In programming we achieve this by writing comments within our code. There are two types of comments, single line comments and multiline comments.

Single line comments begin with two forward slashes (*//*) while multiline comments sit in between the following symbols: */**/*

Examples of comments:

```
// Test Code

/* Line 1 of Comments
Line 2 of Comments */
```

Declaring variables

All variables must be declared or defined before they are used.

To declare/define a variable you just need to specify a data type and a variable name followed by a semicolon:

When you declare a variable without giving it a value, we say that the variable is *uninitialized.*
Uninitialized variable will have a random value in it.

Giving an uninitialized variable a value is known as *initializing* it.

You can also declare and initialize a variable at the same time.

In this example we are going to make use of comments and declare some variables whose value we will print to the console

Create a new project in Code::Blocks, write the following code, build and run it.

Example code

```
#include <iostream>
  using namespace std;

  int main() {

/*
    This is a multiline comment
    As can be seen , it spans
    multiple lines
*/
      int length; // declaring the variable length
      int width; // declaring the variable width

      length = 20; // initializing the variable ler
      width = 20;// initializing the variable widt

      int depth = 40; // declaring and initializin

      cout << length << endl;
      cout << width << endl;
      cout << depth << endl;

      return 0;
  }
```

Explanation

In the above program, in the main block of code, we first begin by writing a multiline comment by writing in between /**/.
We then declare two variables of type int which are *length* and *width* without initializing them, which we do later.

We then declare and initialize the variable *depth* of type int to 40.
Finally, we print the values of length, width and depth to the console each on its own separate line.

Exercise

1. Write a program that contains statements that output the values of five or six variables that have been defined, but not initialized. Compile and run the program. What is the output? Explain.
2. Create a string variable with your name and print it to the console.
3. Create a char variable and print it to the console
4. Create a bool variable and print it to the console
5. Create a float variable and print it to the console
6. Create a long variable named, time of day, in camel case and print it to the console

Mathematics Operations

In this section we will make a small calculator that only performs multiplication of two numbers. The program will ask us for two numbers to multiply and print the result of multiplication.

First, we will go through how to perform mathematic operations in C++

Addition

Addition is done using the + operator

Addition Example code

main.cpp

```
#include<iostream>
using namespace std;

int main(){

    int x = 1;
    int y = 2;
    int sum = x + y ;
    cout << sum ;
    return 0;
}
```

The output of the code will be **3**, which is the sum of x and y.

Subtraction

Subtraction is done using the - operator

Subtraction Example code

main.cpp

```
#include<iostream>
using namespace std;

int main(){

    int x = 1;
    int y = 2;
    int difference = x - y ;
    cout << difference ;
    return 0;
}

```

The output of the code will be **-1**

Multiplication

Multiplication is done using the * operator

Multiplication Example code

main.cpp

```
#include<iostream>
using namespace std;

int main(){

    int x = 3;
    int y = 2;
    int multiplication = x * y ;
    cout << multiplication ;
    return 0;
}
```

The output of the code will be **6**

Division

Division is done using the / operator, this returns the quotient of the division

Division Example code

main.cpp

```
    #include<iostream>
using namespace std;

int main(){

    int x = 3;
    int y = 2;
    int quotient = x / y ;
    cout << quotient ;
    return 0;
}
```

The output of above code will be 1.5

Remainder

In order to get the remainder of a division use the modulo operator which is represented by the symbol **%**.

```
main.cpp

#include<iostream>
using namespace std;

int main(){

    int x = 3;
    int y = 2;
    int remainder = x % y ;
    cout << remainder ;
    return 0;
}
```

The output of the code will be **1**, which is the reminder when x is divided by y.

Getting Input from users

So far, we have just been printing things to the console without any input from the user. In this section we are going to make our program more exciting by asking for input from users.

cin

cin is use to accept input from the keyboard, it can be thought of as standing for console input

Example code

main.cpp

```
#include <iostream>
  using namespace std;

  int main() {
    int num;

    cout << "Enter a number: ";

    // take integer input
    cin >> num;

    cout << "You entered: " << num;

    return 0;
}
```

Explanation

Here we first create a variable called *num* of type int which we will use to store the value we get from the keyboard input.

We the ask the user for some input, and just print it back to the console: 'You entered: 1', if you type in 1 in the console

A simple calculator

We will have to ask the user for two numbers to multiply, and the show the result of multiplication to the user.

Example Code

main.cpp

```
#include <iostream>
 using namespace std;

 int main() {
   int num1;
   int num2;

   // prompt to enter num1
   cout << "Enter a num1: ";

   cin >> num1;

   // prompt to enter num2
   cout << "Enter a num2: ";

   cin >> num2;


   int multiplication = num1 * num2;
   cout << "Result of multiplication:  " << multiplication;

   return 0;
}
```

Explanation

We first declare two int type variables that will store the use input that is num1 and num2

We prompt the user for num1, then store it in the corresponding variable using cin. We do the same to num2

We then perform multiplication on the two and display the result to the user

Exercise

1. Convert each of the following mathematical formulas to a C++ expression, each variable getting its value from the user input
    1. 3x
    2. 3x + y
    3. (x + y)/7
    4. (3x + y) / (z + 2)

2. Write a program that takes in school marks in 6 subjects using 6 input variables. Calculate total marks and average marks for the subjects

3. Write a program that takes in a integer from the user and determines whether it is an even number or an odd number. Hint: Use modulo

Functions

A function is a group of lines of code that perform a given task. Each function has been assigned a name and will be referenced by that name in the program.

In C++ functions are expected to return a value and the data type of the value to be returned is usually indicated when defining a function.

In this section we will write a function that calculates the area of a rectangle

Example of a function

The area of a rectangle is equal to its length multiplied by width, so below is a function to calculate it

Write this before the main function as so:

main.cpp

```
1  #include <iostream>
2  using namespace std;
3
4  //defining the function named areaOfRectangle
5  int areaOfRectangle( int length , int width){
6      int area = length * width;
7      return area;
8  }
9
10 int main() {
11
12     return 0;
13 }
14
15
16
```

Explanation

int is the data type of the value to be returned, so we expect the function to give us back an integer when we run it. This is indicated by the line ***return area;*** just above the closing curly brace in line 7. Notice the variable ***area*** is declared as an integer type since that is the variable that the function returns.

areaOfRectangle is the name we give to our function. Notice that it is written in camel case.

What follows the name of a function is a pair of parentheses, in the parenthesis we declare two variables, and these variables are known as **parameters.** In the example above, **length** and **width** are the parameters.

They will hold values we pass to the function when we run it and they can be accessed with the function's block of code.

We then have our code in curly braces so as to mark it as the lines of code associated with that function name.

Finally, we have the ***return*** statement.

Running a function

Look at the code below

main.cpp

```
#include <iostream>
using namespace std;

int areaOfRectangle( int length , int width){
  int area = length * width;
  return area;
}
  int main() {

    // calling the areaOfRectangle function
    // length = 4 and width = 5

    int area = areaOfRectangle(4,5);

    cout << "Area is: " << area << endl;
    return 0;
}

```

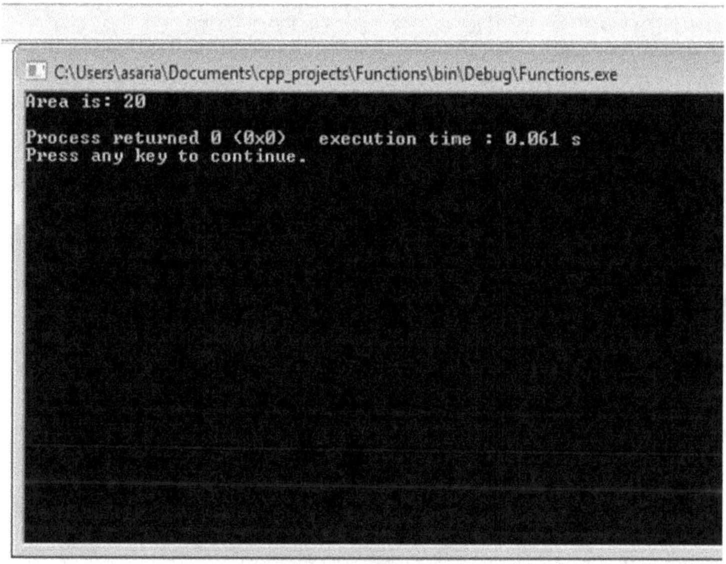

Explanation

When we want to run a function, we usually say that we are **calling** that function.

Some functions take in values when there are being called like ours does, we call these values ***arguments*** of the function.

Notice the syntax used to pass arguments to functions, we first write the function name and in between an opening and closing parenthesis we write the arguments, separated by commas.

So, in our example, we are calling the function ***areaOfRectangle*** passing in the two arguments, that is, 4 and 5.

We expect the function to return a value, which is the area that has been calculated and the value of the area calculated to be of the data type integer.

For this reason, we assign the returned value to the variable named *area* of type i*nt*.

We then print the result to the screen. In this case, the area of the rectangle is 20 so that is the output shown on the screen.

Void Functions

The functions known as void functions are functions that do not return anything after being called

Example code

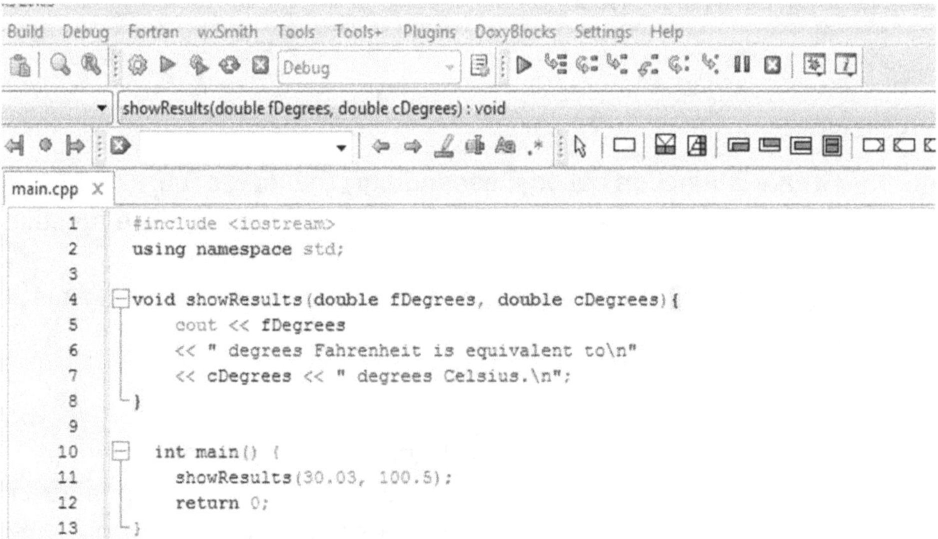

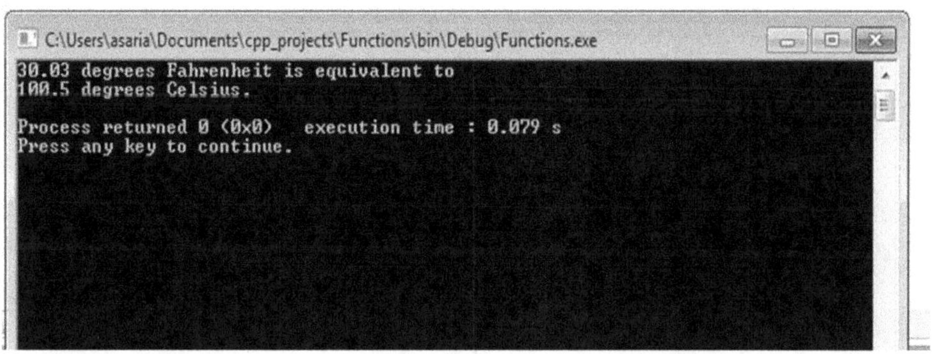

Explanation

Notice that the specified return type is void and that we do not use the return keyword in the body of the function.

Apart from that there are not any other differences with the way we define other non-void functions.

Exercise

1. Create a function called Descending() that takes four arguments. Each argument is a number of type int. The function returns true if the four numbers are in descending order; otherwise, it returns false. For example, Descending(4, 3, 3, 1) and Descending(3, 2, 2, 1) both return true, whereas Descending(2, 1, 3, 2) returns false.

2. Create a function called isOdd()that takes in one argument of type int and returns a Boolean value. The function returns true if the input is an odd number. It returns false if it is an even number.

3. What is the output of the following program?

```
#include <iostream>
using namespace std;
void sayhi();
void hide(int audiencenumber);
int main()
{
        sayhi();
        hide(6);
        cout << "Extra time:\n";
        hide(2);
        sayhi();
```

```
        cout << "End of program.\n";
        return 0;
}
void sayhi()
{
        cout << "Hello\n";
}
void hide(int audiencenumber)
{
        if (audiencenumber < 5)
        return;
        cout << "Bye\n";
}
```

4. Write a function that calculates the perimeter of a circle, that has a parameter called radius of type int and returns type double. Use pi as a double variable of value 3.142.

A Short message from the Author:

Hey, are you enjoying the book? I'd love to hear your thoughts!

Many readers do not know how hard reviews are to come by, and how much they help an author.

I would be incredibly thankful if you could take just 60 seconds to write a brief review on Amazon, even if it's just a few sentences!

>> Click here to leave a quick review

Thank you for taking the time to share your thoughts!

Conditional Statement

We usually want to do something only when a certain condition is true. For example, if it is sunny outside then we go out and play, else we stay at home.

The statement, it is sunny outside, can only either be true or false.

In programming we have a data type that can only store the value true or false, this data type is known as a **boolean**. In C++ we usually shorten it to **bool**.

In addition, we sometimes want to run lines of code only when a certain condition is true, and we achieve this using **if** statement. Let's do an example, which will make it easier to understand

Example Code

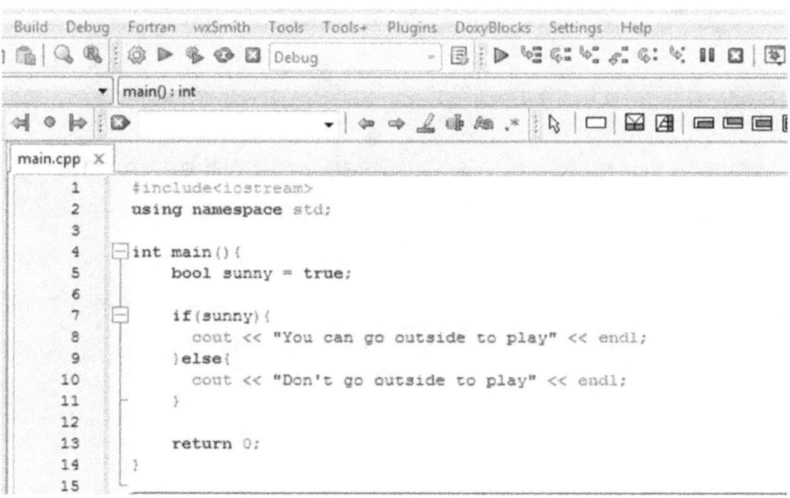

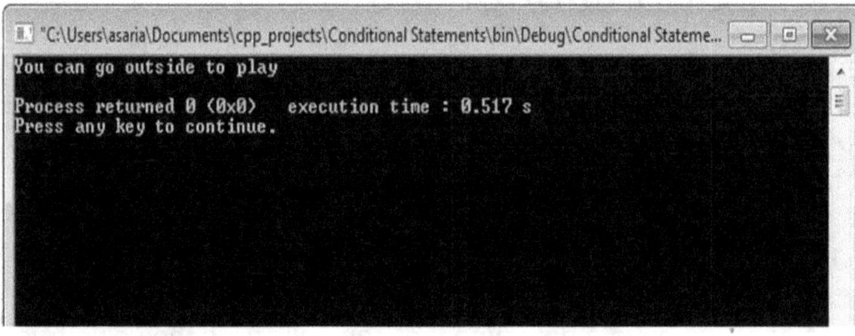

Explanation

In the above example, we first create a variable called *sunny* that holds a boolean value since it has the data type *bool.*

Using the *if* statement we check whether it is true that it is sunny, if it is, we print "You can go outside to play" to the screen else we print "Don't go outside to play"

Exercise

Change the variable *sunny* to be *false* and see what will be printed.

Comparison Operators

Comparison operators compare two values and return either true or false

Examples of comparison operators are:

Less than (<)
It returns true if the value on the left is less than the value on the right. Otherwise, it returns false.

Greater than (>)
It returns true if the value on the left is greater than the value on the right. Otherwise, it returns false.

Less than or equal to (<=)
It returns true if the value on the left is less than or equal to the value on the right. Otherwise, it returns false.

Greater than or equal to (>=)
It returns true if the value on the left is greater than or equal to the value on the right. Otherwise, it returns false.

Equal to (==)
It returns true if the value on the left is equal to the value on the right. Otherwise, it returns false.

Not equal to (!=)
It returns true if the value on the left is not equal to the value on the right. Otherwise, it returns false.

Example of use of comparison operators

Let's say you want to print to the screen the string 'x is greater than 5' if x is indeed greater than 5 else you print 'x is less than or equal to 5'

main.cpp

```
#include<iostream>
using namespace std;

int main(){
    int x = 3;

    if(x > 5){
        cout << "x is greater than 5" << endl;
    }else{
        cout << "x is less than or equal to 5" << endl;
    }
    return 0;
}
```

"C:\Users\asaria\Documents\cpp_projects\Conditional Statements\bin\Debug\Conditional Stateme...

```
x is less than or equal to 5

Process returned 0 (0x0)   execution time : 0.021 s
Press any key to continue.
```

Building Boolean Expressions

A **Boolean expression** is any expression that has one of two values. It is either true or false. It is basically an expression that compares two values and returns true/false.

Two comparisons can be combined using the "and" operator, which is **&&** in C++. For example, the following Boolean expression is true provided a is bigger in value than 5 and a is smaller than 10:

(5 < a) && (a < 10)

The above operation returns true if a is between 5 and 10 (not including 5,10).

When two comparisons are connected using a **&&**, the entire expression is true, provided both comparisons are true; otherwise, the entire expression is false.

You can also combine two comparisons using the "or" operator, which is spelled || in C++. For example, the following is true provided b is less than 2 or b is greater than 9:

(b < 2) || (b > 9)

The above expression returns true if b is less than 2 or b is greater than 9.

In an expression that uses || operation, the expression is true provided that either of the comparisons is true. If both expressions are false, then the expression is false.

A Boolean expression can be negated using the ! operation. For example,

!(a > b)
Returns true if “a is not greater than b”.

In most cases, there is no need to use the exclamation (!) operator.

For example,
!(a > b) is the same as to a <= b

Truth Tables

The following are known as truth tables. It indicates all the possibilities that a combination of each expression can be and the resulting boolean value.

AND

expression1	expression2	expression1 && expression2
true	True	True
true	False	False
false	True	False
false	False	False

OR

expression1	expression2	expression1 || expression2
true	True	True
true	False	True
false	True	True
false	False	False

NOT

expression	! expression
true	False
false	True

Example of Boolean expressions

Let's say that you only buy food when you are hungry, and you have money. To represent this in code it will be something like this.

Example

main.cpp X

```
#include<iostream>
using namespace std;


int main(){

    bool isHungry = true;
    bool hasMoney = true;

    if( isHungry && hasMoney){
        cout << "I will buy food" << endl;
    }else{
        cout << "I can't but  food" << endl;
    }

    return 0;
```

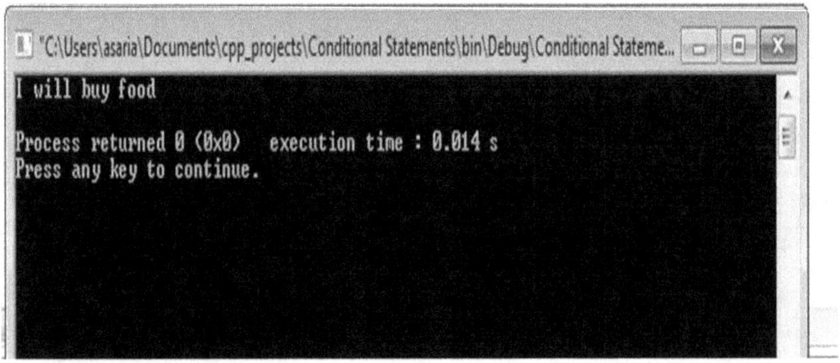

Explanation

The string 'I will buy food' only gets printed when the variables **isHungry** and **hasMoney** are true. Otherwise, the string 'I can't buy food' is printed.
Change the program to print 'I will buy food' if **isHungry** is true or **hasMoney** is true.

Exercise

1. Write a program that outputs the word **Small** if the score is less than 10 and **Big** if the value of the score is bigger than 100.

2. Write a program that outputs the word **Success** provided the variable **test** is greater than or equal to 50 and the value of the variable **codingPrograms** is greater than 5. Otherwise, the programs output the word **failure**. The variables **test** and **codingPrograms** are both of type int.

3. Write a program that outputs the word **Danger** if the variable **temp** is greater than 37, or the value of the variable **press** is

greater than 1, or both. Otherwise, the program prints the word **Great**. The variables **temp** and **press** are both of type int.

Loops

Loops enable us to repeat a set of instructions a fixed number of times. It can also be repeated forever if we wanted to.

There are usually two types of loops, *finite loops* and *infinite loops.*

Finite loops repeat the set of instructions a countable number of times while infinite loops repeat a set of instructions forever.

How we specify loops

In C++ there are two ways of declaring loops.
One way is to use the **for** keyword and the other is to use the **while** keyword.

For loops

Let's say you want to print out your name 10 times to the console, you might think of writing out the instruction *'cout << "My name"<< endl;'* 10 times.
Using For loops is a good way to prevent repetition of the same statement and shorten the code.

Example

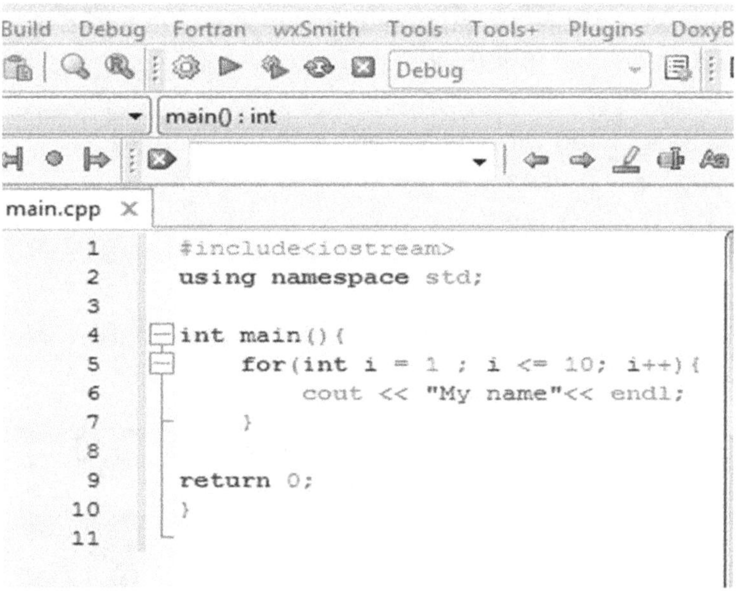
Build Debug Fortran wxSmith Tools Tools+ Plugins DoxyB
Debug
main() : int
main.cpp
#include<iostream>
using namespace std;
int main(){
for(int i = 1 ; i <= 10; i++){
cout << "My name"<< endl;
}
return 0;
}

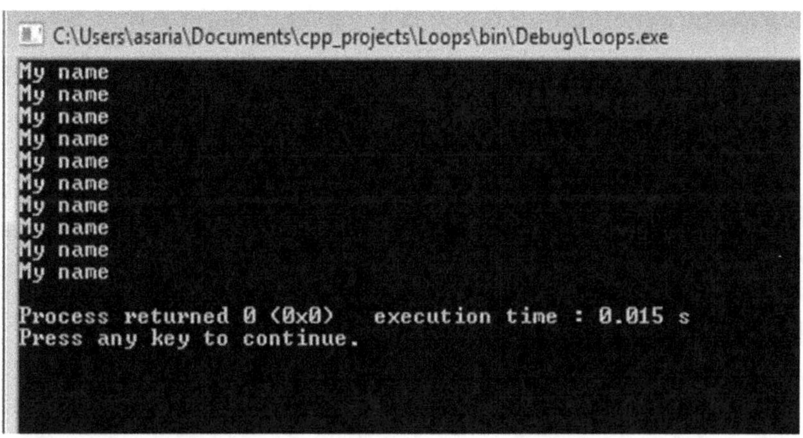
C:\Users\asaria\Documents\cpp_projects\Loops\bin\Debug\Loops.exe
My name
My name
My name
My name
My name
My name
My name
My name
My name
My name
Process returned 0 (0x0) execution time : 0.015 s
Press any key to continue.

Explanation

To use the **for loop** we specify the number of times we want to run the block of code associated with that for loop.

The block of code associated with the for loop is in between the opening and closing curly braces
{
}

In our code the associated block of code has only the line: cout << "My name" << endl;

Inside the opening and closing parenthesis associated with the *for* keyword we specify three important things separated by two semicolons

The first is what number to begin counting at, for us, we begin counting from 1 so we declare the integer variable **i** holding the value 1.

The second, separated from the first by a semicolon, is the condition that should be true in order for the block of code associated with for loop to be executed. We usually use comparison operators such as >, <, <=, >= in this section.

In our case , **i <= 10**, means only run the block of code if the value of the variable i is less or equal to 10, otherwise stop the loop and proceed with the rest of the program.

Finally, the third part, separated by a semicolon from the second part, increments the count variable, in our case we increment by 1 using the special notation **i++**

In addition, this increment occurs after the block of code runs

Exercise

1. Change the program to loop over our text 100 times

Example Using Counter Inside Loop

We can use our declared integer inside the associated block of code, for example, we could print the value 1 to 10 with the code below.

main.cpp

```
#include<iostream>
using namespace std;

int main(){


    for(int i = 1 ; i <= 10; i++){
        cout << i << endl;
    }

return 0;
}
```

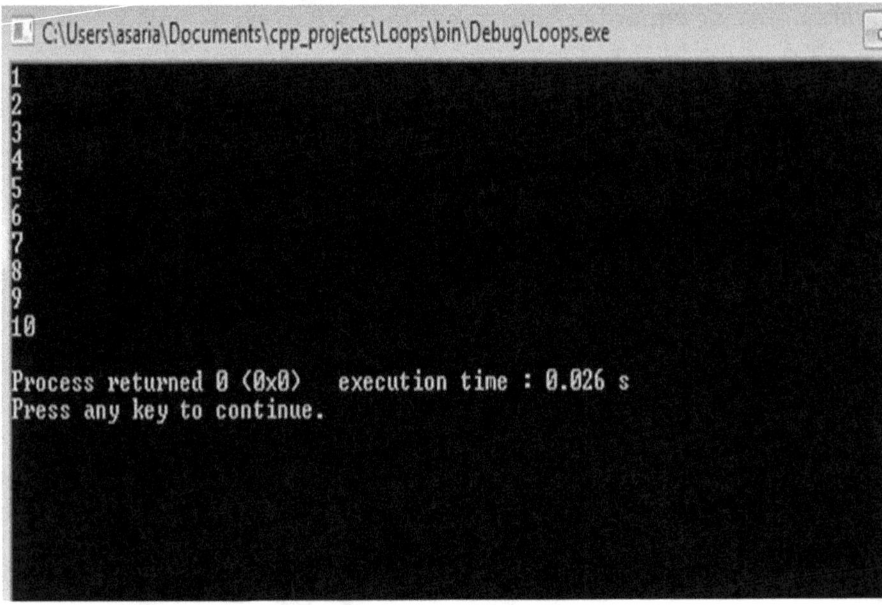

while loops

while loops are similar to *for* loops, with the only difference being that it is only the condition to be met that is in the parenthesis associated with the while keyword.

Example

main.cpp

```
#include<iostream>
using namespace std;

int main(){

    int i = 1;

    while( i <= 10){
      cout << "Hi from the while loop"<< endl;
      i++;
    }

    return 0;
}
```

Explanation

We first declare where we will start counting from in the line: **int i = 1;**

while(i <= 10), means while the value of the variable ***i*** is less or equal to 10 run the associated block of code.

Notice that just before the closing brace we increment the value of i by 1.

The while loop then repeats to check whether i is less or equal to 10, if it is, it executes the associated block of code. If i is greater than 10, the block of code is not executed, and the program goes to the next instructions

Infinite loops

Infinite loops occur when the condition that *for* loop or *while* loop checks in order to decide whether to run their associated block of code, is always **true**.

So, it basically runs forever.

Example

main.cpp

```
#include<iostream>
using namespace std;

int main(){


    while( true ){
      cout << "Hi from the infinite while loop"<< endl;

    }

    return 0;
}
```

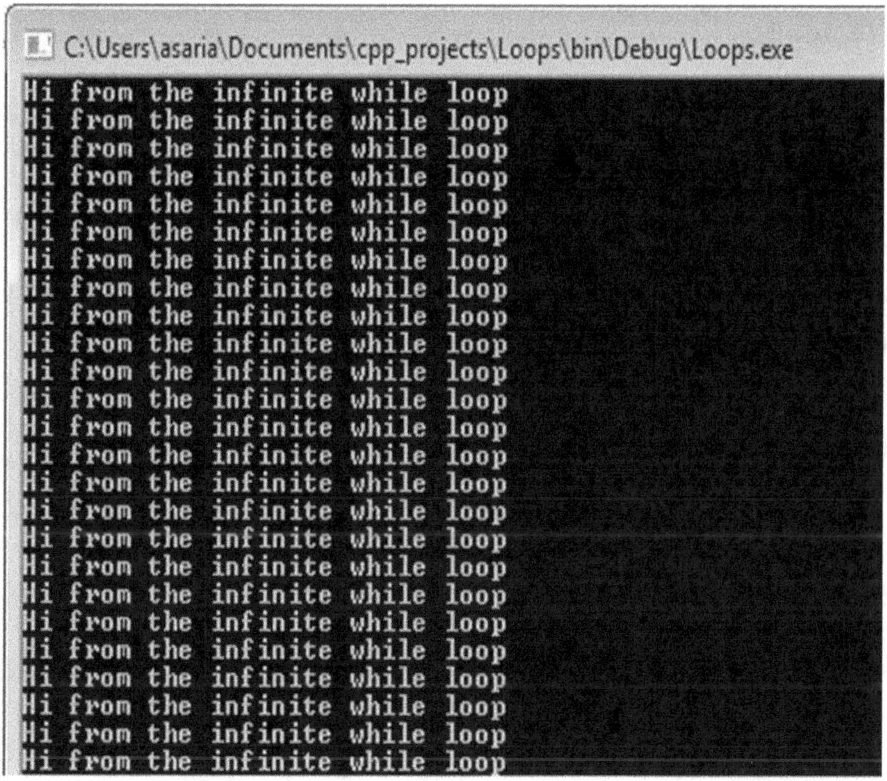
C:\Users\asaria\Documents\cpp_projects\Loops\bin\Debug\Loops.exe
Hi from the infinite while loop
Hi from the infinite while loop
Hi from the infinite while loop
Hi from the infinite while loop
Hi from the infinite while loop
Hi from the infinite while loop
Hi from the infinite while loop
Hi from the infinite while loop
Hi from the infinite while loop
Hi from the infinite while loop
Hi from the infinite while loop
Hi from the infinite while loop
Hi from the infinite while loop
Hi from the infinite while loop
Hi from the infinite while loop
Hi from the infinite while loop
Hi from the infinite while loop
Hi from the infinite while loop
Hi from the infinite while loop
Hi from the infinite while loop
Hi from the infinite while loop
Hi from the infinite while loop
Hi from the infinite while loop
Hi from the infinite while loop
Hi from the infinite while loop

Explanation

This will run forever as the condition is always true

Infinite For Loop

An infinite for loop is defined as shown below:

main.cpp X

```
#include<iostream>
using namespace std;

int main(){


    for(;;){
      cout << "Hi from the infinite for loop"<< endl;

    }

    return 0;
}

```

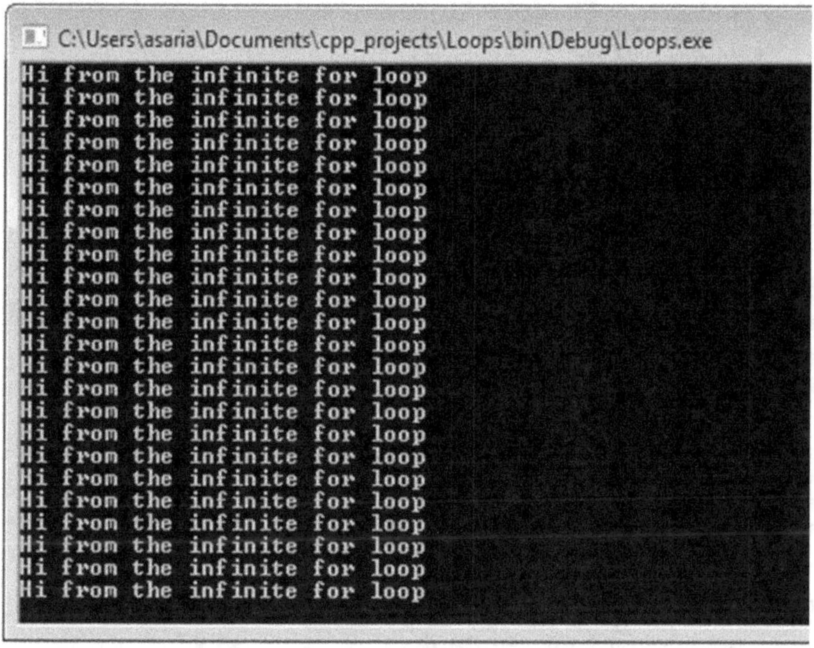

Explanation

Notice that to declare an infinite for loop, you just need to have two semicolons in the parentheses associated with the for keyword, that is:

```
for(;;){
  //this code will run infinitely
}
```

Exercise

1. Rewrite the following loops as for loops.

a.

```
int x = 2;
while(x <= 200)
{
```

```
        if (x < 10 && x != 1)
        cout << 'YY';
        x=x+2;
}
```

b.

```
int a = 2;
while(a <=21)
{
        cout << 'YY';
        a++;
}
```

2. What is the output of the following (when embedded in a complete program)?

```
for (int ctr = 2; ctr < 15; ctr++)
        cout << (3 + ctr) << endl;
```

3. What is the output of the following?

```
for (int b = 50; b > 2; b = b - 3)
{
        cout << "Hi ";
        cout << b << endl;
}
```

4. Write a program that create prints out your name an infinite number of times using a for loop.

Arrays

An array is a collection of values of the same data type.

Each value in the collection has an index associated with it that can be used to retrieve the value.

Indices in C++ start from 0 not 1, this is known as ***zero based indexing.*** It is like starting to count from 0 and not 1.

Exercise

How many items do I have, if I gave them labels from 0 to 4?

Answer: 5

Declaring an array

When declaring an array, we begin by specifying the data type of the values that the array will hold followed by the variable name of the array then by the number of elements it will hold in square brackets.

For example:

```
int size[4];
size = {1,2,3,4};
```

Explanation

Above we have declared an array with the variable name *size* which holds 4 values of the data type integer

```
int size[4];
```

int -> data type of elements held by the array
size -> name of the array
[4] -> specification of the number of elements held by the array

The statement, size = {1, 2, 3, 4}, initializes an array, which simply means assigning a value to the array variable.

You can also declare and initialize an array at the same time as shown below:

Example

```
int size[4] = { 1,2,3,4};
int size[] = { 1,2,3,4};
```

If the arguments are less, the rest are initialized to the zero value of the data type.

Retrieving values from an array

Values are retrieved from an array by specifying the location of the needed value using an index

Example

Let's say we want to retrieve the first element in an array, our code would be:

main.cpp X

```
#include<iostream>
using namespace std;

int main(){
    int size[4] = { 1,2,3,4};
    int firstElement = size[0];

    cout << firstElement ;
    return 0;
}
```

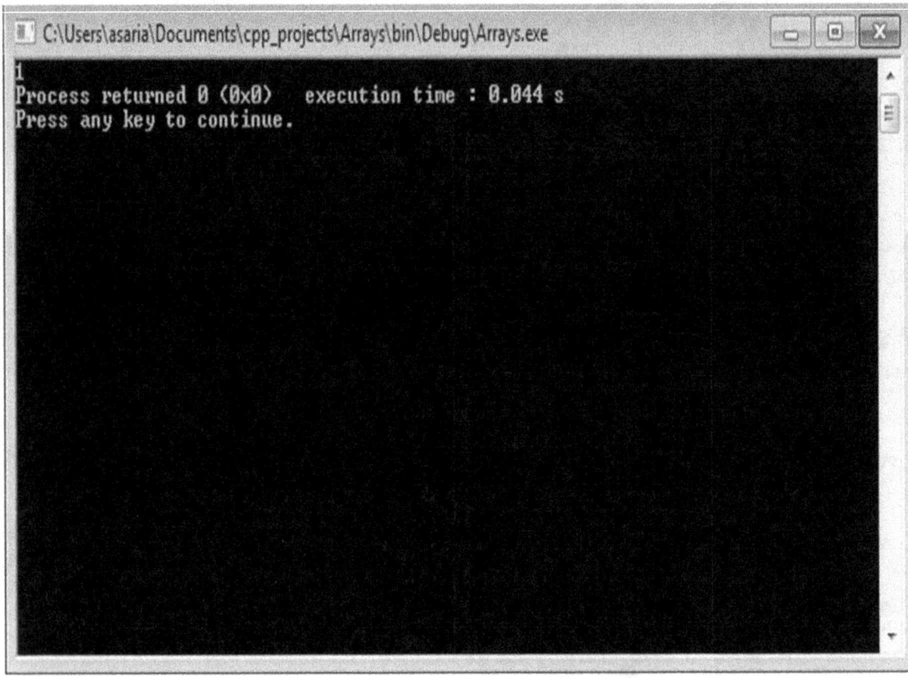

Explanation

The line, **int firstElement = size[0];** , retrieves the first element in the array.

Notice that since in C++ we start counting from 0, the index of the first element in the array is 0.
The program prints out 1 since the 1st element in size is 1.

Exercise

Retrieve the fourth element. (Hint the index is not 4)

Looping through elements in an array

If we want to retrieve all the elements in an array, we can use loops to do that.
We will use *for* loop since it is the simplest way to go about it.

Example

main.cpp

```
#include<iostream>
using namespace std;

int main(){
   int size[4] = { 1,2,3,4};

   for(int i = 0 ; i < 4; i++){
        cout << size[i] ;
   }
   return 0;
}
```

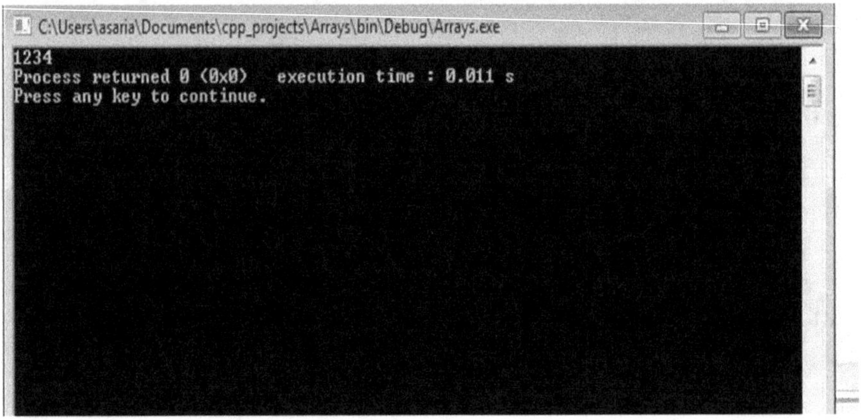

Explanation

Notice that we start our counter from 0 and our condition is that the value of the counter *i* should be less than 4, which is the size of the array.

Exercise

This is to be done in one file:

1. Write a function that calculates the area of a circle.
2. Create an array that holds 10 circle radii that you want to know the areas of.
3. Loop through the array to calculate the areas of the circles and print the result to the screen
4. Calculate only the area of the circle in the fourth position in the array.
5. Create an array of the character of your name and print all of the characters to the screen.

Structures

A structure is a group of values that enables you to order data in a logical manner, that is, in a manner that makes sense to you.

Let's say that you want to collect information about your friends' age, weight and height.

With the current knowledge we have we would do it something like this:

Example code

main.cpp

```
#include<iostream>
using namespace std;

int main(){
    int kevinAge = 10;
    int kevinWeight = 30;
    int kevinHeight = 1;

    int jesiccaAge = 15;
    int jesiccaWeight = 28;
    int jesiccaHeight = 1;
}

```

Structures make grouping such information easier.

Let's first define a structure.

Structure definition

main.cpp

```
#include<iostream>
using namespace std;

struct PersonInfo{

    int age;
    int weight;
    int height;
};

int main(){

    return 0;
}

```

Explanation

A structure is defined outside any function definition, including the main function.

We use the keyword **struct** to define a structure followed by the name we want to give the structure, this name is known as a *structure tag*

Inside the curly braces associated with the structure tag, we declare structure variables which are also known as *member names.* In the above example, **age**, **weight** and **height** are *member names*.

Notice that there is a semicolon after the closing curly brace.

Initializing structures

main.cpp

```
#include<iostream>
using namespace std;

struct PersonInfo{

    int age;
    int weight;
    int height;
};

int main(){

    // initializing the structure
    PersonInfo kevin = {10,30,1 };
    PersonInfo jesicca = {15,28,1 };

    return 0;
}

```

Explanation

By creating a structure, we have created a new data type.

As we usually do when we declare any variables, we start with the data type that it will hold.

In curly braces we pass in the arguments to be values for the declared structure variables.

The order of the arguments is important.

You will get an error if there are more initializer values than structure members.

If the values are less, the last ones that aren't in the list are initialized to zero.

Accessing struct member values

To access a structure's member variables value, you use the dot operator as shown below

Example code

main.cpp

```
#include<iostream>
using namespace std;

struct PersonInfo{

    int age;
    int weight;
    int height;
};

int main(){

    // initializing the structure
    PersonInfo kevin = {10,30,1 };
    PersonInfo jesicca = {15,28,1 };

    cout << kevin.age << endl;
    cout << jesicca.age << endl;

    return 0;
}
```

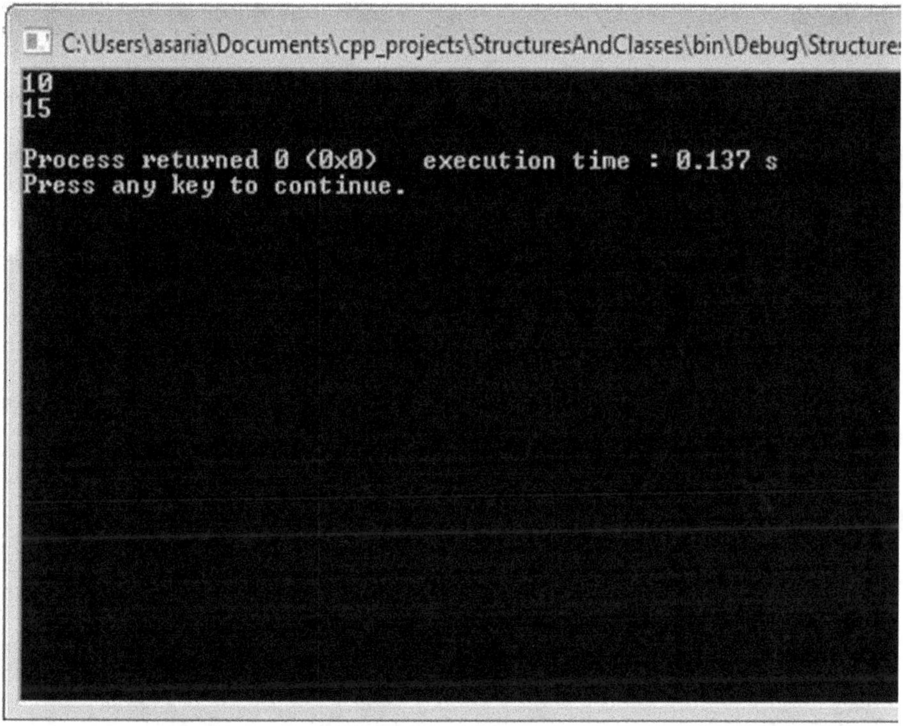

The output for **kevin.age** and **jessica.age** are 10 and 15 in the output above. Age is the first member of the structure. 10 and 15 are the first numbers in the structure initialization, thus they reference Kevin and Jessica's age.

Exercise

Create a structure called Date, that has the member variables year, month and day. Initialize it with your current date and print all the values to the screen.

Final Project

In the final project, we aim to utlize a lot of the skills we've learned throughout the book.

Tasks

Design a student management system. New students are added with information entered including their name and registration number. The user can search the particular student on the basis of registration number. The user can check the entire list of students and delete a particular student in the basis of registration number and exit the program.

The code below performs the task; and all the tasks are explained clearly after the program.

Code

```
#include<iostream>
using namespace std;
#include <string>

// search record function to search the record of the student if it is exist and then print record
void searchRecord(string name[], string regnum[], string reg,int in) {

    // is found variable to check wether a record is exist or not in the array if exist set it true
        bool isfound = false;

        // loop till array to check a wether a record exist or not
        for(int index = 0; index < in; index = index + 1) {

            // check the every record in array if match then
            if ( regnum[index] == reg ) {

                // record is found
                isfound = true;

                // printing the record
                cout << "Student Registration Number   :  "
                << regnum[index]    << "\t\t" <<  " Student Name : "  << name[index] << endl;
                cout << endl;


                // terminating from loop
                break;

            }
        }

        // if a particular record is not exist then
        if (isfound == false) {

            // display that record is not exist
            cout <<" Record is not found : " <<endl;
            cout << endl;
        }
    }

int  main()
{
    // loop control variable set it true when the user exist from the programme set cont false
    bool cont = true;

    // registration number array to store the user registration number
    string registrationNum[100];
```

```
// student name array to store the student registration number
string name[100];

// declaring variable to store the user entered option
int selectedNumber;

// indext to count the total number of added student
int index = 0;

// loop till user exit the programme
while(cont) {

    // printing menu
    cout << "[1] Create New Record \n"
    <<"[2] Search A Record \n[3] View All Record \n[4] Delete a Record \n[5] Exit  \n"<<endl;

    // prompt user to enter the number
    cout << "Select Number : ";

    // store the user entered number in selectedNumber
    cin >> selectedNumber;

    // if the selectedNumber is 1 then add record into array


    if ( selectedNumber == 1) {

        // declare nam and regNum variable to store the user entered nam and regNum
        string nam;
        string regNum;

        // prompt user to enter name
        cout << "Enter your name : ";

        // store the user enter name into nam variable
        cin >> nam;

        //prompt user to enter the registration number
        cout << "Enter your Registration Number : ";
        cin >> regNum;

        // storing the user entered name and regNum into their respective array
        registrationNum[index] = regNum;
        name[index] = nam;

        // incrementing index
        index = index + 1;
        cout << endl;
```

```
}

// check if user entered 2 then
else if ( selectedNumber == 2)
{

    // check if there is at least one record in the array then
    if ( index >= 0) {

        // prompt user to enter registration number
        string renum;
        cout << "Enter Your Registration Number :";

        // storing the user entered registration number into renum variable
        cin >> renum;

        // calling the function which fine a record and print it
        searchRecord(name,registrationNum,renum,index);

    }

    // if there is no record in the array then
```

```
    else {

        // simply print there is no record in the system
        cout << "There is no Record In the System" <<endl;
        cout << endl;
    }
}

// check if the user entered number 3 then
else if ( selectedNumber == 3 ) {

    // Printing all the records of students
    for (int i = 0; i < index; i++) {

        // if there is null in the array which record is deleted
        if ( name[i] == "null" )
        {
            // just ignore that index
            continue;
        }

        else {
```

```
            // printing all the record of student
            cout << "Student Registration Number  :  " <<  registrationNum[i]   <<
            "\t\t" <<   " Student Name : "  << name[i] << endl;
        }

    }

    // adding space
    cout << endl;

}

// check if the user entered the number 4 then
else if ( selectedNumber == 4 ) {

    // check there is any record in the array then
    if ( index >= 0) {

        // declare the variable renum to store the user registartion number
        string renum;

        // prompt user to enter registration number
        cout << "Enter Your Registration Number :";
        cin >> renum;
```

```
        // is found variable which check if the record is found or not in array
        bool isfound = false;

        // loop till the end of number of record
        for(int ind = 0; ind < index; ind = ind + 1 ){

            // check if the user entered registration is equal to registration num in array
            if ( registrationNum[ind] == renum ) {

                // set the value of found to true
                isfound = true;

                // adding the null to arrays where value is found
                name[ind] = "null";
                registrationNum[ind] = "null";

                // just print that record deleted successfully
                cout << " Record deleted successfully : " <<endl;
                cout << endl;
            }

        }

    // if the user entered registration number is not found then
```

```
            if (isfound == false) {

                // print record id not found
                cout <<" Record is not found : " <<endl;
                cout << endl;

            }
        }

        // if there is no record in the array then
        else {

            // print record is not exits
            cout <<" There is no record in the system: " <<endl;
            cout << endl;
        }

    }

    // check if the user entered the number 5 then
    else if( selectedNumber == 5 ) {

        // print take care
        cout <<" Take Care " <<endl;


        // set cont to flase so that programme terminate
        cont = false;

    }

    else {

        // if the user did not enter any number from 1-5 then print please enter valid number
        cout <<" Invalid entry : " <<endl;
        cout << endl;
        }
}
        return 0;

}
```

Output

```
[1] Create New Record
[2] Search A Record
[3] View All Record
[4] Delete a Record
[5] Exit

Select Number : 1
Enter your name : john
Enter your Registration Number : 44

[1] Create New Record
[2] Search A Record
[3] View All Record
[4] Delete a Record
[5] Exit

Select Number : 1
Enter your name : jimmy
Enter your Registration Number : 66

[1] Create New Record
[2] Search A Record
[3] View All Record
[4] Delete a Record
[5] Exit

Select Number : 1
Enter your name : hussain
Enter your Registration Number : 12

[1] Create New Record
[2] Search A Record
[3] View All Record
[4] Delete a Record
[5] Exit

Select Number : 2
Enter Your Registration Number :12
Student Registration Number  :  12               Student Name : hussain
```

```
[1] Create New Record
[2] Search A Record
[3] View All Record
[4] Delete a Record
[5] Exit

Select Number : 3
Student Registration Number  :  44             Student Name : john
Student Registration Number  :  66             Student Name : jimmy
Student Registration Number  :  12             Student Name : hussain

[1] Create New Record
[2] Search A Record
[3] View All Record
[4] Delete a Record
[5] Exit

Select Number : 4
Enter Your Registration Number :66
 Record deleted successfully :
```

```
[1] Create New Record
[2] Search A Record
[3] View All Record
[4] Delete a Record
[5] Exit

Select Number : 3
Student Registration Number  :  44             Student Name : john
Student Registration Number  :  12             Student Name : hussain

[1] Create New Record
[2] Search A Record
[3] View All Record
[4] Delete a Record
[5] Exit

Select Number : 5
 Take Care


--------------------------------
Process exited after 40.77 seconds with return value 0
Press any key to continue . . .
```

Add a record in array

We have declared two arrays for student names and student registration numbers. The two arrays are called ***registrationNum*** and ***nam***.

If the user enters the number '1' then program will ask user to enter student name and registration number. The user then enters the name and registration number. It is stored in their respective array. There is count variable called ***index*** which counts the number of students which are created. The index is increased by 1 each time a student is added. The process of adding the record is shown in the part of the code below.

```
if ( selectedNumber == 1) {

    // declare nam and regNum variable to store the user entered nam and regNum
    string nam;
    string regNum;

    // prompt user to enter name
    cout << "Enter your name : ";

    // store the user enter name into nam variable
    cin >> nam;

    //prompt user to enter the registration number
    cout << "Enter your Registration Number : ";
    cin >> regNum;

    // storing the user entered name and regNum into their respective array
    registrationNum[index] = regNum;
    name[index] = nam;

    // incrementing index
    index = index + 1;
    cout << endl;
```

Search record from the array

A user can search a particular student using their enrolled registration number by pressing '2' at the start of the program.
The program first checks if the student array is empty. If the array is not empty, the user then enters the registration number. The program compares the user-entered registration with registration numbers existing in array. It does this using the function ***searchRecord()***.

```
}

// check if user entered 2 then
else if ( selectedNumber == 2)
{

    // check if there is at least one record in the array then
    if ( index >= 0) {

        // prompt user to enter registration number
        string renum;
        cout << "Enter Your Registration Number :";

        // storing the user entered registration number into renum variable
        cin >> renum;

        // calling the function which fine a record and print it
        searchRecord(name,registrationNum,renum,index);

    }

    // if there is no record in the array then
```

The function ***searchRecord()*** takes in an array of names ***(name[])*** and an array of registration numbers ***(regnum[])*** as arguments. It also takes in two variables for registration number ***reg*** and index ***in***.
reg is the registration number we are using to search for the student record, while ***in*** is the number of records.
The function search the array ***regum[]*** using a for loop for the registration number ***reg***.
If ***reg*** is found, the function prints out the student registration number and name.
If ***reg*** is not found, the function prints out "Record is not found"

```
// search record function to search the record of the student if it is exist and then print record
void searchRecord(string name[], string regnum[], string reg,int in) {

    // is found variable to check wether a record is exist or not in the array if exist set it true
        bool isfound = false;

        // loop till array to check a wether a record exist or not
        for(int index = 0; index < in; index = index + 1) {

            // check the every record in array if match then
            if ( regnum[index] == reg ) {

                // record is found
                isfound = true;

                // printing the record
                cout << "Student Registration Number  :  "
                << regnum[index]   << "\t\t" <<  " Student Name : "  << name[index] << endl;
                cout << endl;



                // terminating from loop
                break;

            }
        }

        // if a particular record is not exist then
        if (isfound == false) {

            // display that record is not exist
            cout <<" Record is not found : " <<endl;
            cout << endl;
        }
```

View all the records

To view all the record of students, the user presses '3' at the start of the program. There is count variable called ***index*** which count the number of students. A for loop is used to retrieve each student record and print out each student name and registration number. The loop continues till it reaches the value of ***index*** which indicates that we are at the end of the array.

```
// check if the user entered number 3 then
else if ( selectedNumber == 3 ) {

    // Printing all the records of students
    for (int i = 0; i < index; i++) {

        // if there is null in the array which record is deleted
        if ( name[i] == "null" )
        {
            // just ignore that index
            continue;
        }

        else {


            // printing all the record of student
            cout << "Student Registration Number  :  " << registrationNum[i]   <<
            "\t\t" <<  " Student Name : "  << name[i] << endl;
        }

    }

    // adding space
    cout << endl;

}
```

Delete a record

If the user presses '4' at the start of the program, the user can delete a particular student on the basis of registration number.
The user first enters the registration number into a variable called ***renum***. The program will check if student array is empty then display there is no record in the system if it is empty. If the array is not empty then the program compares the ***renum*** with registration numbers which

are in array ***registrationNum***. This is done using a for loop that iterates through the array. If the student is found then the record is deleted from the array by declaring the relevant name and registrationNum to null.

If the student record is not found then the program prints “Record is not found”.

```
// check if the user entered the number 4 then
else if ( selectedNumber == 4 ) {

    // check there is any record in the array then
    if ( index >= 0) {

        // declare the variable renum to store the user registartion number
        string renum;

        // prompt user to enter registration number
        cout << "Enter Your Registration Number :";
        cin >> renum;
        // is found variable which check if the record is found or not in array
        bool isfound = false;

        // loop till the end of number of record
        for(int ind = 0; ind < index; ind = ind + 1 ){

            // check if the user entered registration is equal to registration num in array
            if ( registrationNum[ind] == renum ) {

                // set the value of found to true
                isfound = true;

                // adding the null to arrays where value is found
                name[ind] = "null";
                registrationNum[ind] = "null";

                // just print that record deleted successfully
                cout << " Record deleted successfully : " <<endl;
                cout << endl;
            }

        }
        // if the user entered registration number is not found then
    // if there is no record in the array then
    else {

        // print record is not exits
        cout <<" There is no record in the system: " <<endl;
        cout << endl;
    }

}
```

Exit

If the user enter the number '5' then simply break from the loop. The variable ***cont*** is set to false. This terminates the program as the program is in a while loop that continues while ***cont*** is true.

```
// check if the user entered the number 5 then
else if( selectedNumber == 5 ) {

    // print take care
    cout <<" Take Care " <<endl;

    // set cont to flase so that programme terminate
    cont = false;

}
```

Conclusion

Thanks for reading this book.
I hope this has helped you get started with programming in C++.

If you'd like to take the next steps in C++, I'd suggest the books below on Amazon.

Learn C++ Quickly
https://www.amazon.com/Learn-Quickly-Beginners-Programming-Hands-ebook/dp/B08DZ3NY6Z/

Programming: Principles and Practice using C++
https://www.amazon.com/Programming-Principles-Practice-Using-2nd/dp/0321992784/

If you're interested in Javascript or Python, I have a few books on my product page below.

Bob Mather product page
https://www.amazon.com/kindle-dbs/entity/author/B07HHQZC4Y

The end… almost!

Reviews are not easy to come by.

As an independent author with a tiny marketing budget, I rely on readers, like you, to leave a short review on Amazon.

Even if it's just a sentence or two!

So if you enjoyed the book, please...

>> Click here to leave a brief review on Amazon.

I am very appreciative for your review as it truly makes a difference.

Thank you from the bottom of my heart for purchasing this book and reading it to the end.

Book 2:

Coding for Kids Ages 9-15

Basic html, css and JavaScript from Scratch

Introduction

It was a bright summer afternoon in Atlanta; and I grabbed my laptop to watch the latest episode of 'Game of Thrones' on the porch outside. As I sat on the three-legged chair; I felt a wobble on the rear leg. The leg just came off the stool and I crashed to the ground on my back. Hearing the loud thud on the porch, both my wife, Isabelle, and son, Arnad, came out. "Are you ok?" Isabelle gasped. I was shaken, but fine, as Isabelle helped me up. I walked inside and grabbed a glass of water to get me back to my senses. To my amazement, I noticed, through the window, my 9-year-old son, Arnad try to figure out how to piece it together. He assembled the leg back in and noticed that the chair was still wobbling. He then switched out the screw with the one on the good leg; and the chair was still wobbling. He finally glued the sliding mechanism that held the screw in place; and that magically fixed the chair. Wow!!

Next, we can talk about Betty. Our neighbour's daughter, Betty, struggled with Social Sciences for the longest time. Her parents were used to failing grades in this topic; and were relieved each time she got a 'D'. So, imagine their shock when Betty came back one day with a report card that showed an 'A' in social science. Yeah, Betty was a hardworking girl and she did do well in some of her subjects; but this turnaround was unexpected. Then, Betty showed her parents her social science improvement plan in the last three months. She broke down the list of topics she would work on every week; and how she would simplify some of the harder topics with documentaries and group study sessions. She systematically moved on from topic to topic till she addressed all of them.

And finally, we address Carl. Carl was a tennis player at the start of high school. He was a lot smaller and weaker than his opponents. As a result, he lost pretty badly in his first tournament. He struggled to even get a few points. While he was upset, he realized that his loss was not a loss due to lack of skill; it was based of circumstances. He analysed the situation; and realized that he needed to improve his skill and positional play on the court. He analysed the movement of his opponents on the court; and adapted his shots to always make sure they played him off balance. He did plenty of yoga and other stretching exercises to improve his flexibility, balance and speed. He started improving month after month. Every month, he practiced a different shot. In a couple of years, he grew into his frame and was much stronger and wider. And due to his hard work, he was much more skilled than his opponents. In his third year of high school, he won the annual tournament with really no competition at all.

All of these situations are hypothetical and can happen due to innate characteristics of certain kids. Also, coding does not guarantee that you will learn these skills. But, all of these situations demonstrate skills that can be learnt during coding. Arnad systematically examined the chair and its different components; and worked through each component to find the problem. This is the same as a process called ‘debugging’ in programming. Debugging is what happens when a program doesn’t work. It requires systematic analysis of the code to find the problem and make it work.

Betty looked at a problem; and organized it into different parts that are required to achieve a result. This is similar to problem solving in programming. This is understanding what is required to solve a coding problem; and structure the code into different sections to make the program work.

Carl is doing the same thing as Betty; he is structuring a problem into different parts so it can be solved in a simple manner. But, in addition, he is prioritizing different skills on the tennis court. He spent time figuring out which skills are more important to beating his opponent and worked on those first. Prioritization is an important skill in programming after a code is properly structured. Coders want to prioritize more vital tasks in the code to test first.

All these skills are vital to programming; and your kids should learn these if they learn how to code well. It doesn't really matter if they become programmers. The skills will benefit your kids for life. Programming also helps kids improve at basic math and reading; in addition to better logic and problem-solving skills.

These skills, combined with communication skills they learn in high school, are the reason why software engineers are paid a median annual salary of $112000 (as of 2018) in America. This is over double the average salary in America.

Despite this, high schools all over the world, even in affluent areas, lack the staff and technical resources to handle this task. According to a 2000 K-12 teacher survey done by Tech Republic, only 8% of teachers felt reasonably confident to teach children programming. 50% of kids in America do not have access to the internet at home. The statistics are even worse for girls and children of color in America; who have less resources and role models to look up to.

So, you need to take to take this into your own hands.

What Not To Do

You might be wondering what you need to do to get started. There's a couple of things I advise against doing. I would advise against hiring a programmer who has no experience in teaching kids. They are experts in the topic; but it's been decades since they started programming; so, they can't relate to a kid who hasn't learnt programming before and who's learning basic Mathematics. The next thing to avoid is to search for the latest textbook on JavaScript; and read it out for your kid. These are as useful for learning programming; as a dictionary is for learning a language. They are expensive, and more useful as a reference tool for existing programmers. I also recommend against coding camps. These can work for a minority of students; but most students get lost in the large group of kids that are learning. One to one attention is the best way to get going.

First Steps to Get Started

This book is the best way to get started. I've broken down programming into a series of basic chapters; and relate it to the real world. The first chapter will help you set up your JavaScript and html files for you to get started.

I also have code for every chapter that you can copy and paste to get working. Every aspect of the code is well explained;

and I have exercises that you can complete yourself with the concepts in the chapter.

I also have a recommended one on one tutor at the end of the book; and additional books you can use to build on your knowledge.

SET UP WORKSPACE

What You Need

A Laptop/Desktop Computer
Internet Connection
Web browser installed (Firefox, Chrome or Internet Explorer)

Download and Install Notepad++

Download the latest version of a text editing software. I recommend Notepad++. You can download the latest version below:
https://notepad-plus-plus.org/downloads/

How to Start using NotePad++

Open Notepad++ from your Desktop or Start Menu

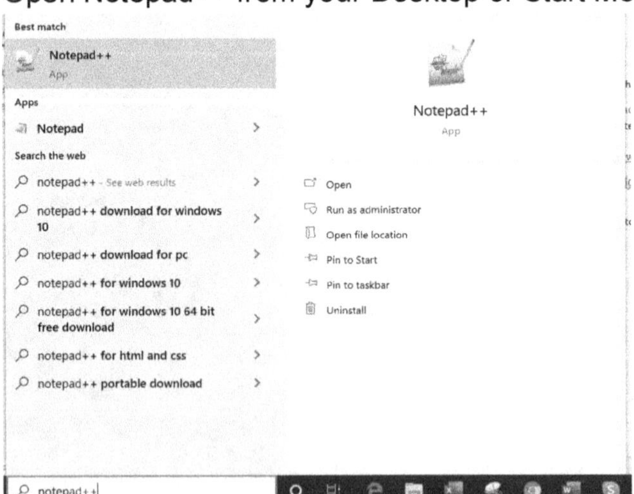

Once NotePad++ is open, go to File>New to open a New File.

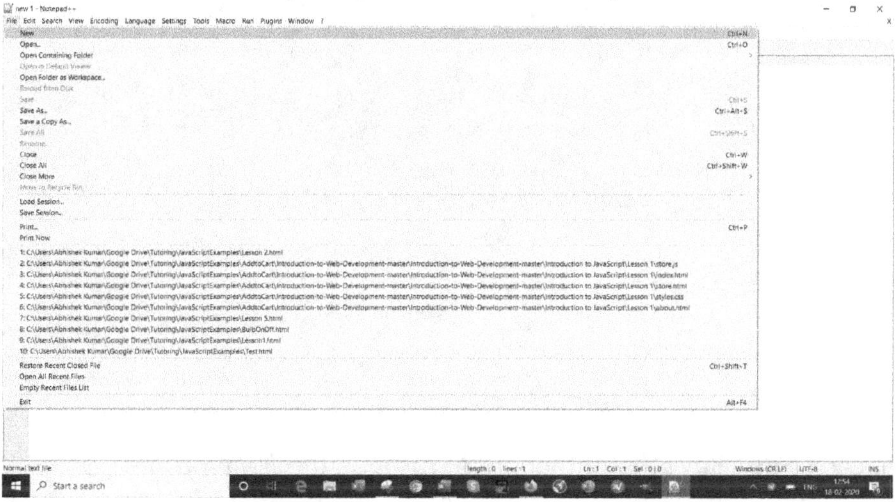

Now, click **File>Save** As and choose **.html** as the file type

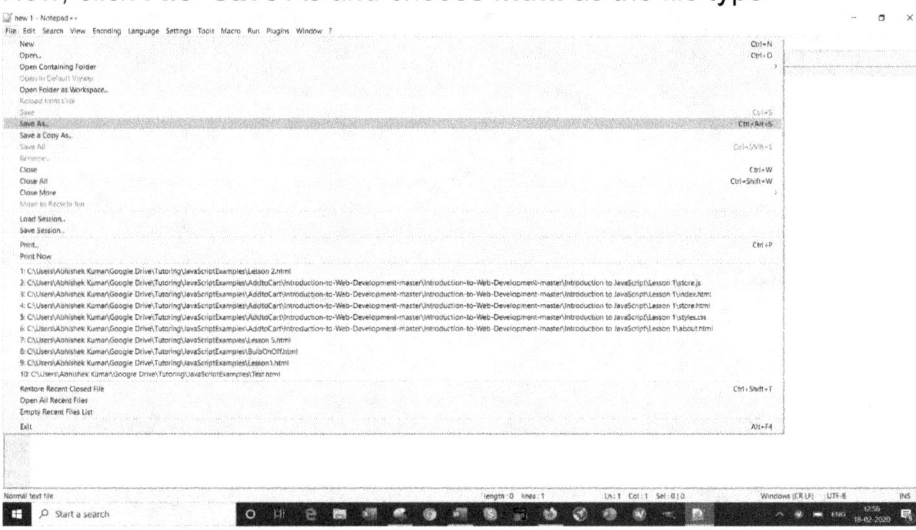

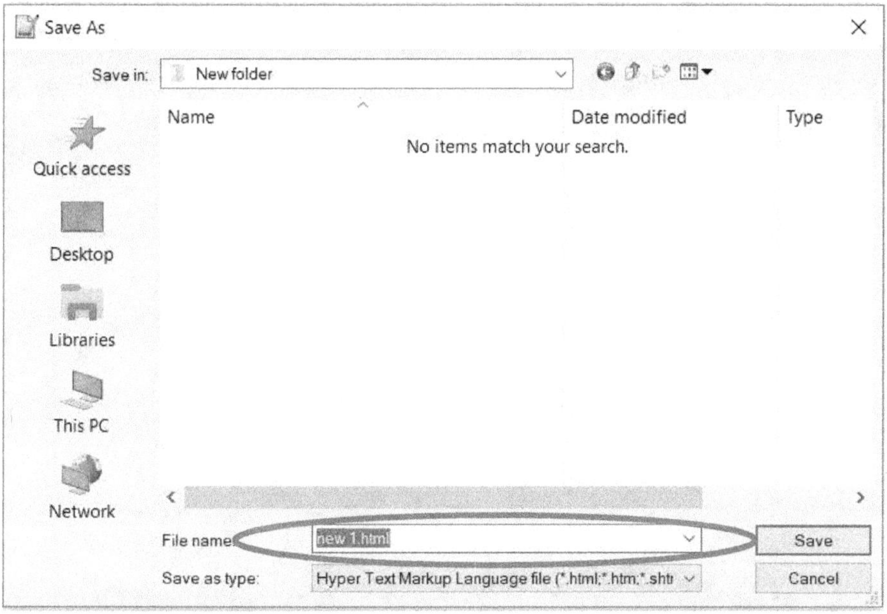

This ensures that you can run your program on a html browser like Firefox or Chrome.

Test Program

There's a simple way to test the program and see if it connects to your browser.

Just type in random text in your file. In my file, I've typed **"Testing 1,2,3……."**

Then click **File>Save**.

After that, click **Run>Launch in Firefox/Chrome/IE** depending on which browser you are using.

If it is working, the text that you typed in should show in the browser window.

File Edit Search View Encoding Language Settings Tools Macro Run Plugins Window ?
Testing 1,2,3

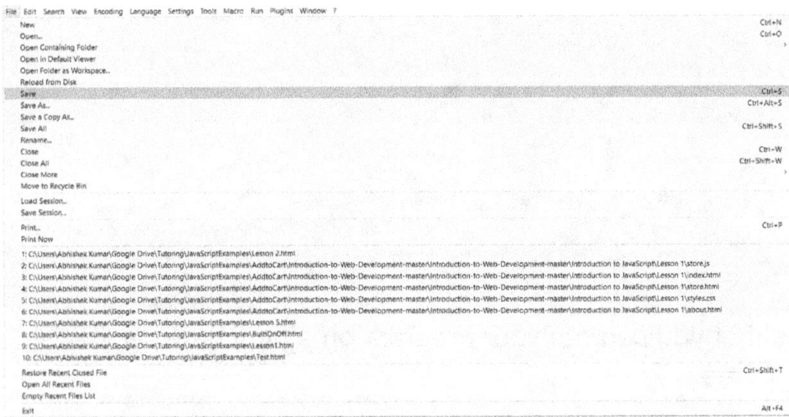
File Edit Search View Encoding Language Settings Tools Macro Run Plugins Window ?
New Ctrl+N
Open... Ctrl+O
Open Containing Folder
Open in Default Viewer
Open Folder as Workspace...
Reload from Disk
Save Ctrl+S
Save As... Ctrl+Alt+S
Save a Copy As...
Save All Ctrl+Shift+S
Rename...
Close Ctrl+W
Close All Ctrl+Shift+W
Close More
Move to Recycle Bin
Load Session...
Save Session...
Print... Ctrl+P
Print Now
Restore Recent Closed File Ctrl+Shift+T
Open All Recent Files
Empty Recent Files List
Exit Alt+F4

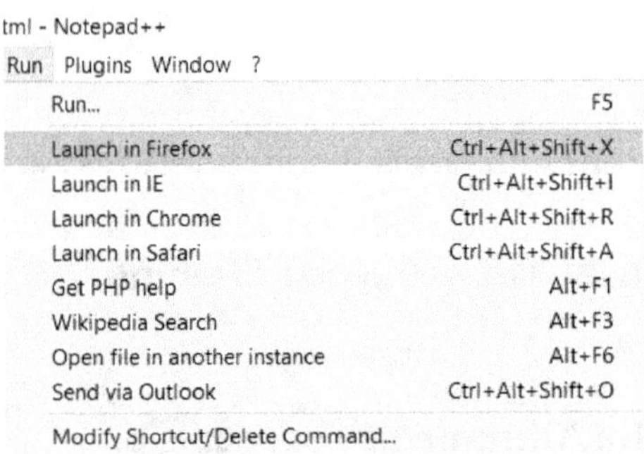
tml - Notepad++
Run Plugins Window ?
Run... F5
Launch in Firefox Ctrl+Alt+Shift+X
Launch in IE Ctrl+Alt+Shift+I
Launch in Chrome Ctrl+Alt+Shift+R
Launch in Safari Ctrl+Alt+Shift+A
Get PHP help Alt+F1
Wikipedia Search Alt+F3
Open file in another instance Alt+F6
Send via Outlook Ctrl+Alt+Shift+O
Modify Shortcut/Delete Command...

Result:

I know that it may be a simple test for some; but it is important to make sure that everything is working before we get on to actual programming.

Intro to html

What is html?

Html stands for Hyper Test Markup Language
Html is the language that humans use to connect with web browsers like Chrome, Internet Explorer, Firefox etc.
Sometimes, it is assisted by css and JavaScript; but the basic structure of a web page is defined by html.
It is pretty simple and easy to grasp for even beginners to programming and young kids.
Html is done using simple tags that look like the ends of an arrow.

Example of a html tag

Here's what a html tag looks like:
<p> - Example of a tag
Every html tag has an extra tag that signals the end of the tag. The ending of a tag has a slash in it in addition to the two ends of a tag. See below for a simple example.

<p> - Tag starts
</p> - Tag ends

Basic html tags and What They're Used For

<html>
This is the tag that starts every piece of html code.

<head>
This is the code that is executed first before anything else.

<title>
This is the code written in the top ribbon of the browser.

<body>
Includes the information that appears on the page.

<p>
This is used for a paragraph of text that appears on the body.

<h1>, <h2>, <h3>, <h4>, <h5>, <h6>
These are used for headings on text in descending order of size. <h1> is the largest size heading, and <h6> is the smallest.

<strong>
This is used to bold text

<ul>
This is used for unordered lists such as bulleted items

<li>
Used to add a bullet icon before a line of text

<ol>
This is used for unordered lists such as items number from 1,2,3...

<div>
These are larger sections of content; that generally contain several paragraphs, headings, etc.

<a>
This is used to hyperlink text. Hyperlink is what happens when you click on a piece of underlined text and it links to another page

<img>
This is used for adding images to a web page.

Now, you might be wondering that it's a lot to learn. Don't worry. You don't need to memorize any of it for now.
Just use it as a reference for when you code.
We're going to go through an examples that will explain everything better.

Html example:

```
<html>
<head>
<title>Greeting to html......</title>
</head>
<body>
<h1>Welcome to your first html website</h1>
<h2>Time to get started....</h2>
<p>Hi. My name is Bob. I am excited to learn about programming a website. Here's a few things we will learn.</p>
<ul>
<li>Basics of html</li>
<li>CSS</li>
<li>JavaScript</li>
</ul>
</body>
</html>
```

Same code below: (that you can copy and paste)

```
<html>
<head>
<title>Greeting to html......</title>
</head>
```

```
<body>
<h1>Welcome to your first html website</h1>
<h2>Time to get started....</h2>
<p>Hi. My name is Bob. I am excited to learn about programming a
website. Here's a few things we will learn.</p>
<ul>
<li>Basics of html</li>
<li>CSS</li>
<li>JavaScript</li>
</ul>
</body>
</html>
```

Here's What We Get as An Output

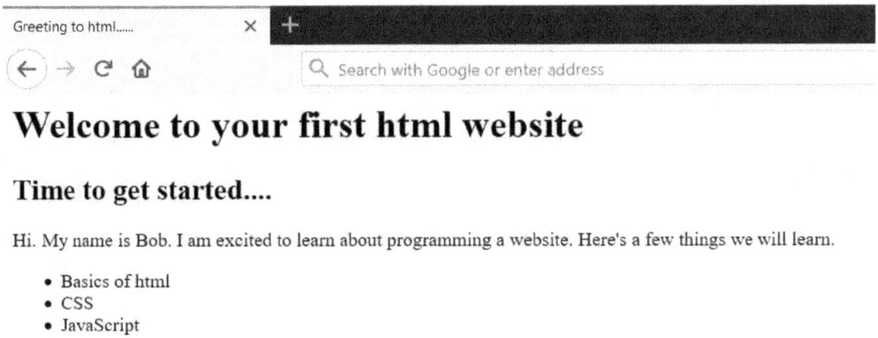

And let's link the output to the tags in the code.

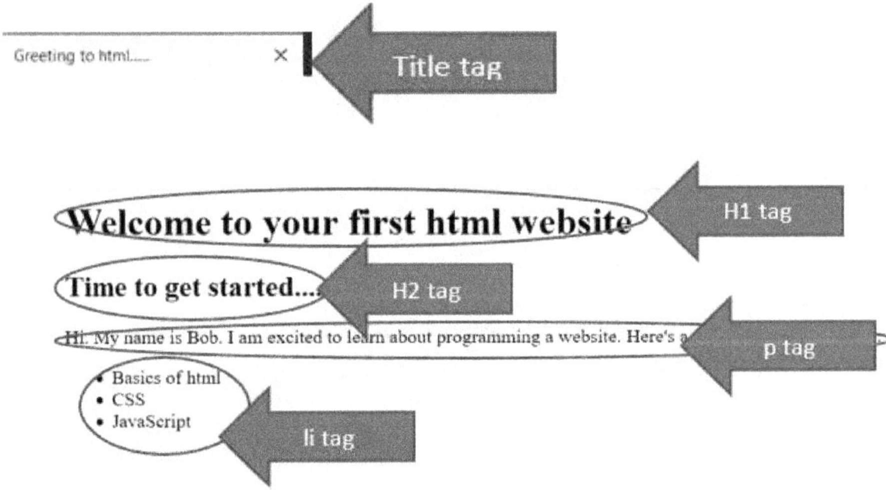

Exercises to Practice

1. Create a html website that introduces yourself. Create a title tag that says 'Introduction'. Create a headline for yourself using a

h1 and h2 tag. Then create a paragraph where you talk about yourself, your age, school, and hometown. Then finally, create a bulleted list of your hobbies.

2. Create a html website that talks about your favorite sports team or TV show. Create a title tag that says the name of the show/sports team. Create a headline using a h1 and h2 tag. Then create a paragraph where you talk about why you like the team/TV show and why they are so awesome. Then finally, create a bulleted list of your favorite players/people on the show.

The Bulb Example - html

What This Project Does

This is a simple html project that creates a button that can switch a light bulb on the page on/off. We are going to use two bulb images to make this happen. The button will switch between the two images.

Concepts to Understand for this Chapter

We'll need to understand button tags and image tags for this example.

Button Tag
<button onclick=Action >Button text</button>
The button element has two elements. An Action and Button Text. The Button Text is the text that shows on the button; and the Action is what happens when the user clicks on the button

Image Tag
<img id=ImageId src=ImageUrl style=ImageSize>
The Image Tag has three elements.
The ImageId is the name you assign to the image. This name is used to reference the image in the code.
Imageurl is the url of the image that the tag is referencing. If the image is in the same folder as the html file, then you can use the file name only instead of the entire url.
ImageSize sets the width and height of the Image.

Files

Include the two images of bulbs on and off in the same folder as the html code we are using. You can get the files by clicking on link below and downloading:

Bulb On Picture

Bulb Off Picture

Code

```
<html>
<head>
<title> The Bulb Project</title>
</head>
<body>

<h2>Bulb Light with JavaScript</h2>
<button onclick="document.getElementById('myImage').src='bulb_off.JPG'">Bulb Off</button>
<img id="myImage" src="bulboff.JPG" style="width:100px">
<button onclick="document.getElementById('myImage').src='bulb_on.JPG'">Bulb On</button>

</body>
</html>
```

Same code below (that you can copy and paste)

```
<html>
<head>
<title> The Bulb Project</title>
</head>
<body>

<h2>Bulb Light with JavaScript</h2>
<button
onclick="document.getElementById('myImage').src='bulb_off.JPG'">Bu
lb Off</button>
<img id="myImage" src="bulboff.JPG" style="width:100px">
<button
onclick="document.getElementById('myImage').src='bulb_on.JPG'">Bu
lb On</button>

</body>
</html>
```

Output

Initial:

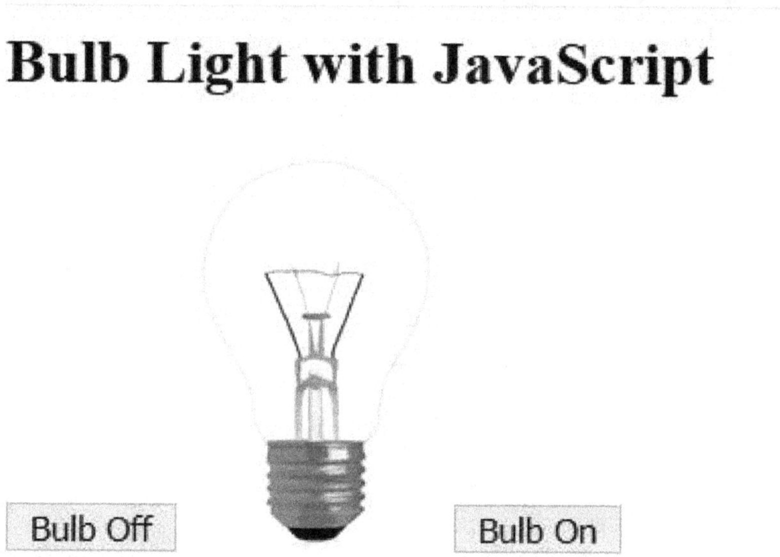

After Clicking **Bulb On** Button:

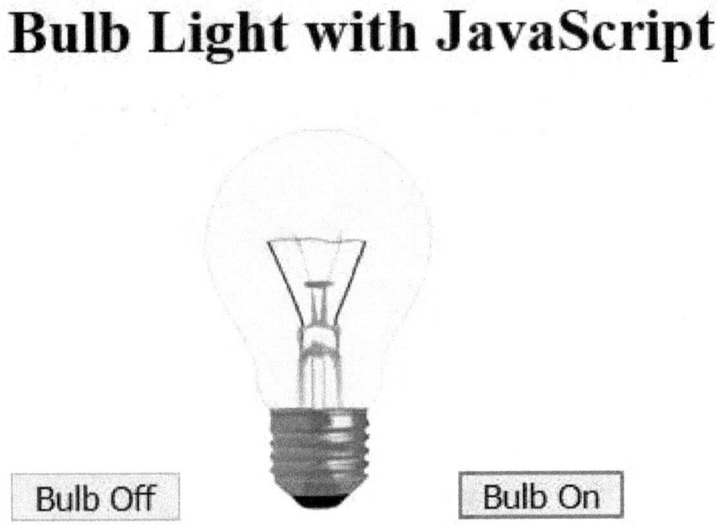

After Clicking **Bulb Off** Button:

Exercises to Practice:

1. Create a program with 2 buttons with 2 buttons; titled 'Day' and 'Night'. When you click on Day button, a picture of the sun shows up; when you click on night, a picture of the moon shows up.
2. Create a program that has 4 buttons that alternate between 4 different wild animals. Each button has 'Tiger', 'Lion', 'Boar' and 'Elephant' as Text. And when you click on each button, the relevant animal picture shows up.

A Short message from the Author:

Hey, are you enjoying the book? I'd love to hear your thoughts!

Many readers do not know how hard reviews are to come by, and how much they help an author.

I would be incredibly thankful if you could take just 60 seconds to write a brief review on Amazon, even if it's just a few sentences!

>> Click here to leave a quick review

Thank you for taking the time to share your thoughts!

Your review will genuinely make a difference for me and help gain exposure for my work.

html Forms

What are html forms?

Html forms are empty boxes on the web page that you can enter information in.
It's those forms that you see online where you enter your name, age, password etc.
Here's what a form looks like:

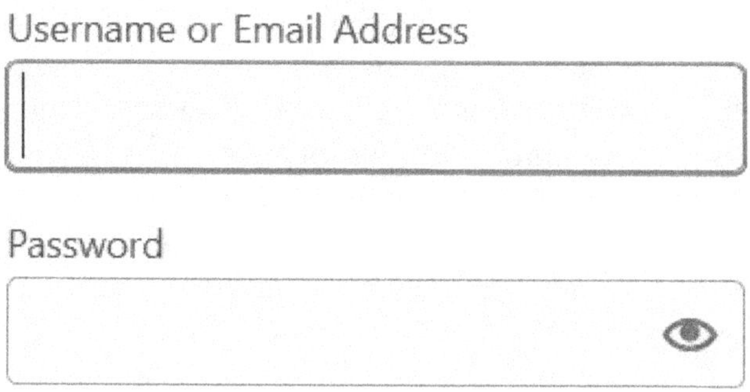

Form Html Tag format

Below is an example of a form html tag that takes in name, occupation and gender.

```
<form id="form1">
Name: <input name="Enter Name" type="text" id="name" size="20"><br>
Occupation: <input type="text" id="occupation" size="20"><br>
Age: <input type="number" id="gender" size="20"><br>
</form>
```

Once you run the program, the output looks like below. You can type anything in the empty boxes in the output. The empty boxes are also called textboxes.

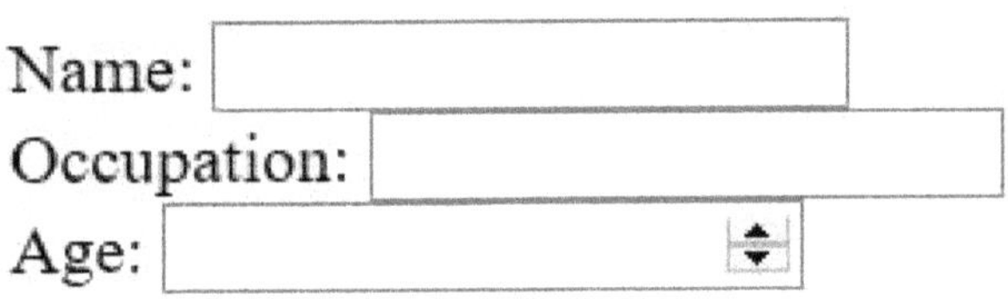

Different parts of form html tag

<form id="form1">

The form id tag is the name of the form that will used as a reference in the rest of the code.

Name:
Occupation:
Age:

This is the text that's written at the left of the box. It is used to describe to the user what to put in the box.

input type="text"

This means that what you type in the box is a type of text or string. For example, name and occupation uses text because you type letters in the box.

input type="number"

This means that what you type in the box is a number. For example, age and phone would use text because it is entirely numbers.

id="name"

id="occupation"

id="gender"

The id is what the box is called in the rest of the program. We will use the id in the rest of the program to reference the box.

size="20"

This means that the length of the box is 20 pixels. To change this, change the value of size. For example, if you want to double the length of the box, change the size to 40.

JavaScript Example

What is JavaScript?

JavaScript is a high-level programming language. It is most commonly used to perform user actions on a html page.
It also helps to enhance interactions of users on a web page.

How to Use JavaScript in html

There are two ways to use JavaScript on a html page:
The first way is to just include JavaScript code within <script> tags. It would be like below:

```
<html>
<head>
<title> </title>
</head>
<body>
<script>
</script>
</body>
</html>
```

The JavaScript code would be within the two script tags shown in red above.

The second way is to create a Javascript file and save it as a .js file. Then you would reference the Javascript file in the html code. This is shown below.

```
<html>
<head>
<title> </title>
</head>
<body>
<script src="newfile.js"></script>
</body>
</html>
```

You would include all the JavaScript code in the newfile.js file.

JavaScript Terms You Need to Know

We are going through a couple of JavaScript html code examples next. We need to know the following terms to understand the code.

function

A JavaScript function is any set of lines of code that performs a task. A function is normally made to execute tasks that need to happen when you click on a html button. Every function has a name and is referenced in the html code. An example is below:

```
function abcd()
```

abcd is the name of the function that performs a specific task. It will be referenced in html code as abcd.

Variable

A variable is used to store names or numbers in JavaScript. Think of it as a box that can store one value. That box is referenced each time you need that value. It is defined as below:

```
var flag=1;
```

flag is the name of the variable and it stores the value of 1. So anytime flag is referenced in the JavaScript program; it has a value of 1 (unless you change the value of flag). This value of flag can be used to define other variables. For example:

```
var king=flag*2;
```

king now has a value of 1*2=2. So variables are a good way of dealing with unknown quantities.

document.getElementbyID().value

This javascript term is used to get the value of an item in a html form textbox. So, if you fill out a form textbox with your name and click on a button, the document.getElementbyID() gets the value of what you typed in the box. As an example:

```
var yname=document.getElementById("name").value;
```

"name" is the id of the form textbox that is defined in html. To see how this is done in html, check out the section on html tags in the previous chapter.

Whatever is typed in the textbox is stored in a variable called yname. It will be referenced in javascript from now on as yname.

Document.write()

This function is used to print anything on the web browser.

For example,

```
document.write("xyz");
```

Prints **xyz** on the screen

You can also add two different terms by using the "+" button.

```
document.write("xyz"+"123");
```

Prints **xyz123** on the screen.

This is useful when you want to add text to a variable. For example.

```
var yname=document.getElementById("name").value;
document.write("My name is "+yname);
```

If you typed in "Matt" in the textbox, it prints out **"My name is Matt"** on the screen.

parseint()

parseint changes the number to a whole number, whether it is a decimal or not. For example,
parseint(2.8) would equal 3.
Parseint(2) would just be 2.

parsefloat()

parsefloat() does the opposite of parseint(). It changes the number to decimal. For example,
parseint(2) would equal 2.0
Parseint(3.1) would just be 3.1

JavaScript Example 1

The code below creates a html form that accepts name, age and hobby of a person. There is a html button that produces JavaScript code when clicked.
The JavaScript code prints out the name, age and hobby of the person when clicked. The JavaScript code is within the <script> tags.
The code is shown below with the output; and then a few of the lines are explained later as well.

```
<html>
<head>
<title>Print Name and Age......</title>
</head>
<body>
<form id="form1">
Enter Name: <input name="Enter Name" type="text" id="name" size="20"><br>
Enter Favorite Hobby: <input type="text" id="hobby" size="20"><br>
Enter Age: <input type="number" id="age" size="20"><br>
</form>
<button onclick="writename()">Print Intro</button>
<script>
function writename()
{
    var nameValue=document.getElementById("name").value;
    var hobbyValue=document.getElementById("hobby").value;
    var ageValue=document.getElementById("age").value;

    document.write("This is "+nameValue+". I am "+ ageValue+" years old.My favorite hobby is "+hobbyValue);
}
</script>
</body>
</html>
```

Output:

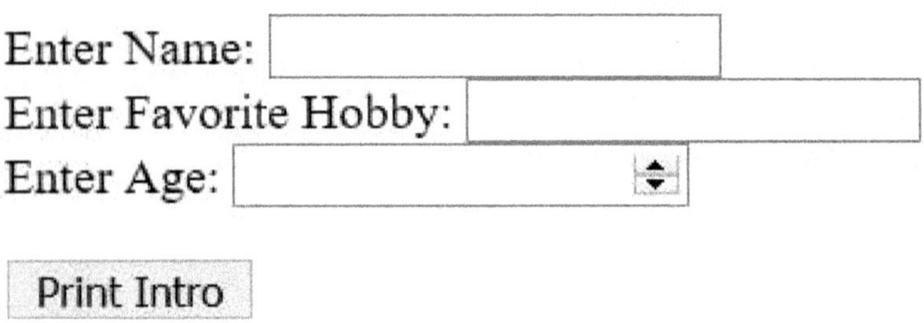

Output (Filled):

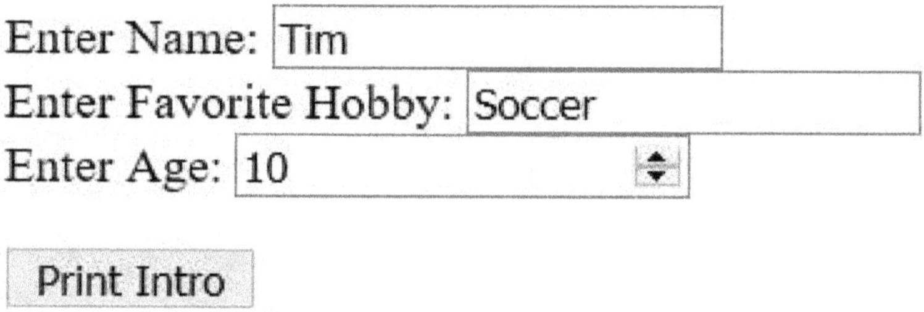

Output (After Clicking 'Print Intro' button)

This is Tim. I am 10 years old.My favorite hobby is Soccer

Breaking down the code:

```
<form id="form1">
Enter Name: <input name="Enter Name" type="text" id="name"
size="20"><br>
Enter Favorite Hobby: <input type="text" id="hobby" size="20"><br>
Enter Age: <input type="number" id="age" size="20"><br>
</form>
```

The html code creates a form with 3 form elements for name, hobby and age. They all have a length of 20 pixels. They are referenced by ids; with id's of name, hobby and age.

```
<button onclick="writename()">Print Intro</button>
```

This html buttons activates the JavaScript function called writename() and the text on the button is Print Intro.

```
function writename()
{
        var nameValue=document.getElementById("name").value;
        var hobbyValue=document.getElementById("hobby").value;
        var ageValue=document.getElementById("age").value;
        document.write("This is "+nameValue+". I am "+ ageValue+"
years old.My favorite hobby is "+hobbyValue);
}
```

The above Javascript code is activated when the button is pressed. nameValue, hobbyValue and ageValue store the values of stuff that is typed into the form elements with id "name", "hobby" and "age". document.write writes out the intro on the screen.

JavaScript Example 2

The code below creates a html form that accepts two numbers and then creates 4 html buttons.
There are 4 Javascript function that add, subtract, multiply or divide the two numbers. A particular JavaScript code is selected based on which buttons are clicked.
The code is shown below with the output; and then a few of the lines are explained later as well.

```
<html>
<head>
<title>Mini Calculator......</title>
</head>
<body>
<form id="form1">
Enter Number 1: <input type="number" id="num1" size="20"><br>
Enter Number 2: <input type="number" id="num2" size="20"><br>
</form>
<button onclick="sum()">+</button>
<button onclick="subtract()">-</button>
<button onclick="multiply()">*</button>
<button onclick="divide()">/</button>

<script>

function sum()
{
    var number1=parseFloat(document.getElementById('num1').value);
    var number2=parseFloat(document.getElementById('num2').value);
    var total=number1+number2;
    document.write("The sum is "+total);
}
function subtract()
{
    var number1=parseFloat(document.getElementById('num1').value);
    var number2=parseFloat(document.getElementById('num2').value);
    var diff=number1-number2;
    document.write("The difference is "+diff);
}
function multiply()
{
    var number1=parseFloat(document.getElementById('num1').value);
    var number2=parseFloat(document.getElementById('num2').value);
    var multi=number1*number2;
    document.write("The product is "+multi);
}
```

```
function divide()
{
    var number1=parseFloat(document.getElementById('num1').value);
    var number2=parseFloat(document.getElementById('num2').value);
    var div=number1/number2;
    document.write("The quotient is "+div);
}
</script>
</body>
</html>
```

Output:

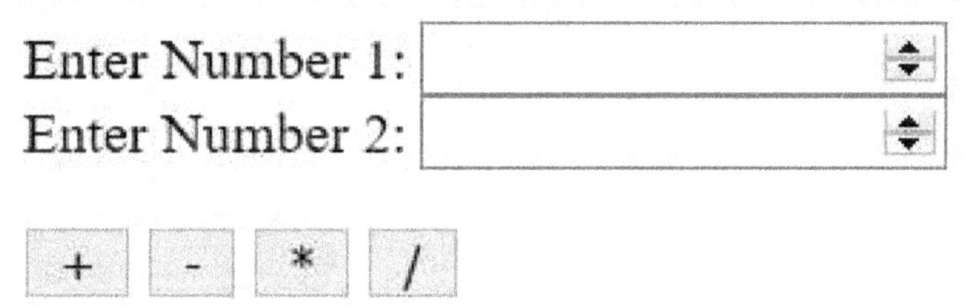

Output Filled:

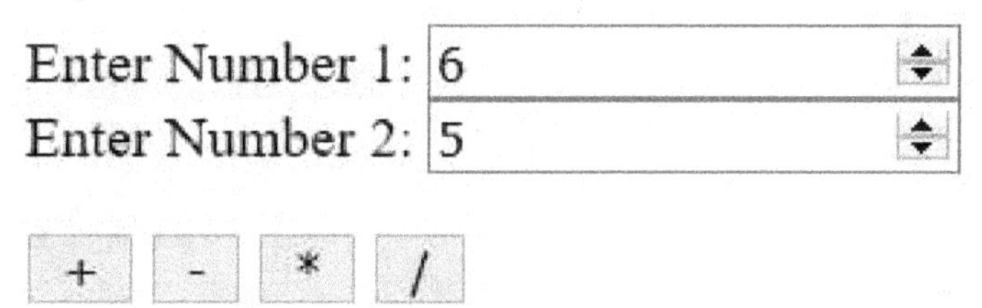

Answers (+ button):

The sum is 11

Answers (- button):

The difference is 1

Answers (* button):

The product is 30

Answers (/ button):

The quotient is 1.2

Breaking Down the Code

```
<form id="form1">
Enter Number 1: <input type="number" id="num1" size="20"><br>
Enter Number 2: <input type="number" id="num2" size="20"><br>
</form>
```

The above code creates a form that accepts two numbers, with ids of num1 and num2.

```
<button onclick="sum()">+</button>
<button onclick="subtract()">-</button>
<button onclick="multiply()">*</button>
<button onclick="divide()">/</button>
```

The above code creates 4 buttons. Each of the 4 buttons activates the functions sum(), subtract(), multiply() and divide().

```
function sum()
{
            var
number1=parseFloat(document.getElementById('num1').value);
        var
number2=parseFloat(document.getElementById('num2').value);
        var total=number1+number2;
        document.write("The sum is "+total);
}
```

number1 and number2 store the numbers that were entered in the form using ids of num1 and num2

Total stores the sum of the two numbers

document.write writes the total on the screen.

Exercises to Practice

You can copy the code above and play around with it. Once you understand the code, you can create your own JavaScript html functions. Here's a couple you can try.

1. Write a program that takes in school marks in 6 subjects using 6 textboxes. Write two Javascript functions that calculate total marks and average marks for the subjects.
2. Write a JavaScript program that takes in 5 different student names and hobbies and prints out names and hobbies of those students.

Conditional Statement

What is the conditional statement?

It is a statement that checks if a certain condition is true. It can be as simple as checking if a number is less than 10 to something as checking medical samples from patients for certain medical conditions. In Javascript, the conditional statement is done using IF ELSE statements.

So, it basically checks that if something is true, then perform an action. If it's not true, then do something else. As an example,

```
IF (George=="Hungry")
        {
        Document.write('Give George a Snack);
        }
ELSE
        {
        Document.write('No snack for George');
        }
```

In the above example, the code checks if George is hungry and performs one of two actions. If George is hungry then it prints 'Give George a snack'. If not, then print 'No snack for George')

This is a simple example of a conditional in JavaScript using IF ELSE statement.

IF ELSE Loop – Example 1

```
<html>
<head>
<title>Check if sum of two numbers is greater than 15......</title>
</head>
<body>
<form id="form1">
Enter Number 1: <input type="number" id="num1" size="20"><br>
Enter Number 2: <input type="number" id="num2" size="20"><br>
</form>
<button onclick="check10()">Check the sum</button>

<script>

function check10()
{
var num1=parseFloat(document.getElementById("num1").value);
var num2=parseFloat(document.getElementById("num2").value);
    if ((num1+num2)<15)
    {
        document.write('Sum of two numbers is less than 15');
    }
    else
    {
        document.write('Sum of two numbers is greater than or equal to 15');
    }
}

</script>
</body>
</html>
```

Output:

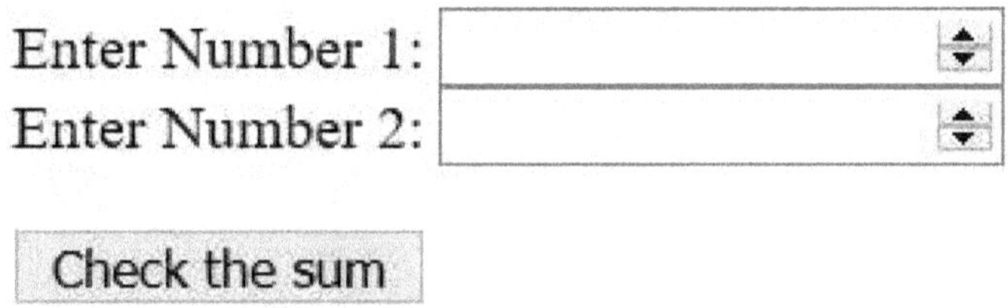

Output (User Filled):

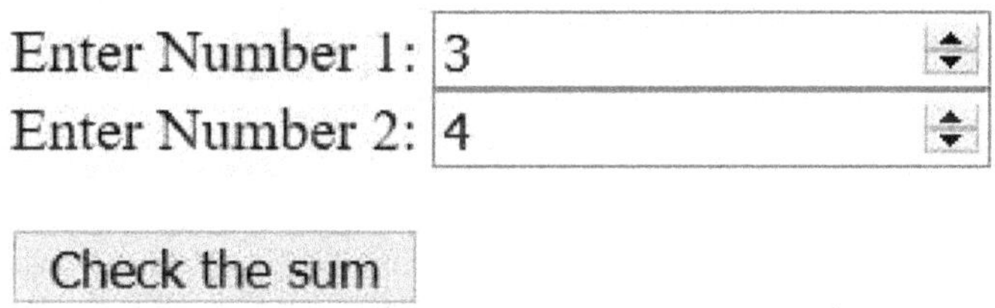

Output (After clicking 'Check the sum' button):

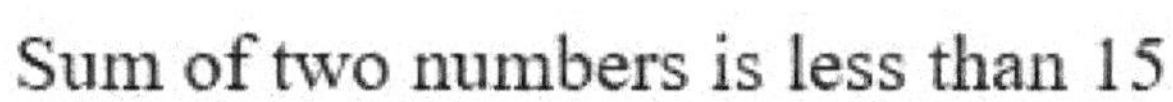

Output (2nd set of numbers filled)

Enter Number 1: 14

Enter Number 2: 3

Check the sum

Output (After Clicking 'Check the Sum' button)

Sum of two numbers is greater than or equal to 15

Breaking down the code:

```
var
num1=parseFloat(document.getElementById("num1").value);
var
num2=parseFloat(document.getElementById("num2").value);
```

These lines store the values of the two numbers filled in by the user in two variables num1 and num2.

```
if ((num1+num2)<15)
```

This checks if the sum of both numbers is greater than 15.

```
{
document.write('Sum of two numbers is less than 15');
}
```

The above loop activates if the sum is less than 15 and prints out 'Sum of two numbers is less than 15.'

```
else
{
document.write('Sum of two numbers is greater than or equal to 15');
}
```

The above loop activates if the sum is greater than 15 and prints out 'Sum of two numbers is greater than or equal to 15.'

IF ELSE Loop – Example 2

```
<html>
<head>
<title>Check if number is divisible by 2......</title>
</head>
<body>
<form id="form1">
Enter Number: <input type="number" id="num1" size="20"><br>
</form>
<button onclick="checkdivby2()">Check div</button>

<script>
function checkdivby2()
{
var number=parseFloat(document.getElementById("num1").value);
if ((number%2)==0)
{
    document.write(number+" is divisible by 2");
}
else
{
    document.write(number+" is not divisible by 2");
}

}
```

Output:

Output (Filled 1):

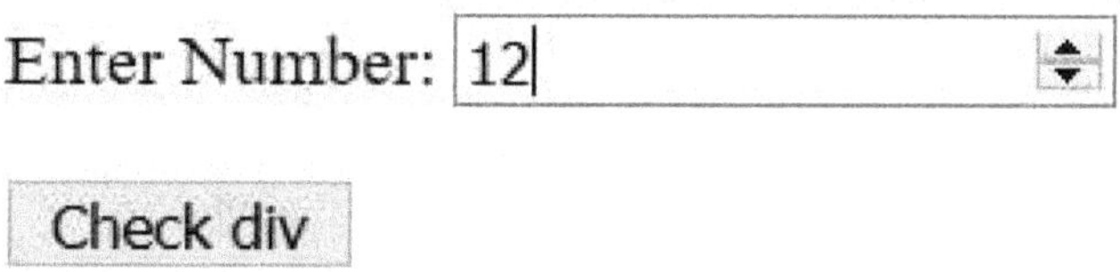

Output (After clicking 'Check div' button)

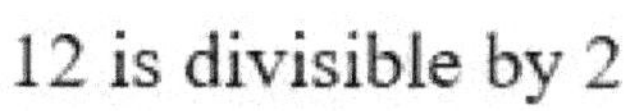

Output (Filled 2):

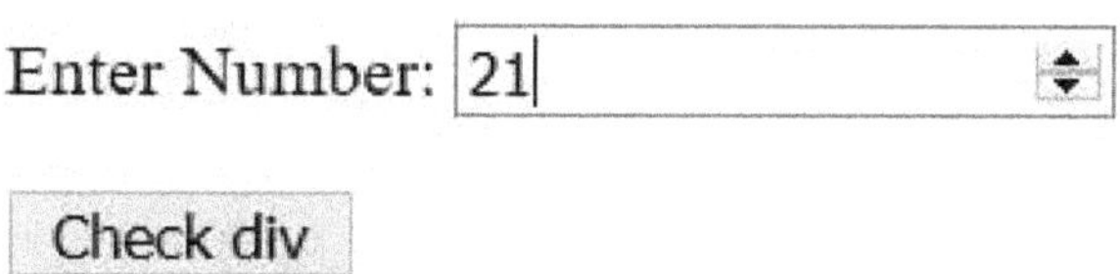

Output (After clicking 'Check div' button)

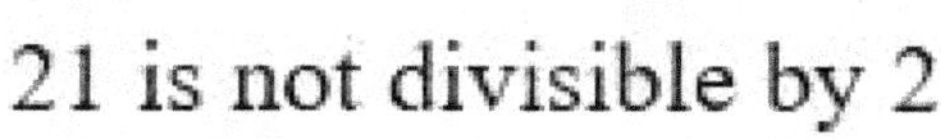

Breaking down the code:

```
if ((number%2)==0)
```

Above line of code checks if number is divisible by 2

```
{
        document.write(number+" is divisible by 2");
}
```

Above section of code is activated if number is divisible by 2. It prints out that the number is divisible by 2.

```
else
{
        document.write(number+" is not divisible by 2");
}
```

Above section of code is activated if number is not divisible by 2. It prints out that the number is not divisible by 2.

Exercises to Practice

You can copy the code above and play around with it. Once you understand the code, you can create your own JavaScript html functions. Here's a couple you can try.

1. Write a program that takes in school marks in 6 subjects using 6 textboxes. Write a JavaScript function that checks the average and then checking if the student passes or fails. If the score is less than 60, then the student fails.
2. Write a program that takes in a year and checks if it is a leap year.

Nested Conditional Statements

These are basically conditional statements within conditional statements. These are also called nested loops.

Let's say that you want to check if two conditions are true in Javascript, before you take an action; then you put two if loops within each other.

Let's take the example from the previous chapter. We want to check if George is hungry and has money to give him a snack.

not true, then do something else. As an example,

```
IF (George=="Hungry")
{
        IF (George=="Has Money")
        {
        Document.write('Buy George a Snack);
        }
        ELSE
        {
        Document.write('Make George a Snack');
        }
}
ELSE
{
        Document.write('No snack for George');
}
```

In the above example, the code checks if George is hungry first. If George is hungry then it performs a 2nd check. It checks if George has money. If George has money, it prints 'Buy George a snack'. If he's hungry but doesn't have money, then print 'Make George a snack').

If he's not hungry, then print 'No snack for George').

This is a simple example of a nested IF ELSE statement in JavaScript.

NESTED IF ELSE LOOP EXAMPLE

In this example, we are going to take a 4 digit year as an input and check if it is a leap year. Now, this is a little more complicated than we think.

We know that every 4 years is a leap year. So that is our first check. So a year like 1996 would be a leap year.

But, every 100 years, there is no leap year. So, 1800 and 1900 are not leap years.

Also, there is another exception. Every 400 years, it is not a leap year. So 1600 and 2000 are not leap years. So there are 3 checks.

```
<html>
<head><title>Leap Year Check</title></head>
<body>
<form id="form1">
Enter Year: <input type="number" id="year" size="20"><br>

</form>
<button onclick="leapyear()">Leap Year?</button>

<script>


function leapyear()
{
var yr=parseInt(document.getElementById("year").value);
var lpyear=0;
    if ((yr%4)==0)//First loop that checks if the year is divisible by 4
    {
        lpyear=1;
        if((yr%100)==0)//Second loop that checks if the year is divisible by 4
        {
            lpyear=0;
            if((yr%400)==0)//Third loop that checks if the year is divisible by 4
            {
                lpyear=1;
            }
        }
    }
if (lpyear==1)
{
    document.write(yr+" is a leap year");
}
else
{
    document.write(yr+" is not a leap year");
}
}
}
</html>
```

Output:

Enter Year: [ ]

[Leap Year?]

Run #1

Enter Year: 1992

[Leap Year?]

Output:

1992 is a leap year

Run #2

Enter Year: 1995

[Leap Year?]

Output:

1995 is not a leap year

Run #3

Enter Year: 1900

Leap Year?

Output:

1900 is not a leap year

Run #4:

Enter Year: 2000

Leap Year?

Output:

2000 is a leap year

As you can see from the above code and results, it properly calculates the leap year through the use of 3 nested if loops.
1992 is a leap year since it is divisible by 4.
1995 is not a leap year since it is not divisible by 4.
1900 is not a leap year since it is divisible by 100.
2000 is a leap year since it is divisible by 400.

Exercises to Practice

You can copy the code above and play around with it. Once you understand the code, you can create your own JavaScript html functions. Here's a couple you can try.

1. Three sensors are attached to a printing device, with three alarms attached to the sensors. The first sensor, "A," detects if the device needs ink. The second sensor, "B," detects if the device needs repair. The third sensor, "C," detects if the device should jam. An alarm sounds if 2 or more problems occur.

2. Schools are given snow days given specific circumstances. If there is ice on the roads, but no salt, then a snow day is given. If there is salt however, then a snow day is not given. Regardless of whether or not there is salt, whenever there is >2 inches of snow, then a snow day is given.
3. A computer chip controls whether or not children are allowed to watch a specific TV show. If the time is before 5PM, then the TV always works. However, if it's after 5PM, then the shows rating is used. If the rating is for General Audiences, then the TV will work; however, if the rating is for Mature Audiences, then the TV does not turn on.

Loops

A loop is a set of instructions that is repeated a certain amount of times. In most cases, a certain process is done and there is a count of the process that increases by 1. At the end of the process, we check if the count is over the number of times we need the process done. If it has reached the number of times we need, then we stop the loop.

For example, let's say you want to print the numbers 1 to 10 on the screen. Then use a loop which counts from 1 to 10. It prints the count on the screen each time.

In JavaScript, we use a function called FOR to implement this loop. We'll go through a simple example below.

Example #1

```
<html>
<head><title>Print 1 to 20</title></head>
<body>


<button onclick="printtotwenty()">Print To 20</button>

<script>

function printtotwenty()
{

for (i=1;i<=20;i++)
{
    document.write(i+"<br>");
}

}

</script>


</body>
</html>
```

In this function we create a function printotwenty that prints the numbers from 1 to 20. The button titled ‘Print To 20’ activates the function.

In the function there is a for loop:

For (i=1;i<=20; i++)

The line above means that the loop runs from 1 to 20; and it increases by a value of 1 each time.

The Document.write prints the value of i each time.

Here’s a look at the results below:

After clicking the button, we get:

```
1
2
3
4
5
6
7
8
9
10
11
12
13
14
15
16
17
18
19
20
```

Prints 1 to 20 as planned. So, next, we're going to do a different version of the same program. Instead of printing just 1 to 20; we're going to let you choose how many numbers you want to print. Just put the length of the loop in the textbox and it will print it out.

Example #2

```
<html>
<head><title>JavaScript Greetings......</title></head>
<body>
<form id="form1">
Loop Length: <input type="number" id="loop" size="20"><br>
</form>

<button onclick="printtotwenty()">Print To 100</button>
<button onclick="printlooplength()">Print Loop Length</button>

<script>

function printtotwenty()
{

for (i=1;i<=20;i++)
{
    document.write(i+"<br>");
}

}

function printlooplength()
{
var looplength=parseInt(document.getElementById("loop").value);

var j=1;
for (j=1;j<=looplength;j++)
    {
    document.write(j+"<br>");
    }
}


</script>


</body>
</html>
```

Now, after running the program, we get:

So, now click **'Print Loop Length'**

So, it prints from 1 to 50. If you want to print 1 to 100, then enter 100 in the textbox and click the same button.

The program above has an extra textbox and extra button. The textbox is for accepting the length of the loop and the button links to a function called printlooplength () that prints the star loop. The variable looplength stores the value that you put in the textbox. The FOR loop runs from 1 to looplength. In the above example, looplength is 50; so it runs from 1 to 50. Each time it runs, it prints the counter using document.write function.

Example #3

Now, we're going to do something even cooler with loops. We're going to print a star pattern based on the loop length.

```
<html>
<head><title>JavaScript Greetings......</title></head>
<body>
<form id="form1">
Loop Length: <input type="number" id="loop" size="20"><br>
Star Loop Length: <input type="number" id="starloop" size="20"><br>
</form>

<button onclick="printtotwenty()">Print To 100</button>
<button onclick="printlooplength()">Print Loop Length</button>
<button onclick="looplengthstar()">Print Star Loop</button>

<script>

function printtotwenty()
{

for (i=1;i<=20;i++)
{
    document.write(i+"<br>");
}

}

function printlooplength()
{
var looplength=parseInt(document.getElementById("loop").value);

var j=1;
for (j=1;j<=looplength;j++)
    {
    document.write(j+"<br>");
    }
}
function looplengthstar()
{
var looplength=parseInt(document.getElementById("starloop").value);

for (i=1;i<=looplength;i++) {
    for (j=1;j<=i;j++)
    {
    document.write("*");
    }
    document.write("<br>");
```

```
function looplengthstar()
{
var looplength=parseInt(document.getElementById("starloop").value);

for (i=1;i<=looplength;i++) {
     for (j=1;j<=i;j++)
     {
     document.write("*");
     }
     document.write("<br>");
     }
}


</script>


</body>
</html>
```

The output below:

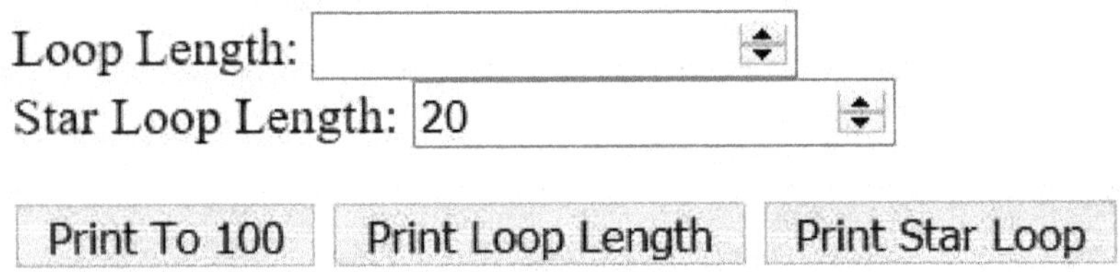

After entering 20, and clicking ‘Print Star Loop’ we get:

*

**

***

****

*****

******

****

****

****

****

****

****

****

****

****

****

****

****

****

****

The program above has an extra textbox and extra button. The textbox is for accepting the length of the starloop and the button links to a function called looplengthstar() that prints the star loop.

Looplengthstar() is a nested FOR loop, which means that it has 1 loop within the other. The variable looplength stores the value of the star loop length that you entered. The first FOR loop goes from 1 to looplength. So, in the example above, the first loop is from 1 to 20. So, within that, there is another FOR loop. The second loop basically prints '*' in one line. The number of times it prints * depends on the counter in the first loop.

For example, if the first loop counter is 5 (i=5); then the second loop prints star 5 times. Something like this – '*****'.

So, the second loop does this each time the first loop is increased and moves to the next line.

Exercises to Practice:

You can copy the above examples and once you are able to run them and understand the code; you can try a few of the problems below.

1. The Fibonacci series is a set of numbers like this 0,1,1,2,3,5,8,13.... Every number is the sum of the previous two numbers. Using a FOR loop, print the first 20 numbers of the sequence.
2. Write a program that takes in a number in a textbox and prints a reverse star loop.
3. Write a program that takes in a number in a textbox and prints the sum of its digits.

Arrays

What is An Array?

An array is basically a group of items that are stored in a single name. They are accessed using different indexes of the name. For example, in Javascript:

var name[5] is an array of size 5. The first element is name[0], the second element is name[1] and so on.....

So, if we want to assign values to the array:

var name[5]=["Abhi","Bob","Aaron","Steve","Mark"]

The above creates an array of size 5. To print the first element in JavaScript, we do:

document.write(name[0]);

This prints out Abhi, which is the first element of the array.

If we do:

document.write(name[4]);

This prints out Mark, which is the last element of the array.

If we want to add an element to the array use the push function as below:

name.push("Carl");

document.write(name[5]);

This prints out Carl, which is the new element of the array.

Now, let's go through a couple of examples:

Example 1

In this example, we create 3 arrays and assign them values in JavaScript, and then print them on the screen.

```
<html>
<head><title>Arrays 1</title></head>
<body>

<button onclick="createarray()">Create Array</button>


<script>

function createarray()
{
var name = ["Bob","Peter","Nick"];
var age=[32,10,11];
var loc=new Array("New York","Rockford","Kansas");// 2nd way to start array
document.write(name[0]+' lives in '+loc[0]+' and age is '+age[0]+"<br>");
document.write(name[1]+' lives in '+loc[1]+' and age is '+age[1]+"<br>");
document.write(name[2]+' lives in '+loc[2]+' and age is '+age[2]+"<br>");
name.push("Steve");
age.push(20);
loc.push("Miami");
document.write(name[3]+' lives in '+loc[3]+' and age is '+age[3]+"<br>");
}

</script>


</body>
</html>
```

The above example, createarray() creates 3 arrays name, age and loc. Each array has three elements assigned. They are printed on the screen using document.write().

After that we add a 4th element using push for all 3 arrays and then that is printed out as well.

Create Array

Once we click the "Create Array" button:

Bob lives in New York and age is 32
Peter lives in Rockford and age is 10
Nick lives in Kansas and age is 11
Steve lives in Miami and age is 20

We basically just print out all the elements of an array.
Now that we know how to create an array, let's do it with info that we enter into textboxes.

Example 2

```
<html>
<head><title>Arrays 2</title></head>
<body>
<form id="form1">
Enter Name:<input name="name" type="text" id="name" size="20"><br>

Enter Work Day 1:<select style="width: 280px" id="day1" name="Day 1">
<option value='Sunday'>Sunday</option>
<option value='Monday'>Monday</option>
<option value='Tuesday'>Tuesday</option>
<option value='Wednesday'>Wednesday</option>
<option value='Thursday'>Thursday</option>
<option value='Friday'>Friday</option>
<option value='Saturday'>Saturday</option>
</select>
<br>

Enter Work Day 2:<select style="width: 280px" id="day2" name="Day 2">
<option value='Sunday'>Sunday</option>
<option value='Monday'>Monday</option>
<option value='Tuesday'>Tuesday</option>
<option value='Wednesday'>Wednesday</option>
<option value='Thursday'>Thursday</option>
<option value='Friday'>Friday</option>
<option value='Saturday'>Saturday</option>
</select>
<br>

</form>

<button onclick="assignarray()">Info Array</button>
<script>
function assignarray()
{
var name=document.getElementById("name").value;
var day1=document.getElementById("day1").value;
var day2=document.getElementById("day2").value;
var employeeobj=[name,day1,day2];
document.write(employeeobj[0]+" works on "+employeeobj[1]+" and "+employeeobj[2]);
}
}
</script>
</body>
</html>
```

The above code takes user input from 1 textbox and 2 select boxes. The select boxes are set up so you can choose between 7 work days (Sunday-Wednesday) as shown below:

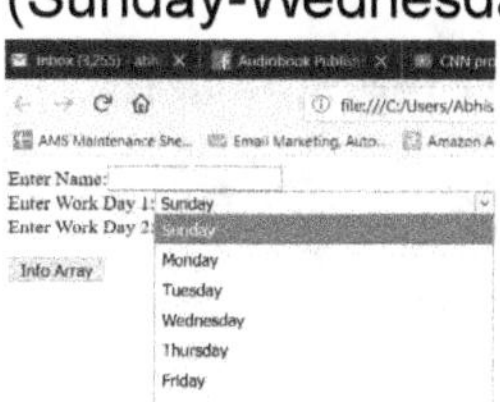

Once the “Info Array” button is clicked, the assignarray() function takes in the 3 inputs and creates 1 single array called employeeobj.
employeeobj[0] is the first element and is assigned the name.
employeeobj[1] is the first element and is assigned the name.
employeeobj[2] is the first element and is assigned the name.
Then we use document.write to print all 3 on the screen. Now, let’s run the program.

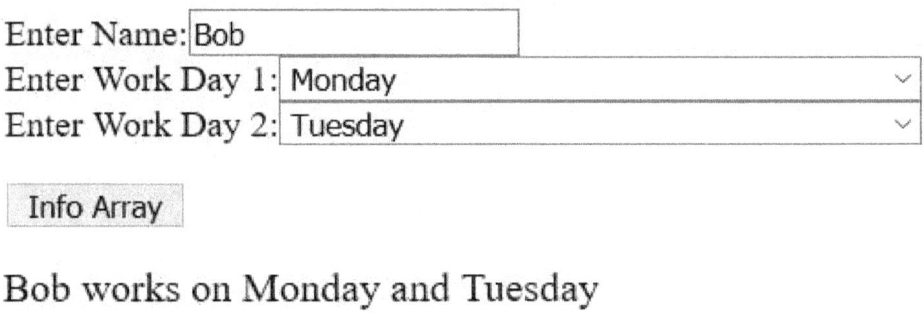

You can copy the above code, and implement the same program on your computer. Now, once you’re able to do that; let’s do some more problems:

Exercises to Practice

You can copy the above examples and once you are able to run them and understand the code; you can try a few of the problems below.

1. Create 5 arrays for your school. The first array stores the value of a student’s name; second stores their mark in Math; third stores their mark in History; and 4th stores their mark in English. Now, calculate the average and store it in the 5th array. The

name and 3 marks are input through text boxes and the function will print out the student's name and average.

2. Create an array of size 12 that stores the months of the year. The user can input the number of the month through a textbox; and the function should link the number with the actual month using the array. Then print out the relevant month in the array.

Having Fun with Strings

Strings and String Variables

We've touched on this in the previous chapters. A string is any piece of text that is used in a program. As an example, "abcd" is a string; while the number 7 is not a string. It is an integer.

A string variable is a place to store a string. As an example, st is a string variable below that stores the value of "abcd".

var st="abcd";

Now, let's have some fun with strings using our knowledge of JavaScript and loops.

Finding Length of a String

Now, let's input a string in a textbox and find the length of the string.

```
<html>
<head><title>JavaScript Lesson 4 - Strings</title></head>
<body>
<form id="form1">
Enter Name:<input name="name" type="text" id="name" size="20"><br>
</form>
<button onclick="strlength()">Name Length</button>
<script>

function strlength()
{
var name2=document.getElementById("name").value;
document.write(name2.length);
}
</script>

</body>
</html>
```

The code below lets you input your name through a textbox. When you click the button, it runs the function strlength() that calculates the length of your name.
name2 is the variable that stores the value of your name.
name2.length gets the length of the string (number of letters in your name).
Let's look at the output:

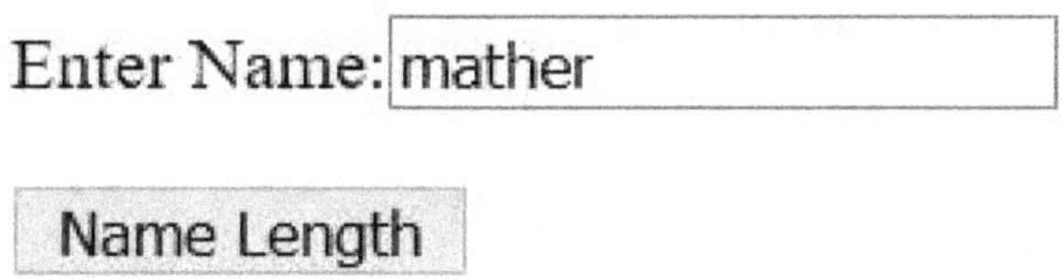

After clicking the button **'Name Length',** we get:

6

Let's do another example:

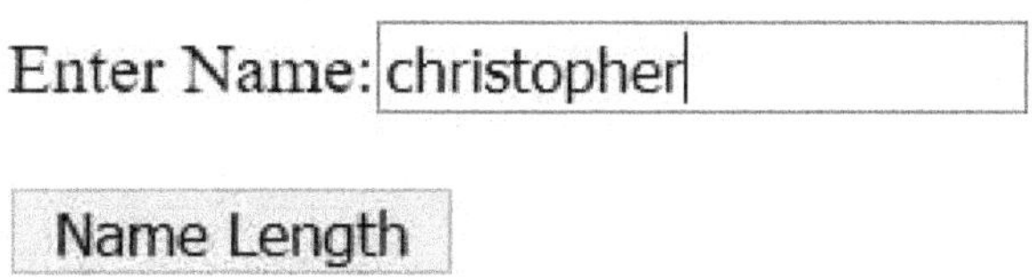

After clicking the button **'Name Length',** we get:

11

So, now that we know how to find the length of a string, let's use that knowledge to reverse your name. The code below does that.

```
<html>
<head><title>JavaScript Lesson 4 - Strings</title></head>
<body>
<form id="form1">
Enter Name:<input name="name" type="text" id="name" size="20"><br>
</form>
<button onclick="strlength()">Name Length</button>
<button onclick="namereverse()">Name Reverse</button>
<script>

function strlength()
{
var name2=document.getElementById("name").value;
document.write(name2.length);
}

function namereverse()
{
var name2=document.getElementById("name").value;
len=name2.length;
for (i=len-1;i>=0;i--)
{
document.write(name2[i]);
}
}

</script>

</body>
</html>
```

The code below lets you input your name through a textbox. When you click the button, it runs the function namereverse() that reverses your name.

Name2 stores the value you entered for your name

len stores the number of letters in your name.

Then we create a loop than runs from len-1 to 0. The reason we use 0 is because name2 is an array of letters. The first index of the array is 0 in JavaScript. So the first character is name2[0].

In the loop, we go backwards and decrease the count by 1 each time. And, within the loop, we print the value of the character that is indexed by the count.

Now, let's run the program:

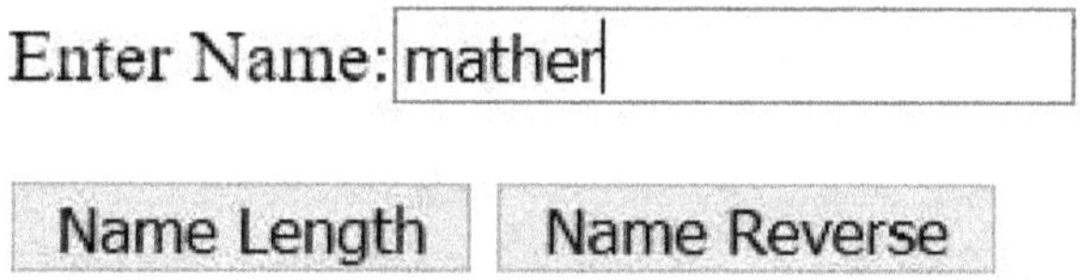

After clicking **Name Reverse** button, we get

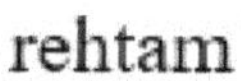

Now, what if you have a lot of spaces at the end of a string. Let's fix that by trimming strings.

Splitting Strings

Now, did you know that you can split a string into an array of elements. You can achieve this using the split function. Now, let's try an example. In the code below, you take a list of 3 animals as input into a textbox which are separated by commas.
The split function separates this into an array of 3 elements and you can print out each element using document.write function.

```
<html>
<head><title>Splitting Strings</title></head>
<body>
<form id="form1">
Enter List of 3 Animals separated by commas:<input name="name" type="text" id="ani" size="20"><br>

</form>
<button onclick="strsplit()">Get Animals</button>

<script>

function strsplit()
{
var animal=document.getElementById("ani").value;
aniarray=animal.split(",");           // Split on commas
document.write("The first animal is "+aniarray[0]+"<br>");
document.write("The second animal is "+aniarray[1]+"<br>");
document.write("The third animal is "+aniarray[2]+"<br>");
}

</script>
</body>
</html>
```

Now, let's check out the output:

Enter List of 3 Animals separated by commas: tiger, lion, wolf

Get Animals

After clicking the button **Get Animals** we have:

The first animal is tiger
The second animal is lion
The third animal is wolf

The above code works if you have 3 animals as input. You might ask if there's a code that can work for more than 3 animals. Yes, it can. You need to find the length of the string array using length function and then use a FOR loop when printing the animals. In the forloop, we use aninumber to keep track of the animal count; and aniarray[i] to keep track of the actual animals to print.

Note that aninumber is always 1 more than i, because i starts from 0 in a JavaScript array.

Here's the code below:

```
<html>
<head><title>Splitting Strings</title></head>
<body>
<form id="form1">
Enter List of Animals separated by commas:<input name="name" type="text" id="ani" size="20"><br>
</form>

<button onclick="strsplit()">Get Animals</button>

<script>

function strsplit()
{
var animal=document.getElementById("ani").value;
aniarray=animal.split(",");          // Split on commas
var len=aniarray.length;
var aninumber;
for (i=0; i<=len-1;i++)
{
aninumber=i+1;
document.write("Animal "+aninumber+" is "+aniarray[i]+"<br>");
}
}

</script>
</body>
</html>
```

And, here's the output below.

Enter List of Animals separated by commas: ı, tiger, wolf, rhino, dog

Get Animals

We enter names of 5 animals and click the **Get Animals** button.

Animal 1 is lion
Animal 2 is tiger
Animal 3 is wolf
Animal 4 is rhino
Animal 5 is dog

Replacing Strings

Now, let's say you have a long paragraph and you want to replace a particular word with another. You use the function .replace.

In the below example, we replace "Atlanta" with "Charleston". Please remember that this works for only 1 instance of Atlanta.

We use a html form element called textarea. Textarea is a bigger form of textbox which can take multiple lines of text from the user. And then we write the modified sentence on the screen.

```
<html>
<head><title>Replacing Strings</title></head>
<body>
<form id="form1">
What was your day like?: <textarea name="sentence" cols="20" rows="5" id="sentence"></textarea><br><br>

</form>

<button onclick="strreplace()">Fix Sentence</button>

<script>

function strreplace()
{
var daydesc=document.getElementById("sentence").value;
var daydescmod=daydesc.replace("Atlanta","Charleston");
document.write(daydescmod);
}

</script>
</body>
</html>
```

Now, let's run the program.

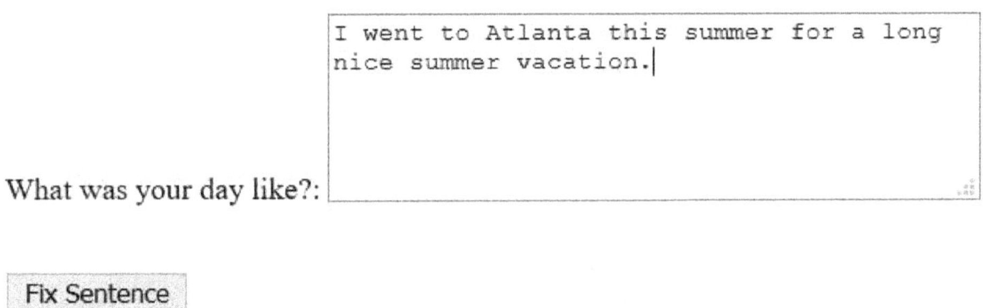

Once we click **Fix Sentence** button, we get:

I went to Charleston this summer for a long nice summer vacation.

Substrings and String Index

There are a couple of other string manipulation techniques that I would like to discuss before we move on. These are string index and substring.

String Index gives you the position within a certain string that another string occurs. For example, the string index of boy in the string "The boy climbed the tree" is 4, because boy starts at the 4th character of the overall string.

A substring lets you extract a section of an existing string. For example, in the same string "The boy climbed the tree"; if we do a substring from 6 to 10 we get "oy cl" because those are the characters between 6 and 10.

Now, let's look at an example below:

```
<html>
<head><title>Substrings and String Index</title></head>
<body>
<form id="form1">
What was your day like?: <textarea name="sentence" cols="20" rows="5" id="sentence"></textarea><br><br>
What String would you like to find the String Index Of?:<input name="test string" type="text" id="tstr" size="20"><br><br>
</form>

<button onclick="strindex()">Find Index</button>

<script>

function strindex()
{
var daydesc=document.getElementById("sentence").value;
var str = document.getElementById("tstr").value;
var ind=daydesc.indexOf(str);
document.write("The String Index is "+ind);
}

</script>
</body>
</html>
```

In the above example, daydesc is the large string and str is the string we need to find the string index for. The variable ind stores the value of the string index and then we print the answer using document.write.

Now, let's run the program:

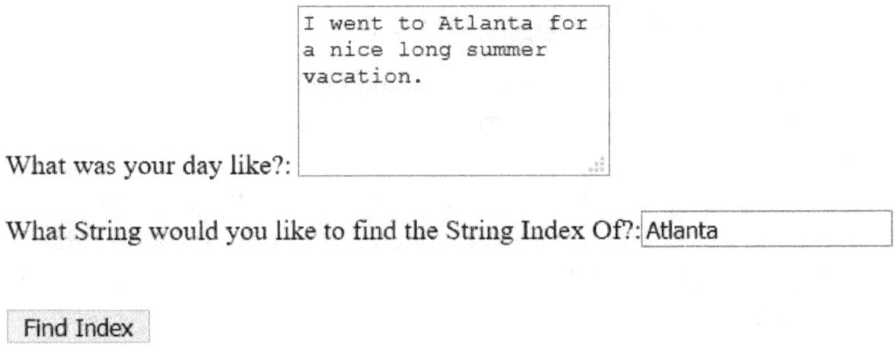

Once we click **Find Index**, we get:

The String Index is 10

Alright, now let's look at an example of Substrings below:

```
<html>
<head><title>Substrings and String Index</title></head>
<body>
<form id="form1">
What was your day like?: <textarea name="sentence" cols="20" rows="5" id="sentence"></textarea><br><br>
Substring From?:<input name="test string" type="number" id="tstr1" size="20"><br><br>
Substring To?:<input name="test string" type="number" id="tstr2" size="20"><br><br>
</form>

<button onclick="substr()">Find SubString</button>

<script>

function substr()
{
var daydesc=document.getElementById("sentence").value;
var strnum1 = document.getElementById("tstr1").value;
var strnum2 = document.getElementById("tstr2").value;

var sstr=daydesc.substring(strnum1,strnum2);
document.write("The SubString is "+sstr);
}

</script>
</body>
</html>
```

In the code above, strnum1 and strnum2 are variables that store the first and last element of the substr. These are inputs from the user. sstr is the substring that goes from strnum1 to strnum2 and is printed out on the screen.

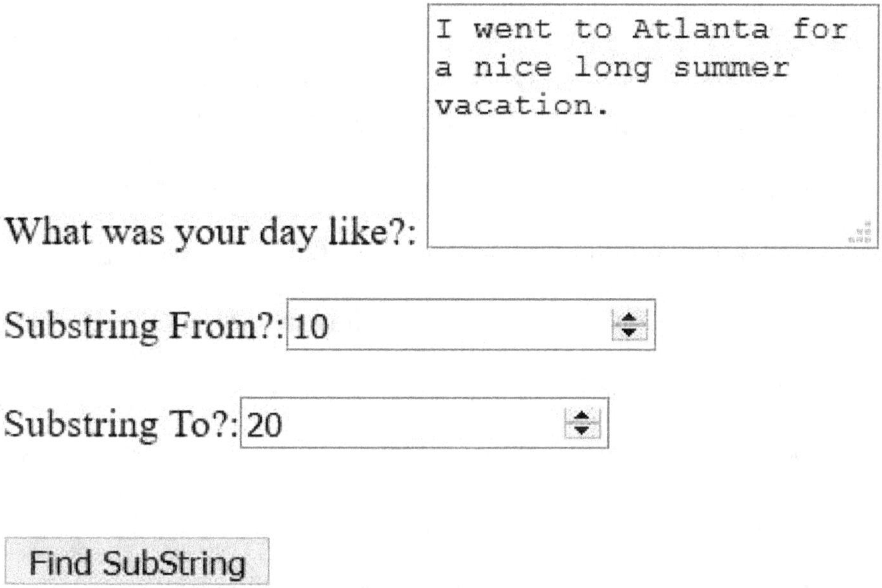

Once we click **Find SubString**, we get the answer:

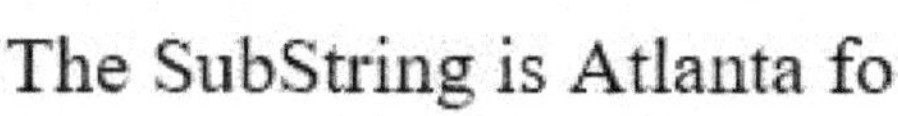

The answer above is 10 characters if we include the space.

Exercises to Practice:

You can copy the above examples and once you are able to run them and understand the code; you can try a few of the problems below.

1. Write a program that find how many times a particular string occurs within a bigger string that is input in a textbox?
2. Write a program that takes in a string that includes a name, math mark, English mark, physics mark and geography mark. Use the split function to separate the string and find the average score for the person. For example, “Mark, 90, 34, 56, 65” would find the average of 90, 34, 56, 65 for Mark.

   Hint: You can use parseint() to convert the scores into numbers.

Introduction to CSS

What is CSS?

CSS stands for cascading style sheets. CSS is used to set up the design and style of your website – including the fonts, colors, layouts, shading and schemes. They work great in partnership with html and JavaScript.

How to Use CSS in a html website

The best way to use CSS is to create a separate css file and refer to it in the html header file.
Now, let's create a css file.

1. Open a blank Notepad++ document.

2. Click 'Save As' and choose file type as 'CSS'. Let's name this file as style

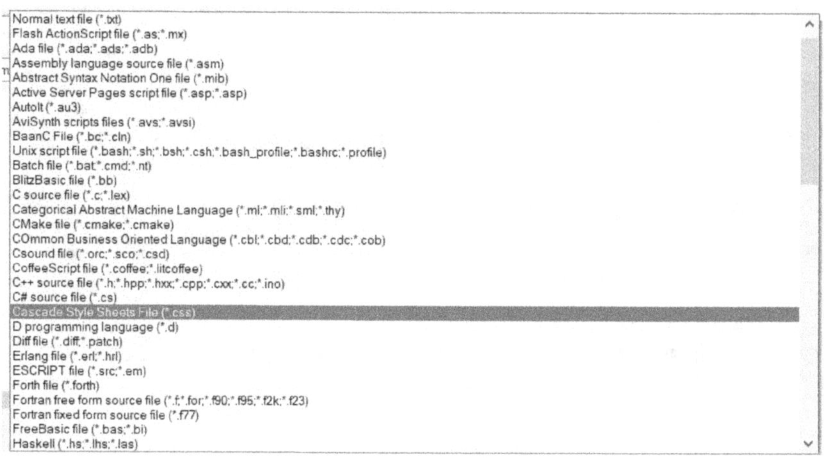

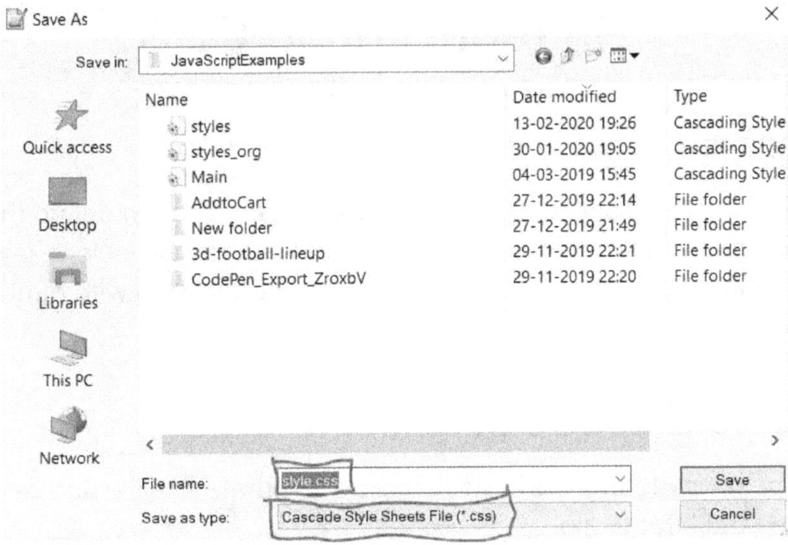

3. Click 'Save'

4. Go to the relevant html and include the line below in the header file.

```
<link rel="stylesheet" href="style.css" />
```

5. (Optional) If you want to include any button css elements, you need a define a button class as below:

```
<button class ="btn str" onclick="substr()">Find SubString</button>
```

Now, let's insert the style sheet in the example from last chapter.

```
<html>
<head>
<title>Substrings and String Index</title>
<link rel="stylesheet" href="style.css" />
</head>
<body>
<form id="form1">
What was your day like?: <textarea name="sentence" cols="20" rows="5" id="sentence"></textarea><br><br>
Substring From?:<input name="test string" type="number" id="tstr1" size="20"><br><br>
Substring To?:<input name="test string" type="number" id="tstr2" size="20"><br><br>
</form>

<button class ="btn str" onclick="substr()">Find SubString</button>

<script>

function substr()
{
var daydesc=document.getElementById("sentence").value;
var strnum1 = document.getElementById("tstr1").value;
var strnum2 = document.getElementById("tstr2").value;

var sstr=daydesc.substring(strnum1,strnum2);
document.write("The SubString is "+sstr);
}

</script>
</body>
</html>
```

Great. Now our CSS sheet is linked to our html file.

CSS Terms

html{}

The above term is used to define css for the entire html file. Any thing that is within the bracket will be used in the html code.

body{}

Defines the style for the body of the html code.

.btn{}

Sets the style for any buttons in the web page. You have to define a class called 'btn' in your html code for the button. See code above for example of that.

.btn:hover{}

sets the style for the button when you hover the mouse over the button in the web page.

background-color:

Background color of the website.

text-decoration:

Used to add decoration to the text such as wavy, dotted, curved etc.

text-transform:

Used the capitalize and un-capitalize entire words or parts of a word

text-align:

Can align the text at the left, right or center of the page.

color:

Sets the color of the text on the page

padding:

Sets the gap between the edge of the page and the text/button elements.

line-height:

Sets the height of the line for the text.

font-family:

Sets the type of font that you want to use for the text.

font-size:

Sets the size of the font.

font-weight:

Can set the font as bold when needed.

These are some of the CSS properties we will use in our example. But, there are 1000's of CSS properties available for a variety of different purposes. If you want to learn more, you can check them out here: https://www.tutorialrepublic.com/css-reference/css3-properties.php

So, let's look at an example for our CSS file:

CSS Example

```
html, body {
     text-decoration: none;
     text-transform: capitalize;
     text-align: center;
     margin: 0;
     padding-top: 100px;
     min-height: 100%;
     color: black;
     background-color: cyan;
     line-height: 1;
     font-family:serif;
     font-size: 20px;
     font-weight: bold;

}
.btn {
   background-color: Crimson;
   border: none;
   color: black;
   padding: 10px 24px;
   text-align: center;
   text-decoration: none;
   display: inline-block;
   font-size: 16px;
}
.btn:hover {
   background-color: MidnightBlue;
   color: white;
}
```

In the html and body of the css code, the text is set to center of the page and capitalized. It is 100 px from the top and black in color with a line height of 1. It is bold in color with font size of 20px. The background of the page is cyan (light blue).

There is a separate css set up for the button. It is Crimson (Red) in color with black text. The text is 10 px from the top and 24 px from the sides. It is center aligned with a 16px font size.

When we hover the button with the mouse, the background of the button changes to MidnightBlue (Blue) and the text changes to White. We can see what it looks like below. Let's look at our website in 2 ways, once before CSS is applied; once after CSS file is linked.

Output (Without CSS):

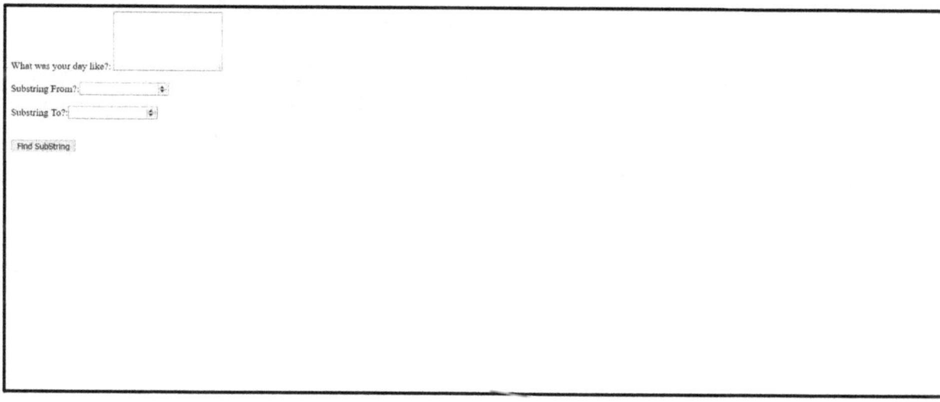

Output (with CSS):

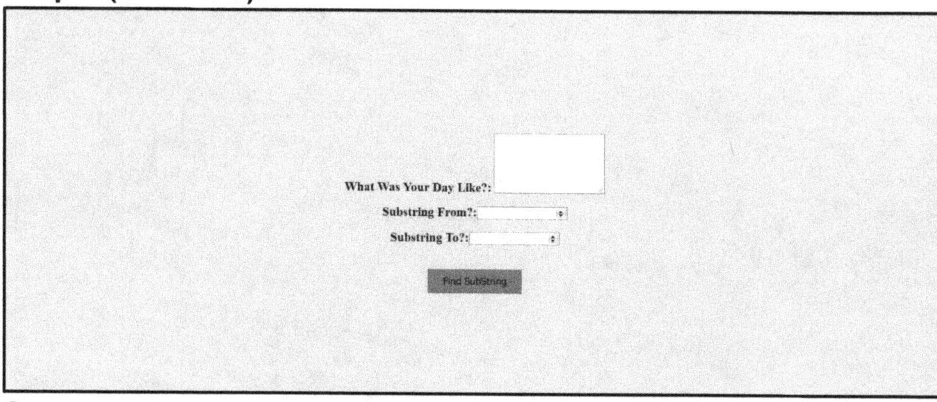

Output (with CSS and mouse hovering over button):

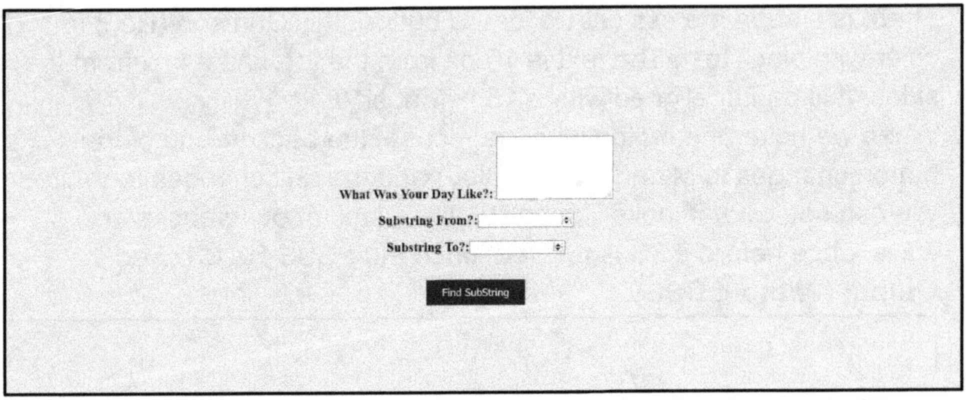

As you can see, it makes a huge difference to the visual appeal of the website. You can customize all these elements yourself with different colors for the text, background and buttons.

Exercises to Practice:

You can copy the above examples and once you are able to run them and understand the code; you can try a few of the problems below.

1. Modify the style elements to find the elements that look the best for you. Try 5 different color fonts, different text sizes and different text forms to find the best-looking website.
2. Use the style.css file to create a style sheet for all the programs you have written so far.

Linking Multiple Web Pages

Now, you have a web page set up with CSS linked up. But you may notice that the web page switches back to the original design when you click the Find Substring button. This is because the JavaScript section is not linked to the webpage yet.

To refresh your memory, the code we are talking about takes in a string and prints a substring based on the preference of the user. The user specifies the start and end of the substring. Here's the code below:

```
<html>
<head>
<title>Substrings and String Index</title>
<link rel="stylesheet" href="style.css" />
</head>
<body>
<form id="form1">
What was your day like?: <textarea name="sentence" cols="20" rows="5" id="sentence"></textarea><br><br>
Substring From?:<input name="test string" type="number" id="tstr1" size="20"><br><br>
Substring To?:<input name="test string" type="number" id="tstr2" size="20"><br><br>
</form>

<button class ="btn str" onclick="substr()">Find SubString</button>

<script>

function substr()
{
var daydesc=document.getElementById("sentence").value;
var strnum1 = document.getElementById("tstr1").value;
var strnum2 = document.getElementById("tstr2").value;

var sstr=daydesc.substring(strnum1,strnum2);
document.write("The SubString is "+sstr);
}

</script>
</body>
</html>
```

As you can see the code is linked to the style.css sheet to get the current design.

So, we get an output below:

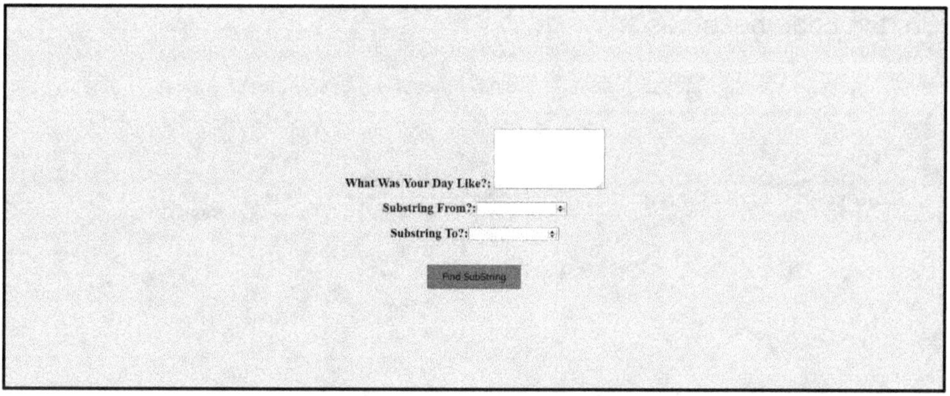

Now, let's run the program:

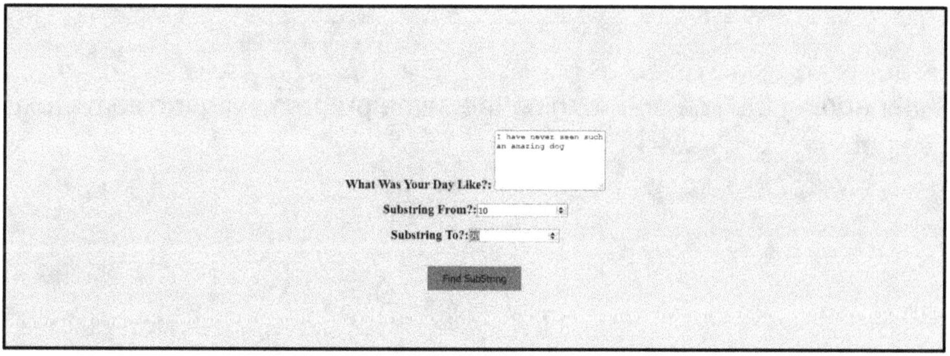

On clicking, Find Substring, we get:

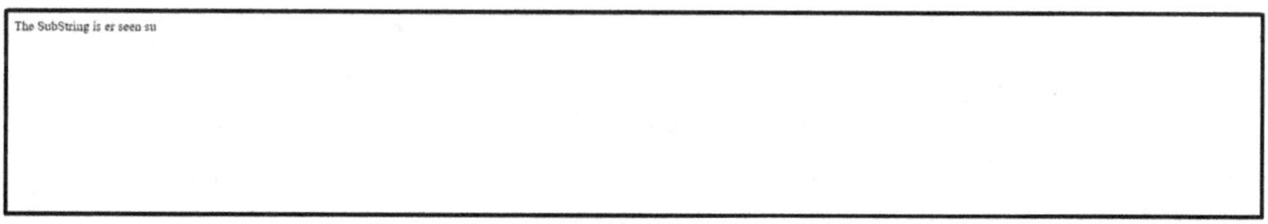

As you can see, it reverts back to the old design. Now, let's fix this. We just add the below code to the Javascript function before document.write.

Document.write('<link rel="stylesheet" type="text/css" href="styles.css" />');

This code basically writes the stylesheet onto the Javascript function.

So, the code becomes:

```
<html>
<head>
<title>Substrings and String Index</title>
<link rel="stylesheet" href="styles.css" />
</head>
<body>
<form id="form1">
What was your day like?: <textarea name="sentence" cols="20" rows="5" id="sentence"></textarea><br><br>
Substring From?:<input name="test string" type="number" id="tstr1" size="20"><br><br>
Substring To?:<input name="test string" type="number" id="tstr2" size="20"><br><br>
</form>

<button class ="btn str" onclick="substr()">Find SubString</button>

<script>

function substr()
{
var daydesc=document.getElementById("sentence").value;
var strnum1 = document.getElementById("tstr1").value;
var strnum2 = document.getElementById("tstr2").value;

var sstr=daydesc.substring(strnum1,strnum2);
document.write('<link rel="stylesheet" type="text/css" href="style.css" />');
document.write("The Substring is "+sstr);
}
```

After adding the line and running the same program with the same text, we get:

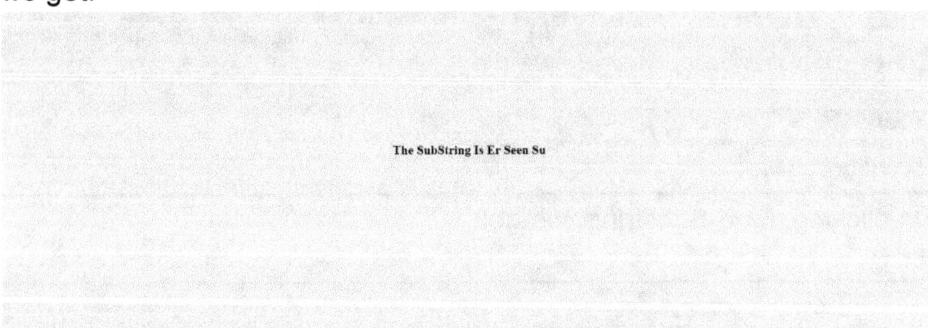

So, that's great, we have the JavaScript output with the same css.
Now, you might want to create another substring. How do we do that?
We need a Home button.
Let's create that. The code below helps with that.

```
<html>
<head>
<title>Substrings and String Index</title>
<link rel="stylesheet" href="styles.css" />
</head>
<body>
<form id="form1">
What was your day like?: <textarea name="sentence" cols="20" rows="5" id="sentence"></textarea><br><br>
Substring From?:<input name="test string" type="number" id="tstr1" size="20"><br><br>
Substring To?:<input name="test string" type="number" id="tstr2" size="20"><br><br>
</form>

<button class ="btn str" onclick="substr()">Find SubString</button>

<script>

function substr()
{
var daydesc=document.getElementById("sentence").value;
var strnum1 = document.getElementById("tstr1").value;
var strnum2 = document.getElementById("tstr2").value;

var sstr=daydesc.substring(strnum1,strnum2);
document.write('<link rel="stylesheet" type="text/css" href="style.css" />');
document.write("The SubString is "+sstr);
document.write("<br>");
document.write('<button class = "btn home" onClick="redirect()">Home</button>');
}

function redirect()
{
window.location.replace("strcomma.html");
}
```

document.write("<br>") creates a space after the substring and moves to the next line.

```
document.write('<button class = "btn home"
onClick="redirect()">Home</button>');
```

The above line creates a button that implements the redirect function on clicking.

We create a function that redirects the user to our original webpage.

```
function redirect()
{
window.location.replace("strcomma.html");
}
```

Strcomma.html is the name of the file. So it basically restarts the file.
Alright, now lets run the program. After doing so and using the same text, we get:

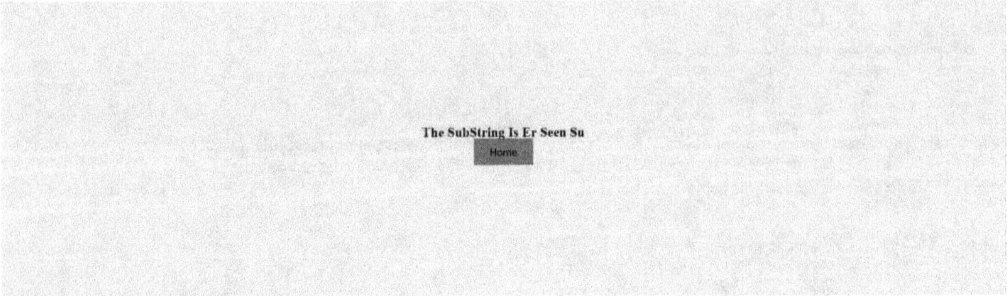

After clicking Home, we get:

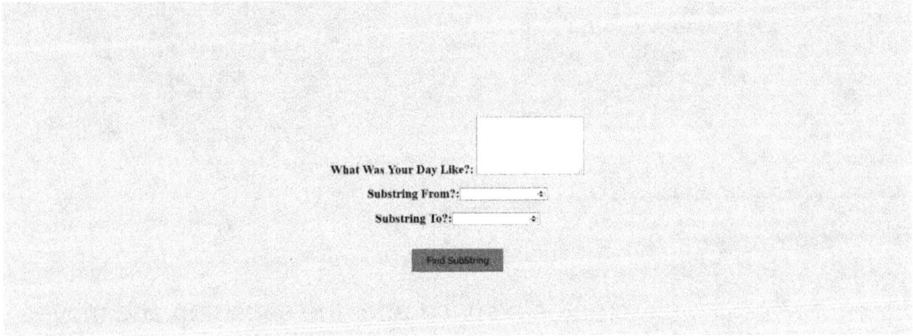

So, now we know how to get back to the original webpage.
There is another way to link web pages; which is used when you create two separate web pages. Let's say you want to add a link from Page A on Page B.
So, in Page B you would add the link using:

```
<a href="PageB.html">
```

We can also link any external web pages using the same html code:

```
<a href=www.google.com>
```

Exercises to Practice:

You can copy the above examples and once you are able to run them and understand the code; you can try a few of the problems below.

1. Add a home button and link your best css design to every web page that you've designed in this book.
2. Create a program that links to external web pages based on user preference.

Math Functions

This is amazing so far. But what if you want to make a mini calculator? Or teach math to kids? Learning how to code Math functions is a great way to also increase the pace at which your kids understand Math. You can set up Math tests for your kids and verify them with JavaScript functions.

Let's get started with some basic Math functions that we can implement in JavaScript.

Math.Round()

Math.Round() rounds a decimal number to the nearest whole number. For example, Math.Round(1.635) rounds to 2; while Math.Round(1.43) rounds to 1

Math.ceil()

Math.ceil() round to the higher number. It basically rounds up to the higher whole number. For example, Math.ceil(1.67) returns 2; while Math.ceil(2.01) returns 3.

Math.floor()

Math.floor() rounds to the lower whole number. It basically removes the decimal points from a decimal number. So, Math.floor(1.47) returns 1; and Math.floor(2.34) also returns 2.

Math.Sqrt()

Math.Sqrt() returns the square root of a number. So, Math.sqrt(9) returns 3; while Math.sqrt(16) returns 4.

Math.min()

Math.min() returns the minimum value of an array. Just put the array inside the bracket. So, if

a=[13,11,34,54,9];

Math.min(A) returns 9

Math.max()

Math.min() returns the maximum value of an array. So for the above example, Math.max(A) returns 54.

Math.Random()

Math.Random() is a cool function. It returns a random decimal number between 0 and 1; not including 1.

So, Math.Random() could include 0.95 the first time and 0.43 the second time.

So, you could play a guess the number game between 0 and 10. Just do this below:

Math.Round(Math.Random()*10) gives you a random whole number between 0 and 10.

Conclusion

Thank you for taking the team to read this book.
I hope you have found it useful; and learnt the basics of html, css and JavaScript. If you've been through the practices you have build several html pages and also learnt how to design them with basic css.
If you liked my book and you'd like to learn more, watch my Author page below. I'll have another book out soon that shows how to create a shopping cart from scratch using html, css and JavaScript.
I'd also recommend looking at the other books in the section, especially the ones on how Artificial Intelligence will take over the world.
If you'd like any clarification regarding the topics; or any suggestions; please email me at: abiprod.pty.ltd@gmail.com
I also do one-one coaching online if you are interested in personalized help.

Book 3:

Coding for Kids Ages 10 and Up

Coding for Kids and Beginners using html, css and JavaScript

Introduction

Rob had been in front of his computer for a few hours. He was in the middle of programming the next version of his JavaScript game. After making a lot of progress in the last month, he was now stuck. He tried a lot of different things, but still just cannot make it work. This is a common problem in coding. Learning the basics of coding is a good start. Rob read my first coding book (Coding for Kids Ages 9-15) a few months ago and he was very excited. Not only did learn the basics well and successfully went through all the exercises; he also implemented some of his own programs and fun coding games. He loved programming; and he was hooked.

After a couple of months, however, Rob got stuck. He was getting tired and bored. He kept doing similar programs over and over. He struggled with more advanced topics. The story of Rob is similar to those of thousands of kids across America and the world. These kids have the resources and money available to move forward. Some of their parents have spent a month's salary (sometimes even more) to get their child a laptop to program with. However, both the parents and their kids realize that they need more to get going. There is something missing. Something that is hard to quantify.

The story of Rob and others inspired me to write the next Javascript book. While Rob might seem to be struggling, he needs to be commended for his effort. Too many of us give up at the first sight of difficulty. We move on from activity to activity with the mindset of a kitten playing with a ball of yarn. The truth is that there is no movement forward in any activity without a little bit of effort and pain. Rob just needs that little bit more, and that's contained in this book.

This book starts off with some of the basics to ensure that you have the basic knowledge needed to more forward. We'll talk about setting up your workspace and doing basic programming and testing. However, this book does have a strong emphasis on coding games, activities and puzzles. These are meant to embed a deeper love for what programming can accomplish. We realize how important these kind of coding games are to the learning process. It imbibes a sense of fun and curiosity which is very exciting for everyone involved. There is also a very important section on the softer side of programming. This chapter talks about how to improve your coding through self-discovery, teamwork, self-discipline and healthy habits. These are the soft skills that would really help Rob move forward in programming.

Soft Skills of Coding

My experiences with teaching kids coding, and also from hearing from Rob have convinced me that soft skills are just as important as technical knowledge in coding. These soft skills also help you with all other aspects of life moving forward. So, it's a win-win all the way around.

So, what exactly are soft skills? Soft skills relate more to how people work. This is different from hard technical skills which focus on what people work on. Soft skills relate to how people deal with mental, physical and interpersonal problems. In combination with good technical knowledge, soft skills can take your performance to a higher level. Here are some of the skills that I am talking about:

1. **Focus and Concentration:** Ability to focus on a single task at hand is a tough skill to master in a world dominated by social media and other distractions. Multi-tasking may seem cool; but in the long run it takes away from quality work and quality education.

    a. A new tool to help you focus is something called isochronic tones. This is specific music that gets your mind in the right frame and helps you focus. You can check out these tones for free by searching 'isochronic tones' on Youtube or Google.

b. Another tool is daily meditation. Meditation for 5 minutes at the start of the day can help you build focus over time.

c. And finally, breaking your work down into periods of 20-30 minutes can make a big difference. Take a 5-10 minute walk between each session and come back refreshed.

2. **Perseverance:** The ability to persist and learn from failures is very important in coding. It's common practice among programmers to try to break the code (or make the code fail) so they can learn the weak points in a program, and make it improve. You can do the same for your program and for your programming skill.

3. **Teamwork:** Going at coding alone is necessary when starting off; but will hold you back in the long run. You can learn a lot faster from the mistakes of others; than from your own mistakes. You can join a local programming club in your own city; hire a programming tutor; join relevant facebook coding groups; post on redditt threads and learn from Github code. It's

important to be active on these groups and recognized as a positive contributor.

4. **Physical Health:** This is a very underrated and undervalued trait by many programmers. But in the long run, it really hurts people in the industry. Back problems, obesity, carpal tunnel syndrome are common health issues that programmers encounter after working in the industry for 5-10 years or more. Here's a few ways to take better care of your health.
    a. Maintain a good sitting posture: Sit upright. Make sure your laptop is close to eye level, so you don't have to bend your neck down. Make sure your feet are in line with your knees.
    b. Take frequent breaks: I recommend taking breaks every 20-30 minutes. Take a walk in between periods.
    c. Diet: Maintain a healthy diet high in good fats, protein and complex carbs. Minimize simple carbs and sugar.
    d. Exercise: Maintain a regular exercise regime or play a sport. It's important to exercise at least 3-4 times a week (maybe more).

e. Sleep: Get at least 7-8 hours of sleep every night. If you're unable to sleep, ask a qualified doctor how you can improve your sleep.

One can write entire books on each of the above topics; but this is a coding book, so I will leave it there. Just remember that the above soft skills are very important and you can work on them while you are coding as well.

Setting Up Your Workspace

What You Need

You need a laptop/desktop with an internet connection, and a web browser installed. I recommend using Mozilla Firefox or Google Chrome.

Download/Install Text Editing software

Download the latest version of a text editing software. I recommend downloading NotePad++. Once you download, double click the Setup.exe file and follow the installation prompts.
https://notepad-plus-plus.org/downloads/

Start using NotePad++

Open Notepad++ from your Desktop or Start Menu

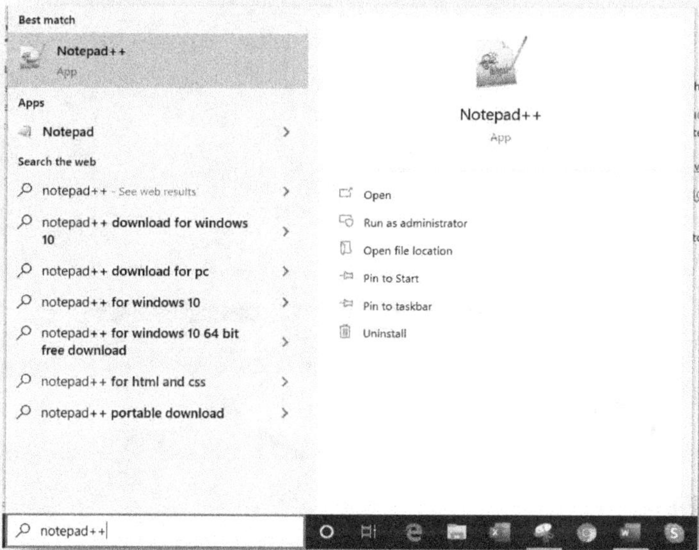

Now, click **File>New** to open a New File.

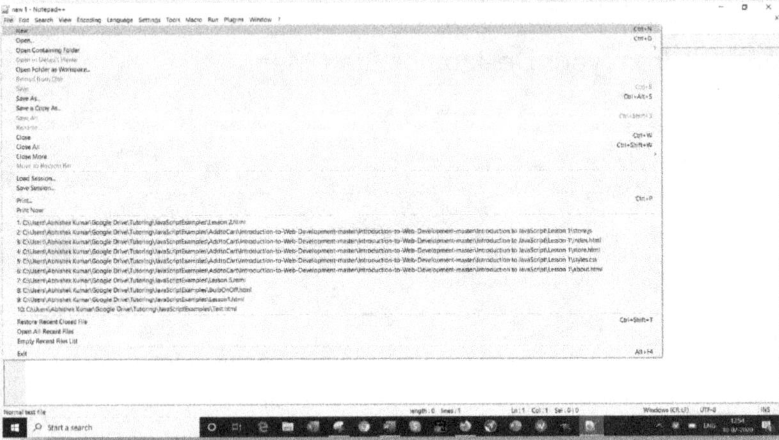

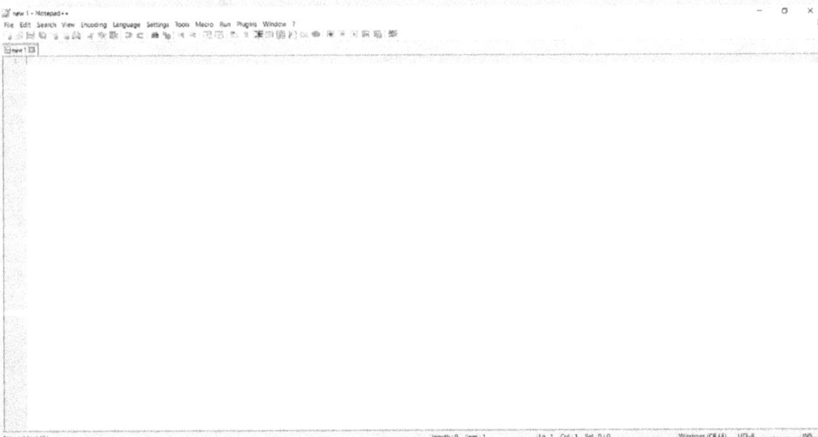

Now, choose **File>Save** As and choose **.html** as the file type

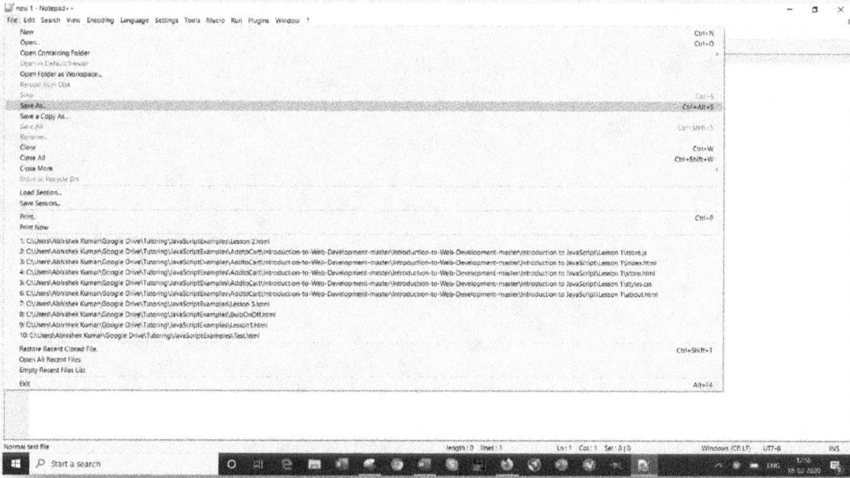

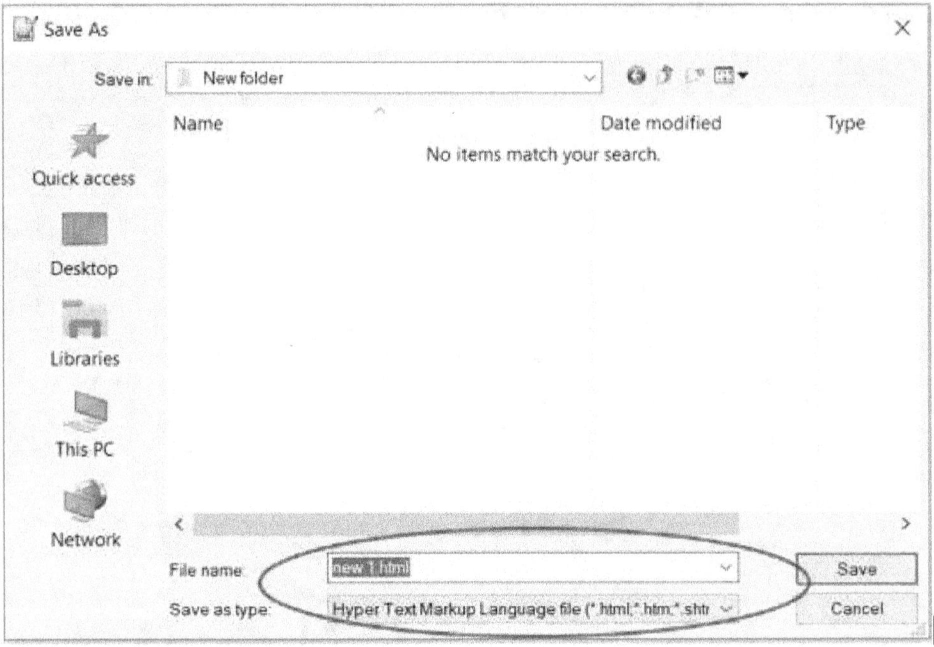

Test Program

Now, let's test if the program connects with the browser.
Just type in random text in your file. In my file, I've typed **"This is a Test Message."**
Now **File>Save**.
After that, click **Run>Launch in Firefox/Chrome/IE** depending on which browser you are using.
If it is working, the text that you typed in should show in the browser window.

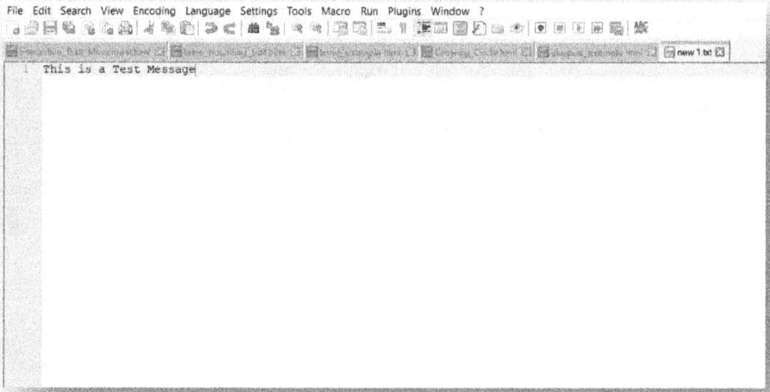
File Edit Search View Encoding Language Settings Tools Macro Run Plugins Window ?
new 1.txt
This is a Test Message

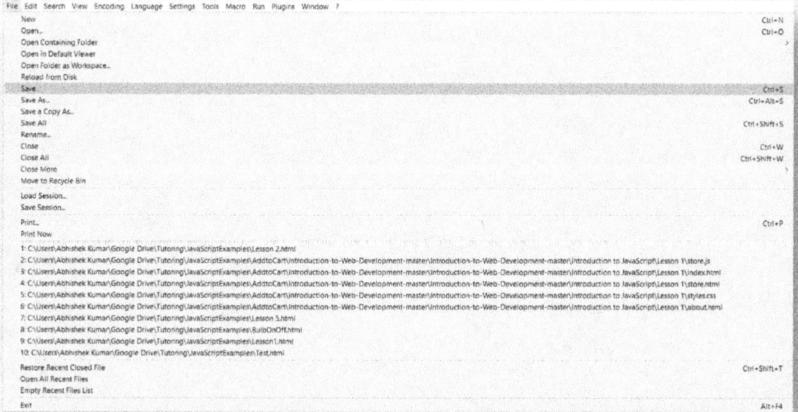
File Edit Search View Encoding Language Settings Tools Macro Run Plugins Window ?
New Ctrl+N
Open... Ctrl+O
Open Containing Folder
Open in Default Viewer
Open Folder as Workspace...
Reload from Disk
Save Ctrl+S
Save As... Ctrl+Alt+S
Save a Copy As...
Save All Ctrl+Shift+S
Rename...
Close Ctrl+W
Close All Ctrl+Shift+W
Close More
Move to Recycle Bin
Load Session...
Save Session...
Print... Ctrl+P
Print Now
Restore Recent Closed File Ctrl+Shift+T
Open All Recent Files
Empty Recent Files List
Exit Alt+F4

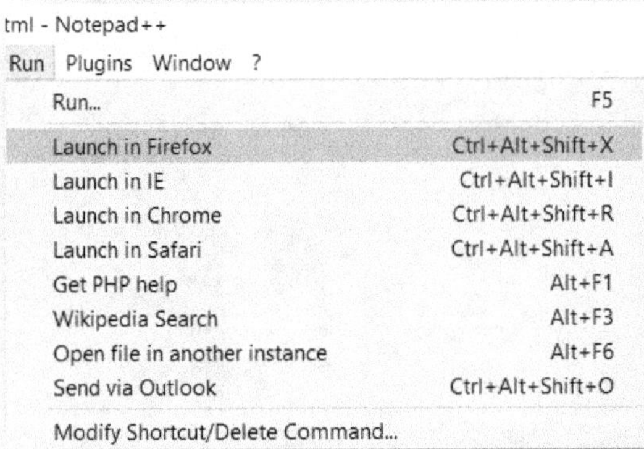

Result:

This is a great simple way to ensure that your program is working before moving forward.

Aside:

One issue that some students have encountered is that the run browser option sometimes does not work and gives an error. This is because the path is not set right. If, for some reason, it doesn't work, you can still run the program.

1. Just save the Notepad++ as a html document.
2. Close the Notepad++ file.
3. Go the folder where the html document is.
4. Double click on the html file and it should work.

What is html?

html stands for Hyper Text Markup Language.
It is the programming language that we use to interact with the internet through web pages. The basic structure of all web pages is defined by html.
It is simple enough for beginner programmers to grasp quickly.
Most html programming is done by items called tags. These tags start with **<>**
And end with **</>**. For example, a common tag is the paragraph tag which begins with **<p>** and ends with **</p>.**

Common html Tags

<html> - This tag is used at the start of every webpage to denote the start of html code

<head> - This piece of html code is executed before the rest of the program
<title> - This tag is used the title the web page. It writes the text on to the top ribbon of the webpage.

<body> - This is the information on the body of the web page.

<h1> - Used to denote a heading tag. This is the largest size heading tag.

<h2>,<h3>,<h4>,<h5>,<h6> - Used to denote subheadings of decreasing size.

<p> - Used to denote paragraphs of text

<img> - This shows an image on the web page. This image either links to an external web page or to an internal file.

<strong> - Added to make text bold
<ul> - This is for an unordered list. An example of this would be a list of items in bullet form.

<li> - Adds a bullet item to an unordered list.

<ol> - This is for ordered lists such as numbered lists from 1,2,3....

<div> - Used to denote larger sections of text; that contain several paragraphs..

<a> - Used to link items in a web page to another web page.

**
** - Adds a line break to the code and moves to the next line.

Example of html code

Below is an example of basic html code. It has examples of all the above html codes. You can type these out or copy paste the example below that.

```
<html>
<head>
<title>My first html website......</title>
</head>
<body>
<h1>Welcome to Programming in Javascript (this is a h1 tag)</h1>
<h2>Let's get started (this is a h2 tag)</h2>
<h3>This is the start of bigger things (this is a h3 tag)</h3>
<p>We're going over a few basic html tags here but you can feel free to play around them and experiment.
There are 1000's of html tags that you can learn in the long run. Here's a list of topics you can learn below (This is a paragraph tag)</p>

<ul> Below is the example of an unordered bulleted list
<li>Basics of html</li>
<li>CSS</li>
<li>JavaScript</li>
<li>Loops</li>
<li>Arrays</li>
<li>Canvas</li>
</ul>

<a href="https://www.google.com">Example of hyperlink to Google</a><br>
<a href="https://www.facebook.com">Example of hyperlink to Facebook</a><br>
<a href="https://www.amazon.com">Example of hyperlink to Amazon</a><br>

</body>
</html>
```

Copy Paste Version of html code

You can copy and paste below code into your html browser to see if it works

```
<html>
<head>
<title>My first html website......</title>
</head>
<body>
<h1>Welcome to Programming in Javascript (this is a h1 tag)</h1>
<h2>Let's get started (this is a h2 tag)</h2>
<h3>This is the start of bigger things (this is a h3 tag)</h3>
<p>We're going over a few basic html tags here but you can feel free to play around them and experiment.
There are 1000's of html tags that you can learn in the long run. Here's a list of topics you can learn below (This is a paragraph tag)</p>
```

```
<ul> Below is the example of an unordered bulleted list
<li>Basics of html</li>
<li>CSS</li>
<li>JavaScript</li>
<li>Loops</li>
<li>Arrays</li>
<li>Canvas</li>
</ul>
<a href="https://www.google.com">Example of hyperlink to
Google</a><br>
<a href="https://www.facebook.com">Example of hyperlink to
Facebook</a><br>
<a href="https://www.amazon.com">Example of hyperlink to
Amazon</a><br>
</body>
</html>
```

Code Output

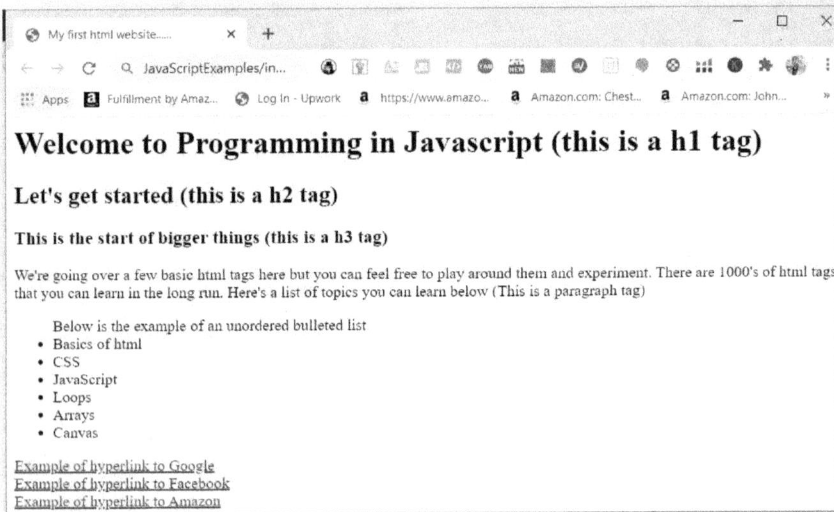

Now, let’s break down the different elements:
Below is the title tag <title>

Below are the heading tags <h1>,<h2>,<h3>

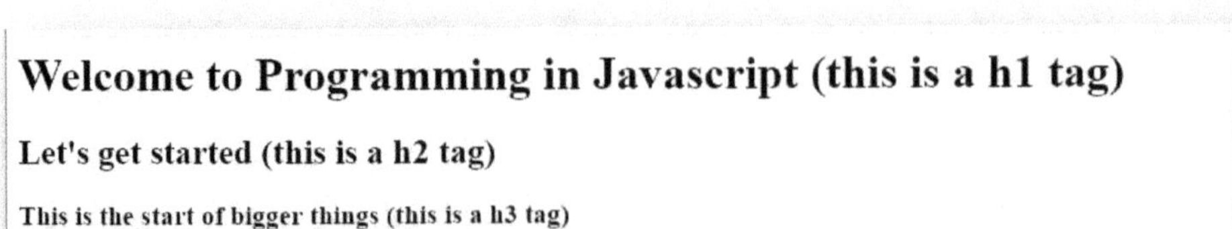

Below is the paragraph tag <p>

We're going over a few basic html tags here but you can feel free to play around them and experiment. There are 1000's of html tags that you can learn in the long run. Here's a list of topics you can learn below (This is a paragraph tag)

Below is an unordered bulleted list <ul> <li>

- Basics of html
- CSS
- JavaScript
- Loops
- Arrays
- Canvas

Below are 3 hyperlink tags to 3 popular websites <a href>

Example of hyperlink to Google
Example of hyperlink to Facebook
Example of hyperlink to Amazon

Practice Problems

1. Make a website with a title tag that has a list of grocery items in an unordered list. Use a paragraph tag to indicate any special instructions you may have for particular items. At the end of the list, use a hyperlink tag to link to the website of the closest grocery store.
2. Create a website with a list of all the players on your soccer team. Use a title, heading and paragraph tag to welcome users

to your website and describe the team and the philosophy of the team. Use an ordered list to list the players.

3. Make a website that lists all your favorite restaurants and coffee shops in your area in an unordered list. Use a title, heading and paragraph tag to introduce yourself and the dining experience in your area.

Sample html Program

What This Project Does

This html project creates two buttons. These two buttons switch between two images of Day and Night. The two buttons are labelled 'Day' and 'Night'
This is a simple html project that creates a button that can switch a light bulb on the page on/off. We are going to use two bulb images to make this happen. The button will switch between the two images.

Concepts to Understand for this Chapter

We'll need to understand button tags and image tags for this example.
Button Tag
<button onclick=**Action** >**Button text**</button>
The button element has two elements. An Action and Button Text. The Button Text is the text that shows on the button; and the Action is what happens when the user clicks on the button
Image Tag
<img id=**ImageId** src=**ImageUrl** style=**ImageSize**>
The Image Tag has three elements.
The **ImageId** is the name you assign to the image. This name is used to reference the image in the code.
Imageurl is the url of the image that the tag is referencing. If the image is in the same folder as the html file, then you can use the file name only instead of the entire url.
ImageSize sets the width and height of the Image. The width and height are in pixels.

Files

Here are the two files that you need to use for the next project. You can download these and save it in the same folder that you are going to create the html file.

Day Picture

Night Picture

Code

```
<html>
<body>

<h2>Day and Night Buttons</h2>

<button onclick="document.getElementById('myImage').src='DayImage.jpg'">Day</button>

<img id="myImage" src="DayImage.jpg" style="width:200px">

<button onclick="document.getElementById('myImage').src='NightImage.jpg'">Night</button>

</body>
</html>
```

Output

Initially, the default is set to Day Image.

Once, you click the **Night** button, you get:

Then, when you click **Day** button again, you get:

Day and Night Buttons

Day  Night

Code Explained

```
<img id="myImage" src="DayImage.jpg" style="width:200px">
```

The above html element is an image tag. It has 3 elements; id, src and style.
id is a label for the image. In this case, it is labelled as “myImage”. The id is used to reference the image throughout the program.
src is the source of the image the tag loads. The image “DayImage.jpg” is in the same folder as the html file.

```
<button
onclick="document.getElementById('myImage').src='DayImage.jpg'">Day</button>
```

The above element is a button element. It has a parameter called **onclick** which describes what action is done when clicking the button.
document.getElementById obtains the element with id ‘myImage’. So it displays ‘DayImage.jpg’ on ‘myImage’ when you click the button.
‘Day’ is the text written on the button.

```
<buttononclick="document.getElementById('myImage').src='NightImage.jpg'>Night</bu
tton>
```

document.getElementById obtains the element with id ‘myImage’. So, it displays ‘NightImage.jpg’ on ‘MyImage’ when the button is clicked.
‘Night’ is the text written on the button.

Practice Problems

1. Find 3 images of a person running, walking and standing still.

   Write a program with 3 buttons where the person runs, walks or

   stands till based on the button your press.

2. Find 3 images of a traffic light with red, green and orange light on. Write a program with 3 buttons that say 'STOP', 'GO' and 'WATCH'. The traffic light switches to red when 'STOP' button is pressed; switches to green when 'GO' button is pressed; and to yellow when 'WATCH' button is pressed.

html forms

Remember those forms you see online where you enter your name and age and date of birth? Those are html forms.
Today, we're going to learn how to make those.
Before we start making forms, we need to learn about a few basic form elements:
Button <button> - It is an element that allows the user to perform an action when clicked.
Textbox <input> - This element allows the user to type text into a box on the browser screen. It's used to collect small text items like name, city etc.
Textarea <textarea> - This allows the user to input larger quantities of text. It is bigger in size than the textbox. It's used for larger text items like address, comments etc.
Option Select<select> - This element allows the user to select between several available options. It's basically a drop-down box.
Date Input<input type="date"> - This elements allows the user to choose a date from a calendar drop down.
Now, let's go through each of these examples through a sample form below.

Sample Form

```
<html>
<head><title>Sample Form</title></head>
<body>
<form id="form1">
Enter First Name:<input name="frstname" type="text" id="frstname" size="20"><br>
Enter Last Name:<input name="lname" type="text" id="lname" size="20"><br><br>
Enter Address: <textarea name="TextBox" cols="40" rows="5" id="tstr2"></textarea><br><br>
Enter Country: <select id="country" name="country">
               <option value="USA">USA</option>
               <option value="Mexico">Mexico</option>
               <option value="Canada">Canada</option>
               <option value="Australia">Australia</option>
               </select><br>
Date of Birth: <input type="date" id="start" name="trip-start"
               value="2020-07-22"
               min="1918-01-01" max="2020-06-31"><br>
<button onclick="">Submit</button>

</body>
</html>
```

Now, let's go through each part of the code.

```
<form id="form1">
```

Each form starts with the <form> html element. The id **"form1"** is the name that you give the form. The id is used to reference the form in the rest of the program.

```
Enter First Name:<input name="frstname" type="text" id="frstname" size="20"><br>
Enter Last Name:<input name="lname" type="text" id="lname" size="20"><br><br>
```

The above 2 lines are textboxes for first and last name. The type is assigned to **"text"** because name is a form of text. The id **"frstname"** and **"lname"** will be used to reference the code if we need to later. The size is set to **"20"** which means it can accept 20 characters. You can change it to a larger or shorter size as needed.

```
Enter Address: <textarea name="TextBox" cols="40" rows="5" id="tstr2"></textarea><br><br>
```

The above element is a textarea element for the address. It has 5 rows (rows="5") and 40 characters per row (cols="40"). It is labelled as "tstr2".

```
Enter Country: <select id="country" name="country">
               <option value="USA">USA</option>
               <option value="Mexico">Mexico</option>
               <option value="Canada">Canada</option>
               <option value="Australia">Australia</option>
               </select><br>
```

The above element is a select option element for choosing a country. It allows you to select between a drop-down menu of 4 different options; USA, Mexico, Canada and Australia. It is labelled as “country” **(id=”country”)**.

```
Date of Birth: <input type="date" id="start" name="trip-start"
               value="2020-07-22"
               min="1918-01-01" max="2020-06-31"><br>
```

The above element is an input date element, that lets you choose a date of birth between 1918 (**min=”1918-01-01”**) and 2020(**max=“2020-06-31”)**. It is named as “start” **(id=”start”)** and is set to a value of 2020-07-22 **(value=”2020-07-22”)**.

```
<button onclick="">Submit</button>
```

The above element is a button element. It has the text “Submit” written on it. It does nothing on clicking as the onclick function is empty.
Now, let’s have a look at what happens when we run the program.

Output:

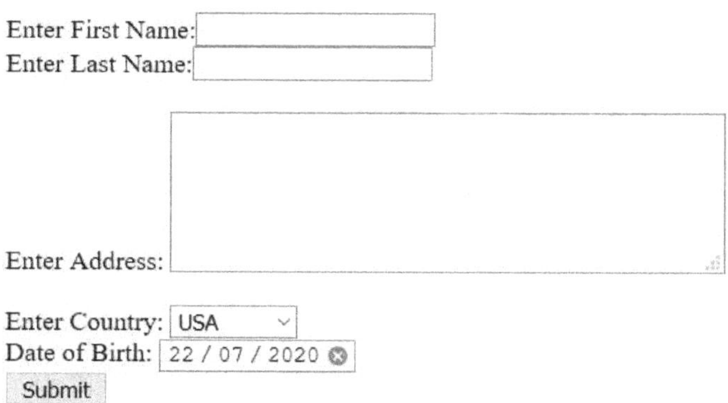

I hope you learned a bit about the basics of html forms with this example. In the next few chapters, we’ll learn how to use the information we input using JavaScript. In fact, we’ll use this same example and print it out using JavaScript.

Practice Problems

1. Write a html form that is a resume for a university student. It accepts first name, last name, university name through a textbox; university year through a drop down. Then there are 3 activities/internships/co-ops. Each activity has a from date element, to date element and a textarea large enough to describe the experience. End with a submit button.
2. Write a html form for a grocery list. It accepts first name, last name, date of shopping, address and city. It has 5 drop down with 30 common grocery items to choose form. And finally, it has a submit button.

Each of the above will be expanded on with JavaScript in the coming chapter.

What is JavaScript?

JavaScript is a high-level programming language that is used to make web pages more interactive and dynamic. It is text-based and user-friendly.

While html is used to create a web page structure and css is for web page style, JavaScript is used to make the web page more interactive with the user. It allows different html elements to interact with each other, performs calculations, animations etc. In other words, it makes web page programming fun.

Using JavaScript with html

There are two ways to use JavaScript in a html web page. The first way is to just add the code within script tags in html. This is shown in the blue portion of the code below.

```
<html>
<head><title>Test file 1</title>
</head>
<body>
<script>
//Enter JavaScript code here
</script>
</body>
</html>
```

The 2nd way is to create an external JavaScript file that contains the code and save it as a .js file. Then you can link the file to the html content. For example, let's say you create a file called 'test.js'. You can link it using the blue portion of the code below:

```
<html>
```

```
<head><title>Test file 2</title>
</head>
<body>
<script src=" test.js"></script>
</body>
</html>
```

JavaScript Elements

With that basic knowledge, let's have a look at some basic JavaScript elements.

functions

A function in JavaScript is a set of lines of code that performs a certain task.

It is defined in JavaScript within the script tags as:

```
function afunc()
{
//Enter function code here
}
```

The name of the function is afunc and the code within the curly brackets is executed each time afunc is called on.

It is useful to have functions when we want to perform the same task several times in the same program. We can just call on the function instead of writing the same lines of code several times.

Variables

A variable in JavaScript is a placeholder that takes on a certain value. The value can be changed throughout the program and can be used in other parts of the code. Let's take an example:

```
var x=5;
```

x is the variable defined. It starts with a value of 5.

Later on, in the program, it can be changed to a different value, as in:

```
x=10;
```

Now, x has a value of 10. And, if we do:

```
x=x-1;
```

Then x becomes 9. What we just showed is an integer variable. We can also have string variables used to store text values, as in:

```
var b="abcd"
```

b is a variable that holds the value abcd.

And finally, we can have Boolean variables that holds only true/false values. For example:

```
var c = true;
var d = (7>5);
var e = (7<6);
```

Variables c,d and e are all Boolean variables. Variable c is assigned to true. Variable d is true (because 7 is greater than 5). Variable e is false (because 7 is not less than 6).

document.write()

document.write() is used to print elements on the web page. Anything that is within the brackets is printed on the web page. For example:

```
document.write("Example print");
```

The above line prints the words **"Example print"** on the screen.

We can also print variables on the screen. For example,

```
var a=7;
document.write(a)
```

Above line prints 7 on the screen.

And, we can combine different elements also using "+" operator. For example:

```
var a=7;
document.write("The number printed is "+a);
```

The above line prints "The number printed is 7".

alert()

Alert puts a pop-up on the screen with a particular message. For example,

```
alert("Hello")
```

The above message has a pop-up message that says "Hello"

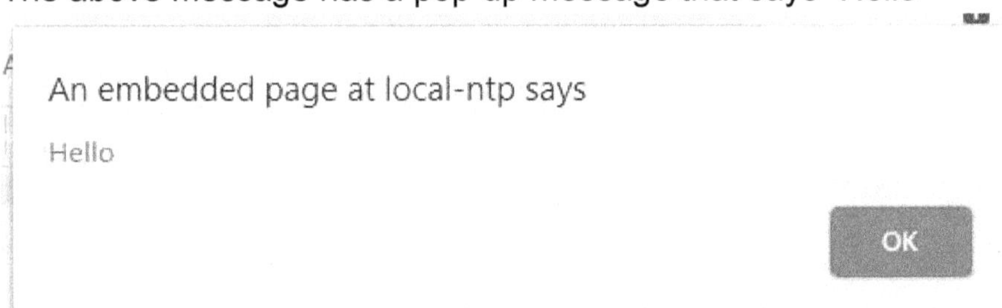

prompt()

prompt has the same popup but what a textbox that allows user input. The user input can be stored in a variable. For example:

```
var name = prompt("What is your name");
```

It shows a pop-up. Once the user enters his name and says ok, it stores the value in the variable name.

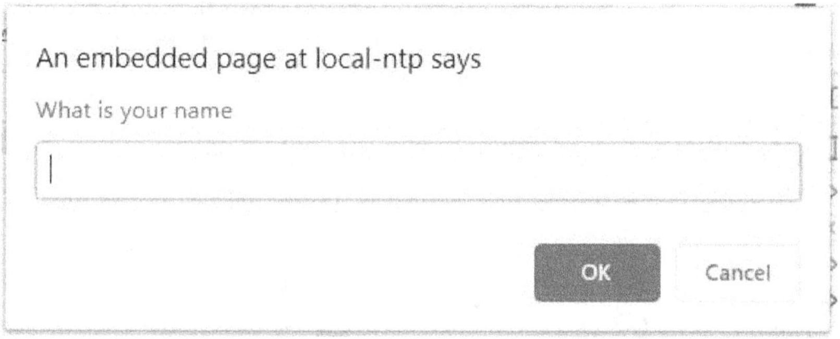

document.getElementById().value

Document.getElementById().value is used to get html elements into JavaScript variables. So, we need to use the id of the html element and put it in between brackets. Let's look at an example.

Let's look at below html element:

```
Enter number: <input name="x" type="number" id="test"
size="20"><br>
```

JavaScript code:

```
var testv=document.getElementById("test").value;
```

The html element is a form textbox that accepts a number from the user.

In Javascript, the number that the user assigns is set to the variable testv.

How to add Comments

Comments are items that you add to the code to document or explain the code. Comments cannot be executed and do not effect the program. Comments in JavaScript are added using two double backslash in front of the comment ("//")

```
<html>
<head>
<title>Print Name and Age......</title>
</head>
<body>
<form id="form1">
Enter Name: <input name="Enter Name" type="text" id="name" size="20"><br>
Enter Favorite Hobby: <input type="text" id="hobby" size="20"><br>
Enter Age: <input type="number" id="age" size="20"><br>
</form>
<button onclick="writename()">Print Intro</button>

<script>

function writename()
{
    //Creating variables
    var nameValue=document.getElementById("name").value;
    var hobby=document.getElementById("hobby").value;
    var age=document.getElementById("age").value;

    //Prints name on screen
    document.write("This is "+nameValue+". I am "+ age+" years old.My favorite hobby is "+hobby);

}

</script>
</body>
</html>
```

Below is an example of comments. The comments are in green and circled in red.

Example 1

Now, let's start looking at some examples. We'll start with the html form in the previous chapter. We're going to assign all the user inputs into variables and print them on the web browser using JavaScript.
The code below is the similar to the example in the previous chapter. A JavaScript function has been added to print the first name and country of the person who submitted the form.

```
<html>
<head><title>Sample Form</title></head>
<body>
<form id="form1">
Enter First Name:<input name="frstname" type="text" id="frstname" size="20"><br>
Enter Last Name:<input name="lname" type="text" id="lname" size="20"><br><br>
Enter Address: <textarea name="TextBox" cols="40" rows="5" id="tstr2"></textarea><br><br>
Enter Country: <select id="country" name="country">
               <option value="USA">USA</option>
               <option value="Mexico">Mexico</option>
               <option value="Canada">Canada</option>
               <option value="Australia">Australia</option>
               <option value="India">Australia</option>
               </select><br>
Date of Birth: <input type="date" id="dbirth" name="trip-start"
               value="2020-07-22"
               min="1918-01-01" max="2020-06-31"><br>
<button onclick="printcountry()">Submit</button>

<script>
function printcountry()
{
var fname = document.getElementById("frstname").value;
var lname = document.getElementById("lname").value;
var address = document.getElementById("tstr2").value;
var country = document.getElementById("country").value;
var dob = document.getElementById("dbirth").value;
document.write (fname+" lives in "+country);
}
</script>


</body>
</html>
```

Output:

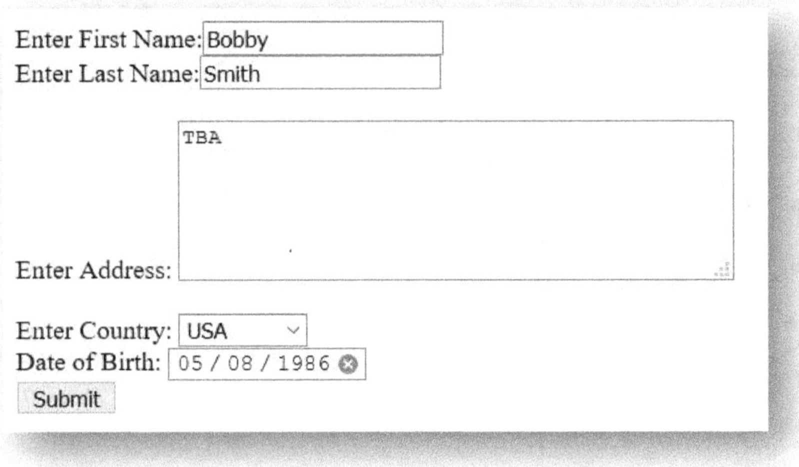

After clicking **submit**, we get:

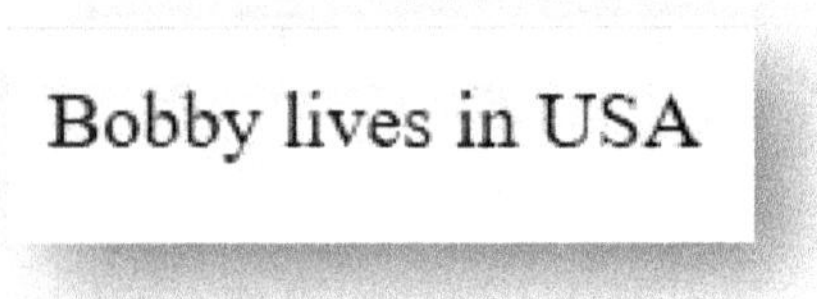

The Code Explained

So the main part that we added was the function printcountry(). We also added the function to the onclick element of the button. (onclick="printcountry()").

```
<button onclick="printcountry()">Submit</button>

<script>
function printcountry()
{
var fname = document.getElementById("frstname").value;
var lname = document.getElementById("lname").value;
var address = document.getElementById("tstr2").value;
var country = document.getElementById("country").value;
var dob = document.getElementById("dbirth").value;
document.write (fname+" lives in "+country);
}
</script>


</body>
</html>
```

In this function, we declare five variables fname, lname, address, country, dob. Each of these variables is assigned to the values of first name, last name, address, country and dob entered in the form respectively. This is done using the document.getElementById().value JavaScript element.

Finally, we use document.write() to print out first name and dob entered in the form.

Example 2

In the second example, we create a simple JavaScript function that takes in 3 numbers and multiplies them together.

Output:

```
<html>
<head><title>Sample Form</title></head>
<body>
<form id="form1">
Enter First Number:<input name="number1" type="number" id="num1" size="20"><br>
Enter Second Number:<input name="number2" type="number" id="num2" size="20"><br><br>
Enter Third Number: <input name="number3" type="number" id="num3" size="20"></textarea><br><br>

<button onclick="multiplynum()">Submit</button>

<script>
function multiplynum()
{
var n1 = document.getElementById("num1").value;
var n2 = document.getElementById("num2").value;
var n3 = document.getElementById("num3").value;
document.write("The product of the three numbers is "+n1*n2*n3);
}
</script>


</body>
</html>
```

Once we click, submit we get:

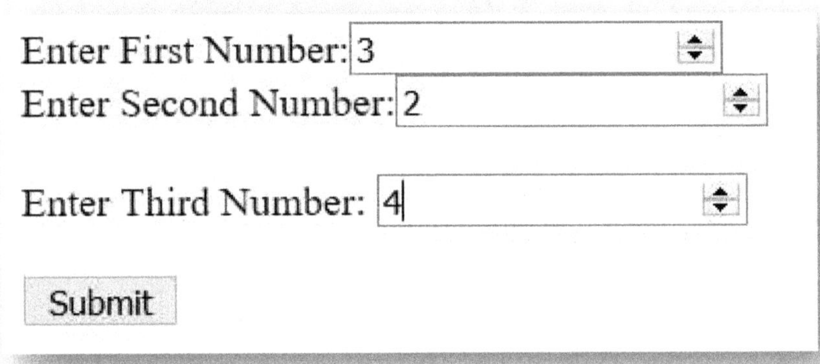

Code Explained:

In the above code, we take in three numbers in the form with id's of num1, num2 and num3.

The button runs the **multiplynum()**Javascript function when it is clicked.
In the function three variables of n1,n2,n3 are assigned to the 3 numbers in the form with id's of num1, num2 and num3 respectively. Finally, we print out the product of the three numbers n1*n2*n3 using document.write() in the final line.

Practice Problems

1. Create the form in practice problem 1 of the previous chapter. Print out all the information in the form like a proper resume on the web page. Feel free to print it out and hand it over to an employer if it looks good enough 😊.
2. Create the form in practice problem 2 of the previous chapter. Print out the entire grocery list on the html web page. Then you can print it out on a sheet of paper and go shopping.
3. Create a form that takes in two numbers. It has 4 buttons with button text of Add, Subtract, Multiply and Divide. Each of these 4 buttons executes 4 different functions that adds, subtracts, multiplies and divides the two numbers and prints out the result.

A Short message from the Author:

Hey, are you enjoying the book? I'd love to hear your thoughts!
Many readers do not know how hard reviews are to come by, and how much they help an author.

I would be incredibly thankful if you could take just 60 seconds to write a brief review on Amazon, even if it's just a few sentences!

>> Click here to leave a quick review

Thank you for taking the time to share your thoughts!
Your review will genuinely make a difference for me and help gain exposure for my work.

Introduction to CSS

What is CSS?

CSS is an acronym for Cascading Style Sheets. It allows the user to set and modify the style of your html website. 'Style' is a term used for font type, font color, background color, shading etc. CSS elements can be accessed through html and JavaScript.

Create CSS file and link to html file

There are 5 steps to create a CSS file and link it to a html document.

1. To create a css file, open a black html document and save as 'CSS' file type. In this case, we're going to name it 'samplestyle'.

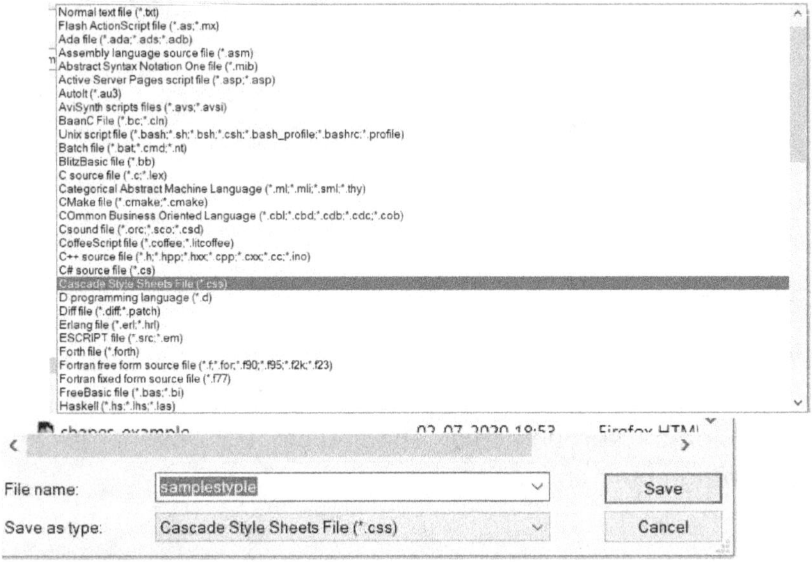

2. Go to the relevant html and include the line below in the header file. You can do so with the line below.

```
<html>
<head><title>Sample Form</title></head>
<body>
<link rel="stylesheet" href="samplestyle.css" />
<form id="form1">
Enter First Number:<input name="number1" type="number" id="num1" size="20"><br>
Enter Second Number:<input name="number2" type="number" id="num2" size="20"><br><br>
Enter Third Number: <input name="number3" type="number" id="num3" size="20"></textarea><br><br>

<button onclick="multiplynum()">Submit</button>

<script>
function multiplynum()
{
var n1 = document.getElementById("num1").value;
var n2 = document.getElementById("num2").value;
var n3 = document.getElementById("num3").value;
document.write("The product of the three numbers is "+n1*n2*n3);
}
</script>


</body>
</html>
```

3. (Optional) To make your button editable in css add the text class="btn" to the html button line as shown below:

<button class = "btn submit" onclick="multiplynum()">Submit</button>

Now, Let's insert the style sheet in the example from last chapter.

```
<html>
<head><title>Sample Form</title></head>
<body>
<link rel="stylesheet" href="samplestyle.css" />
<form id="form1">
Enter First Number:<input name="number1" type="number" id="num1" size="20"><br>
Enter Second Number:<input name="number2" type="number" id="num2" size="20"><br><br>
Enter Third Number: <input name="number3" type="number" id="num3" size="20"></textarea><br><br>

<button class = "btn submit" onclick="multiplynum()">Submit</button>

<script>
function multiplynum()
{
var n1 = document.getElementById("num1").value;
var n2 = document.getElementById("num2").value;
var n3 = document.getElementById("num3").value;
document.write("The product of the three numbers is "+n1*n2*n3);
}
</script>


</body>
</html>
```

Great.

Now our CSS sheet is linked to our html file.

CSS Terms

html{}, body{}: The code within the html brackets defines the styling for the entire html files. The body code within the brackets is the code for the body of the html file.
text-decoration: Can modify the text design by making it wavy, dotted, curly etc.
text-transform: Can capitalize parts or the whole text
text-align: Can align the text at the center, right or left
margin: Margin is the space between elements. It is expressed in terms of pixels. For example, margin: 5px specifies a margin of 5 pixels.
padding: Padding is the space within an element from the outer boundary. It is specified in pixels as well.
display: Can be used to completely turn off an element. (e.g. display: none switches off the element completely)
hidden: Can he used to hide an element while it still takes up space in the layout.
font-size: Specifies the size of the font.
background-color: Specifies the background color of the element. Any of the wide variety of colors in the link below can be chosen.
https://www.quackit.com/css/css_color_codes.cfm
color: Specifies the color of the written text.
border: Specifies the presence and type/style of border around an element. There can be a hidden, dotted, double border; or there can also be no border.
font-weight: Specifies the boldness of a font.
min-height: Specifies the minimum height of an element. Height is in pixels.
line-height: Specifies the height of a line of text. Height is in pixels.

CSS Button Elements

.btn{} – This specifies the styling for any buttons defined in html. To make a button accessible in css, we have to include the class name in the html definition as we did in the previous example.
.btn:hover{} – Did you know that you can specify the style of a button when the mouse hovers over it? Cool, isn't it? All items within the brackets can specify the style of the button and text within the button. To get a look at the 1000's of CSS properties out there to style your web-page look at the link below:
https://www.htmlhelp.com/reference/css/properties.html

CSS Example

```
html, body {
     text-decoration: none;
     text-transform: capitalize;
     text-align: center;
     margin: 10;
     padding-top: 50px;
     min-height: 80%;
     color: white;
     background-color: blue;
     line-height: 1.5;
     font-family:serif;
     font-size: 25px;
     font-weight: normal;

}
.btn {
   background-color: black;
   border: none;
   color: white;
   padding: 10px 24px;
   text-align: center;
   text-decoration: none;
   display: inline-block;
   font-size: 16px;
}
.btn:hover {
   background-color: Crimson;
   color: black;
}
```

Code Explained

We first define the html and body of the code. The text is capitalized and set to the center. It is white in color against a blue background. It is 50 pixels from the top of the margin. It is normal un-bolded sans-serif font of 25 px.
The button style is defined with .btn{}. The button has white text with a black background. The text font is 16 px and is aligned to the center of

the button. The style changes when we hover the mouse over the button. It changes to black text with a Crimson red background.
The css file is linked to one of our sample forms in the previous chapter. We show you the output before and after linking the css file. We see what a difference a CSS styling makes. It's like a makeover 😊

Output (Without CSS):

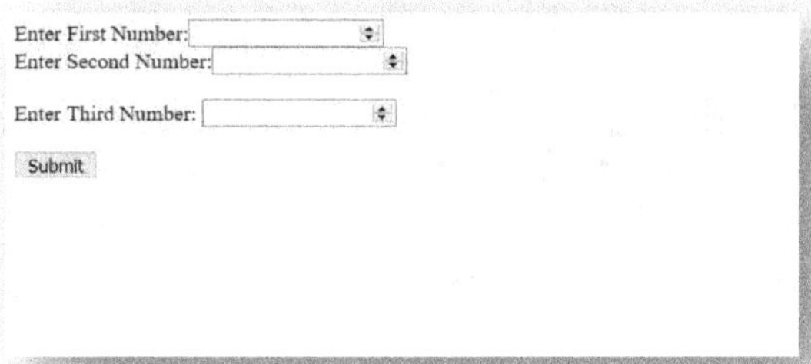

Output (with CSS):

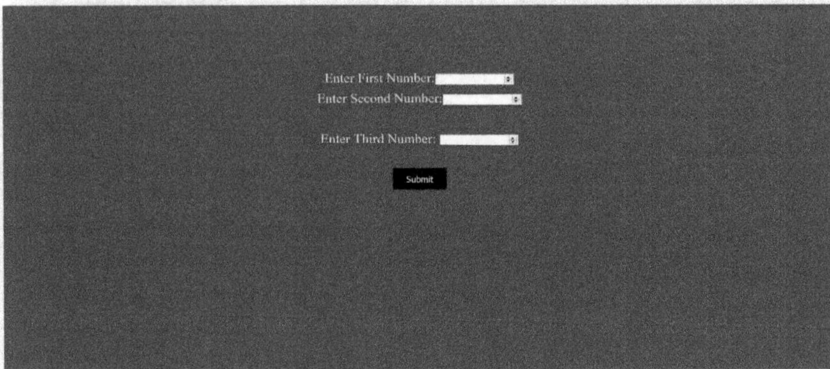

Output (with CSS and mouse hovering over button):

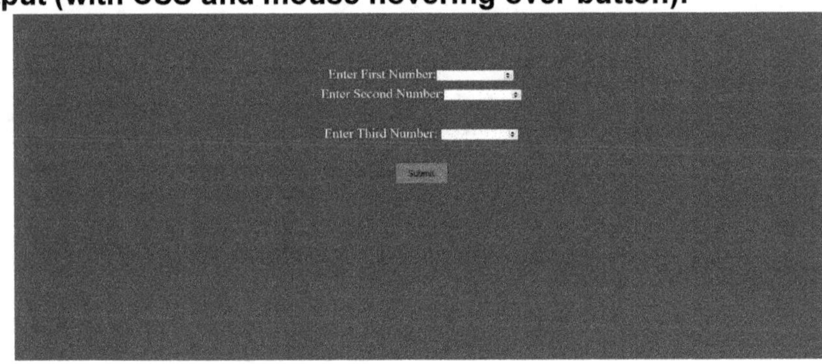

CSS And JavaScript

If a html form is linked to CSS, and JavaScript starts printing text on the web page, you notice that it is no longer linked to CSS.

What you need to do is relink the CSS in the JavaScript code using the line below:

```
document.write('<link rel="stylesheet" type="text/css"
href="samplestyle.css" />');
```

Enter this code right before the start of every function in JavaScript. This ensures that css is shown for the entire program. See the example in the text below:

```
<html>
<head><title>Sample Form</title></head>
<body>
<link rel="stylesheet" type="text/css" href="samplestyle.css" />
<form id="form1">
Enter First Number:<input name="number1" type="number" id="num1" size="20"><br>
Enter Second Number:<input name="number2" type="number" id="num2" size="20"><br><br>
Enter Third Number: <input name="number3" type="number" id="num3" size="20"></textarea><br><br>

<button class = "btn submit" onclick="multiplynum()">Submit</button>

<script>
function multiplynum()
{
var n1 = document.getElementById("num1").value;
var n2 = document.getElementById("num2").value;
var n3 = document.getElementById("num3").value;
document.write('<link rel="stylesheet" type="text/css" href="samplestyle.css" />');
document.write("The product of the three numbers is: "+n1*n2*n3);
}
</script>


</body>
</html>
```

Output (before adding CSS line to JavaScript):

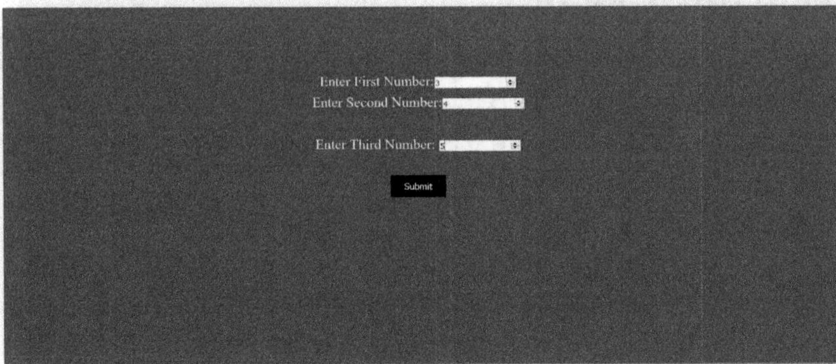

On clicking **Submit** button:

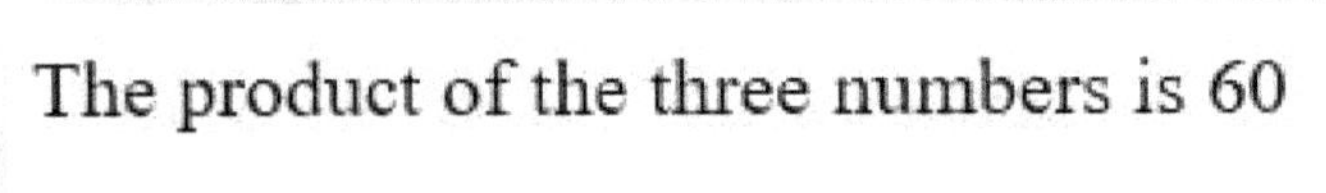

Output (after adding CSS line to JavaScript):

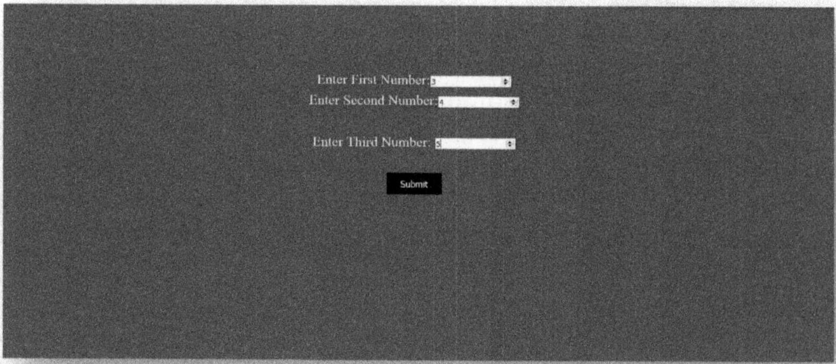

On clicking **Submit** button:

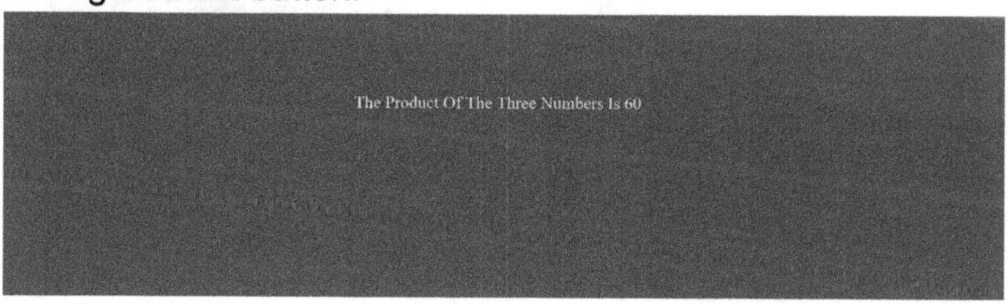

Practice Problems

1. Create a css stylesheet that specifies a style for all form elements and buttons. Link it all the previous practice problems and marvel at your creation.
2. Create a html form with 2 buttons. Create two css sheets. The 2 html buttons switch between the two stylesheets.

Doing Math with JavaScript

JavaScript is a great programming language to perform calculations and analyse data from users. We'll go over a few functions that help get you going with JavaScript.
Now, this section is not for everyone. It's only for those who are interested in implementing a lot of math in their programs, or like math and would like to see it implemented in JavaScript.

ParseInt/ParseFloat

parseInt – ParseInt takes in a string variable and returns an integer. It also takes in decimal numbers and converts them to integers.
ParseFloat – ParseFloat is similar to parseInt but works with decimal numbers.
Let's look at an example below.
In the example, we put 3 of the numbers through parseInt and the same numbers through parseFloat. And we see the outputs.

```
<html>
<head><title>Sample Form</title></head>
<body>
<form id="form1">

<button onclick="multiplynum()">Parse Integers</button>

<script>
function multiplynum()
{
xi=parseInt("5.2");
yi=parseInt(5.01);
zi=parseInt(5.65);
xf=parseFloat("5.2");
yf=parseFloat(5.01);
zf=parseFloat(5.65);
document.write("xi= "+xi+"<br>");
document.write("yi= "+yi+"<br>");
document.write("zi= "+zi+"<br>");
document.write("xf= "+xf+"<br>");
document.write("yf= "+yf+"<br>");
document.write("zf= "+zf+"<br>");
}
</script>


</body>
</html>
```

Output:

```
xi= 5
yi= 5
zi= 5
xf= 5.2
yf= 5.01
zf= 5.65
```

We can see that the results are different for parseInt and parseFloat. For xi and yi, we pass the string "5.2". It is considered a string because it is within quotes. Even though there is a number within the quotes, we cannot use it in any mathematical operations without actually doing a parseInt or parseFloat. After completing a parseInt or parseFloat, it becomes a number.

We also note that for all the values parseInt removes the decimal points and makes it a whole number. It does not round up or round down, just removes the decimal.

ParseFloat retains the decimal value. So, if you want to work with decimals; use ParseFloat. If you want no decimal, then use ParseInt.

Rounding numbers – Math.ceil(), Math.floor() and Math.round()

Next, let's talk about rounding numbers. We use the functions **Math.Ceil()**, **Math.Floor()** and **Math.Round()**. Math.Ceil() rounds to the upper decimal value, Math.Floor() to the upper decimal value and Math.Round() to the nearest value (whether it's upper or lower). Let's look at a sample program.

```
<html>
<head><title>Sample Form</title></head>
<body>
<form id="form1">

<button onclick="multiplynum()">Round numbers</button>

<script>
function multiplynum()
{
xc=Math.ceil(5.2);
yc=Math.ceil(7.8);
zc=Math.ceil(4.5);
xf=Math.floor(5.2);
yf=Math.floor(7.8);
zf=Math.floor(4.5);
xr=Math.round(5.2);
yr=Math.round(7.8);
zr=Math.round(4.5);
document.write("Example of Math.ceil<br>");
document.write("xc= "+xc+"<br>");
document.write("yc= "+yc+"<br>");
document.write("zc= "+zc+"<br>");
document.write("Example of Math.floor<br>");
document.write("xf= "+xf+"<br>");
document.write("yf= "+yf+"<br>");
document.write("zf= "+zf+"<br>");
document.write("Example of Math.round<br>");
document.write("xr= "+xr+"<br>");
document.write("yr= "+yr+"<br>");
document.write("zr= "+zr+"<br>");
}
</script>


</body>
</html>
```

In the code, we put 3 decimal numbers through Math.floor(), Math.ceil() and Math.round() and the output demonstrates how the functions work.

Output:

```
Example of Math.ceil
xc= 6
yc= 8
zc= 5
Example of Math.floor
xf= 5
yf= 7
zf= 4
Example of Math.round
xr= 5
yr= 8
zr= 5
```

Add, subtract, multiply, divide

It might seem self-explanatory, but because of how vital it is to do any basic calculation, I have to go over the 4 basic mathematical operations.

```
<html>
<head><title>Sample Form</title></head>
<body>
<form id="form1">
Enter First Number:<input name="number1" type="number" id="num1" size="20"><br>
Enter Second Number:<input name="number2" type="number" id="num2" size="20"><br><br>

<button onclick="test()">Calculate</button>

<script>
function test()
{
var n1 = parseInt(document.getElementById("num1").value);
var n2 = parseInt(document.getElementById("num2").value);
var sum=n1+n2;
var difference=n1-n2;
var product=n1*n2;
var quotient=n1/n2;

document.write("The sum is "+sum+"<br>");
document.write("The difference is "+difference+"<br>");
document.write("The product is "+product+"<br>");
document.write("The quotient is "+quotient);

}
</script>


</body>
</html>
```

In the code, we accept two numbers using a html form. The two numbers are assigned to two variables n1 and n2.
Then we calculate the sum, difference, product and quotient and assign them to 4 different variables.
At the end, these 4 variables are printed out using document.write()
Output:

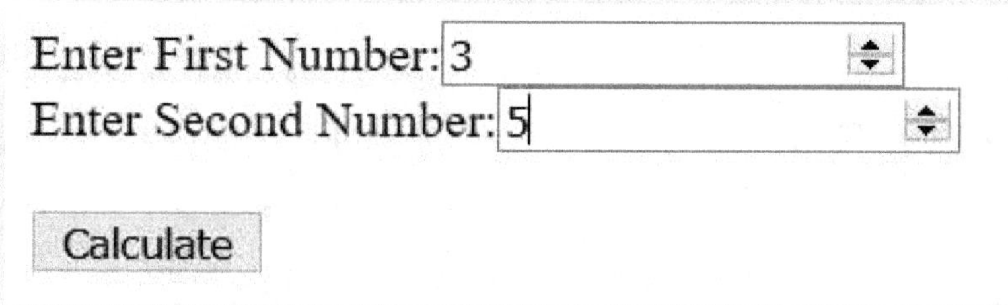
Enter First Number: 3
Enter Second Number: 5
Calculate

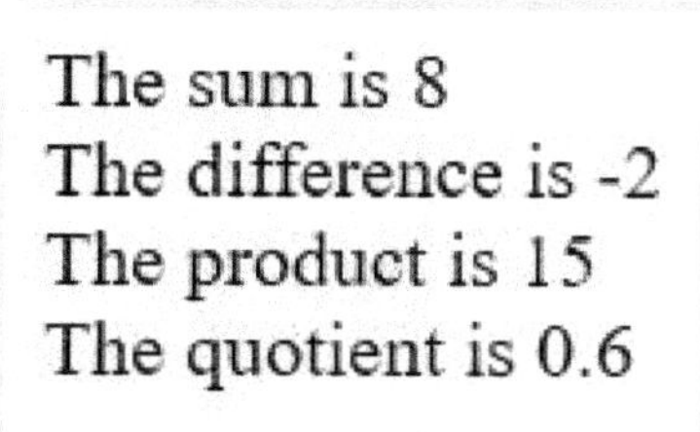
The sum is 8
The difference is -2
The product is 15
The quotient is 0.6

Modulus Operation

The modulus operation returns the remainder between two numbers. It looks like the percentage sign %. Here's an example below:

```
<html>
<head><title>Sample Form</title></head>
<body>
<form id="form1">
Enter First Number:<input name="number1" type="number" id="num1" size="20"><br>
Enter Second Number:<input name="number2" type="number" id="num2" size="20"><br><br>

<button onclick="test()">Calculate Remainder</button>

<script>
function test()
{
var n1 = parseInt(document.getElementById("num1").value);
var n2 = parseInt(document.getElementById("num2").value);
var remainder=n1%n2;

document.write("The remainder when "+n1+"is divided by "+n2+" is "+remainder+"<br>");


}
</script>


</body>
</html>
```

The above code takes in two numbers via a html form and finds the remainder between the two; as shown in output below.

Output:

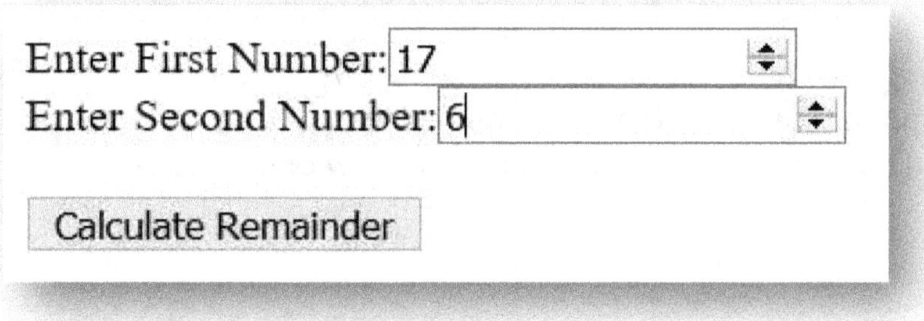

After hitting the button **"Calculate Remainder"**

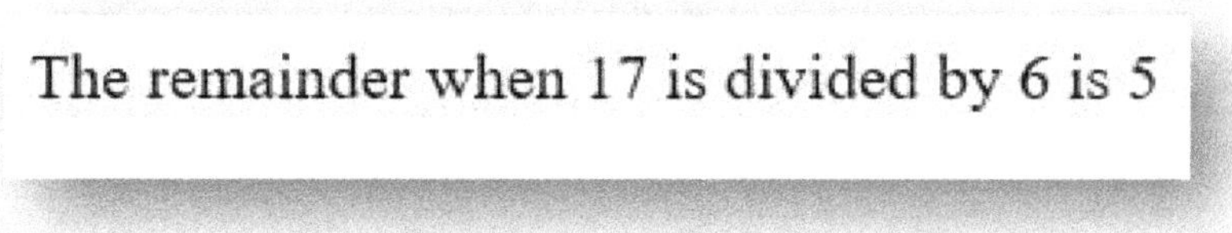

Math.Random()

Math.Random() returns a random number between 0 and 1. If we want to get a random between 0 and 10, we multiply by 10 and round the answer (using Math.round()). Let's look at a few examples.

```
<html>
<head><title>Sample Form</title></head>
<body>

<button onclick="test()">Random Numbers</button>

<script>
function test()
{
var n1 = Math.random();
var n2 = Math.round(Math.random()*50);
var n3 = Math.round(Math.random()*50);
var n4 = Math.round(Math.random()*1000);

var remainder=n1%n2;

document.write("Random number between 0 and 1 = <strong>"+n1+"</strong><br>");
document.write("1st Random number between 0 and 50 = <strong>"+n2+"</strong><br>");
document.write("2nd Random number between 0 and 50 = <strong>"+n3+"</strong><br>");
document.write("Random number between 0 and 1000 = <strong>"+n4+"</strong><br>");



}
</script>


</body>
</html>
```

In the above example, n1 is a random number between 0 and 1.
n2 and n3 are two different random numbers between 0 and 50. You should probably see that n2 and n3 are different because both numbers are randomized.
n4 returns a random number between 0 and 1000.
We can see the results in the output below. As the numbers are randomized we should get a different result each time we run the program.
Math.Random() is a fun function and we are going to be using it in quite a few games this book.
Output:

Random number between 0 and 1 = **0.20604429056114348**
1st Random number between 0 and 50 = **21**
2nd Random number between 0 and 50 = **6**
Random number between 0 and 1000 = **866**

Exponent and Logarithms

Exponents in Javascript are done using the Math.pow() function and natural logarithms are done using Math.log(). If we want logarithm to the base10 we use Math.log10().

```
<html>
<head><title>Sample Form</title></head>
<body>

<button onclick="test()">Random Numbers</button>

<script>
function test()
{
var n1 = Math.pow(6,2);
var n2 = Math.pow(7,3);
var n3 = Math.log(100);
var n4 = Math.log10(100);


document.write("6 raised to the power 2 = <strong>"+n1+"</strong><br>");
document.write("7 raised to the power 3 = <strong>"+n2+"</strong><br>");
document.write("The natural logarithm of 100 is = <strong>"+n3+"</strong><br>");
document.write("Logarithm (to the base 10) of 100 is = <strong>"+n4+"</strong><br>");



}
</script>


</body>
</html>
```

In the code above, we have two examples of exponents using Math.pow(x,y). Basically, x is raised to the power of y in both both cases. n1 and n2 give exponents. n3 shows a natural logarithm of 100 and n4 shows logarithm to base 10 of 100.

Output:

6 raised to the power 2 = **36**
7 raised to the power 3 = **343**
The natural logarithm of 100 is = **4.605170185988092**
Logarithm (to the base 10) of 100 is = **2**

Square root

Math.sqrt() is used the find square root and Math.Abs() is used to find the absolute value of a number.
Here's a few examples:

```
<html>
<head><title>Sample Form</title></head>
<body>

<button onclick="test()">Test</button>

<script>
function test()
{
var n1 = Math.sqrt(36);
var n2 = Math.sqrt(75);
var n3 = Math.abs(13);
var n4 = Math.abs(-14);


document.write("The square root of 36 = <strong>"+n1+"</strong><br>");
document.write("The square root of 75 = <strong>"+n2+"</strong><br>");
document.write("The absolute value of 13 is = <strong>"+n3+"</strong><br>");
document.write("The absolute value of -14 = <strong>"+n4+"</strong><br>");



}
</script>


</body>
</html>
```

In the above code, n1 and n2 are examples of the square root function; while n3 and n4 are examples of the absolute function.
If you haven't heard of the absolute value function, it basically returns a positive value whether the number is +ve or -ve. So, 13 and -13 would both return an absolute value of 13.
Output:

The square root of 36 = **6**
The square root of 75 = **8.660254037844387**
The absolute value of 13 is = **13**
The absolute value of -14 = **14**

Trigonometry

Yes, JavaScript can be used for trigonometric functions as well. Here's a few of them.

Math.sin(x) returns the sine value of x radians. If we want to find the sine of x degrees, then we have to convert it to radians. So, we should change the function to Math.sin(x*MATH.PI/180).

Also, keep in mind that in Javascript, we represent the value of π as Math.PI

We can also do cos and tan function using Math.cos(x) and Math.tan(x), where x is in radians.

Let's look at an example program below:

```
<html>
<head><title>Sample Form</title></head>
<body>

<button onclick="test()">Test</button>

<script>
function test()
{
var n1 = Math.sin(5);
var n2 = Math.sin(5*Math.PI/180);
var n3 = Math.sin(90*Math.PI/180);
var n4 = Math.cos(10);
var n5 = Math.cos(10*Math.PI/180);
var n6 = Math.cos(0*Math.PI/180);
var n7 = Math.tan(30);
var n8 = Math.tan(30*Math.PI/180);
var n9 = Math.tan(45*Math.PI/180);

document.write("The sine of 5 radians = <strong>"+n1+"</strong><br>");
document.write("The sine of 5 degrees = <strong>"+n2+"</strong><br>");
document.write("The sine of 90 degrees = <strong>"+n3+"</strong><br>");
document.write("The cos of 10 radians = <strong>"+n1+"</strong><br>");
document.write("The cos of 10 degrees = <strong>"+n2+"</strong><br>");
document.write("The cos of 0 degrees = <strong>"+n3+"</strong><br>");
document.write("The tan of 30 radians = <strong>"+n7+"</strong><br>");
document.write("The tan of 30 degrees = <strong>"+n8+"</strong><br>");
document.write("The tan of 45 degrees = <strong>"+n9+"</strong><br>");

}
</script>

</body>
</html>
```

In the above code, we show 3 examples of sine, cos and tan values. And we show the difference between calculating trigonometric values of degrees and radians. For example, for n1, we calculate the value of sin(5 radians) and in n2 we calculate the value of sin(5 degrees). In n2, we had to convert 5 degrees into radians by doing sin(5* π/180).

Output:

The sine of 5 radians = **-0.9589242746631385**
The sine of 5 degrees = **0.08715574274765817**
The sine of 90 degrees = **1**
The cos of 10 radians = **-0.9589242746631385**
The cos of 10 degrees = **0.08715574274765817**
The cos of 0 degrees = **1**
The tan of 30 radians = **-6.405331196646276**
The tan of 30 degrees = **0.5773502691896257**
The tan of 45 degrees = **0.9999999999999999**

Practice Problems

1. Write a program that calculates the total salary payment cost for a team. Create a form that takes in two inputs; number of employees and average hours worked per employee. Use parseInt to ensure that the number of employees is an integer. Round the average hours worked to the top hour (So, 5.2 and 5.6 hours would both become 6 hours). Multiply the two inputs and print out the total salary paid to employees.
2. Let's get started and make a demo calculator with all that we've learned. Create a form that takes in two numbers in 2 textboxs and has 15 buttons. Each buttons links to a JavaScript button that does a calculation. Create a button each for addition, subtraction, multiplication, division, remainder, exponent, natural logarithms, logarithms (to base 10), square root, sine, cos, tan, cosec, sec, cot. Some of these buttons only need one number to operate (trig functions, square root, logarithms) while others need two numbers.
3. Create a program that calculates the height of a building you are looking at using trigonometry. The program takes in two

user inputs in a form. The first is the distance from the building; and the second is the viewing angle to the top of the building. Use trigonometry (tan value to be specific) to calculate the height of the building.

Loops

Loops in coding are a sequence of instructions that are repeated a certain number of times.
Think of a loop like an escalator. The steps run in a direction again and again till someone pushes the stop button.
There are 3 types of loops based on the conditions of execution. They are:

a. **IF Loops:** IF loops contain a sequence of instructions that are executed if a certain condition is met. If the conditions are not met, the loop is not executed.

b. **FOR Loops:** FOR loops contain a sequence of instructions that are executed for a certain number of times. For example, a FOR loop from 1 to 10 executes the code inside the loop 10 times.

c. **WHILE Loops:** WHILE loops is a sequence of instructions that are executed till a certain condition is met.

Now, let's look at the elevator example through each of these loops.
Let's say we want the elevator to run only when there are more than 1000 people in the building. Then we use an IF loop that checks the number of people in the building and then runs the elevator function if that is the case.
The IF Loop Example:

```
if(people>1000)
{
```

```
Runelevator();
}
```

Now, if we want to do a 1000 run test on the elevator to see if it can hold a certain weight; we use a FOR loop. The FOR loop below starts at 0 and ends at 999, thus running the elevator a 1000 times.

```
for (i=0;i<1000;i++)
{
Runelevator();
}
```

Finally, if we want to keep running the elevator till 6 PM, we use a WHILE loop.

```
While (checktime!=18:00)
{
Runelevator();
}
```

These are simple examples of the 3 loops to explain the concepts of loops. This concept is very important in coding.
Now, let's do some examples in JavaScript.

IF LOOP EXAMPLE 1

IF loops are also called conditionals. A conditional is a piece of code that checks if a certain condition has been fulfilled. For example, an insurance company might want to give you a lower rate if the combined ages of your two kids is higher than 15. So, you check for those condition. Let's look at it using an IF loop below.

```
<html>
<head><title>Insurance Test</title></head>
<body>
Enter Age of 1st Kid:<input name="a1" type="number" id="age1" size="20"><br>
Enter Age of 2nd Kid:<input name="a2" type="number" id="age2" size="20"><br><br>

<button onclick="checkinsuranceprice()">Check Price</button>

<script>
function checkinsuranceprice()
{
var inscost=0;
var a1 = parseInt(document.getElementById("age1").value);
var a2 = parseInt(document.getElementById("age2").value);

//Check condition
if ((a1+a2)>15)
{
inscost=inscost+300;
}
else
{
inscost=inscost+600;
}
document.write("Your annual car insurance is $"+inscost);
}
</script>

</body>
</html>
```

In the above a html form allows the user to enter two ages with ids' "age1" and "age2". The JavaScript variables a1 and a2 store the values of the variables. The IF statement checks if the sum of the two is greater than 15. If it's greater than 15, insurance cost is $300; otherwise it's $600. Finally, we print out the value of the insurance. Here's the output below.

Output #1:

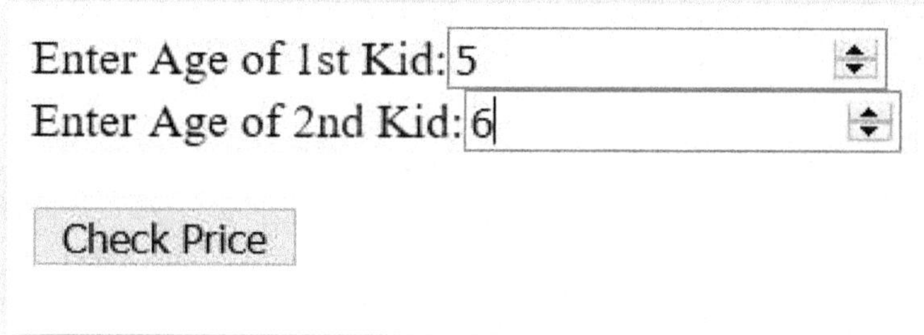

On clicking **Check Price**:

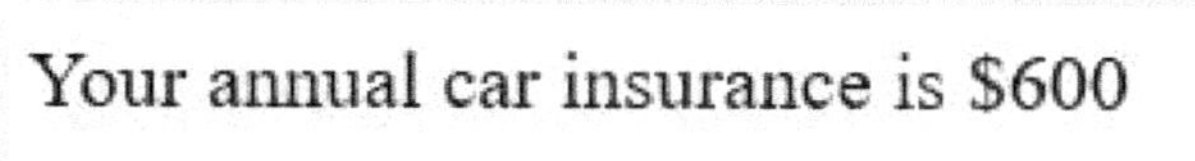

Output #2:

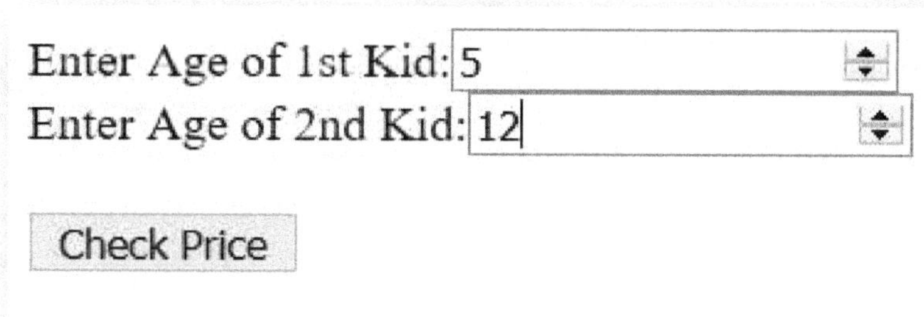

On clicking **Check Price**:

Your annual car insurance is $300

IF LOOP EXAMPLE 2

Let's take another example. How about if you are looking to figure out which gym to sign up for. You want to sign up for gyms that are within 5 miles and cost less than $60 per month. So, you have two IF loops that check for each condition. The loops are within each other. This is called a Nested Loop. Let's have a look below.

```
<html>
<head><title>Gym Test</title></head>
<body>
Enter Name of Gym:<input name="g1" type="text" id="gname" size="20"><br>
Enter Gym Distance from home:<input name="g2" type="number" id="dist" size="20"><br>
Enter Monthly Membership Costs:<input name="g3" type="number" id="memc" size="20"><br><br>

<button onclick="checkgym()">Check Gym</button>

<script>
function checkgym()
{
var name = document.getElementById("gname").value;
var gymdistance = parseInt(document.getElementById("dist").value);
var memberprice = parseInt(document.getElementById("memc").value);


//Check condition
if (gymdistance<5)
{
    if(memberprice<60)
    {
    document.write(name+" is a possible gym");
    }
    else
    {
    document.write(name+" does not work for me");
    }
}
else
{
    document.write(name+" does not work for me");
}

}
</script>

</body>
</html>
```

In the above a html form allows the user to enter a gym name with id="gname", a gymdistance with id="dist" and a gym price with id="memc". The JavaScript variables name, gymdistance and memberprice store the values of the user inputs. One IF statement checks if gymdistance is less than 5. If it's greater than 5, the gym is not good. If it's less than 5, then we use another IF to check if monthly membership price is less than $60. If yes, then this is one possible gym; otherwise it is no good. Here's a few sample outputs below.

Output #1:

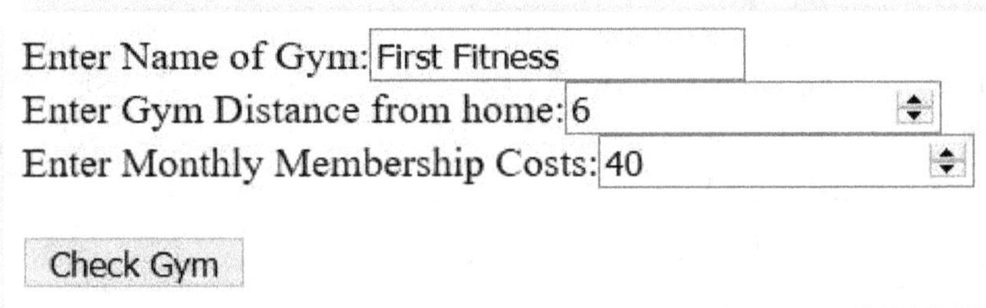

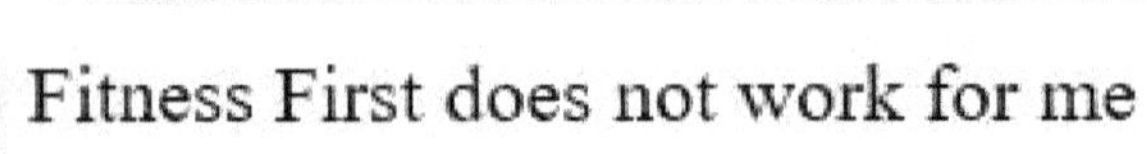

Output #2:

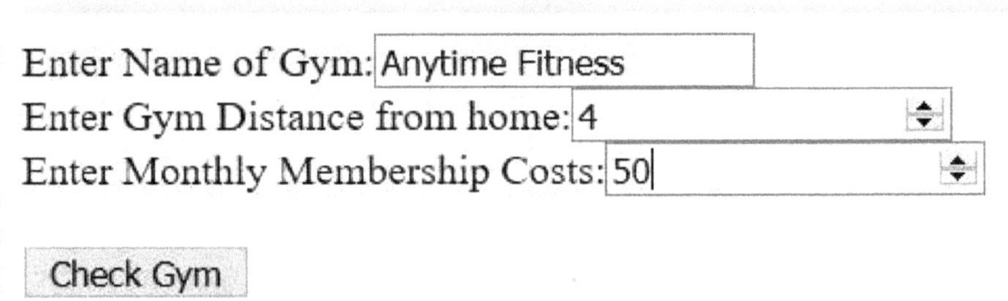

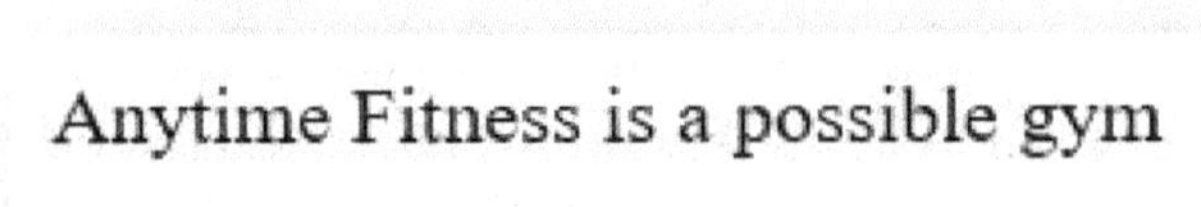

Output #3:

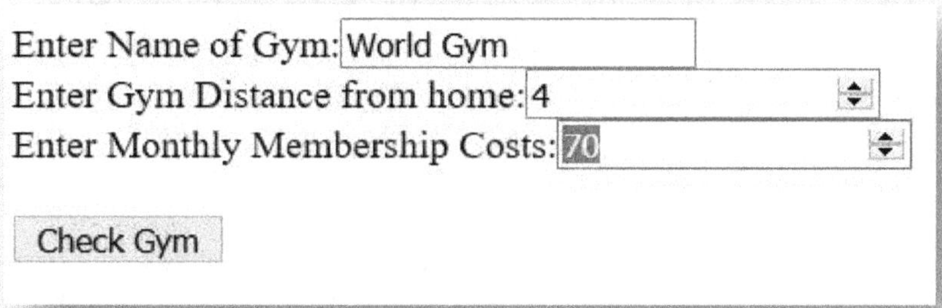

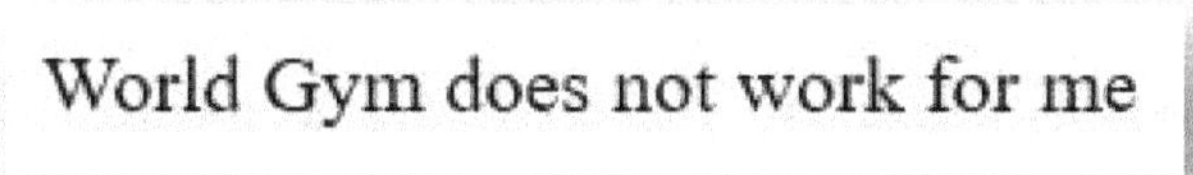

FOR LOOP Example 1

A simple example of a For Loop is a program that counts to 10.

```
<html>
<head><title>Loops......</title></head>
<body>


<button onclick="printtoten()">Print To 10</button>


<script>

function printtoten()
{

for (i=1;i<=10;i++)
{
    document.write(i+"<br>");
}
}

</script>


</body>
</html>
```

The above code is a simple example of a for loop. It has a button that runs the function printtoten(). Printtoten() has a for loop that prints numbers 1 to 10 on the screen through document.write().

For (i=1;i<=10; i++)

The line above means that the loop starts from 1 (i=1). It is increasing by 1 each time (i++). The loop ends when i reaches 10 (i<=10).

Output:

Once you click the button on the output, you see the numbers 1 to 10 printed on the screen.

```
1
2
3
4
5
6
7
8
9
10
```

FOR LOOP Example 2

Now, let's do a slightly different version of this. In this example, we're going to use a form that takes in a number for the loop. That means we can make the loop as long as we want.

```
<html>
<head><title>Loops......</title></head>
<body>

<form id="form1">
How long do you want the loop?: <input name="Loop Number" type="number" id="loop" size="20"><br>

</form>

<button onclick="printtoten()">Print To 10</button>
<button onclick="printlooplength()">Print Loop Length</button>


<script>

function printtoten()
{

for (i=1;i<=10;i++)
{
    document.write(i+"<br>");
}
}
function printlooplength()
{
var looplength=parseInt(document.getElementById("loop").value);


for (i=1;i<=looplength;i++)
{
    document.write(i+"<br>");
}
}
</script>


</body>
</html>
```

A html form was added to this program

The form takes in a number input and stores in a variable called **"loop".**

There is a second button labelled **"Print Loop Length"** which runs the **"printlooplength()"** function.

In the function, we assign the form variable "loop" to another variable **"looplength"**. And we run the loop from 1 to **"looplength".** The loop prints the numbers between 1 and **"looplength".**

In the example below, we put 35 in the form; and as we can see, it prints out numbers between 1 and 35.

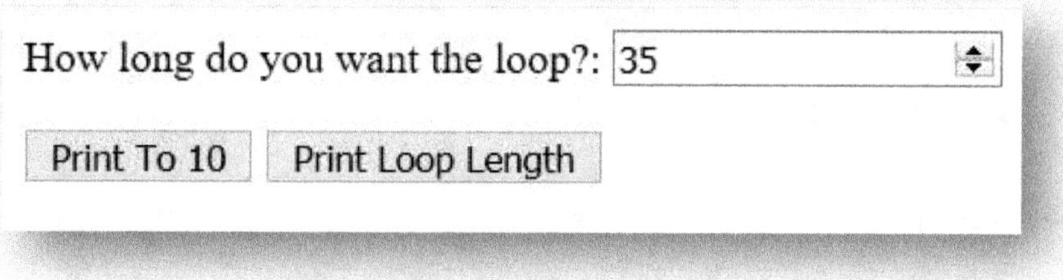
How long do you want the loop?: 35
Print To 10
Print Loop Length

FOR Loop Example 3 – Nested Loops

In the final example, we use FOR loops to create a star pattern.
So, we create a 2nd button labelled 'Print Star Loop' which runs **starloop()** on clicking. In the function, again, looplength has the value of the loop we enter in the form.
So, first, we create a FOR loop that goes from 1 to looplength. The variable i holds the count value of the loop and increases by 1 each time.
Then, we create another FOR loop within that goes from 1 to i. The second FOR loop prints the star("*") i times.
So, for example, if you're going through the first loop for the 5th time, i=5. The second loop prints * from 1 to 5 (i.e. 5 times).
In the example, below, we print the star loop for a looplength of 23.

Output

```
<html>
<head><title>Loops......</title></head>
<body>
<form id="form1">
Loop Number: <input name="Loop Number" type="number" id="loop" size="20"><br>
</form>
<button class="btn printoten" onclick="printtoten()">Print To 10</button>
<button class="btn printoten" onclick="printlooplength()">Print Loop Length</button>
<button class="btn printoten" onclick="starloop()">Print Star Loop</button>
<script>

function printtoten()
{
for (i=1;i<=10;i++)
{
    document.write(i+"<br>");
}
}
function printlooplength()
{
var looplength=parseInt(document.getElementById("loop").value);


for (i=1;i<=looplength;i++)
{
    document.write(i+"<br>");
}
}
function starloop()
{
var looplength=parseInt(document.getElementById("loop").value);

for (i=1;i<=looplength;i++)
    {
    for (j=1;j<=i;j++)
    {
    document.write("*");
    }
    document.write("<br>");
    }
}
</script>
</body>
</html>
```

```
*
**
***
****
*****
******
*******
********
*********
**********
***********
************
*************
**************
***************
****************
*****************
******************
*******************
********************
*********************
**********************
***********************
```

WHILE LOOP EXAMPLE 1

A while loop runs while a certain condition is met. If the condition is no longer met, it breaks out of the loop. In the below example, the program executes a while loop that takes in a user input via the prompt function. The while loop keeps running and printing the user text. The loop stops when the user inputs the word **'STOP'**. Once the word is input, that's the end of the while loops and the program stops.

```
<html>
<head><title>While Loop Test</title></head>
<body>

<button onclick="testwhileloop()">Test</button>

<script>
function testwhileloop()
{
var inputtext = "";
while (inputtext != "STOP")
{
   inputtext = prompt("Enter what you want to do now (Enter in ALL CAPS");
   document.write("Next Activity = "+inputtext+"<br>");
}

}
</script>

</body>
</html>
```

Here's the output below that shows how this works.

Output:

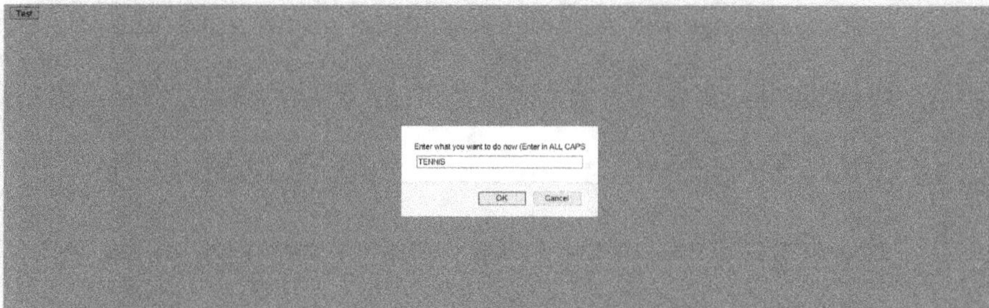
Test
Enter what you want to do now (Enter in ALL CAPS
TENNIS
OK
Cancel

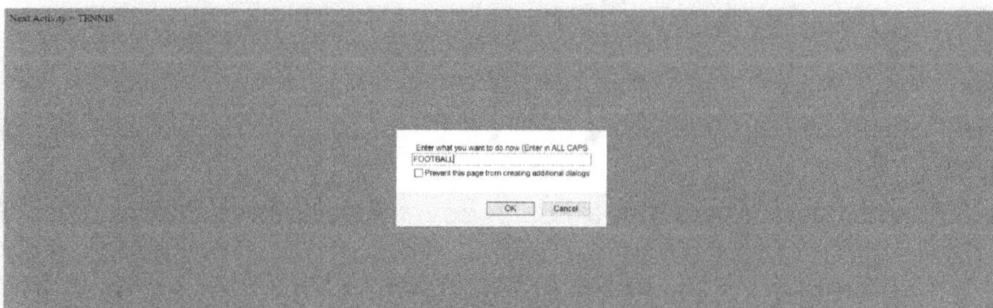
Next Activity = TENNIS
Enter what you want to do now (Enter in ALL CAPS
FOOTBALL
Prevent this page from creating additional dialogs
OK
Cancel

Next Activity = TENNIS
Next Activity = FOOTBALL
Next Activity = STOP

Practice Problems

1. Write a program that inputs a number via a form and checks if its divisible by 3.
2. Write a program that takes a user input and outputs the following pattern below. For example, if the user inputs the number '5' it outputs:

1
22
333
4444
55555

3. Write a program that takes in seven user inputs that are different animals. Then write a function that checks if any of these animals is a tiger, and then print out which number animal is the tiger.
4. Write a program that is a filter for a car dealership. It takes in the name and price of a car via prompt function. The program prints out the name of the car each time. It stops when the sum of all the cars exceed a value of $50000; as that is the upper limit of their budget.

5. Write a program that takes in two user number inputs via prompt function. Keep making the user input two numbers till their sum is greater than 20. Once the user inputs two numbers whose sum is greater than 20, the program stops.
6. Write a program that takes in the vote of a person via user prompt. There are 3 candidates. It checks if the vote is any of the candidates and adds to the candidate vote total. There is a final prompt that asks if there are any more votes and it accepts the values of 'Y/N'. If 'N', then it stops the program and prints out the winner. If 'Y', then it asks for the vote again and repeats the process.
7. Write a program that takes a user input and outputs the following star pattern below. For example, if the user inputs the number '6' it outputs:

```
******
*****
****
***
**
*
```

8. Write a program that takes in a user input and prints out the sum of numbers from 1 to that number. For example, if the user inputs 3; the sum is 1+2+3=6.

Game Time - Loops

Now, it's time to design a few games based on what we've learned so far.
There's no better way of learning concepts than applying them; and even better to apply them to something fun.
Before, getting started, let's talk about one concept; which is adding html elements using Javascript.

Adding html Elements using JavaScript

What if want to add a button or textbox in the middle of the JavaScript program. Yes, you can do that within JavaScript using the document.write() function. For example, you can create a button using:

```
document.write('<button onClick="afunction()">Restart</button>');
```

In the above line, we create a button with text 'Restart' on it. On clicking the button, **afunction()** is run. This is very useful in games where we have the option to keep running the program instead of stopping. Now, let's look at a similar program below.

```
<html>
<head><title>Sample Form</title></head>
<body>
<link rel="stylesheet" type="text/css" href="samplestyle.css" />
<form id="form1">
Enter First Number:<input name="number1" type="number" id="num1" size="20"><br>
Enter Second Number:<input name="number2" type="number" id="num2" size="20"><br><br>
Enter Third Number: <input name="number3" type="number" id="num3" size="20"></textarea><br><br>

<button class = "btn submit" onclick="multiplynum()">Submit</button>

<script>
function multiplynum()
{
var n1 = document.getElementById("num1").value;
var n2 = document.getElementById("num2").value;
var n3 = document.getElementById("num3").value;
document.write('<link rel="stylesheet" type="text/css" href="samplestyle.css" />');
document.write("The product of the three numbers is "+n1*n2*n3);
document.write('<hr>');
document.write('<button onClick="redirect()">Home</botton>');
}

function redirect()
{
window.location.replace("form_JavaScript.html");
}

</script>

</body>
</html>
```

The program above is the form in the previous chapter. We just added two lines and a function.

The two lines create a Home button which runs the function **redirect().**

The **redirect()** function runs the program again.

'form_JavaScript.html' is the name of the file we are running. You should change 'form_JavaScript' to whatever you have named your html file.

Output #1

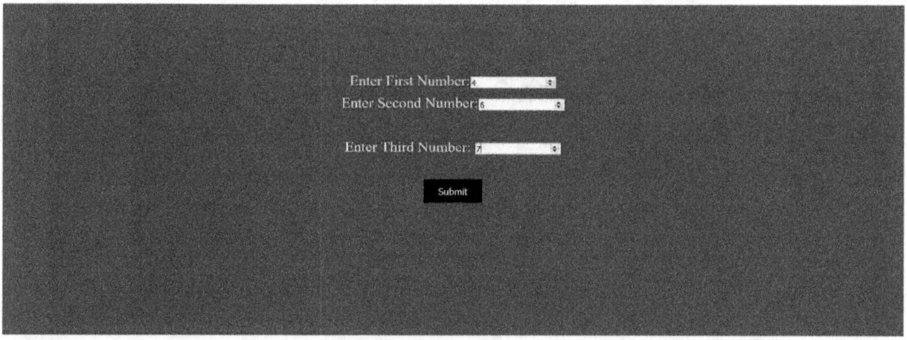

After entering numbers and clicking Submit, we get:

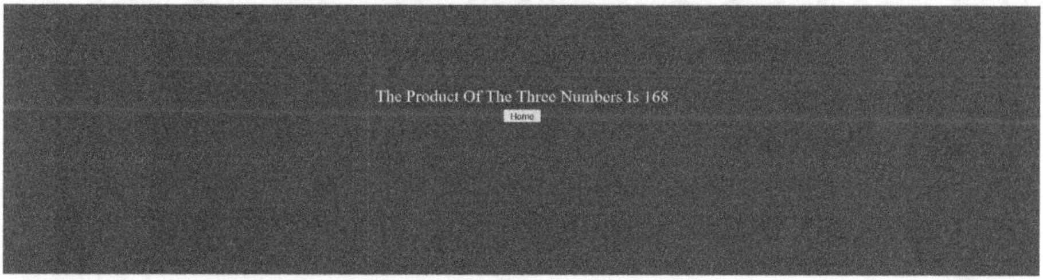

And now, after clicking Home button, we get:

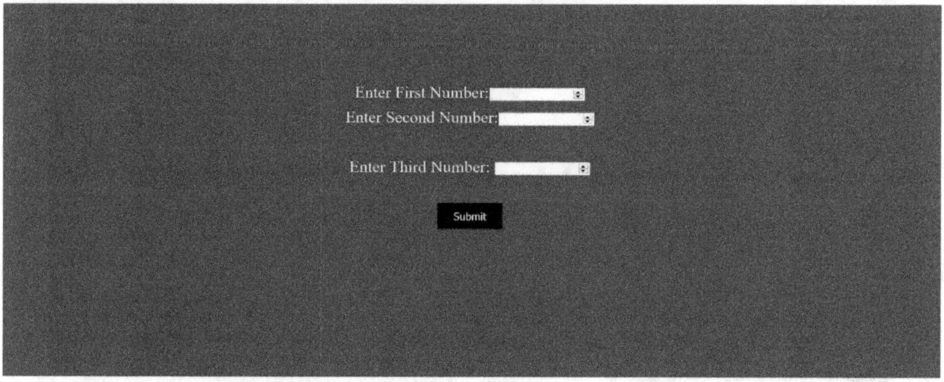

So, it basically restarts the html program.
Now, let's get started with our first game.

Game 1 – Guess Random Numbers

In this game, we're going to create a form that takes in a number via a textbox. The number is between 0 and 10. Then we compare that number to a random number generated via JavaScript (using Math.random). If it is the same, then the guessed number is correct. If not, then we give them the right number. The user has the option to click the Home button and try again. See the code and output below.

```
<html>
<head><title>Guess Number</title>
<link rel="stylesheet" href="samplestyle.css" />
</head>
<body>
<form id="form1">
Guess Number between 0 and 10:<input name="name" type="number" id="num1" size="20"><br>
</form>
<button class="btn a" onclick="guessnumber()">Check</button>
<script>

function guessnumber()
{
var guess=document.getElementById("num1").value;
var rand=Math.floor(Math.random()*10);
if (guess==rand)
{
    document.write("Congratulations. You guessed the right number");
}else{
    document.write("Sorry. You guessed wrong. The correct number is "+rand);
}


document.write('<link rel="stylesheet" type="text/css" href="samplestyle.css" />');
document.write('<br>');
document.write('<button onClick="redirect()">Home</button>');



}
function redirect()
{
window.location.replace("GuessNumber.html");
}

</script>

</body>
</html>
```

Output:

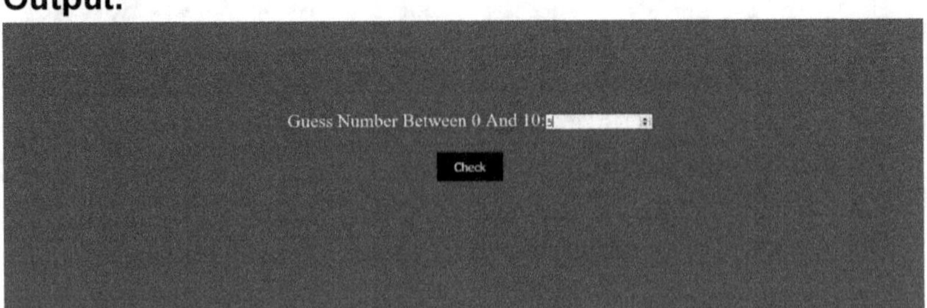

If we click **Home**, we can play the game again.
This program is a good way to practice conditional loops and random number generators.

Game 2 – Math Quiz Game

This is a bit of a longer program, so I've broken it up into 2 pictures. It basically prints out 5 simple math problems and takes in answers to these problems via a form (they have id's of **num1,num2,num3,num4,num5**). The answers are stored as variables in JavaScript **(answer1,answer2,answer3,answer4,answer5).** These answers are compared to the real answers using IF functions. A counter is incremented by 1 each time the user gets a correct answer and finally the counter is printed to see how many correct answers the user got.

```
<html>
<head><title>Math Quiz</title></head>
<link rel="stylesheet" href="samplestyles.css" />
<body>
<form id="form1">
5*2 = :<input name="name" type="number" id="num1" size="20"><br>
7/2 = :<input name="name" type="float" id="num2" size="20"><br>
6*5 = :<input name="name" type="number" id="num3" size="20"><br>
14+29 = :<input name="name" type="number" id="num4" size="20"><br>
17-6 = :<input name="name" type="number" id="num5" size="20"><br>
</form>
<button class="btn" onclick="guessnumber()">Check</button>
<script>

function guessnumber()
{
var correct=0;

var answer1=parseInt(document.getElementById("num1").value);
var answer2=parseFloat(document.getElementById("num2").value);
var answer3=parseInt(document.getElementById("num3").value);
var answer4=parseInt(document.getElementById("num4").value);
var answer5=parseInt(document.getElementById("num5").value);

if (answer1==10)
{
    correct=correct+1;
}
if (answer2==3.5)
{
    correct=correct+1;
}
if (answer3==30)
{
    correct=correct+1;
}
if (answer4==43)
{
    correct=correct+1;
}
if (answer5==11)
{
    correct=correct+1;
}
document.write('<link rel="stylesheet" type="text/css" href="samplestyle.css" />');
document.write("You got "+correct+" answers correct");
}

</script>

</body>
</html>
```

Output:

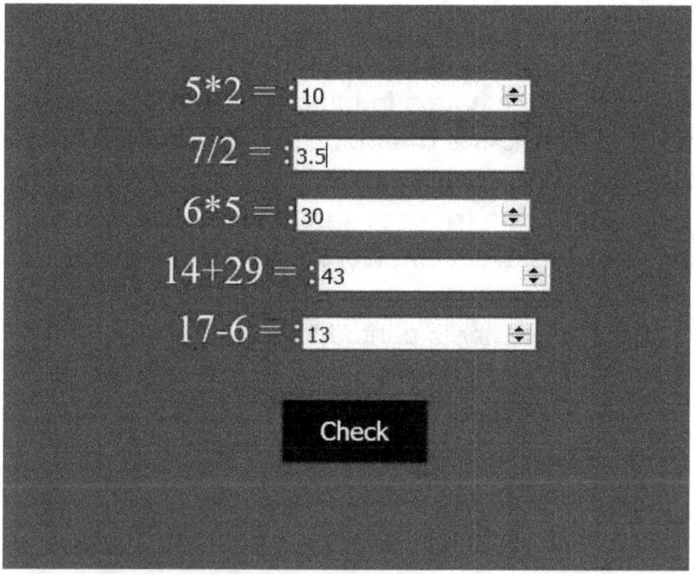

On clicking **Check** button, we get:

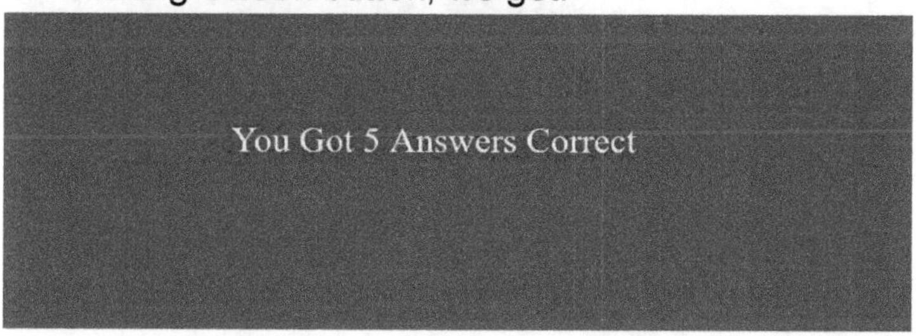

This is a great practice program. But you might be thinking that kids can use this program only once as we always use the same numbers. To fix this problem, we generate random numbers in the next game.

Game 3 – Math Quiz with Random Numbers

In this program below, there are 5 math questions generated by 10 random numbers. The 10 random numbers are variables **number1-number10**. The answers to the questions are calculated and are stored in variables **answer1-answer5**. These 15 variables are called global variables as they are outside any functions. This means that their values can be accessed anywhere in the program by any function. The function **startquiz()** uses the 10 variables **number1-number10** to write the quiz on the screen and create a form that takes in 5 answers with id's **num1-num5**. On clicking the **Check** button, these 5 answers are sent to the function **guessnumber()** and stored as variables **guess1-guess5**. These 5 answers **(guess1-guess5)** are checked against calculated answers **(answer1-answer5)** using 5 different IF functions. Each time there is a correct answer, a counter is incremented. Eventually, the counter is printed to show the number of correct answers. There is also a **Home** button at the end which gives the user the option to restart the program with fresh questions. These questions are randomly generated which means that the user gets different questions each time.

```
<html>
<head><title>Math Quiz</title></head>
<link rel="stylesheet" href="samplestyle.css" />
<body>
<button class="btn" onclick="startquiz()">Start Math Quiz</button>

<script>

var number1=Math.floor(Math.random()*10)+1;
var number2=Math.floor(Math.random()*10)+1;
var number3=Math.floor(Math.random()*10)+1;
var number4=Math.floor(Math.random()*10)+1;
var number5=Math.floor(Math.random()*50)+1;
var number6=Math.floor(Math.random()*50)+1;
var number7=Math.floor(Math.random()*50)+1;
var number8=Math.floor(Math.random()*50)+1;
var number9=Math.floor(Math.random()*50)+1;
var number10=Math.floor(Math.random()*50)+1;
var answer1=number1*number2;
var answer2=number3*number4;
var answer3=number5+number6;
var answer4=number7-number8;
var answer5=number9%number10;

function startquiz()
{
document.write(number1+" * "+number2+" = ");
document.write('<input name="name" type="number" id="num1" size="20"><br>');

document.write(number3+" * "+number4+" = ");
document.write('<input name="name" type="number" id="num2" size="20"><br>');

document.write(number5+" + "+number6+" = ");
document.write('<input name="name" type="number" id="num3" size="20"><br>');

document.write(number7+" - "+number8+" = ");
document.write('<input name="name" type="number" id="num4" size="20"><br>');

document.write(number9+" / "+number10+". Remainder= ");
document.write('<input name="name" type="number" id="num5" size="20"><br>');
document.write('<link rel="stylesheet" type="text/css" href="samplestyle.css" />');
document.write('<br>');
document.write('<button class="btn a" onclick="guessnumber()">Check</button><br>');
}
```

```
function guessnumber()
{
document.body.innerhtml='';
correctanswers=0;
var guess1=document.getElementById("num1").value;
var guess2=document.getElementById("num2").value;
var guess3=document.getElementById("num3").value;
var guess4=document.getElementById("num4").value;
var guess5=document.getElementById("num5").value;
document.write("Answer 1 = "+answer1+'<br>');
document.write("Answer 2 = "+answer2+'<br>');
document.write("Answer 3 = "+answer3+'<br>');
document.write("Answer 4 = "+answer4+'<br>');
document.write("Answer 5 = "+answer5+'<br>');

if (guess1==answer1)
{
    correctanswers=correctanswers+1;
}
if (guess2==answer2)
{
    correctanswers=correctanswers+1;
}
if (guess3==answer3)
{
    correctanswers=correctanswers+1;
}
if (guess4==answer4)
{
    correctanswers=correctanswers+1;
}
if (guess5==answer5)
{
    correctanswers=correctanswers+1;
}

document.write("Number of correct answers = "+correctanswers);
document.write('<br>');
document.write('<button class="btn a" onClick="redirect()">Home</button>');

}

document.write("Number of correct answers = "+correctanswers);
document.write('<br>');
document.write('<button class="btn a" onClick="redirect()">Home</button>');

}


function redirect()
{
window.location.replace("MathQuiz_Random_Numbers.html");
}

</script>

</body>
</html>
```

Output:

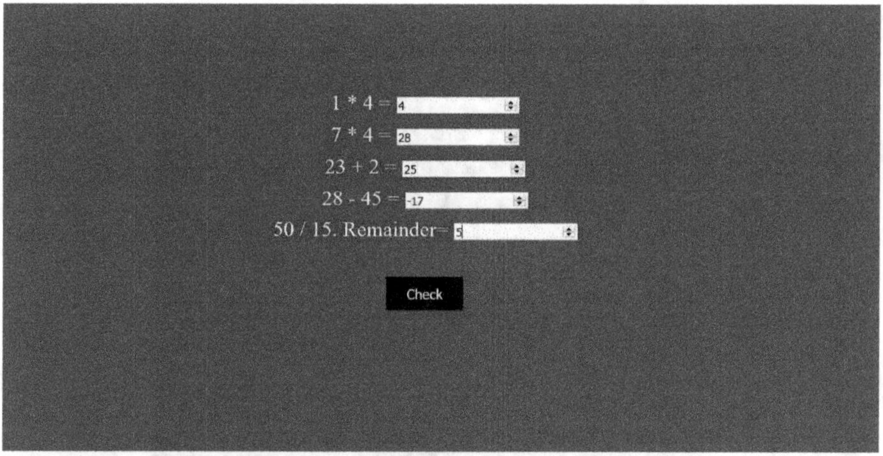

On clicking **Check** button, we get:

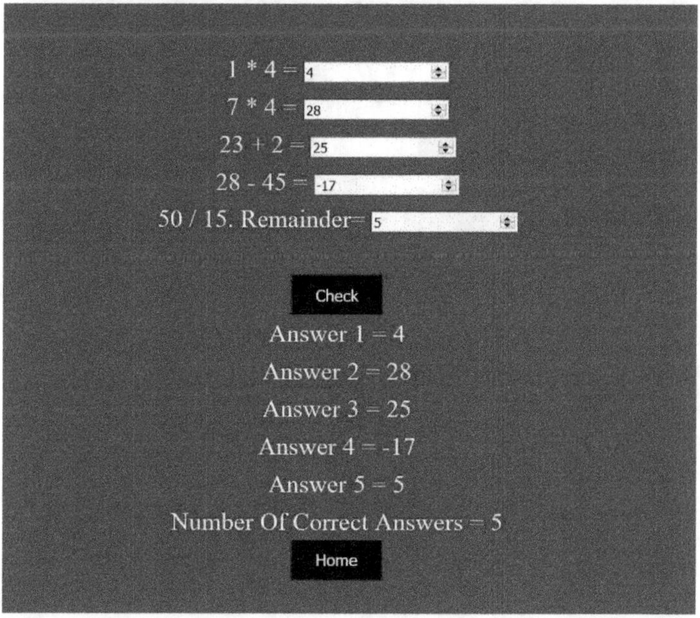

Now, we know that we got all correct answers. Now, let's click **Home** again. We click **Start Math Quiz** to get us here again to do another quiz again. Since the numbers are randomized, we get 5 completely different questions. Brilliant!!

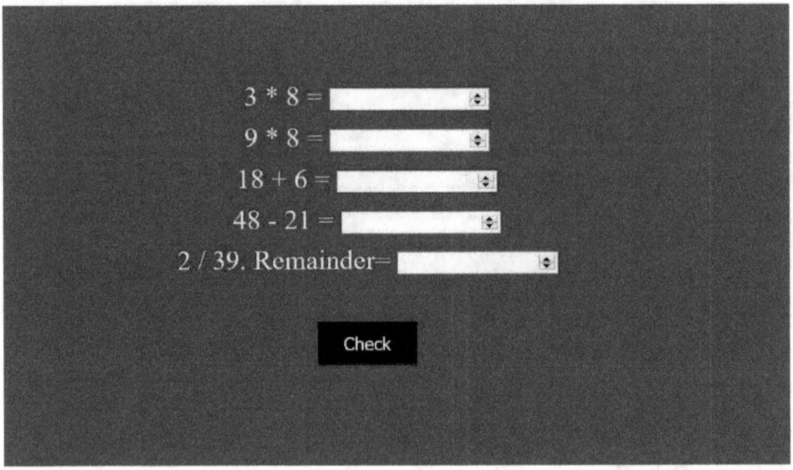
3 * 8 =
9 * 8 =
18 + 6 =
48 - 21 =
2 / 39. Remainder=
Check

Practice Problems

1. Write a program that generates two random numbers between 0 and 10. The program calculates their sum and product. It prints out the sum and product on the screen and asks the user to guess the 2 numbers. The user inputs his guesses through a form and it is checked against the initial two numbers. If he gets it right, then he gets a congratulatory message. If he gets it wrong, the program lets him know the correct answers. At the end, there is the option to restart the program and try again.
2. Write a program that generates a random number between 0 and 20. It squares the number and prints the square on the screen. Then, it asks the user to guess what the number is. The user inputs the number via a form and the program checks whether it is correct or not.
3. Write a program that allows the user to input 3 numbers via a form. These 3 numbers are supposed to be the 3 sides of a triangle. The program then checks if this is a right-angled triangle. The program lets the user know if it is a right-angled triangle (Hint: Use Pythagros theorem to check).

String Variables

A string variable in JavaScript programming is used to store a group of characters.
For example:
var x="awe3t5"
x is a string variable that stores the value of "awe3t5".
It is a string variable of size 6. When we access the string, remember that the values start from 0 instead of 1. For example, x[0] returns a value of a, x[1] returns w and so on.
Strings are very useful in processing text information likes names, addresses etc.
Here's a list of useful functions that can be used to process strings.
length – This returns the length of a string. In the above example, x.length returns 6.
charAt(y) – This returns the character at position y in the string. For example, in the string x; if we want the 5th character, we do x.charAt(5) and that returns t.
indexOf(y) – Checks the index of character y in the string. For example, x.indexOf('a') returns 0.
lastIndexOf(y) – Checks the last index of character y in the string. For example, x.lastIndexOf('e') returns 3. This is only useful if there are multiple occurrences of the same string.
.concat(b) – This join string b to a previous string. For example, if string a = "xyz" and string b = "lmn"; a.concat(b) gives "xyzlmn".
includes(y) – This checks if string y is included in a string and returns a true or false value. For example, if string x= "Hi Peter"; then x.includes("Hi") returns true, but x.includes("Home") returns false.
replace(x,a) – This basically replaces all instances of string x with string a. For example if a string str ="Hi Peter"; then str.replace("Hi","Hello") becomes str="Hello Peter".

startswith(y) – This checks if a string starts with string y. It returns a Boolean variable of **true** or **false** value. In the above example, str.startswith("Hi") returns true while str.startswith("Hello") returns false.
toUpper() – This changes the entire string to upper case. In the above example, str.toUpper() becomes "HI PETER".
toLower() – This changes the entire string to lower case. In the above example, str.Lower() becomes "hi peter".

Example 1 – Playing with Your Name; Reverse name game

In the example below, we enter our name through a form. There are two buttons, one prints the length of your name; and the second reverses your name. The first button runs a function called **strlength()**. **strlength()** gets your name via the form and finds the length using the **.length** function.
The second button executes a function called **namereverse()**. namereverse() gets your name via the form again and finds the length. Then it runs a FOR loop which starts from the last character and keeps subtracting 1 till it reaches the first character. It prints out the character at each loop iteration. This prints out letters from the last character to the first, thus reversing the name.
Below is the code and output.

```
<html>
<head><title>JavaScript Lesson 4 - Strings</title></head>
<body>
<link rel="stylesheet" href="samplestyle.css" />
<form id="form1">
Enter Name:<input name="name" type="text" id="name" size="20"><br>


<button onclick="strlength()">Name Length</button>
<button onclick="namereverse()">Name Reverse</button>

<script>

function strlength()
{
var nm=document.getElementById("name").value;
document.write("Your name is "+nm.length+ " characters long");
document.write('<link rel="stylesheet" type="text/css" href="samplestyle.css" />');
document.write('<br>');
}

function namereverse()
{
var nm=document.getElementById("name").value;
len=nm.length;
document.write("Name Reversed = ");
for (i=len-1;i>=0;i--)
{
document.write(nm[i]);
}
document.write('<link rel="stylesheet" type="text/css" href="samplestyle.css" />');
document.write('<br>');
}


</script>


</body>
</html>
```

Output:

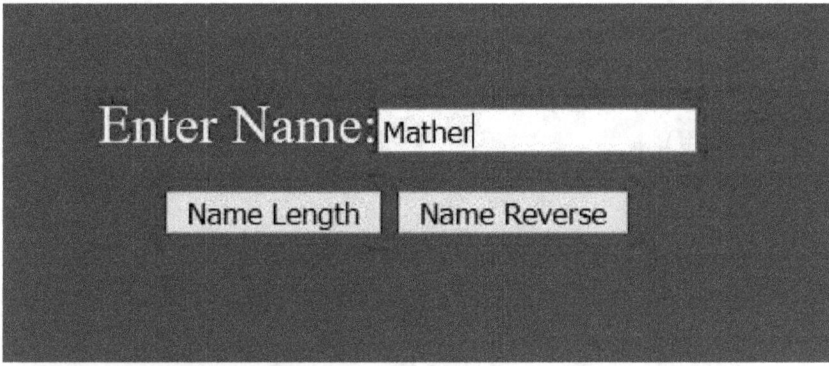

On Clicking **Name Length**

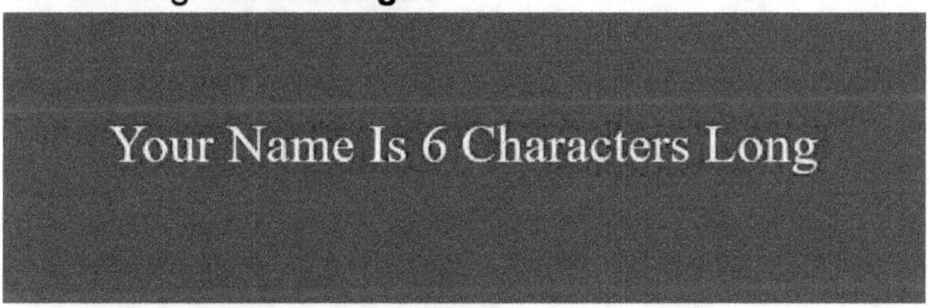

On Clicking **Name Reverse**

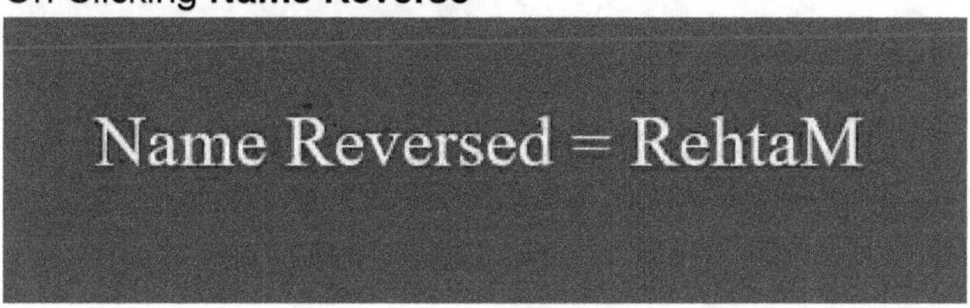

Example 2 –Address Check

In the below program, the user enters a name and an address via a form. The address is entered via a textarea to allow for larger number of characters. It accepts 5 rows of 40 characters each (200 characters in total). So, the goal of this program is to assign all New York residents flying in to a separate hotel. The button runs a function called addcheck(). Addcheck() takes in name and address from the form and assigns them to variables.

An IF function with .includes() checks if the address contains "New York". If it does, then the name string concatenates with the hotel 1 string using .concat().

If it does not contain New York, then the name string concatenates with the hotel 2 string.

We print out the concatenated string in either case.

Here's the code with a couple of outputs below showcasing the 2 different cases.

```
<html>
<head><title>JavaScript Lesson 4 - Strings</title></head>
<body>
<link rel="stylesheet" href="samplestyle.css" />
<form id="form1">
Enter Name:<input name="name" type="text" id="name" size="20"><br>
Enter Address: <textarea name="TextBox" cols="40" rows="5" id="address"></textarea><br><br>


<button onclick="addcheck()">Check Address</button>

<script>

function addcheck()
{
var nm=document.getElementById("name").value;
var address=document.getElementById("address").value;
var len=address.length;
var pstr="";
h1=" stays in Hotel 1";
h2=" stays in Hotel 2";
if (address.includes("New York"))
{
pstr=nm.concat(h1);
document.write(pstr);
}
else
{
pstr=nm.concat(h2);
document.write(pstr);
}
document.write('<link rel="stylesheet" type="text/css" href="samplestyle.css" />');
document.write('<br>');
}


</script>


</body>
</html>
```

Output #1:

On Clicking **Check Address**, it shows Hotel 2 because address is not from New York.

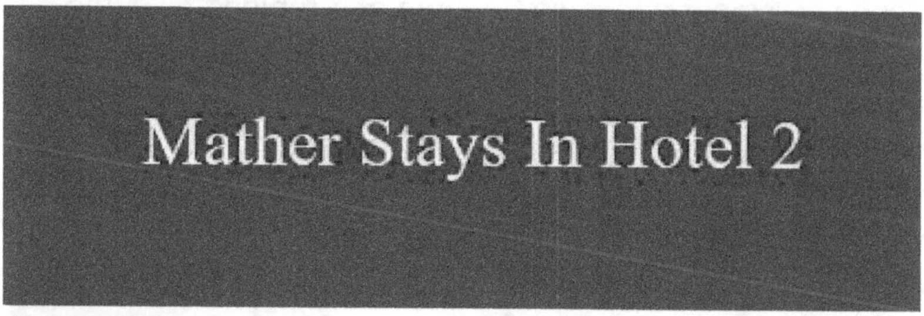

Output #2

On Clicking **Check Address**, it shows Hotel 1 because address is a New York address.

Timmy Stays In Hotel 1

Example 3 – Enter a string and replace all curse words with *****

In the below code, we input a text via textarea and replace all curse words with five stars *****. For censorship's sake, we are using **"Fudge"** as our curse word.
The button runs **filterc()** function. The **filterc()** function takes in the text via the textarea id in the form. An IF function with **.includes** and **.toUpperCase()** checks if the word "Fudge" is found. The **.toUpperCase()** is used because we do not know if the curse word is entered in lower case or Upper case.
If it is the curse word, we use **.replace** to replace the words "Fudge" and "FUDGE" with "*****". At the end, we print out the modified string. We have the code and a couple of output variations below.

```
<html>
<head><title>JavaScript Lesson 4 - Strings</title></head>
<body>
<link rel="stylesheet" href="samplestyle.css" />
<form id="form1">
Enter Name:<input name="name" type="text" id="name" size="20"><br>
Enter Text: <textarea name="TextBox" cols="40" rows="5" id="phrase"></textarea><br><br>


<button onclick="filterc()">Filter Curse Words</button>

<script>

function filterc()
{
var nm=document.getElementById("name").value;
var text=document.getElementById("phrase").value;
var modtext=text;
if (text.toUpperCase().includes("FUDGE"))
{
modtext=text.replace("Fudge","****").replace("FUDGE","*****");
}
document.write("Modified Text ="+modtext);
document.write('<link rel="stylesheet" type="text/css" href="samplestyle.css" />');
document.write('<br>');
}


</script>


</body>
</html>
```

Output #1:

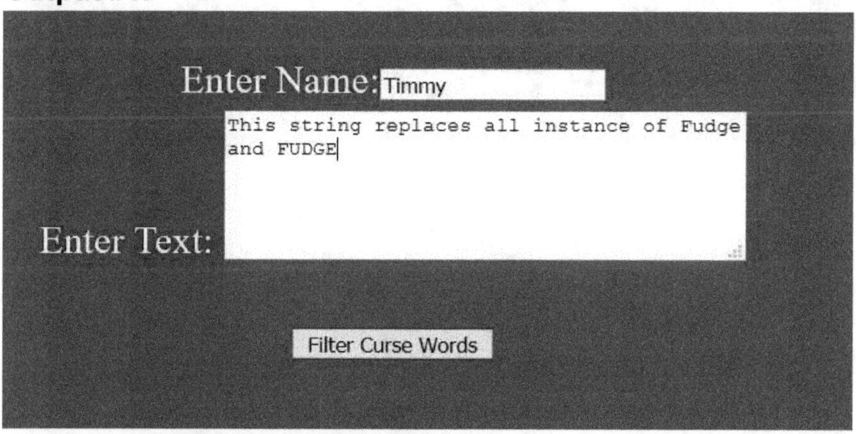

On Clicking **Filter Curse Words**…

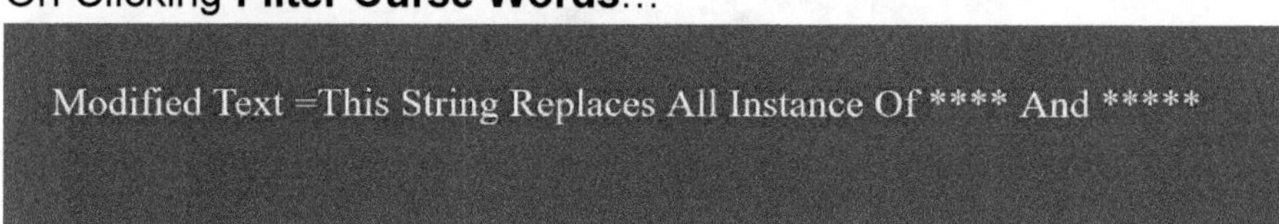

Output #2:

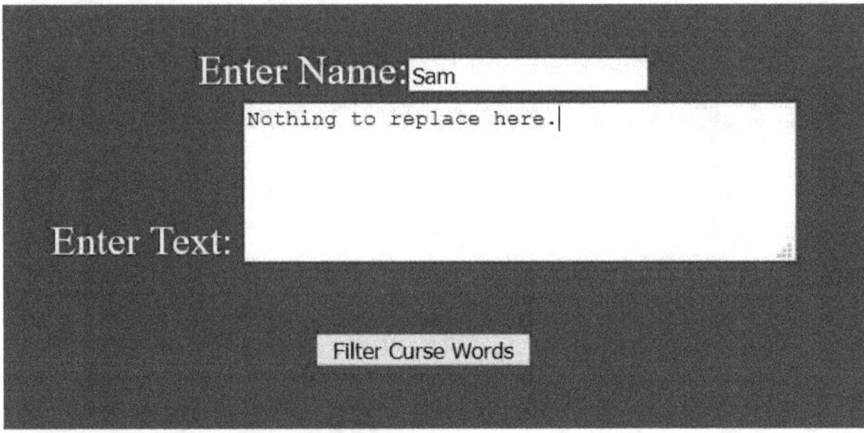

On Clicking **Filter Curse Words**…

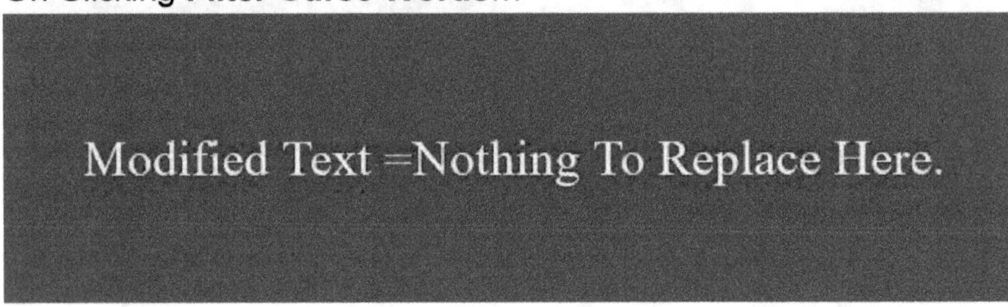

Practice Problems

1. Write a program that takes in a string and prints out every 2nd character in the string. For example "wfwfwkfnfwbej" would print out "ffkbwj".
2. Write a program that takes in a long sentence and replaces all instances of the word "red" with "yellow".
3. Write a program that takes in an address and checks if the zip code contains 5 characters. If it contains more or less, or there is no zip code, print out "Invalid Address".

Arrays

An array in JavaScript is used to store a group of similar variables. Think about how you would store ages of people using variables. Let's say we have three people and their ages. We can store them in variables age1; age2 and age 3.

```
age1=5;
age2=25;
age=45;
```

Now, let's say we have 10 people. We can store it in variables age1, age2….. age10. Now, what if we had to store it for 100 people. You get the picture. There are too many variables to track.

For this reason, we use arrays. For storing 10 ages, we can just use.

```
age=[5,25,45,60,20,23,24,43,34,78];
```

To access the values in Javascript, we use the index of the array. The index of the 1st element is 0, 2nd is 1, 3rd is 2 and so on…. For example,

document.write(age[0]) outputs **5**;

document.write(age[1]) outputs **25**;

document.write(age[5]) outputs **23**.

Example 1 – Creating An Array in JavaScript

Now, let's look at the example below. We create 3 arrays in JavaScript for name, age and state of 5 people. We print these out using array index. And then we add a 6th person using .**push()** feature. Check out the code and output below.

```
<html>
<head><title>JavaScript Lesson 5 - Arrays</title></head>
<body>
<link rel="stylesheet" href="samplestyle.css" />


<button onclick="createarray()">Print Array</button>

<script>

function createarray()
{
document.write('<link rel="stylesheet" type="text/css" href="samplestyle.css" />');
document.write('<br>');

var nm = ["Jim","Tim","Kim","Bim","Sam"];
var age=[7,56,40,34,56];
var state=["Florida","California","Georgia", "Illinois", "Nevada"];
document.write(nm[0]+' lives in '+state[0]+' state and age is '+age[0]+"<br>");
document.write(nm[1]+' lives in '+state[1]+' state and age is '+age[1]+"<br>");
document.write(nm[2]+' lives in '+state[2]+' state and age is '+age[2]+"<br>");
document.write(nm[3]+' lives in '+state[3]+' state and age is '+age[3]+"<br>");
document.write(nm[4]+' lives in '+state[4]+' state and age is '+age[4]+"<br>");
name.push("Yang");//Adding another index to the array
age.push(20);
loc.push("California");
document.write(nm[5]+' lives in '+state[5]+' state and age is '+age[5]+"<br>");



}

</script>


</body>
</html>
```

Output:

On clicking **Print Array**, we get..

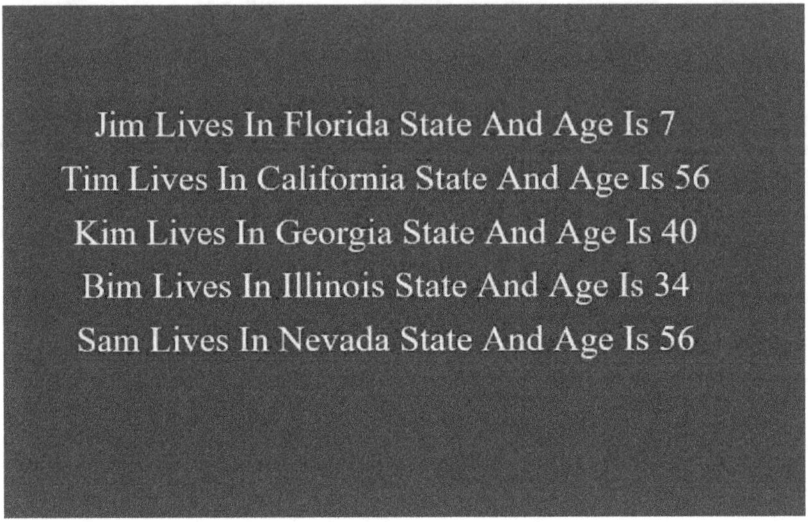

Example 2 – Assigning An Array Through A Form

In this example, we input name, age and state through a html form. In Javascript, we assign the form elements to variables.
3 names, ages and state locations are entered via a form and entered into 3 arrays using **document.getElementById**.
The array is printed at the end using **document.write()**.

```
<html>
<head><title>JavaScript Lesson 5 - Arrays</title></head>
<body>
<link rel="stylesheet" href="samplestyle.css" />
Enter Name1 <input name="name" type="text" id="name0" size="20"><br>
Enter Age1 <input name="age" type="number" id="age0" size="20"><br>
Enter State1 <input name="state" type="text" id="state0" size="20"><br>

Enter Name2 <input name="name" type="text" id="name1" size="20"><br>
Enter Age2 <input name="age" type="number" id="age1" size="20"><br>
Enter State2 <input name="state" type="text" id="state1" size="20"><br>

Enter Name3 <input name="name" type="text" id="name2" size="20"><br>
Enter Age4 <input name="age" type="number" id="age2" size="20"><br>
Enter State4 <input name="state" type="text" id="state2" size="20"><br>
<button onclick="createarray()">Start Program</button>

<script>

function createarray()
{
var nm=[];
var age=[];
var state=[];

nm[0]=document.getElementById("name0").value;
age[0]=document.getElementById("age0").value;
state[0]=document.getElementById("state0").value;
nm[1]=document.getElementById("name1").value;
age[1]=document.getElementById("age1").value;
state[1]=document.getElementById("state1").value;
nm[2]=document.getElementById("name2").value;
age[2]=document.getElementById("age2").value;
state[2]=document.getElementById("state2").value;

document.write('<link rel="stylesheet" type="text/css" href="samplestyle.css" />');
document.write('<br>');
document.write(nm[0] + " is "+age[0]+" years old and lives in "+state[0]+"<br>");
document.write(nm[1] + " is "+age[1]+" years old and lives in "+state[1]+"<br>");
document.write(nm[2] + " is "+age[2]+" years old and lives in "+state[2]+"<br>");

}
```

Output:

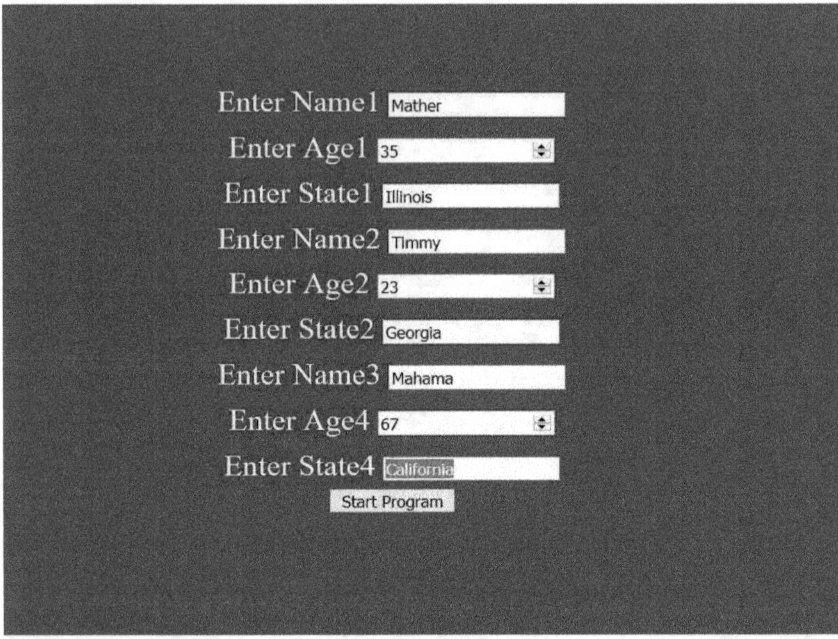

On Clicking **Start Program**, we get:

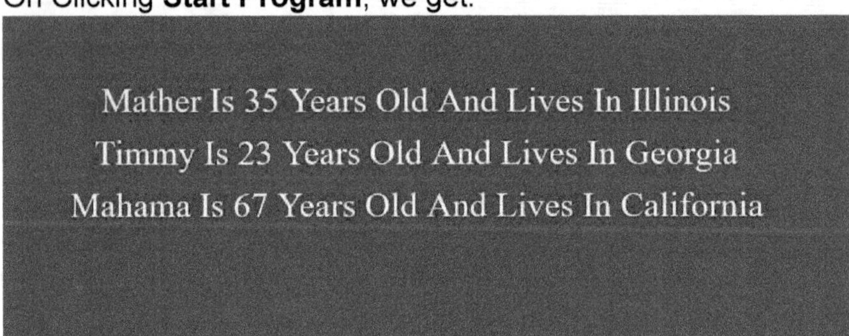

Example 3 – Guess World Capitals

In this program, we code a quiz that asks the user the capital of a random country around the world, and checks if the answer is correct. In the program, the one button runs the **worldquiz()** function. In the function, we declare two arrays. One array contains all the countries around the world; and the other contains all the capitals.

You can get the values for these arrays below:

https://drive.google.com/file/d/1Vbnrllk290oVmh3Vn8Jv2EgFBL1w8vSd/view?usp=sharing

We then chose a random number between 0 and x, x being the length of the array. This random number picks a random country from the array. We do this using **Math.random()** and **Math.floor()**.

We take in a user guess for the capital using **prompt**. We compare the user guess to the actual capital. Then, we send the user a message telling them they're correct or wrong (with the correct capital if they're wrong).

Then, the user has the chance to restart the program with the **Home** button that runs the **redirect()** function. The redirect function runs '**GuessWorldCapitals.html**' which is the name of the file. The code and the outputs are shown below.

```
<html>
<head><title>Guess World Capitals</title>
<link rel="stylesheet" href="styles.css" />
</head>
<body>
<button class="btn a" onclick="worldquiz()">Start Quiz</button>
<script>

function worldquiz()
{

var countries = ["Afghanistan","Albania","Algeria","Andorra","Angola","Antigua and Barbuda","Argentina","Armenia",
var capitals = ["Kabul","Tirana (Tirane)","Algiers","Andorra la Vella","Luanda","Saint John's","Buenos Aires","Yer
var randomcountrynumber = Math.floor(Math.random() * countries.length);
var chosencountry = countries[randomcountrynumber];
var chosencapital = capitals[randomcountrynumber];
var guess = prompt("What is the capital of "+chosencountry+" ?");

if (guess.toUpperCase()==chosencapital.toUpperCase())
{
    document.write("<p>Congratulations. You are correct.</p>");
}else
{
    document.write("<p>Wrong. The capital is "+chosencapital+"</p>");
}

document.write('<link rel="stylesheet" type="text/css" href="styles.css" />');
document.write('<br>');

document.write('<button onClick="redirect()">Home</button>');

}
function redirect()
{
window.location.replace("GuessWorldCapitals.html");
}

</script>
</body>
</html>
```

Output #1:

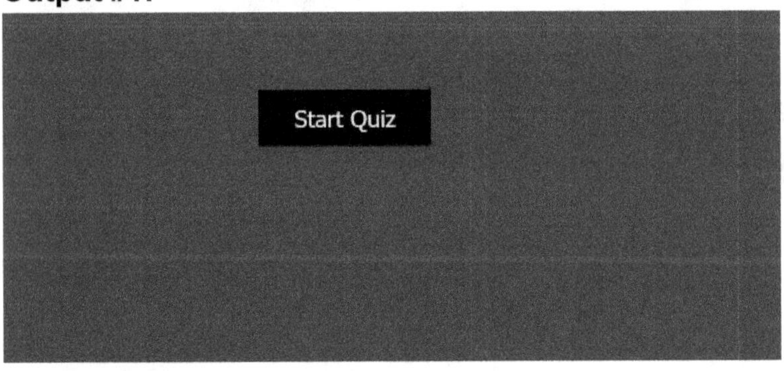

Click **Start Quiz**

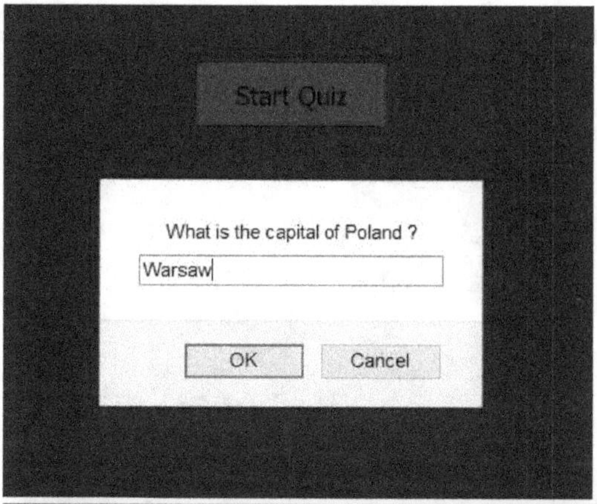
Start Quiz
What is the capital of Poland ?
Warsaw
OK
Cancel

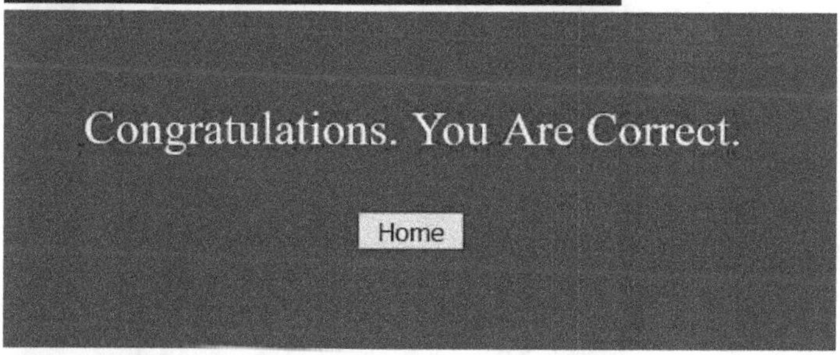
Congratulations. You Are Correct.
Home

Output #2:

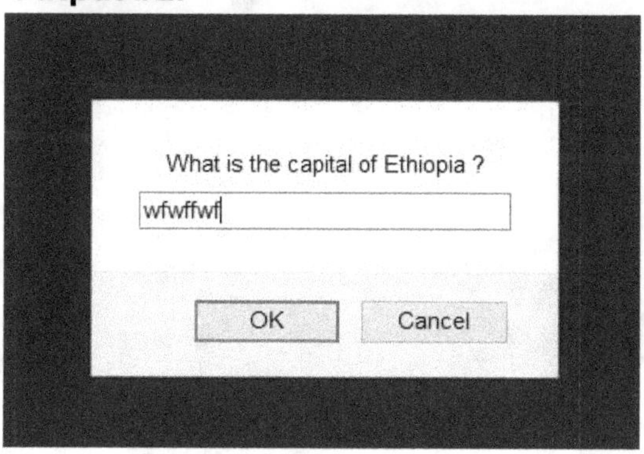
What is the capital of Ethiopia ?
wfwffwf
OK
Cancel

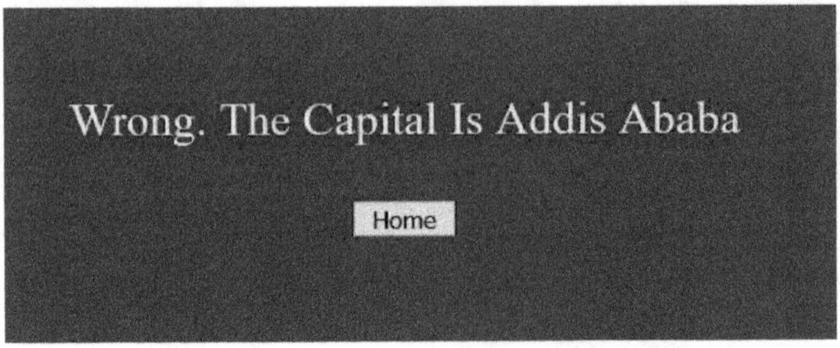
Wrong. The Capital Is Addis Ababa
Home

Example 4 – Random Jokes

This program prints a random joke out a random joke picked from a list of jokes. The one button runs the **writejoke()** function. In the function, we declare an array that contains all the jokes.
You can get the values for the array below:
https://drive.google.com/file/d/1xDN9dt2Gvj-mdPmi5ATCnP1tvOZtZt25/view?usp=sharing
We then chose a random number between 0 and x, x is the length of the array. This random number picks a random country. We do this using **Math.random()** and **Math.floor()**.
We then print out the joke using the **document.write()** function.
Then, the user has the chance to restart the program with the **Home** button that runs the **redirect()** function.

```
<html>
<head><title>Random Duck Jokes</title>
<link rel="stylesheet" href="samplestyle.css" />
</head>
<body>
<button class="btn a" onclick="writejoke()">Get A Duck Joke</button>
<script>
var duckjokes = [
"Why did the duck cross the road?                    It was the chicken's day off",
"Why did the duck detective get promoted?              He quacked the case",
"Why did the tiger cross the road?                 To eat the duck and the hen",
"What did the duck do when he saw the clown?          He started quacking up",
"Why is the duck always standing straight?            To hide his butt-quack",
"Which is the heaviest bird?                 The crane",
"Why did the duck go to prison?                 He became a quackpot.",
"Why did the bee do his own haircuts?             He did buzzcuts",
"Why did the duck lose the race?                Because he was a lame duck",
"What happened after the duck got injured?        He went to a ducktor!",
"Where did the duck eat breakfast?              Quacker barrel",
"Why did the hen keep its nest warm?           Because it was eggstremely cold outside",
"Why did the duck not like the soup?             Because it had no quackers!",
"Why were the two ducks always together?         They were stuck together with duck-tape",
"Why do swans avoid the stock market?            Because they're afraid of the black-swan",
"How do ducks know if it's about to rain?            They checked the feather-forecast",
"What did the duck do on July 4th?             It burst quackers",
]
function writejoke()
{
var chosenjoke = duckjokes[Math.floor(Math.random() * duckjokes.length)];

document.write(chosenjoke);
document.write('<link rel="stylesheet" type="text/css" href="samplestyle.css" />');
document.write('<br>');
document.write('<button onClick="redirect()">Home</button>');
}
function redirect()
{
window.location.replace("RandomJoke.html");
}
</script>

</body>
</html>
```

Output #1:

Output #2:

Example 5 – Animal Hangman

This program codes a fun game of animal hangman. The button in the program below starts the function **animalhangman()**. In the function, we first declare an array that contains all the animals. Then, we pick a random animal using Math.random() and Math.floor().
We create a variable that stores the answer (**answerArray**). It stores the user answer. It is initialized to underscores (_) with the same length as the original animal.
The variable **remletters** is the number of remaining letters to be guessed. A while loop is created to accept user guesses as long as **remletters>0**.
Using prompt, we accept a single letter input from the user. If there is more than one letter input, we set an error message and ask the user to enter only one letter. Once the user enters a letter, we enter a loop that checks each letter of the random animal against the user letter. Each time there is a match, we subtract **remletters** by 1 and update the relevant part of **answerArray** with the matched letters. At the end of the while loop, the user has guessed the animal, and we print out a congratulatory note with the name of the animal.
At any point within the while loop, if the user doesn't enter a letter and tries to proceed, we exit the program loop and print out the animal name.
At the end of the game, the user has the option to restart the program using the **Home** button. Here's the code below with some examples.

```
<html>
<head>
  <title>Animal Hangman</title>
  <link rel="stylesheet" href="samplestyle.css" />
</head>
<body>
 <button class="btn" onclick="animalhangmman()">Start Animal Hangman</button>

<script>
 function animalhangmman()
{
  // Create an array of animals
  var animals = [
  "tiger",
  "lion",
  "monkey",
  "kangaroo",
  "racoon",
  "flamingo",
  "elephant",
  "porcupine"
  ];
  var chosenanimal = animals[Math.floor(Math.random() * animals.length)];
  var answerArray = [];
  for (var i = 0; i < chosenanimal.length; i++) {
  answerArray[i] = "_";
  }
```

```
var remletters = chosenanimal.length;
while (remletters > 0)
{
alert(answerArray.join(" "));
var guess = prompt("Guess a letter, or click Cancel to stop playing.");
if (guess == null)
{
// Exit the game loop
break;
}
else if (guess.length !== 1)
{
alert("Please enter a single letter.");
}
else
{
// Update the game state with the guess
for (var j = 0; j < chosenanimal.length; j++)
{
if (chosenanimal[j] === guess)
{
answerArray[j] = guess;
remletters=remletters-1;
}
}
} // The end of the game loop
}
// Show the answer and congratulate the player
alert(answerArray.join(" "));
alert("Good job! The answer was " + chosenanimal);
}
</script>
</body>
</html>
```

Output #1

Below is the starting point showing the length of the answer.

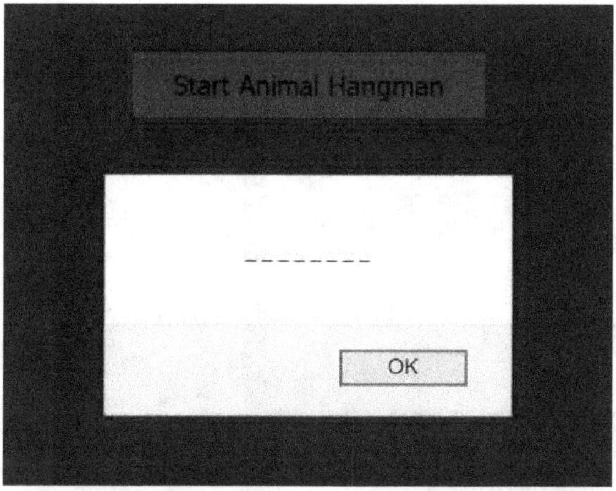

Guess the first letter. The user enters ‘t’

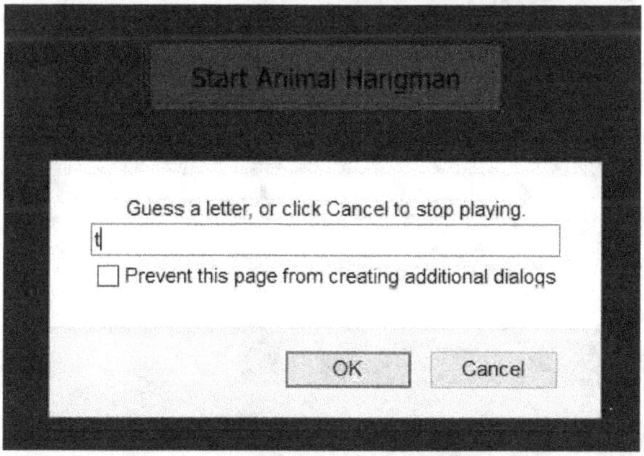

There is no ‘t’. So we try again.

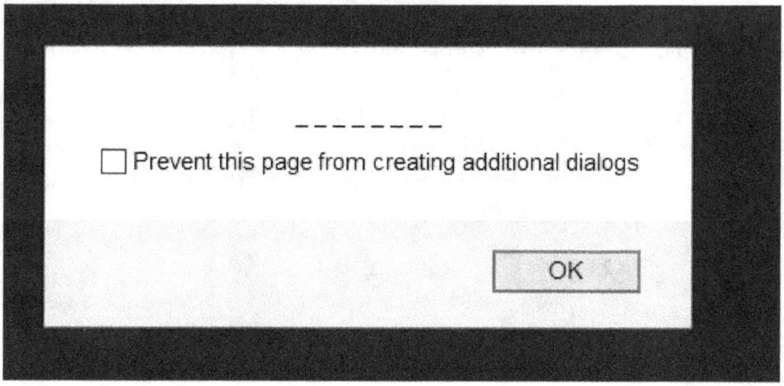

The user enters ‘k’

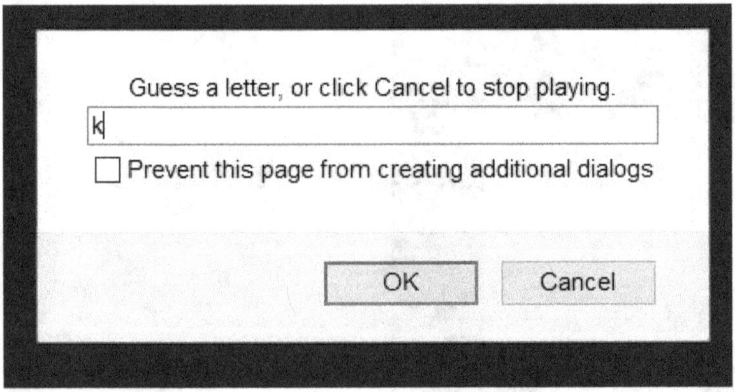

No ‘k’ in the answer. Still no correct guess.

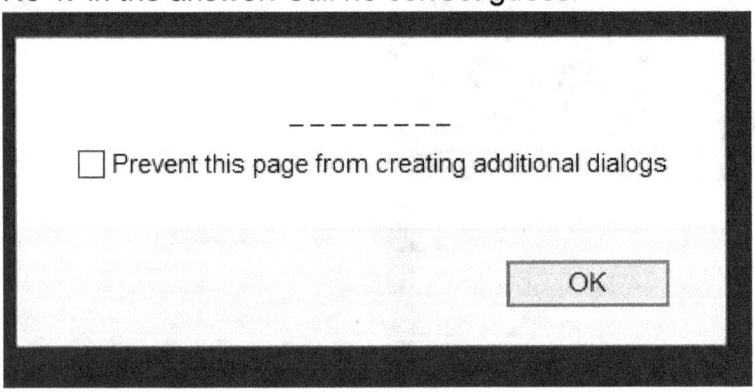

Now, the user enters ‘o’

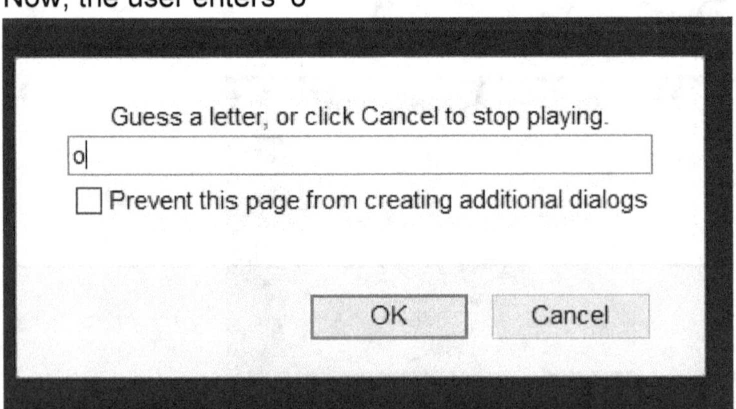

Finally, the user guesses correct. The word ends with 'o' and we see that in the updated answer.

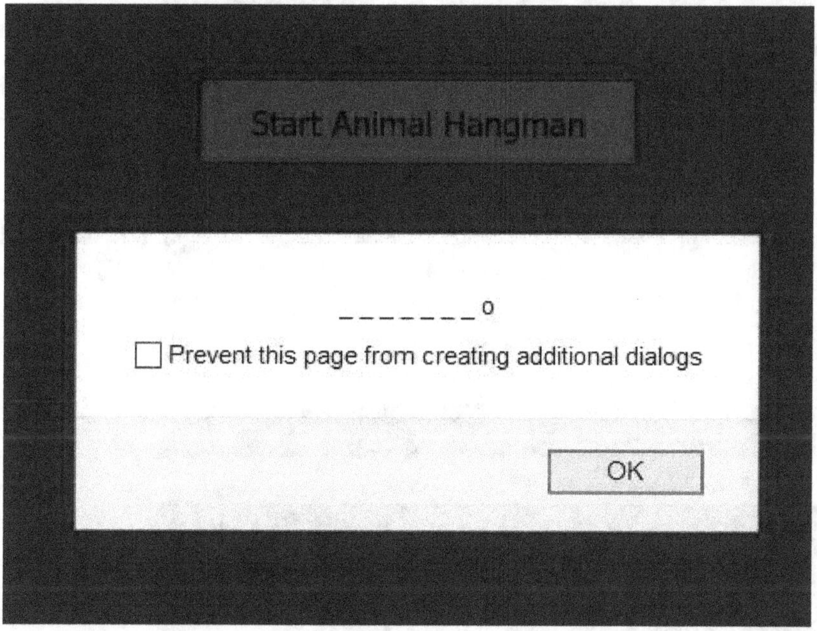

So, after a few more guesses of this, we arrive at answer below. Just one more guess.

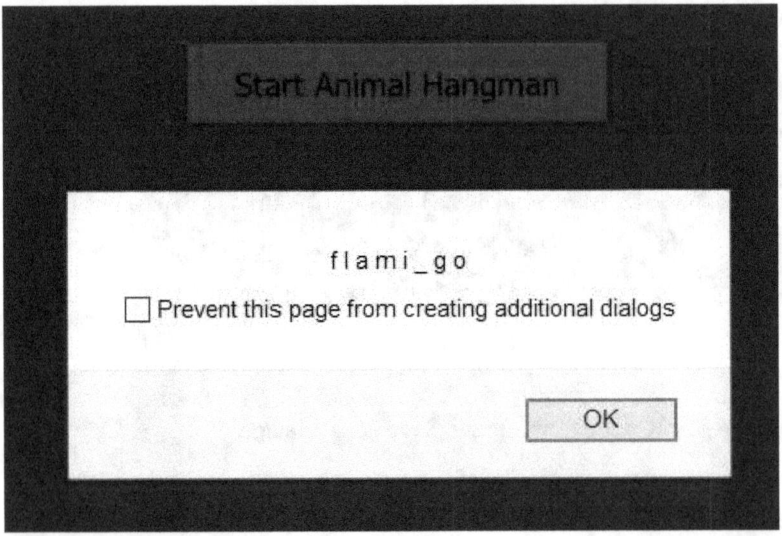

The user guesses ‘n’.

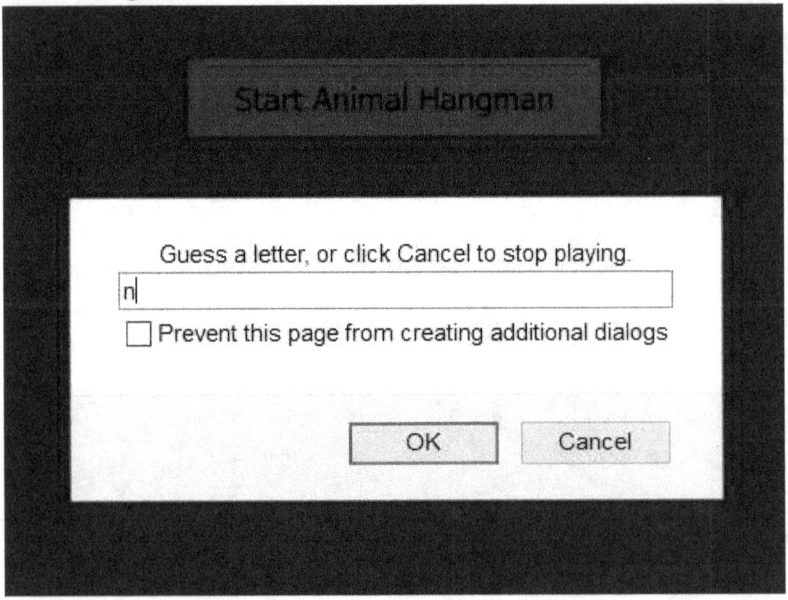

And that is correct. The entire word is flamingo.

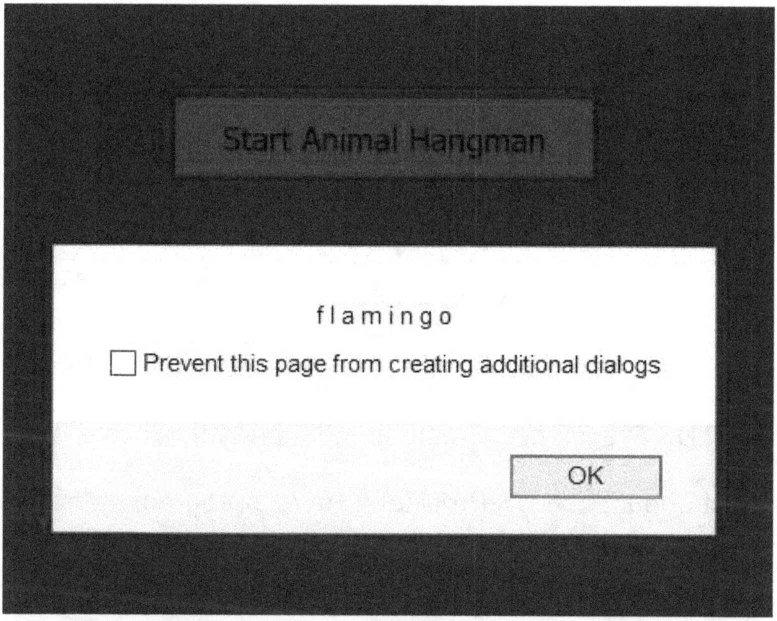

And, the program displays the correct answer below.

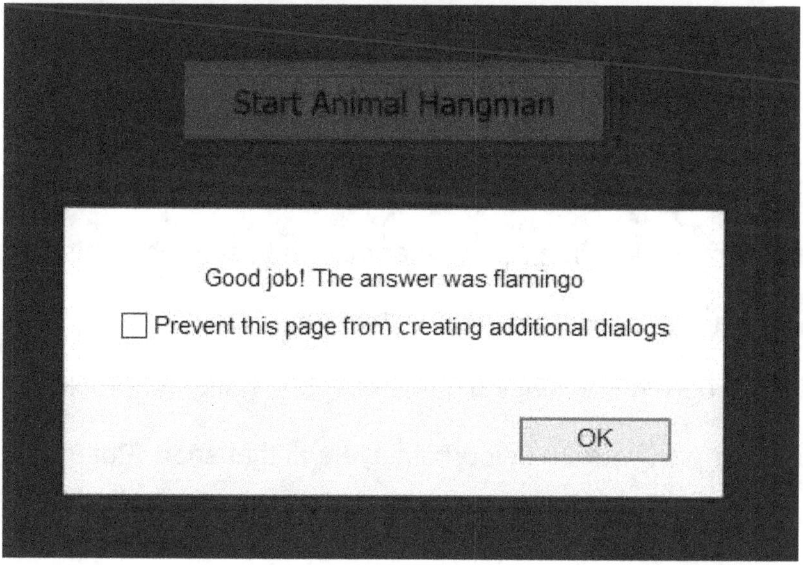

Practice Problems

1. Create a resume that takes in multiple candidates through a form and stores them in separate arrays. One array for names, one for cities, one for university and one for GPA. Print out all the names that are in a particular city.
2. Write a program that is a quiz about US Presidents. Create an array of all US Presidents. Create another array that has a well-known fact about each US President. Have a program that randomly chooses a fact to present to the user; and the user can guess who that is.
3. Write a program that lists all the cars that the dealership has in an array. Another corresponding array has all the prices of those cars; and a third has the year of manufacture in a year. The program takes in a model year from the user and prints all the cars and prices of cars newer than that year.
4. Write a program that plays a game of sports hangman. Pick a sport; and pick your 20 favourite players in that sport. Put the players in an array of size 20 and have the user guess the letters as in a game of hangman.

Objects

An object in programming is a collection of properties with values for each property. These properties need not be the same variable types. For example, we can have an object with both string and numerical properties.

Example 1

In the example below, we create an object for a car. It has 4 different properties, one for name, one for model, one for price, one for license plate. These are accepted through user input via forms.
They are accepted as input in the **entercar()** function and then assigned to an object in printcars() function. In the **printcars()** functions, the user inputs via forms are assigned to 4 separate variables.
These variables are assigned to the object car as shown below. The property and value are separated from one another using: and the different property/values are separated using a comma(,)
In the below example, type, model, license and price are properties; while **carname**, **carmodel**, **carnumber** and **carprice** are the values of the respective properties. The 4 values below are the ones that are from the user form.

```
var car={type:carname,model:carmodel,license:carnumber,price:carprice};
```

And to access the object values, we use the dot(.) operator before the property. For example, **car.type** will give you the value assigned to property '**type**' of object '**car**'.
And thus, we print out car type and price by accessing the object property value.
The code is available below with outputs.

```
<html>
<head><title>Car Check</title></head>
<link rel="stylesheet" href="samplestyle.css" />
<body>
<button class="btn" onclick="entercar()">Start Car</button>
<script>
function entercar()
{
document.write("Car Name: ");
document.write('<input name="name" type="text" id="carname" size="20"><br>');
document.write("Car Model: ");
document.write('<input name="name" type="text" id="carmodel" size="20"><br>');
document.write("License Plate: ");
document.write('<input name="name" type="text" id="carnumber" size="20"><br>');
document.write("Car price: ");
document.write('<input name="name" type="number" id="carprice" size="20"><br>');
document.write('<link rel="stylesheet" type="text/css" href="styles.css" />');
document.write('<br>');
document.write('<button class="btn a" onclick="printcars()">Check</button><br>');
document.write('<link rel="stylesheet" type="text/css" href="samplestyle.css" />');
document.write('<br>');
}
function printcars()
{
var carname=document.getElementById("carname").value;
var carmodel=document.getElementById("carmodel").value;
var carnumber=document.getElementById("carnumber").value;
var carprice=document.getElementById("carprice").value;
var car={type:carname,model:carmodel,license:carnumber,price:carprice};
document.write("Type of car = "+car.type+"<br>");
document.write("Price of car = "+car.price)+"<br>";
}

function redirect()
{
window.location.replace("ObjectsCars.html");
}
</script>
</body>
</html>
```

Output 1:

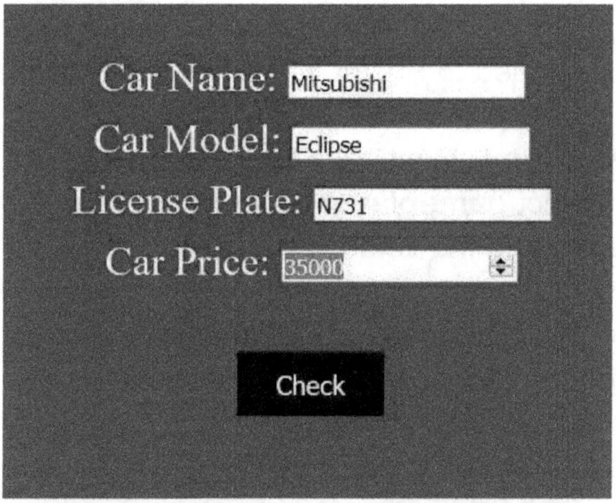

After clicking **Check** button, we get:

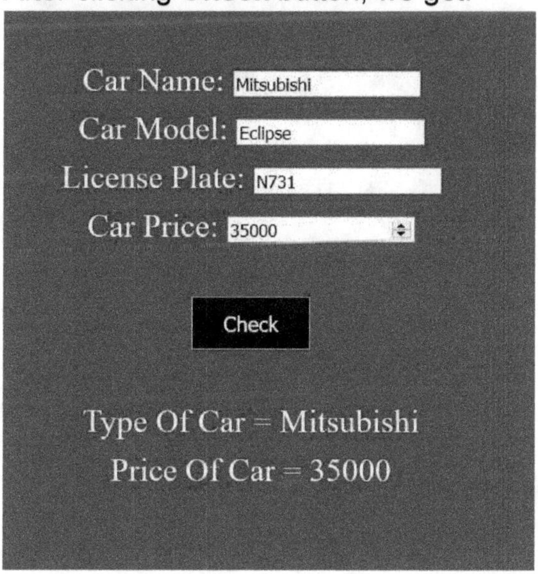

Example 2

In the below example, we simulate a game of dice between 6 players.

Basically, a game of dice is played 10 times; and points are added to the players depending on where the dice falls between 1-6. For example, if it falls on 1, a point is added to Player 1. If it falls on 2, a point is added to Player 2 and so on. The value of the dice is simulated between 1 and 6 using **Math.Random()** function.

At the start of the program, an object **gameplayer** is declared. The property is the name of the player, and the value is the number of points obtained.

In the function **dicegame()**, there is a **FOR** loop that runs **gamecalc()** 10 times. In gamecalc() a random number between 1 and 6 is chosen, which simulates the rolling of the dice. Depending on what value the dice falls on, a player's property value is increased by 10.

At the end of the **FOR** loop, we print out the points obtained by each player below.

The code is below with a sample output.

```
<html>
<head><title>Game Score Keeper</title></head>
<link rel="stylesheet" href="samplestyle.css" />
<body>
<button class="btn" onclick="dicegame()">Start Playing</button>

<script>
var gameplayers={"Adam": 0,"Bob":7,"Carol":0,"Steve":4,"Mark":2,"Tim":0,};

function dicegame()
{

for (i=0;i<10;i++)
{
gamecalc();
}
document.write("<br>");
document.write("Adam scored "+gameplayers["Adam"]+ " points.<br>");
document.write("Bob scored "+gameplayers["Bob"]+ " points.<br>");
document.write("Carol scored "+gameplayers["Carol"]+ " points.<br>");
document.write("Steve scored "+gameplayers["Steve"]+ " points.<br>");
document.write("Mark scored "+gameplayers["Mark"]+ " points.<br>");
document.write("Tim scored "+gameplayers["Tim"]+ " points.<br>");


document.write('<link rel="stylesheet" type="text/css" href="samplestyle.css" />');
document.write('<br>');

document.write('<button class="btn a" onclick="dicegame()">Check</button><br>');

}
```

```
function gamecalc()
{
score=Math.floor((Math.random() * 6) + 1);

if(score==1)
{
gameplayers["Abhishek"]=gameplayers["Abhishek"]+10;
document.write("Abhishek won 10 points.<br>");
}
if(score==2)
{
gameplayers["Bob"]=gameplayers["Bob"]+10;
document.write("Bob won 10 points.<br>");
}
if(score==3)
{
gameplayers["Carol"]=gameplayers["Carol"]+10;
document.write("Carol won 10 points.<br>");
}
if(score==4)
{
gameplayers["Steve"]=gameplayers["Steve"]+10;
document.write("Steve won 10 points.<br>");
}
if(score==5)
{
gameplayers["Mark"]=gameplayers["Mark"]+10;
document.write("Mark won 10 points.<br>");
}
if(score==6)
{
gameplayers["Tim"]=gameplayers["Tim"]+10;
document.write("Tim won 10 points.<br>");
}
}
function redirect()
{
window.location.replace("ObjectsCars.html");
}

</script>
</body>
</html>
```

Output:

The top 10 lines of the output show who won the dice game in the 10 iterations of the loop.
The bottom 6 lines show the final scores obtained by the players.

```
Tim Won 10 Points.
Adam Won 10 Points.
Steve Won 10 Points.
Mark Won 10 Points.
Bob Won 10 Points.
Adam Won 10 Points.
Tim Won 10 Points.
Adam Won 10 Points.
Bob Won 10 Points.
Carol Won 10 Points.

Adam Scored 30 Points.
Bob Scored 27 Points.
Carol Scored 10 Points.
Steve Scored 14 Points.
Mark Scored 12 Points.
Tim Scored 20 Points.

Check
```

Practice Problems

1. Write a program that creates an object for a restaurant menu. The properties are the dish name, time to cook and price of dish. And then access the object values to print out all the dishes that cost below $20 and cook below 20 minutes.
2. Write a program that simulates shooting practice for a basketball game. The name of the player is the property and the points scored is the value assigned to the property. The program checks the name of the player and whether the shot is outside the 3-point circle. Based on the answer, it adds 2 or 3 points to the relevant player.

Creating a Canvas

What is a Canvas?

A canvas is a html element allows that allows the user to draw graphics, shapes, images and run animations using JavaScript. It is a rectangular area on the html page, the size of which we can define.

Canvas Example

The size of a canvas is defined in the unit of pixels. A pixel is the smallest unit of illumination on a computer screen. The most used computer size is 1366 pixels width by 768 pixels height.
Below is the sample canvas, which has a width of 500 pixels and height of 500 pixels. It has a visible border of 2 pixels around the canvas.

```
<html>
<head><title>Sample Canvas</title>
</head>
<body>
<canvas id="myCanvas" width="500" height="500" style="border:2px solid"></canvas><br>
<script>

</script>
</body>
</html>
```

Output:

Drawing (with measurements):
Below is the drawing with the canvas size relative to the regular computer monitor screen. The green measurements are the size of the computer screen, and the black measurements are the size of the canvas. One can only draw on the canvas and not on the rest of the screen.

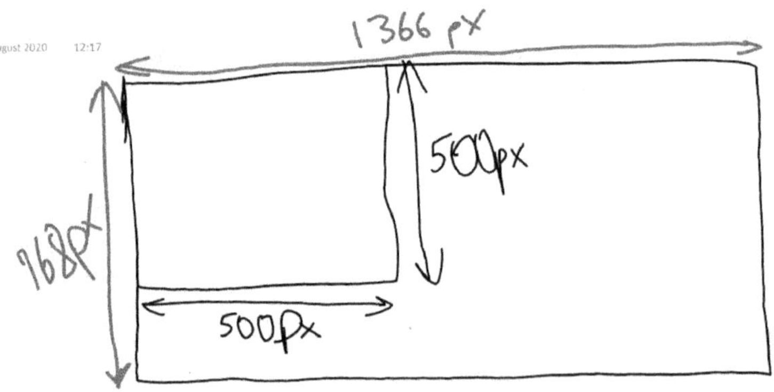

Creating a Circle on the Canvas

A circle in JavaScript is created using 5 steps. That's what we do in the code below.
The first step is to convert the html element to a JavaScript variable using document.getElementByID. Then it is converted to a 2D drawing element variable using getContext("2d"). In the below example, variable c2x is the drawing element.
We can start any drawing in JavaScript with **beginPath()** and then clear the canvas using **clearRect**. Here's how **clearRect** works, as in the below example:
clearRect(a,b,c,d) means that the top left corner of the rectangle starts at an x-coordinate of **a** and y-cooridnate of **b**; it has a width of **c** and a height of **d**. So, we start at **(a,b)**, and clear a canvas of width c and height d. In the example below, we start at **(0,0)**, and clear the entire canvas of width **500** pixels and height **500** pixels. This makes the entire canvas blanks and ready to draw.
Next, we draw the circle using the arc function. So, let's see how that works:
arc(a,b,c,d,e) is how we draw the circle. **(a,b)** is the center of the circle; **a** being the x-coordinate and **b** being the y-coordinate. **c** is the radius of the circle. **d** is the starting part of the arc of the circle. **e** is the ending part of the arc.
d and **e** are measured in radians. For a full circle, d and e would be 0 and 2π respectively. For a half-circle d and e would be between 0 and π.
In the below example, Circle 1 center is at **(50,50)** and has a radius of **20** pixels. Circle 2 is at a center point of **(250,250)** and has a larger radius of **70**. Circle 3 is actually a semi-circle as it goes from 0 to π radians. It is closer to the bottom right hand corner at **(350,350)** and has a radius of **50** pixels.

In the final step we draw the circles using stroke(). If we want to fill the circles, we do so using fill(). And we can change the color using fillStyle().

```
<html>
<head><title>Sample Canvas</title>
</head>
<body>
<canvas id="acanvas" width="500" height="500" style="border:2px solid"></canvas><br>
<button class="btn a" onclick="drawcircle()">Draw Circle</button>

<script>
function drawcircle()
{
var i = document.getElementById("acanvas");
var c2x = i.getContext("2d");

//Circel
c2x.beginPath();
c2x.clearRect(0, 0, 500, 500);
c2x.arc(50,50,20,0,2*Math.PI);
c2x.fillStyle = "red";
c2x.stroke();
c2x.fill();

//Circle2
c2x.beginPath();
c2x.arc(250,250,70,0,2*Math.PI);
c2x.fillStyle = "blue";
c2x.stroke();
c2x.fill();

//Circle3
c2x.beginPath();
c2x.arc(350,350,50,0,1*Math.PI);
c2x.fillStyle = "green";
c2x.stroke();
c2x.fill();
}

</script>
</body>
</html>
```

Output:

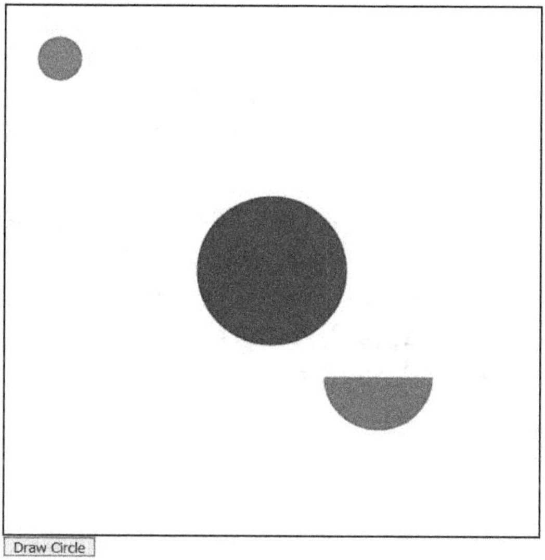

Drawing (Measurements):

Here's Circle 2 (blue circle) measuring using the canvas co-ordinates, just to show an example.

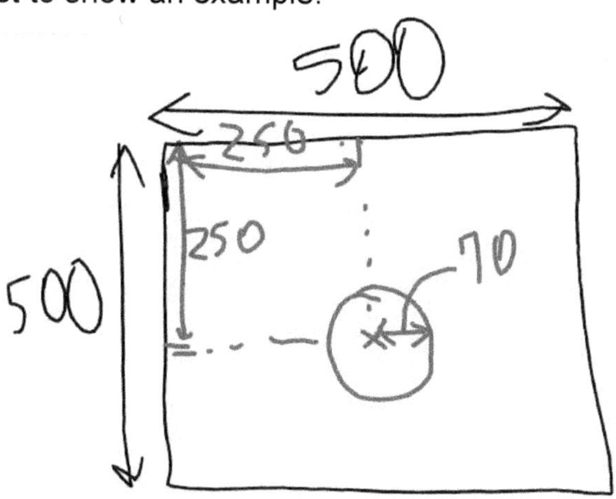

Circle #2

Creating a Rectangle on the Canvas

The drawing of a rectangle begins the same way as of a circle; with the canvas and 2D context variables. Again, we use **beginPath()** and **clearRect()** to start the process. Then we use a function known as **fillRect()** which is shown below:

fillRect(a,b,c,d) means that the top left corner of the rectangle starts at an x-coordinate of **a** and y-cooridnate of **b**; it has a width of **c** and a height of **d**. So, we start at **(a,b)**, and clear a canvas of width c and height d. In the example below, we start at **(0,0)**, and creates a rectangle of width 50 pixels and height 100 pixels. It is a red triangle (since fillRect is red).

There is a second **fillRect()** which creates a square of width 75 pixels (as both width and height are set to the same value of 75). The top left corner of the square starts at **(150,150)**.

In both cases, fillRect() automatically draws and fills the rectangle with the assigned color.

```
<html>
<head><title>Sample Canvas</title>
</head>
<body>
<canvas id="acanvas" width="500" height="500" style="border:2px solid"></canvas><br>
<button class="btn a" onclick="drawsquare()">Draw Square</button>

<script>
function drawsquare()
{
var i = document.getElementById("acanvas");
var c2x = i.getContext("2d");

//Rectangle 1
c2x.beginPath();
c2x.fillStyle = "red";
c2x.clearRect(0, 0, 500, 500);
c2x.fillRect(0, 0, 50, 100);

//Square 1
c2x.beginPath();
c2x.fillStyle = "blue";
c2x.fillRect(150, 150, 75, 75);

}

</script>
</body>
</html>
```

Output:

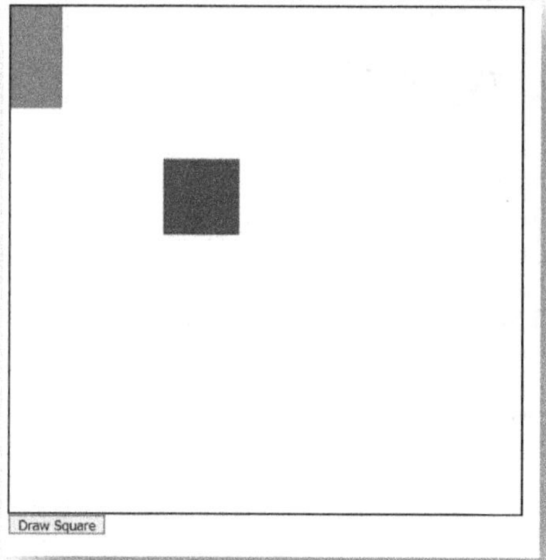

Drawing (Rectangle 2):

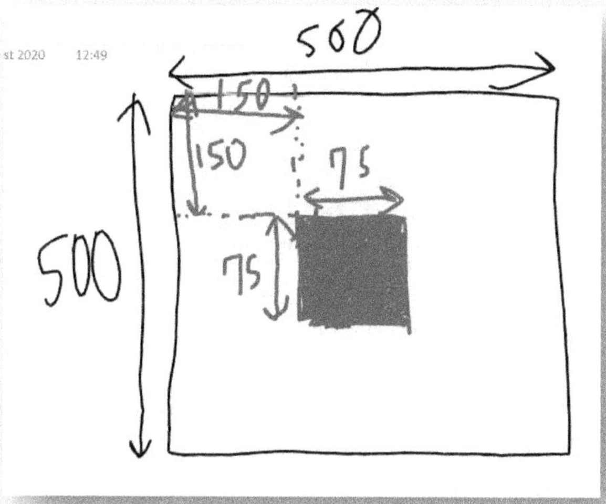

Creating a Smiley Face

In the below example, we use our knowledge of circles and semi-circles to create a smiley face.
First, we do a yellow circle of 75 pixel radius in the center of the screen, which is the face. We then draw 2 small black circles of 10 pixels each which serve as the eyes.
And finally, we do a semi-circle filled with black color of radius 30 pixels. This is the smile.
Pretty cute, huh? You can get creative and make any face you want.

```
<html>
<head><title>Smiley Face</title>
</head>
<body>
<canvas id="acanvas" width="500" height="500" style="border:2px solid"></canvas><br>
<button class="btn a" onclick="drawsquare()">Draw Square</button>

<script>
function drawsquare()
{
var i = document.getElementById("acanvas");
var c2x = i.getContext("2d");

//Yellow Face
c2x.beginPath();
c2x.clearRect(0, 0, 500, 500);
c2x.arc(250,250,75,0,2*Math.PI);
c2x.fillStyle = "yellow";
c2x.stroke();
c2x.fill();

//Black Eyes
c2x.beginPath();
c2x.arc(225,225,10,0,2*Math.PI);
c2x.fillStyle = "black";
c2x.stroke();
c2x.fill();

c2x.beginPath();
c2x.arc(275,225,10,0,2*Math.PI);
c2x.fillStyle = "black";
c2x.stroke();
c2x.fill();

//Black Smile

c2x.beginPath();
c2x.arc(250,275,30,0,1*Math.PI);
c2x.fillStyle = "black";
c2x.stroke();
c2x.fill();

}
```

Output:

Draw Square

Practice Problems

1. Create a canvas of 700 pixels by 500 pixels. Draw 4 circles on the 4 different corners of the canvas. And then draw a 5th circle right on the centre of the canvas. All circles are of different colors. This is a good canvas to get you comfortable with positioning shapes on the screen.
2. Create a canvas of 600 pixels by 600 pixels. Draw different emoticons on the screen. Draw a smiley face at the center of the canvas. Then, do a frowny face right on top of it. Third, do a scared emoticon (with closed eyes and straight mouth) at the right of center. And finally, do an emoticon of your choice to the left.
3. Create a canvas of 600 pixels by 600 pixels. Draw a square right at the center of side 100 pixels. Then draw a second square of 80 pixels. Third, draw a square of 60 pixels.... And so on, tell it can't get any smaller. This is an example of concentric squares. (Hint: A square is just a rectangle with all equal sides).

Timer and Animations

What is a Timer?

A timer in Javascript is used to time Javascript code. It allows the user to execute different portions of the code at different time intervals. **setTimeOut()** and **setTimeInterval()** functions are used to set the timer. **setTimeOut()** allows a fixed break before executing a code; **settimeinterval()** allows the code to be executed multiple times with a fixed interval between each execution. For example:
setTimeOut(a, 1000) executes the function **a** after **1000 ms (1 second).**
setTimeInterval(a, 1000) keeps executing the function with a break of **1000 ms (1 second)** between runs.
These functions are the key to running JavaScript animations.

Timer Example

In our code, we only use the **setInterval()** function. In the example below, we have two buttons that run two separate functions.
The first function **writename()** prints the name "Bob" on the screen every 2500 ms (or 2.5 seconds). The function **fname()** is run using **setinterval(fname, 2500)** and write the name "Bob".
The second function runs the function **setcount()** prints numbers starting from 1 and increments it by 1 each time with a break of 500 ms (0.5 seconds). So, it prints 1,2,3,4 and so on with a break of 0.5 seconds between each print.

```
<html>
<head><title>Counting Timer</title>
</head>
<body>
<link rel="stylesheet" href="samplestyle.css" />
<button class="btn a" onclick="setcount()">Count</button>
<button class="btn a" onclick="writename()">Write Name</button>

<script>
function writename()
{
var name="Bob";
setInterval(fname, 2500);
function fname()
{
 document.write('<link rel="stylesheet" type="text/css" href="samplestyle.css" />');
 document.write(name);
 document.write("<br>");
}
}

function setcount()
{
count=0;
setInterval(timeUp, 500);
function timeUp()
{
 document.write('<link rel="stylesheet" type="text/css" href="samplestyle.css" />');
 count=count+1;
 document.write(count);
 document.write("<br>");

}
}
</script>
</body>
</html>
```

Output 1:

On clicking **Count**,

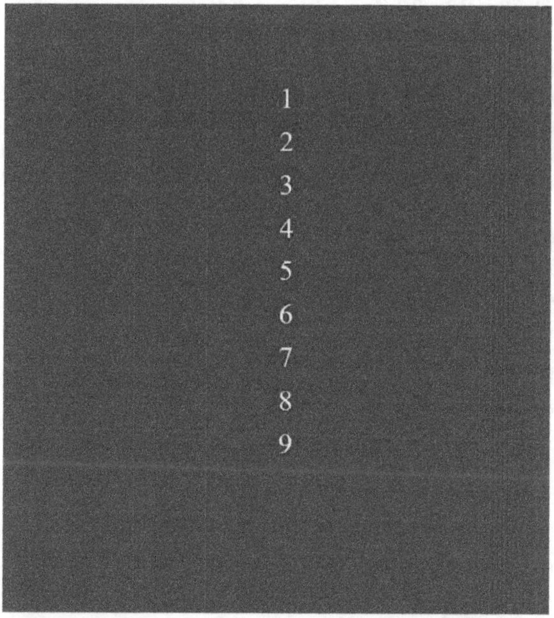

Output #2

On clicking **Count**

Growing Square

We use the **setInterval** and **fillRect** functions to write a program that expands a square. A button when clicked runs the growing square function. In the growing square functions, we do a **setinterval** where we run the function **frame()** every 10 ms (0.01 seconds). We declare a variable size to 10 pixels. **Size** contains the length of the square.
In the function frame, we first clear the entire canvas using **clearRect().** Then we draw a rectangle starting at (0,0) of length '**size**'. **Size** is increased by 5 every time the function is executed. Once size is greater than the 500, it is set back to 10. This ensures that once the square is larger than the canvas, it restarts growing from a small size.

```
<html>
<head><title>Growing Square</title>
</head>
<body>
<canvas id="myCanvas" width="500" height="500" style="border:2px solid"></canvas><br>
<button class="btn a" onclick="growingsquare()">Square</button>
<script>
function growingsquare()
{
var i = document.getElementById("myCanvas");
var c2x = i.getContext("2d");
setInterval(frame, 10);
size=10;
function frame()
{
 if (size>500)
 {
 size=0;
 }
 c2x.clearRect(0, 0, 500, 500);
 c2x.fillRect(0, 0, size, size);
 size=size+5;
}
}
</script>
</body>
</html>
```

Output:

Drawing (Square grows)

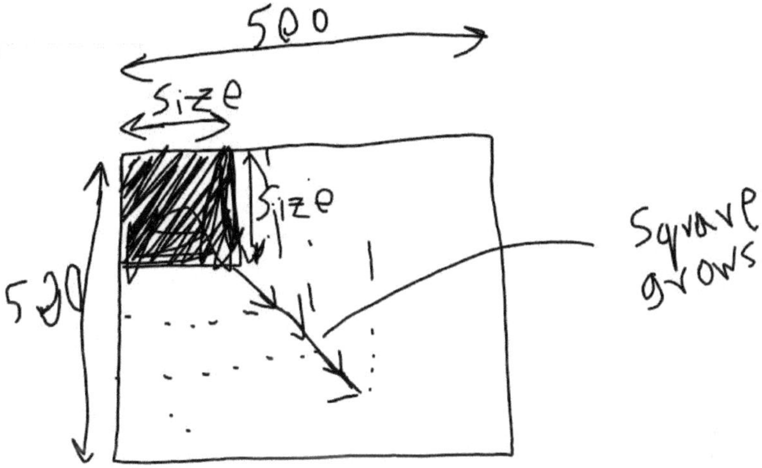

Growing Circle

We use the **setInterval** and **arc** functions to write a program that expands a circle. A button when clicked runs the growing square function. In the growing square functions, we do a **setinterval** where we run the function **frame()** every 50 ms (0.05 seconds). We declare a variable size to 10 pixels. **Size** contains the radius of the circle.
In the function frame, we first clear the entire canvas using **clearRect().** Then we draw a circle starting at the center of (250,250) of radius '**size**'. **Size** is increased by 5 every time the loop is executed. Once size is greater than the 350, it is set back to 10. This ensures that once the circle is larger than the canvas, it restarts growing from a small size.

```
<html>
<head><title>Growing Circle</title>
</head>
<body>
<canvas id="myCanvas" width="500" height="500" style="border:2px solid"></canvas><br>
<button class="btn a" onclick="growingcircle()">Circle</button>
<script>
function growingcircle()
{
var c = document.getElementById("myCanvas");
var ctx = c.getContext("2d");
setInterval(frame, 50);
size=10;
function frame()
{
//Circle
if (size>350)
{
size=10;
}
ctx.beginPath();
ctx.clearRect(0, 0, 500, 500);
ctx.arc(250,250,size,0,2*Math.PI);
ctx.fillStyle = "blue";
ctx.stroke();
ctx.fill();
size=size+5;
}
}
</script>
</body>
</html>
```

Output:

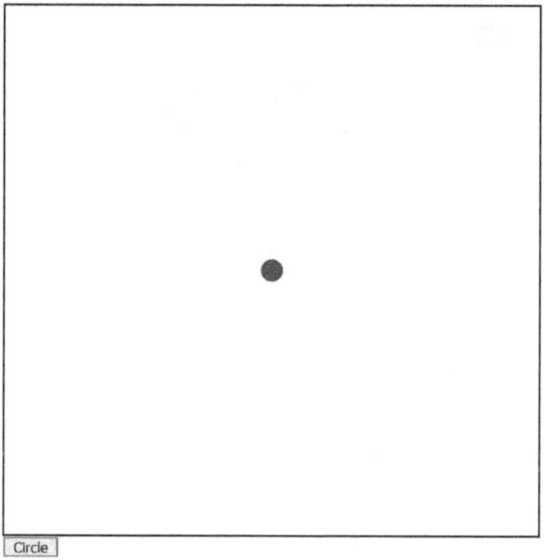

Drawing (Circle)

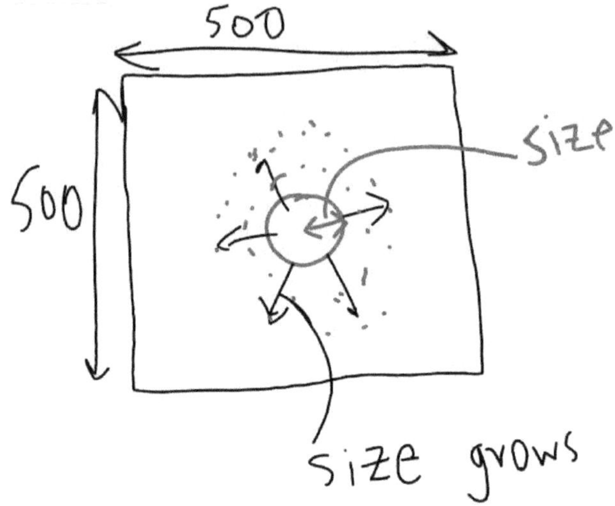

Growing Radial Circle

A radial circle is very similar to a circle. A radial circle controls the color of the circle, the background and can also add an extra color to the border between the circle and the background. In the below example, we create a radial circle of color red with a blue background. And there is a yellow border to the red ball, which acts like an annulus.

In the below example, **createRadialGradient()** is used to create the circle. This is how it works.

createRadialGradiant(a,b,c,d,e,f) creates an inner circle with **center (a,b)** with radius **c**. The second circle creates a circle with **center (d,e)** with radius **f**. If we want an annular circle then we should have them at same center i.e. **(a,b) = (d,e).**

In the below example, we have an inner circle and outer circle at the center of the canvas **(250,250).** The radius of the outer circle is always **20** pixels more than the inner circle.

The inner circle color is set to red using **addColorStop(0,"red")** and the the background is set to blue using **addColorStop(1,"blue").** Finally, the outer circle color is set to yellow using **addColorStop(0.5,"yellow").**

The radial circle keeps growing by 5 pixels every 50 ms (0.5 seconds). If the size of the circle exceeds the canvas, it is set back to 10 pixels.

```
<html>
<head><title>Growing Circle</title>
</head>
<body>
<canvas id="mCanvas" width="500" height="500" style="border:2px solid"></canvas><br>
<button class="btn a" onclick="growingcircle()">Circle</button>
<script>
function growingcircle()
{
var c = document.getElementById("mCanvas");
var c2x = c.getContext("2d");
setInterval(frame, 50);
size=10;
function frame()
{
//Circle
if (size>350)
{
size=10;
}
c2x.beginPath();
var grd = c2x.createRadialGradient(250, 250, size, 250, 250, size+20);
grd.addColorStop(0, "red");
grd.addColorStop(0.5, "yellow");
grd.addColorStop(1, "blue");

// Fill with gradient
c2x.fillStyle = grd;
c2x.fillRect(0, 0, 500, 500);
c2x.stroke();
c2x.fill();
size=size+5;
}
}
</script>
</body>
</html>
```

Output:

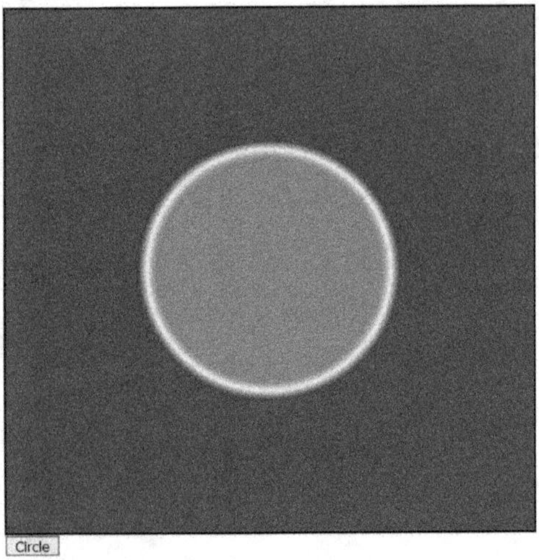

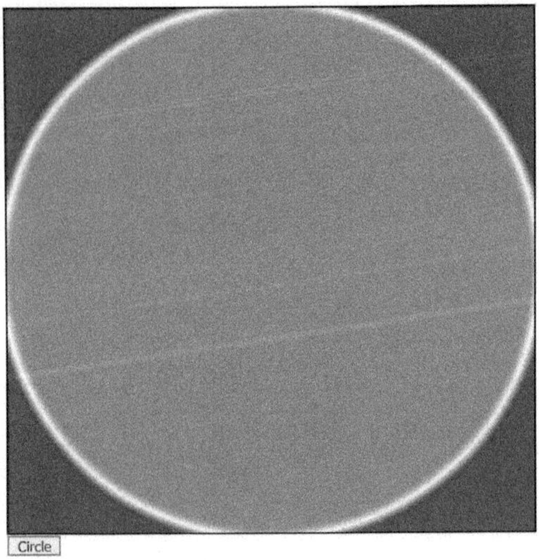

Drawing:

st 2020 12:26

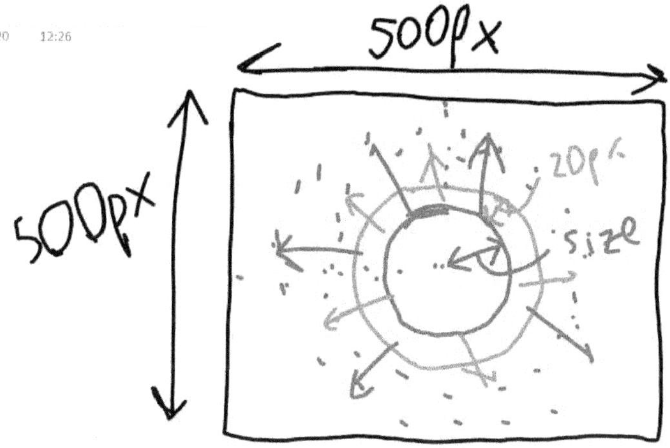

Moving Ball in Different Directions

In the below example, we use the timer and ball functions to move the ball in 4 different directions using 4 buttons. Each button runs the function that moves the ball in a particular direction.

For example, if we press down, it moves the ball down using the **MoveDown()** function. Once the ball reaches the bottom of the canvas, it restarts from the top again.

In each of the functions, we set a position variable to indicate starting point of the ball. In MoveUp() and MoveDown() we set the y position to 500 and 0 respectively. Using the setInterval function we increase/decrease the position variable by 5 pixels to move the ball every 50 ms (0.05 seconds). And, we use the IF function to check if the ball has reached the end of the canvas, and set it back to the original function.

```
<html>
<head><title>Growing Circle</title>
</head>
<body>
<canvas id="myCanvas" width="500" height="500" style="border:2px solid"></canvas><br>
<button class="btn a" onclick="MoveDown()">Down</button>
<button class="btn a" onclick="MoveUp()">Up</button>
<button class="btn a" onclick="MoveRight()">Right</button>
<button class="btn a" onclick="MoveLeft()">Left</button>

<script>
function MoveDown()
{
var c = document.getElementById("myCanvas");
var ctx = c.getContext("2d");
setInterval(frame, 50);
locy=10;
function frame()
{
//Circle
if (locy>500)
{
locy=10;
}
ctx.beginPath();
ctx.clearRect(0, 0, 500, 500);
ctx.arc(250,locy,30,0,2*Math.PI);
ctx.fillStyle = "blue";
ctx.stroke();
ctx.fill();
locy=locy+5;
}
}
```

```
function MoveUp()
{
var c = document.getElementById("myCanvas");
var ctx = c.getContext("2d");
setInterval(frame, 50);
locy=500;
function frame()
{
//Circle
if (locy<0)
{
locy=500;
}
ctx.beginPath();
ctx.clearRect(0, 0, 500, 500);
ctx.arc(250,locy,30,0,2*Math.PI);
ctx.fillStyle = "blue";
ctx.stroke();
ctx.fill();
locy=locy-5;
}
}
function MoveRight()
{
var c = document.getElementById("myCanvas");
var ctx = c.getContext("2d");
setInterval(frame, 50);
locx=10;
function frame()
{
//Circle
if (locx>500)
{
locx=10;
}
ctx.beginPath();
ctx.clearRect(0, 0, 500, 500);
ctx.arc(locx,250,30,0,2*Math.PI);
ctx.fillStyle = "blue";
ctx.stroke();
ctx.fill();
locx=locx+5;
}
}
```

```
function MoveLeft()
{
var c = document.getElementById("myCanvas");
var ctx = c.getContext("2d");
setInterval(frame, 50);
locx=500;
function frame()
{
//Circle
if (locx<0)
{
locx=500;
}
ctx.beginPath();
ctx.clearRect(0, 0, 500, 500);
ctx.arc(locx,250,30,0,2*Math.PI);
ctx.fillStyle = "blue";
ctx.stroke();
ctx.fill();
locx=locx-5;
}
}
</script>
</body>
</html>
```

Output #1: Move Down

Position 1

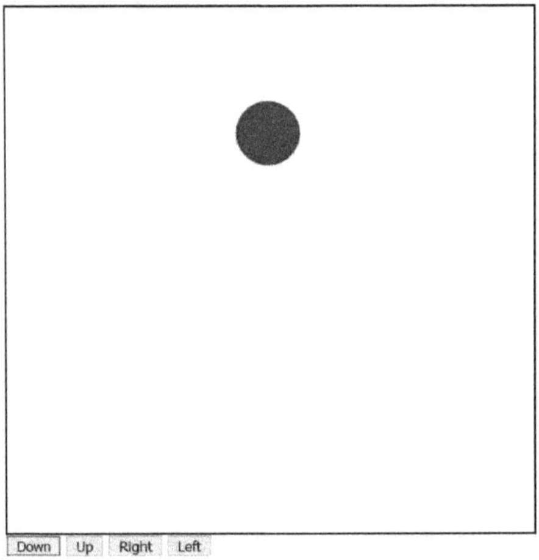

Position 2

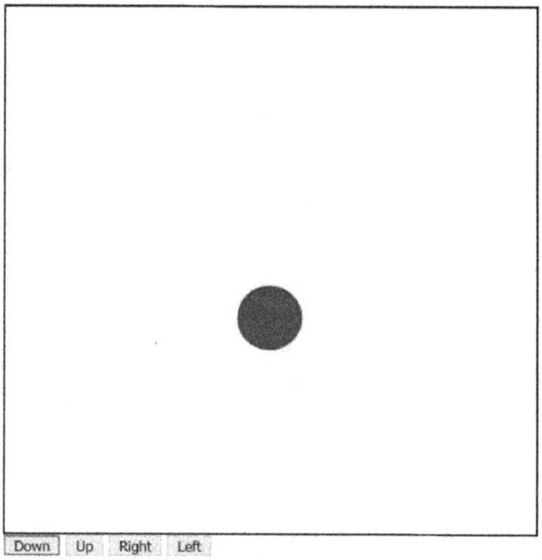

Output #2: Move Left

Position 1

Position 2

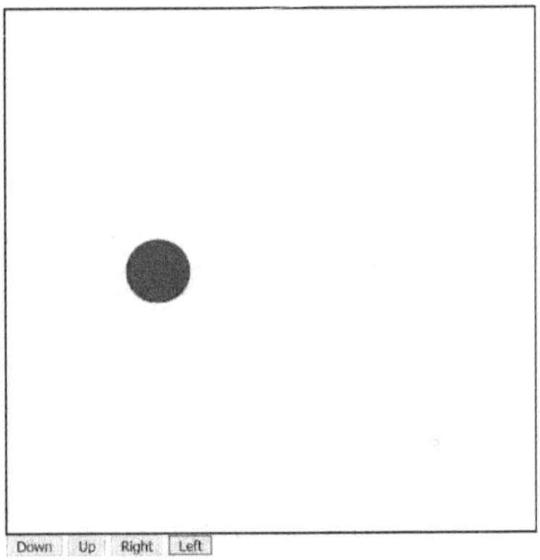

Drawing (Move Down)

As we can see below, locy starts at 10 and keeps increasing to make it move down in the animation.

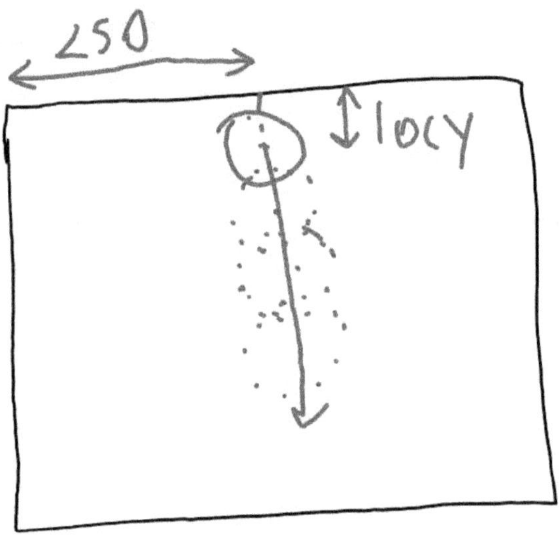

Bouncing Ball

In this example, we move the ball towards the edge of the canvas and the ball bounces back when it hits the canvas.

This is done by modifying the equation that determines the x location and y location of the ball.
Firstly, in this case, we move the ball in both x and y locations at the same time. So, we have two separate variables, **locationx** and **locationy**. There are another 2 variables, that determine the direction in which the ball moves; **snx** and **sny**. If snx is positive, it moves to the right. If snx is negative, it moves to the left. Thus, the equations for locationx and locationy are:
locationx=locationx+snx*5
locationy=locationy+sny*5
So, we move the ball 5 pixels through x (either left or right) and 5 pixels through y (either up or down)
If the ball reaches the side edge of the canvas (**locationy=500** or **locationx =0**), then we change direction of x motion (**snx=snx*-1**).
And, if the ball reaches the upper/lower edge of the canvas (**locationy=500** or **locationy=0**) then we change the direction of y-motion (**sny=sny*-1**).
This change of direction creates the bounce that we see on the screen.

```
<html>
<head><title>Bouncing Ball</title>
</head>
<body>
<canvas id="myCanvas" width="500" height="500" style="border:2px solid"></canvas><br>
<button class="btn a" onclick="bouncingball()">Bounce Ball</button>
<script>
function bouncingball()
{
var c = document.getElementById("myCanvas");
var ctx = c.getContext("2d");
var snx=1;
var sny=1;
setInterval(frame, 10);
locationx=Math.random()*350;
locationy=Math.random()*350;
```

```
function frame()
{
//Circle
ctx.beginPath();
ctx.clearRect(0, 0, 500, 500);
ctx.arc(locationx,locationy,20,0,2*Math.PI);
ctx.fillStyle = "red";
ctx.stroke();
ctx.fill();
if (locationx>=500)
    {
        snx=snx*-1;
    }
if (locationx<=0)
    {
        snx=snx*-1;
    }
if (locationy>=500)
    {
        sny=sny*-1;
    }
if (locationy<=0)
    {
        sny=sny*-1;
    }
locationx=locationx+snx*5;
locationy=locationy+sny*5;
}
}
</script>
</body>
</html>
```

Output

Drawing (Bounce Bottom Wall)

12:49

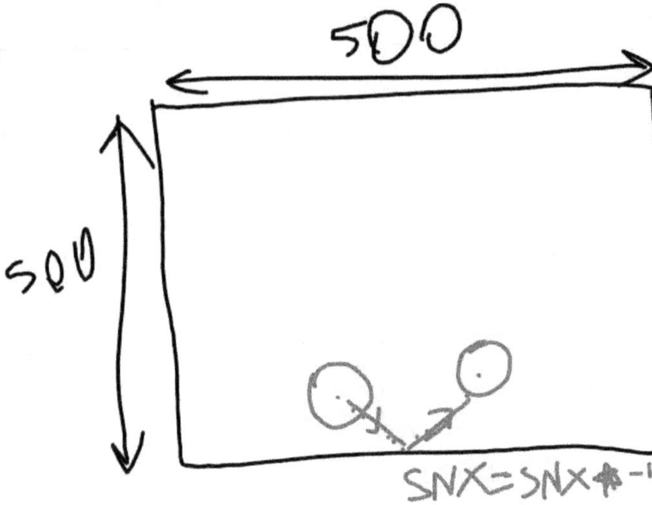

Drawing (Bounce Right Wall)

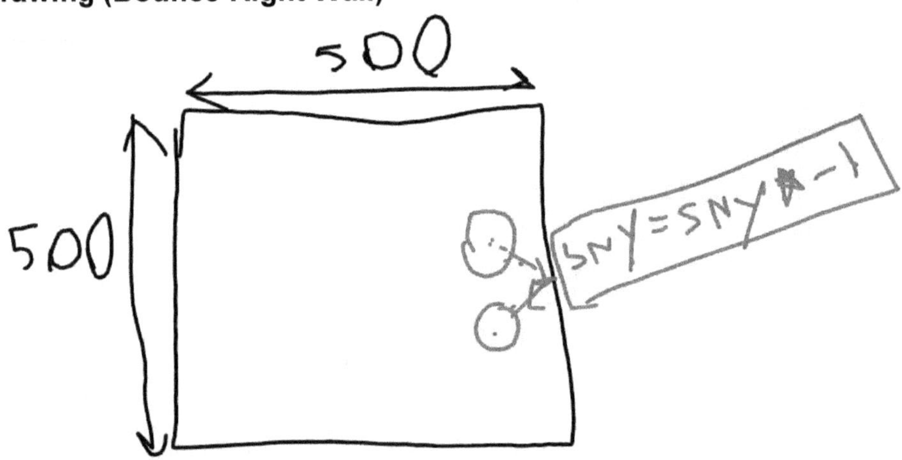

Practice Problems

1. Write a program that accepts a number as input and prints a multiple of that number every 0.5 seconds. For example, if we accept 6 as input; we should print out:

   6
   12
   18
   24...
   And so on, every 0.5 seconds.
2. Modify the **growing square** program so it grows from the centre of the canvas instead of from one corner.

   Hint: You need to add variables for the first 2 co-ordinates of the fillRect function and reduce them by 5 each time to move the corner up and left.
3. Create a shrinking circle problem that starts off at the size of canvas and shrinks to a radius of 5 pixels slowly. When it reaches 5 pixels size, it restarts at the original size and starts shrinking again. So, it's the reverse of our Growing Circle example.

4. Create 2 balls that start at random positions on the canvas; and move in random directions. They bounce off the wall; and if they touch each other, they change directions. (Hint: Create a 2nd

ball in the Bouncing Ball program, and then add in a check for the distance between the two balls. If the distance between the two balls is small, change direction of both balls).

KeyPress and Mouse Click Event

What does a KeyPress Element Do?

A KeyPress element detects when a certain event happens on the keyboard. The action of typing a key is called an event.
A KeyPress Element is part of jQuery. jQuery is a JavaScript library used to handle events, animations etc. Below is a simple example of a keypress element.

KeyPress Example 1

Before we start the program, we upload the jQuery library on to the program using below code:

```
<script src="https://code.jquery.com/jquery-2.1.0.js"></script>
```

In Javascript, we create a variable called **keyc** which contains all the keycodes. The keycodes are numbers assigned to every event that occurs when we type on the keyboard. For example, 32 is the keycode for the event of pressing the spacebar. To get a list of all the event keycodes, we can check them on the link below:
https://keycode.info/
We include only 8 keycodes shown in the program; as this is just a test program. Feel free to include more if you want to. Then we have the below code that runs the function **press(event)** when a key is pressed.
$("body").keydown(press)
Inside the function, we use **keyc[event.keycode]** to access the event that happened when we pressed the button. See some examples below for the output.

```
<html>
<head>
  <title>Keyboard input</title>
</head>
<body>
 <script src="https://code.jquery.com/jquery-2.1.0.js"></script>
<script>
var keyc = {
  16: "shift",
  27: "escape",
  32: "space",
  37: "left",
  38: "up",
  39: "right",
  40: "down",
  46: "delete"
};
$("body").keydown(press);
function press(event)
{
document.write("You just pressed the key: "+keyc[event.keyCode]);
}

</script>
</body>
</html>
```

Output:

You just pressed the key: right

You just pressed the key: space

KeyPress Example 2

In the below program, we create 5 different functions that places a small ball at 5 different parts of the canvas; based on which key is pressed on the keyboard. If the user presses “space” the program runs **centerballposition()** which places the ball in the center of the canvas.
If the user presses “right” the program runs **rightballposition()** which places the ball in the top right corner of the canvas.
If the user presses “left” the program runs **leftballposition()** which places the ball in the left top corner of the canvas.
If the user presses “down” the program runs **downballposition()** which places the ball in the bottom right corner of the canvas.
If the user presses “escape” the program runs **downleftballposition()** which places the ball in the bottom left corner of the canvas.
The code and output is below.

```
<html>
<head>
 <title>Keyboard input</title>
</head>
<body>
 <canvas id="canvas" width="400" height="400" style="border:1px solid #000000;"></canvas>
 <script src="https://code.jquery.com/jquery-2.1.0.js"></script>
 <script>
var canvas = document.getElementById("canvas");
var cx = canvas.getContext("2d");
var w=canvas.width;
var l=canvas.length;
function rightballposition()
{
cx.clearRect(0, 0, 400, 400);
cx.beginPath();
cx.arc(390, 10, 10, 0, Math.PI * 2);
cx.fill();
}
function leftballposition()
{
cx.clearRect(0, 0, 400, 400);
cx.beginPath();
cx.arc(10, 10, 10, 0, Math.PI * 2);
cx.fill();
}
function centerballposition()
{
cx.clearRect(0, 0, 400, 400);
cx.beginPath();
cx.arc(200, 200, 10, 0, Math.PI * 2);
cx.fill();
}
function downballposition()
{
cx.clearRect(0, 0, 400, 400);
cx.beginPath();
cx.arc(390, 390, 10, 0, Math.PI * 2);
cx.fill();
}
```

```
function downleftballposition()
{
cx.clearRect(0, 0, 400, 400);
cx.beginPath();
cx.arc(10, 390, 10, 0, Math.PI * 2);
cx.fill();
}
var keyc = {
 16: "shift",
 27: "escape",
 32: "space",
 37: "left",
 38: "up",
 39: "right",
 40: "down",
 46: "delete"
};
$("body").keydown(press);
function press(event)
{
if (keyc[event.keyCode]=="right")
{
rightballposition();
}
if (keyc[event.keyCode]=="left")
{
leftballposition();
}
if (keyc[event.keyCode]=="space")
{
centerballposition();
}
if (keyc[event.keyCode]=="down")
{
downballposition();
}
 if (keyc[event.keyCode]=="escape")
{
 downleftballposition();
}
}

</script>
</body>
</html>
```

Output:

On pressing right:

On pressing left:

On pressing down:

On pressing space:

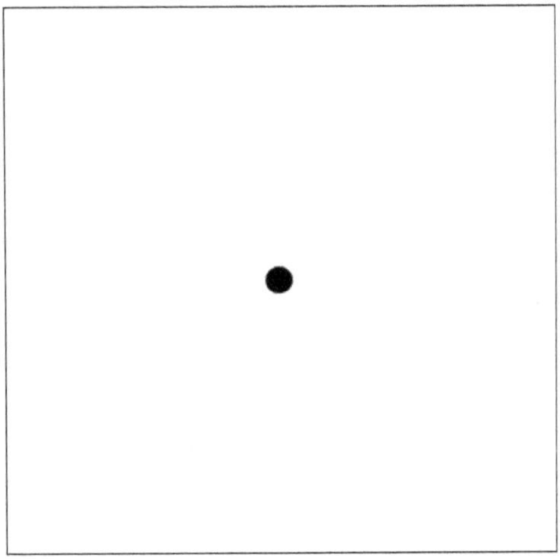

On pressing escape:

What does a MouseClick Element Do?

A Mouse element detects the click/motion of the mouse and the location of the mouse cursor on the html canvas when the event happens. It can also perform a certain function when this happens.

MouseClick Example

In the below example, the user checks if the mouse has been clicked on the canvas. It checks for the click using the line:
$(“#canvas”).click(mousec)
canvas is the name of the html canvas and **mousec** is the name of the function that runs on clicking the mouse. Inside the function, the user writes that the mouse has been clicked.

```
<html>
<head>
  <title>Keyboard input</title>
</head>
<body>
  <canvas id="canvas" width="400" height="400" style="border:1px solid #000000;"></canvas>
  <script src="https://code.jquery.com/jquery-2.1.0.js"></script>
  <script>
 $("#canvas").click(mousec);
 function mousec(event)
 {
 document.write("You just clicked the mouse on the canvas");
 }

 </script>
 </body>
 </html>
```

Output:

After clicking on the canvas:

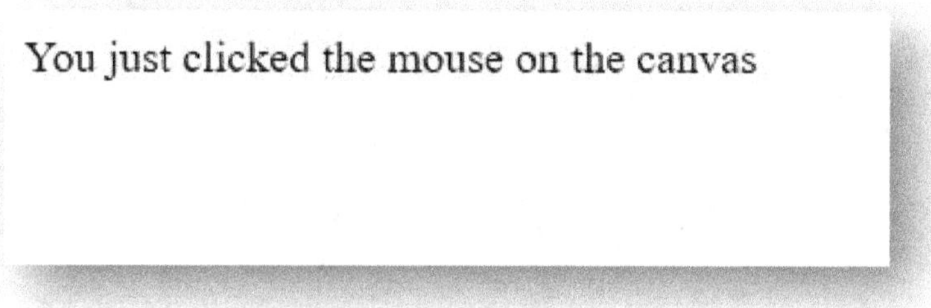

MouseClick – Hide and Seek

In the below example, we upload a html image and choose a random position on the image as the location of "Tim" in our hide and seek game.
Now, we click on different positions within the image. The program calculates how far the click is from Tim using Pythagros theorem. You can get the image using the link below, or use your own image.
Hide and Seek Picture Link:
https://drive.google.com/file/d/1gmPI4Z2Rm9iAA9vEBi7LWehe-uNE2UQ4/view?usp=sharing
In the below code, **timx** and **timy** are two random numbers between 0 and 500 that determine the x and y co-ordinates of where Tim is hidden in this picture.
mousec(event) is the function that runs when the mouse is clicked. Inside the function **event.offsetX** gives the x co-ordinate of the click and **event.offsetY** gives the y-coordinate of the click. **ctr** is a counter that counts the number of clicks and increments by 1 inside the **mousec** function.
The program then uses Pythagros theorem to find the distance between Tim and the mouseclick and prints the distance as an alert. Once the distance is less than 10 pixels; you found Timmy and the program prints out the number of clicks it took.

```
<html>
<head>
 <title>Find Tim</title>
</head>
<body>
 <h1>Find Tim</h1>
 <img id="hidenseek" src="hidenseek.jpg" width="400" height="400" style="border:1px solid #000000;"></canvas>
 <script src="https://code.jquery.com/jquery-2.1.0.js"></script>
 <script>

ctr=0;
var timx=Math.random()*400;
var timy=Math.random()*400;

$("#hidenseek").click(mousec);
function mousec(event)
{
dist=Math.sqrt((event.offsetX-timx)**2+(event.offsetY-timy)**2);
if (dist<10)
{
ctr=ctr+1;
alert("<strong>Congratulations!! You found Tim after "+ctr+" clicks.</strong>");
}else
{
ctr=ctr+1;
alert("Distance from Tim is "+Math.round(dist));
}
}

</script>
</body>
</html>
```

Output:

Find Tim
<strong>Congratulations!! You found Tim after 14 clicks.</strong>
Prevent this page from creating additional dialogs
OK

Hand Calculations (Dist):

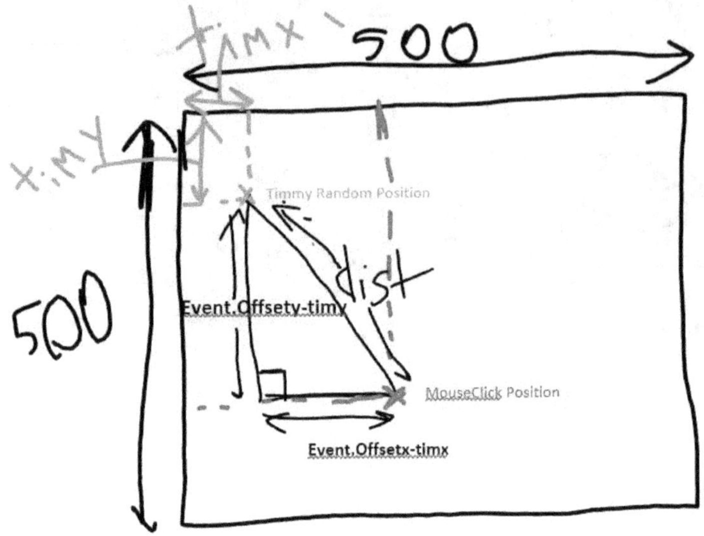

$$Dist = \sqrt{(Event.Offsety - timy)^2 + (Event.Offsetx - timx)^2}$$

MouseClick – Treasure Hunt

The treasure hunt game is very similar to the Hide and Seek Game. There is a different picture, that is the picture of a treasure map. And a random position on the map is the location of the treasure. The program checks for the location of a mouse click and calculates the distance between the clicks and the treasure location. Once the location is within 10 pixels, the treasure is found and the number of clicks taken is printed out.

Treasure Map Link:

https://drive.google.com/file/d/1wPoGYFvwoo2rCJ2eBvA-9HPAGrAX6v_1/view?usp=sharing

```
<html>
<head>
  <title>Treasure Map</title>
</head>
<body>
  <h1>Find the treasure location</h1>
  <img id="hidenseek" src="treasure-map.jpg" width="400" height="400" style="border:1px solid #000000;"></canvas>
  <script src="https://code.jquery.com/jquery-2.1.0.js"></script>
  <script>

ctr=0;
var jimmyx=Math.random()*400;
var jimmyy=Math.random()*400;

$("#hidenseek").click(mousec);
function mousec(event)
{
dist=Math.sqrt((event.offsetX-jimmyx)**2+(event.offsetY-jimmyy)**2);
if (dist<10)
{
ctr=ctr+1;
alert("<strong>Congratulations!! You found the treasure after "+ctr+" clicks.</strong>");
}else
{
ctr=ctr+1;
alert("Distance from target is "+Math.round(dist));
}
}

</script>
</body>
</html>
```

Output:

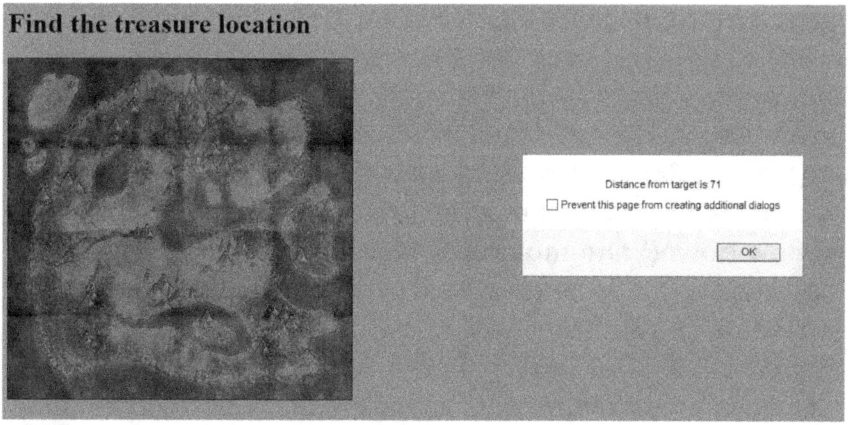

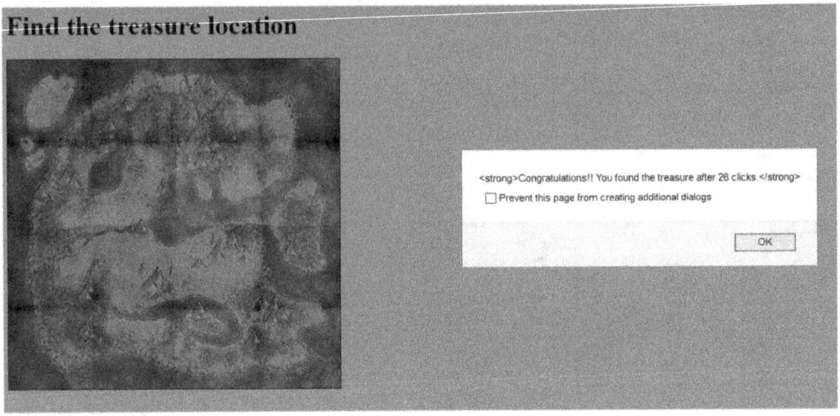

Pong Game

The Pong game is a fun game that builds on the "**Bouncing Ball**" game on Page 215 of this book. So, the program has a ball bouncing around the canvas. We add a bat in the LH corner of the screen that moves up and down. The bat of length 15 pixels is drawn using **clearRect()** and **fillRect()**. It is set to a constant xlocation of 10 and the ylocation is defined by a variable called **yrect**. yrect is defined in functions **movedown() and moveup()**. Moveup() is activated when up button is pressed and it decreases yrect by 30 pixels, which moves the bat up. Movedown() is activated when down button is pressed and it increases yrect by 30 pixels, which moves the bat down.
Also, the function **press(event)** detects the presence of keys pressed and activates moveup() and movedown() when up and down button are pressed respectively.
And we finally have the **frame()** function. It is a function that checks if the ball is next to the top, bottom and right walls. If the x-coordinate of the ball gets close to 500, then it is close to the right wall. Then we change the direction of x-motion to create a bounce back. We do the same thing if the y-coordinate is 0 or 500 (it reaches top/bottom wall), so we change direction of y-motion for the bounce.

And finally, we have a check to see if the ball touches the bat. We calculate the distance dist between bat location and ball location using Pythagros theorem. If the distance (dist) is less than 75 pixels, then we change the direction of x-motion.

```
<html>
<head>
  <title>Pong Game</title>
</head>
<body>
  <canvas id="canvas" width="800" height="600" style="border:1px solid #000000;"></canvas>
  <script src="https://code.jquery.com/jquery-2.1.0.js"></script>
  <script>
var canvas = document.getElementById("canvas");
var cx = canvas.getContext("2d");
var w=canvas.width;
var l=canvas.length;
var yrect=0;
cx.beginPath();
cx.clearRect(0, 0, 800, 600);
cx.rect(10, yrect, 15, 90);
cx.fill();
cx.fillStyle = "black";

setInterval(press , 100);


//Ball variables
var snx=1;
var sny=1;
setInterval(frame, 10);
locationx=Math.random()*350;
locationy=Math.random()*350;
```

```
function movedown()
{
yrect=yrect+30;
if (yrect>570)
{
yrect=yrect-30;
}
cx.beginPath();
cx.clearRect(0, 0, 800, 600);
cx.rect(10, yrect, 15, 90);
cx.fill();
cx.fillStyle = "black";
}
function moveup()
{
yrect=yrect-30;
if (yrect<0)
{
yrect=yrect+30;
}
cx.beginPath();
cx.clearRect(0, 0, 800, 600);
cx.rect(10, yrect, 15, 90);
cx.fill();
cx.fillStyle = "black";
}

var keyc = {
  16: "shift",
  27: "escape",
  32: "space",
  37: "left",
  38: "up",
  39: "right",
  40: "down",
  46: "delete"
};
$("body").keydown(press);
```

```
function press(event)
{
if (keyc[event.keyCode]=="up")
{
moveup();
}

if (keyc[event.keyCode]=="down")
{
movedown();
}
}
function frame()
{
//Circle
cx.beginPath();
cx.clearRect(20, 0, 800, 600);
cx.arc(locationx,locationy,20,0,2*Math.PI);
cx.fillStyle = "red";
cx.stroke();
cx.fill();
dist=Math.sqrt((locationx-10)**2+(locationy-yrect)**2);
//document.write(dist);
if (locationx>=800)
    {
        snx=snx*-1;
    }
if (dist<75)
    {
        snx=snx*-1;
        locationx=locationx+snx*20;
    }
if (locationy>=600)
    {
        sny=sny*-1;
    }
if (locationy<=0)
    {
        sny=sny*-1;
    }
locationx=locationx+snx*5;
locationy=locationy+sny*5;
}
</script>
</body>
</html>
```

Output:

Handwritten calculation (distance between bat and ball)

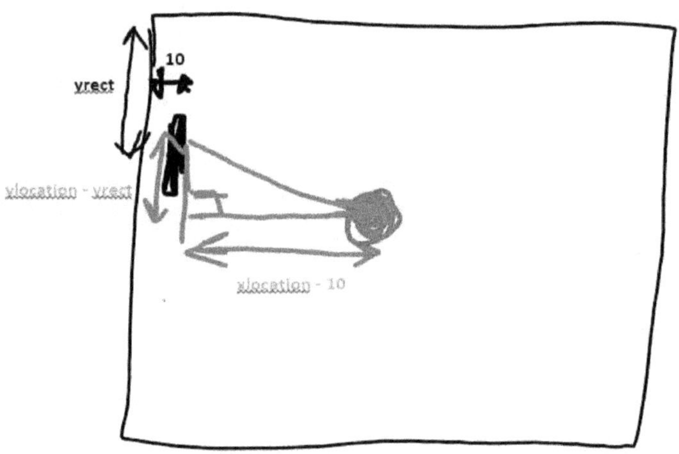

$$Dist = \sqrt{(ylocation - yrect)^2 + (xlocation - 10)^2}$$

Practice Problems

1. Write a program that takes in a user input and prints out pictures of 4 animals based on whether the user presses **p,m,a,t** (peacock, monkey, alligator, tiger). For example, if the user presses p, the program shows a picture of a peacock. (Hint: Save the 4 pictures in the same folder. Use the keypress element to detect the presence of the keys, and then the <img> tag to show the pictures).
2. Write a program that shows a simple color chart to the user. The user clicks on one of the colors, and the program prints out the name of the color (Hint: Use the mouseclick to detect the presence and location of the click; and then check if it is close to a particular color).
3. Draw a circle that moves up, down, left and right on the canvas based on whether the user clicks up, down, left and right.
4. To advance on Problem 3, have a treasure placed randomly on the canvas and if the circle gets to within 5 pixels of the treasure, then send a "Congratulations" message.

Conclusion

Thanks for buying the book. I hope you enjoyed it and learnt a lot from the book.

If you were able to go through the exercises in this book by yourself, you are definitely on the right track.

If you'd like any clarification regarding the topics; or any suggestions; please email me at: abiprod.pty.ltd@gmail.com

I also do one-one coaching online if you are interested in personalized help.

If you'd like a more beginner friendly version of this book, you can download my Coding for Kids using JavaScript Book or my Coding for Kids and Beginners using Python.

Other Recommended Books for further reading:

JavaScript: The Good Parts by Douglas Crawford

A Smarter Way to Learn JavaScript

JavaScript: The Definitive Guide

The end... almost!

Reviews are not easy to come by.
As an independent author with a tiny marketing budget, I rely on readers, like you, to leave a short review on Amazon.
Even if it's just a sentence or two!

So if you enjoyed the book, please...
>> Click here to leave a brief review on Amazon.
I am very appreciative for your review as it truly makes a difference.
Thank you from the bottom of my heart for purchasing this book and reading it to the end.

Free Gift

We do want you to succeed in coding. To ensure your success, we are giving you a free list of projects that you can work on once you are completed with this book.
https://coding.gr8.com/

Coding for Kids and Beginner Using Python

Bob Mather

TABLE OF CONTENTS

Disclaimer

Free Gift

We do want you to succeed in coding. To ensure your success, we are giving you a free list of projects that you can work on once you are completed with this book.
https://coding.gr8.com/

Introduction

Do you want your child to code? I am sure this feels like an impossible endeavor, doesn't it? It is as hard as learning a new language, and this is definitely a daunting experience for a child. It is harder to convince your child to learn to code as well. Every parent has been there. You know how difficult it is to start a new journey. It is quite overwhelming and scary. So, how do you think your child may feel about it? He is going to have a million questions, such as:

- Can I learn how to code?
- Will I ever reach a stage in life where coding is easy?
- When can I use this skill?
- Is it something that will help me in school? If not, why am I even doing it?

These statements stop most of us, so it is going to stop your child, too. The entire process of learning is too tedious. You first need to have a plan in mind, then find the right courses so you learn, make sure you are good enough and then create an app or tool. Having said that, you should first decide what it is you want to learn. You also need to know everything there is to know about the new subject, so you know what the dividend will be. There is no easy way to go about this, and it is a quite challenging task.

A new task may seem impossible when you start off, and it will definitely be hard for you to meet your goals if you do not take the necessary steps. If it is this hard for you, how hard do you think it will be for your child? You need to ensure that you and your child jump in with two feet. If both of you do not commit to learning, it will only lead to frustration. It will also lessen the chance of your child following through with the course and succeeding. It is best to let your child start with something small, take his time to learn and achieve measurable and realistic goals.

If this is what you want to do, you have come to the right place. You will find all the information your child needs to learn more about coding and get involved in it. There are different gamified and fun exercises that will keep your mind engaged. It is quite difficult to engage a young brain and motivate your child to learn something new and complex. However, the information and exercises make coding easy to understand. So, before you coax your child into learning how to code, make sure to do the following:

- Explain to your child why it is important for him to learn to code
- Outline the benefits of coding
- Define some key terms
- Look at different examples
- Choose a programming language and begin!

Coding, in simple terms, is a language used to communicate with computers and machines. You can also use this language to build and run apps, websites and more.

How to Make your Child Code?

This question has numerous answers but let us focus on how it helps your child move forward. This does not mean your child must make giant leaps. If you read the section above, you know it only means your child needs to start off small. The only thing you must focus on is to ensure your child progresses with every move he makes with respect to coding. This gives rise to the question – why should my kid learn to code?

The idea that kids should lean to code was planted years ago, and at the time, you may have believed it was hype. The concept was new, and every educational institute wanted to include coding classes for kids. The idea was not unfounded, but people needed some time to digest the idea that coding will become the most important strength that people must have. Some statistics show that the number of jobs will increase in the years to come, but the majority of those jobs will be in computing. This makes people wonder if coding is difficult to understand and learn.

Your child should not learn how to code for the wrong reasons. Do not tell him he needs to code to look cool. You must explain to him what the results are and how coding will help him land a good job in the future. Make sure to tell him he will be rewarded if he knows how to code. There are so many jobs out there, and they pay quite well. What makes coding better is that it not only helps your child do well in the future, but it helps him become creative, develop problem solving skills, collaborate with other programmers or people to develop new apps, communicate with them and various other skills that help him become a star employee.

Does this mean learning a new language is as easy as learning how to perform other activities or talking to people? Definitely not. Having said that, it is best to use these reasons to get your child moving if he is wary about learning how to code. Give him a set of guidelines, so he knows where to start. These guidelines will also help him determine where he stands. Coding is the language of the future, and thus it is important for your child to know how to code. As mentioned earlier, when your child learns to code, he also develops other skills that will help him in the future.

Python Example, why it's good

What is Python?

When we want the computer to do something, we need to give the computer instructions it can understand, i.e. machine language. Machine Language. Machine Language consists of 0s and 1s. Below is an example of Machine Language:

10011 00011 110001 1001010101 100001 001 0111 0000 11111 11010101

Although the computer might find it easy to read, we humans do not. Therefore, to make instructions readable and easier to understand, we use Programming Languages. We write the instructions for the computer in a programming language, and it is converted to machine language which can be understood by the computer.

Python is an example of a programming language. Below is a piece of code in Python to calculate the average of a student's marks and return their grade base on the average.

```
def grade(marks):
    sum = 0
    for mark in marks:
        if mark > 100:
            return "Invalid Mark"
        sum += mark
    average = sum/len(marks)

    if average >= 90:
        return "A"
    elif average >= 80:
        return "B"
    elif average >= 70:
        return "C"
    elif average >= 60:
        return "D"
    else:
        return "F"
```

Although you may not know Python, you may be able to understand certain parts of the code. That is the beauty of Python. It's easy to read and understand. Python can be used for various tasks. It can be used to predict stock prices, build software to automate daily tasks, develop APIs for websites, developing games etc. It is actively being used in the field of Machine Learning, Data Science and Web Development. Below is a list of companies that use Python as one of their programming languages

- Facebook
- Google
- Netflix

- Spotify
- Reddit

and the list goes on. Google engineers made the decision "Python where we can, C++ where we must."

Install Python on your computer

1. Go to https://www.python.org/downloads/ and click on the "Download Python 3.x.x". In my case, the latest version is 3.8.4, and since I am on Windows, I will be downloading Python for windows. Make sure you download the latest version of Python for your Operating System.

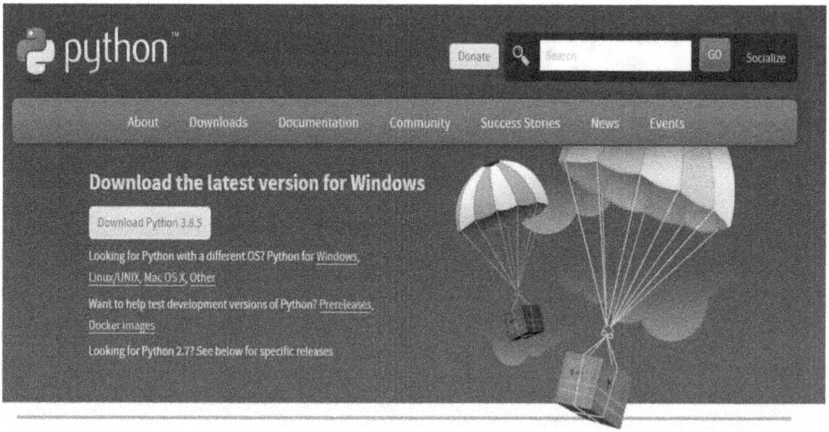

2. Launch the installer and wait for it to load. Check the "Install launcher for all users". Make sure the "Add Python 3.8 to PATH" is also checked. After you have checked the boxes, click on "Install Now" and wait for the installation to be complete.

3. Once the installation is complete, search for "Python Idle" and start Python.

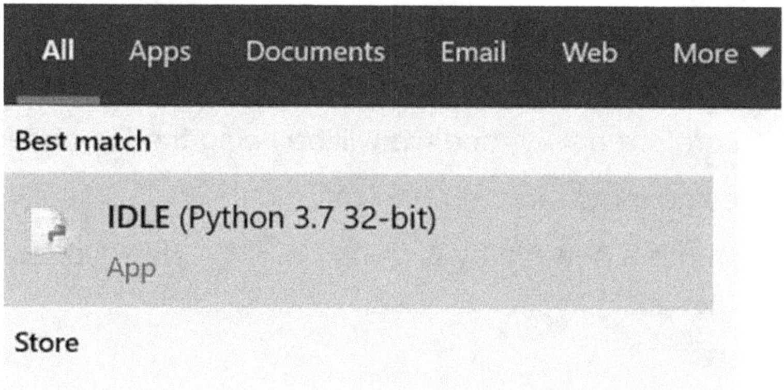

Below is a screenshot of Python idle.

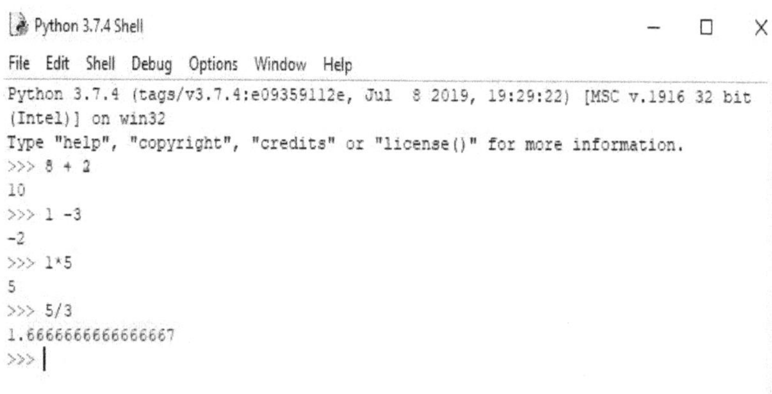

Exploring Python

Try typing out a few simple math expressions like the ones above. The window above is called a Python shell, and in the shell, Python gives an output message after each statement. You can also write all your code in a file and run the file using Python, this is the preferred way, and we will be using the file-based coding moving forward.

You can create a new file by clicking on File > New file.

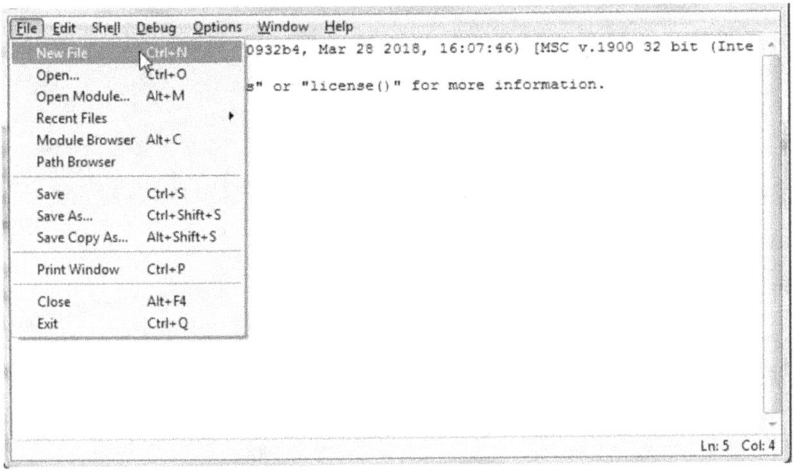

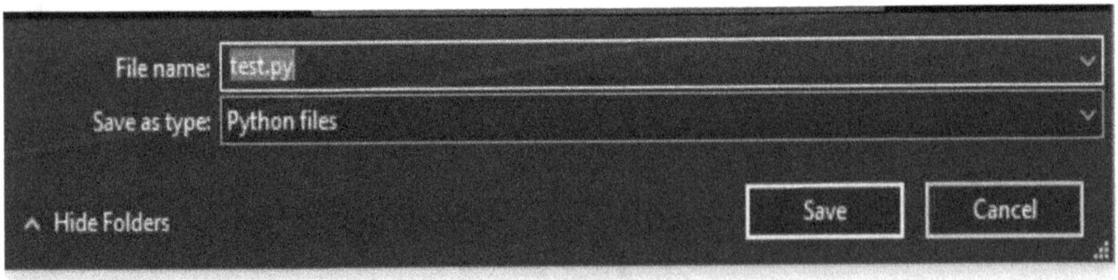

Make sure to save the file with '.py' at the end and the type as "Python files'. This tells the computer that the file contains code which can be executed using Python.

Try typing a few math expressions like in the file. Once done, either press F5 or go the run option and select the run module option. The python shell should open up again, but this time you won't be able to see any output. We need to tell Python to display the output explicitly. We can do so using the print statement, which will be discussed in the below.

Python Keywords

1. **Syntax**

   Syntax is to Python what grammar is to English. It is a set of rules that must be followed while writing code. Ex: there is a syntax to display output, there is a syntax to perform complex math functions etc.

2. **Comments**

   Comments are statements which the Python code will ignore. They are used to explain your code to other users, describe the purpose of a particular piece of code etc. The syntax for adding comments is:

```
# Add your comment
```

Python will ignore the line which is preceded by a #

3. Variable

A variable is used to store names or value(s) in Python. Think of it as a box that can value(s). That box is referenced each time you need that value(s). The syntax for defining a variable is as below:

```
var = 10
```

In the above example, var is the name of the variable, and it stores a value of 10. Anytime, you use the name 'var' in your code, Python will replace it with the value, i.e. 10.

The basic types of values a variable can store are:

String to store text values, ex: var = 'Python is fun'

Integer to store integer values, ex: var = 10

Float to store decimal values, ex: var = 9.81

Boolean to store True/False, ex: var = True

A variable can also store more than one value, and more on that will be discussed later.

4. Function

A function in Python is a set of lines of code with a name assigned to it. A function is used when a certain piece of code needs to be used in multiple places. Instead of typing the lines each time, you can type the function name. When Python sees the function name, it executes the lines of code associated with that function name. First, you have to define a function in the below format:

```
def my_function( input variables ):
        ........ piece of code .........
        return variables
```

A function can take in variables as input known as parameters, do something with the variable such as increasing it by 20, multiplying it with 4 etc. and return the result. The ‘return’ keyword is used to return a result. In the above case, the name of the function is ‘my_function’. A function doesn’t necessarily take parameters and return an output all the time, e.g.:

```
def new_function():
        ......... piece of code ........
```

The above is also a valid definition of a function. Python comes with a broad set of pre-defined or built-in functions which are available for us to use, eg: print(), min(), max() etc.

When we want to use a function, we simply invoke it like this:

```
my_function( input variables)
```

If the function doesn’t take in any parameters, we do not type anything in between the parentheses. If we expect the function to return a result, we need to store the result in a variable :

```
var = my_function()
```

In the above line of code, we assume we have already defined a function named 'my_function' which doesn't take any parameters but returns a result. This result is stored in the variable 'var'

5. Print

print() is a built-in function in Python. It takes a string, a variable or a combination of a string and variables as its input parameters and displays it on the python shell. Below are some examples:

```
print(.' Python is Fun') # Prints 'Python is Fun' in the python shell
print(8+10) # Prints 18 in the python shell

# below are two variables name and age to store the Name and Age of a
# person
name = 'Peter Parker'
age = 29
print(' My name is {} and my age is {} years'.format(name , age)
```

Prints 'My name is Peter Parker, and my age is 29 years' in the shell

To print a variable we replace the variable with {} in the string and use

.format() function with the variable as the parameters. The order matters

and values are replaced respectively

```
# Takes in variables name and age as parameters
def my_function(name , age):
    # Increases age by 10
    new_age = age + 10
    # prints output
    print("Hello {}, your new age is {} years".format(name , new_age) )


n = 'Captain America'
a = 90

# calling my_function with above variables
my_function(n,a)

# calling my_function with new values
my_function('Peter Parker' , 20)
```

We have used all the keywords discussed above in this particular piece of code. Function 'my_function' takes name and age as parameters, increments age by 10 and displays it on the python shell. The result from the first function call and the second function call is

```
Hello Captain America, your new age is 100 years
Hello Peter Parker, your new age is 30 years
>>>
```

When writing code inside the function, the code needs to be indented, i.e. a tab space must precede each line of code. Any line not preceded by a tab space will not be part of the function. Ex: In the above code, the declaration of variables n and a are not a part of

Function my_function.

The Input Function

To make a program interactive, we need to get input from the user.

To take input from the user, we use the input() function. More often than not, we store the input in a variable, below is the syntax for the statement:

name = input("Input your name")

Example

```
def func(color):
    print("Your favorite color is {}".format(color))


c = input("What is your favorite color? ")
func(c)
```

In the above code, we first ask the user for their favorite color and then pass the color as a parameter to the function func(). func() prints the statement "Your favorite color is ________". Below is the output when we input our favorite color as Blue

```
What is your favorite color? Blue
Your favorite color is Blue
>>> |
```

Exercise

1. Write a program in Python to take the user's name and age as input and display it on the python shell. Hint: You will need to use input(), variables and print().
2. Write a program in Python to take three numbers as input, calculate the sum of the three numbers and print the output. Hint: Create three variables a1, a2 and a3 and print a1+a2+a3

Conditional Statement

Conditional Statements are also known as control statements. They help decide the flow of the program. Sometimes we want a specific block of code to execute only if a certain condition is met. Ex: We take the weather as an input from the user and print "Don't forget your umbrella" if it's rainy or prints "Have a nice day" if it is not.

```
weather = input("Input the weather? ")
if weather == "rainy":
        print("Don't forget your umbrella")
else:
        print("Have a nice day")
```

If the user inputs "rainy", print("Don't forget your umbrella" gets executed and python skips the code inside the else block. If the user inputs something other than "rainy", Python skips the code inside the if block and executes the code in the else block. The general syntax is:

```
if *condition is True* :
```

...... execute this code block ....

else:

.... execute this code block ....

Types of condition

Boolean variable

A boolean variable can have either a value of True or False.

```
boolean = True

if boolean:
    print("The  value is True")
else:
    print("The value is False")
```

First, we declare a boolean variable called 'boolean' and set it True. If 'boolean' is True, we print "The value is True". If it is false, we print "The value is False". Below is the output when 'boolean' is set to True

```
The  value is True
>>> |
```

Comparison operators

The different type of comparison operators supported by Python are:

> - greater than

< - less than

== - equal (Note there are two equal signs, a single equal is used to assign values to a variable, two equal signs are used for comparison

!= - not equal to

>= - greater than or equal to

<= - less than or equal to

Comparison can only be made between numbers or string. It is not possible to compare a number to a string. When we take input from the user, we get a string value. If the string contains only numeric characters, we can convert it to an int using int(). Conversion of data types is known as typecasting.

```
number = int (input ("Number? "))

if number > 10:
    print("{} is greater than 10".format(number))
else:
    print("{} is not greater than 10".format(number))
```

In the above code, we take an input from the user and convert it to an integer. We then compare it with 10 and print a statement.

If we enter an input of 8, which is less than 10, we get the following output.

```
Number? 8
8 is not greater than 10
>>> |
```

We can also compare strings like the weather example mentioned at the beginning. Below are a few comparison examples in the Python Shell

```
>>> 100 == 101
False
>>> 100 != 101
True
>>> 10 > 9
True
>>> 10 <9
False
>>> 'a' > 'b'
False
>>> 'b' > 'a'
True
>>> 'hello' == 'hello'
True
>>> 'world' == 'WORLD'
False
>>> |
```

Python is case sensitive, as it can be seen in the last example, 'world' != 'WORLD'.

Combination of conditions

Multiple conditions can be combined using the 'and', 'or' and 'not'.

```
>>> True and True
True
>>> True and False
False
>>> False and False
False
>>> False and True
False
>>> True or True
True
>>> True or False
True
>>> False or True
True
>>> False or False
False
>>> not True
False
>>> not False
True
```

elif keyword

While only one of the if or else code blocks will execute, you may have a case where you want one of many code blocks to execute based on the condition. You can use the elif keyword for such a case. The elif keyword is roughly translated to “else if”.

```
number = int (input ("Number? "))

if number > 10:
    print("{} is greater than 10".format(number))
elif number > 5:
    print("{} is greater than 5".format(number))
else:
    print("{} is not greater than 5 or 10".format(number))
```

The above code is similar to the ‘number-checker’ code we had earlier, but now it also checks if the number is greater than 5. Below is the output when the user inputs 8

```
Number? 8
8 is greater than 5
>>> |
```

Example

1) A function to print the grade based on the mark input by the user

```
def func(mark):
    mark = int(mark)
    if mark >= 90:
        print("Grade A")
    elif mark < 90 and mark >= 80:
        print("Grade B")
    elif mark < 80 and mark >= 70:
        print("Grade C")
    elif mark < 70 and mark >= 60:
        print("Grade D")
    else:
        print("Grade F")


mark = input("Enter the Mark? ")
func(mark)
```

The function ‘func’ takes a variable mark as a parameter. It checks for the following conditions:

- If ‘mark’ is greater than or equal to 90, it prints “Grade A”
- If ‘mark’ is in the range of 80 - 89 (note it’s < 90 and not <= 90), it prints “Grade B”
- If ‘mark’ is in the range of 70 - 79, it prints “Grade C”

- If 'mark' is in the range of 60 - 69, it prints "Grade D"
- If none of the conditions is satisfied, it prints "Garde F"

For every input, only one of the conditions is satisfied, and as a result, only one print statement is executed. Below is the output for user's input 65

```
Enter the Mark? 65
Grade D
>>> |
```

Since 65 is between 60-69, the third elif condition is satisfied.

Below is the output for user's input 90

```
Enter the Mark? 90
Grade A
>>>
```

Since 90 >=90, the if condition is satisfied, and the if block is executed.

Below is the output when the user's input is 50

```
Enter the Mark? 50
Grade F
>>> |
```

50 is not in any of the above ranges. Therefore, none of the conditions is satisfied, and the else block is executed.

2) A Basic Calculator

```
def Calculator(number1 , number2 , operation):
    number1 = int(number1)
    number2 = int(number2)
    if operation == '+':
        return number1 + number2
    elif operation == '-':
        return number1 - number2
    else:
        return "Operator is not supported"


n1 = input("Enter the first number? ")
n2 = input("Enter the second number? ")
op = input("Enter the operator? ")

print(Calculator(n1,n2,op))
```

The above code takes two numbers and an operator as an input from the user. It returns the sum or difference based on the operator the user inputs. The following checks are performed:

- If the operator is '+', we return the sum of the two numbers

- If the operator is '-', we return the difference between the two numbers
- If any other operator is input, we return an error message

Below is the output when the user inputs 10, 20, +

```
Enter the first number? 10
Enter the second number? 20
Enter the operator? +
30
```

Since the operator is '+', the if condition is executed and the sum is returned.

Below is the output when the user inputs 20, 10, -

```
Enter the first number? 20
Enter the second number? 10
Enter the operator? -
10
>>> |
```

Since the operator is '-', the elif condition is executed, and the difference is returned.

Below is the output when the user inputs an invalid operator

```
Enter the first number? 20
Enter the second number? 10
Enter the operator? /
Operator is not supported
>>> |
```

The operator '/' doesn't satisfy the if or the elif condition, therefore, the else code block is executed

Exercise

1) Extend the calculator function above to support multiplication and division operators.

2) Write a function which takes two numbers as input from the user and returns "Yes" if number 1 is divisible by number 2 and "No" if it is not. Hint: Use the modulo operator, '%'. It returns the remainder of number1 divided by number2. If it returns 0, it is divisible.

Nested Conditional Statements

In cases when we want multiple conditions to be checked, using keywords 'and' and 'or' makes code hard to read, therefore, we used nested conditional statements. Nested conditional statements are simply if..else blocks inside an if , elif or else block. Below is the general syntax:

```
        if *condition is True* :
                    if *condition is True* :
                              ...... execute this code block
........
                         elif *conditio is True*:
                              ....... execute this code block
........
                         else:
                              ...... execute this code block
........
                         else:
                    ....... execute this code block ........
```

Example

In this example, we are going to take a 4-digit year as an input and check if it is a leap year. Now, this is a little more complicated than we think. We know that every 4 years is a leap year. So that is our first check. So, a year like 1996 would be a leap year. But, every 100 years, there is no leap year. So, 1800 and 1900 are not leap years. Also, there is another exception. Every 400 years, it is not a leap year. So, 1600 and 2000 are not leap years. So, there are 3 checks.

```
def check_leap(year):
    year = int(year)
    leap = False
    if year % 4 == 0:
        leap = True
        if year % 100 == 0:
            leap = False
            if year % 400 == 0:
                leap = True
    return leap

year = input("Enter the year? ")

if check_leap(year):
    print("It is a leap year")
else:
    print("It is not a leap year")
```

The function check_leap takes the year as a parameter and returns True or False based on the conditions. First, we declare a boolean variable ‘leap’ and initially set it to False. Then we perform the following checks:

- If the year is divisible by 4, we set leap to True and return True. Then we enter the second loop to check if it is divisible by 100.
    - If the year is divisible by 100, we set the leap to False since the year might not be a leap year. If it is divisible by both 4 and 100, we enter the 3rd loop to check if it is divisible by 400.
        - If the year is divisible by 400, it must be a leap year, so we set leap to True and return True.
        - If the year is not divisible by 400, but it is divisible by 100, it is not a leap year. We set leap to False and return False.
    - If the year is not divisible by 100, we return True.
- If it is not, we set it to False since a leap year must be divisible by 4 and return False.

We take the year as input from the user, call the function, passing the input as a parameter, and check if the return value is true or false.

- If check_leap returns True, the year is leap and we print “It is a leap year”.
- If the check_leap returns False, the year is not leap, and we print “It is not a leap year”.

Below are a few executions of the code:

```
Enter the year? 1992
It is a leap year
>>>
Enter the year? 1995
It is not a leap year
>>>
Enter the year? 1900
It is not a leap year
>>>
Enter the year? 2000
It is a leap year
>>>
```

As you can see from the above code and results, it accurately calculates the leap year using 3 nested IF statements.

- 1992 is a leap year since it is divisible by 4.
- 1995 is not a leap year since it is not divisible by 4.
- 1900 is not a leap year since it is divisible by both 100 and 4; but not divisible by 400.

- 2000 is a leap year since it is divisible by 4, 100 and 400.

Exercise

1) Write a program that takes in as user input the number of inches of snow, number of inches of ice and the presence of salt. Check if snow day should be declared or not. It is a snow day if there is more than 15 inches of Snow. However, if there is salt, no snow day is given. If there is ice and snow together, snow day is given irrespective of whether salt is present or not.

2) Write a program that takes in a TV program time, TV program type and whether parents are present. Check if children can watch TV or not. Children can watch TV anytime between 6:00 pm and 7:00 pm. After 7, the rating of the tv show will have to be checked. If it's for a general audience and before 10 pm, they can watch TV. If it's for a mature audience before 10 pm and a parent is present, they can watch it. However, if a parent is not present, they cannot watch it. They cannot watch TV irrespective of the rating and presence of their parents after 10pm.

A Short message from the Author:

Hey, are you enjoying the book? I'd love to hear your thoughts!

Many readers do not know how hard reviews are to come by, and how much they help an author.

I would be incredibly thankful if you could take just 60 seconds to write a brief review on Amazon, even if it's just a few sentences!

>> Click here to leave a quick review

Thank you for taking the time to share your thoughts!

Your review will genuinely make a difference for me and help gain exposure for my work.

Loops

Loops in Python are used when we want a block of code to be repeated. We usually set conditions for the block to be repeated, as long as the condition is satisfied the block of code is repeated. As soon as the condition is no longer satisfied, the loop ends and the code block is no longer repeated.

Python has two kinds of loop:

1) for loop
2) while loop

FOR loop

A FOR loop is used when we know the number of times, we want the loop to be executed. For loops are also used in arrays, which will be discussed in the next chapter. Below is the syntax for a for loop to repeat a block of code 10 times.

```
for i in range(0,10):
```

.... block of code ....

In the above piece of code , the variable 'i' is initially set to 0, and 'i' is incremented by 1 every time the block of code executes. Before executing the block of code , a check is made: if 'i' is less than 10, the loop is executed, if 'i' is greater than or equal to 10 the loop is not executed and Python starts executing the code outside of the loop.
In general, the variable is initially set to the first parameter in range and is incremented by 1 every time the loop is executed until its value reaches the second parameter.

```
for i in range(0,10):
    print(i)
```

In the above code, we print the value of the variable 'i' during each execution of the loop. Below is the output

```
0
1
2
3
4
5
6
7
8
9
>>>
```

After 'i' = 9, 'i' is incremented to 10 and since 'i' is no longer less than 10, we exit the loop.

Example 1

We will write a program which takes an integer as an input from the user and returns the sum of all even numbers between 0 and that number.

```
def sum_even(number):
    number = int(number)
    sum = 0
    for i in range(0,number):
        if i%2 == 0:
            sum = sum + i
    return sum

number = input("Please input the number? ")
print(sum_even(number))
```

The function sum_even takes in a number as a parameter and returns the sum of all the even numbers up to that number, excluding the number. The following steps are performed:

1. We set variable ‘sum’ to 0
2. A loop is created which starts at ‘i’ =0 and runs till ‘i’ = number input by user with increments of 1

3. Inside the loop a check is performed to determine if 'i' is even or not
4. If 'i' is even, we update the value of 'sum' to the 'sum' + i
5. Once i is equal to the input number, we exit the loop and return the sum.

Below is the output when input is 10

```
Please input the number? 10
20
>>> |
```

The numbers which are even between 0 and 10 are 2,4,6,8 and 2+4+6+8 = 20. Below is the output when input is 20

```
Please input the number? 20
90
>>>
```

The numbers which are even between 0 and 20 are 2,4,6,8,10,12,14,16,18 and 2+4+6+8+10+12+14+16+18 = 90. Therefore, our code works as expected

Example 2

We will write a function which will print a *n x n* square filled with stars (*).

```
def print_square(number):
    n = int(number)
    for row in range(n):
        for col in range(n):
            print("*",end='')
        print('')

number = input("Please enter the value of n:")
print_square(number)
```

The function print_square takes in a number as a parameter and prints a
n x n square filled with *.

1. First, we need a loop to iterate through each row of the square, this iterator is called “row” and goes from 0 to n-1.

   Note: when no starting point provided for range(), it will start from 0 and go up to n-1

2. Next, we need to iterate through each column, we call this iterator col.

3. Using these 2 iterators, we can think of the square as an *n x n* table in which we have to fill in each block.
4. Now we have to print the "*" for each column in a row. We need to ensure that we specify end='' because otherwise python would move to a new line after every print causing all the * to be on a separate line.
5. After iterating through every column of a row, we need to move to a new line before going to the next row, thus we use print('')

Output for n = 3:

```
Please enter the value of n:3
***
***
***
```

Output for n = 10:

```
Please enter the value of n:10
**********
**********
**********
**********
**********
**********
**********
**********
**********
**********
```

While loop

A while loop is used when we do not know the number of times we want the loop to be executed. A while loop keeps on running as long as a predefined condition is True, once False it exits the loop. Below is the general syntax for a while loop

```
while condition:
    ......... block of code .........
```

A for loop can also be written as a while loop. If we want to print the numbers between 0 to 10, excluding 10, below is the code:

```
i = 0

while i<10:
    print(i)
    i = i+1
```

First we set a variable ‘i’ to 0 and increment it by 1 every time the block of code inside the loop is executed. Before executing the block of code, we check if the value of i is less than 10. If the condition evaluates to True, we execute the code, if it evaluates to False, we exit the loop. Below is the output:

```
0
1
2
3
4
5
6
7
8
9
>>>
```

Like before, when i = 9, the loop is executed, i.e we print i and increment i by 1. When i = 10, the condition evaluates to false and we exit the loop.

Example 1

Below is a function that takes an input from the user and prints it. This keeps on being repeated till the user inputs the word 'exit'.

```
def func():
    status = True
    while status:
        word = input("Enter the word? ")
        if word == 'exit':
            status = False

func()
```

We define a function func to take input from the user and print it to the console repeatedly. We stop once the user inputs 'exit'. First we declare a boolean variable 'status' and set it to True. The while loop keeps on running as long as the boolean variable has a value True

```
Enter the word? test
Enter the word? Loop
Enter the word? Python is cool
Enter the word? Hello world
Enter the word? exit
>>>
```

As you can see, when we input 'test', 'Loop', 'Python is cool', 'Hello world' Python keeps on asking us for input but as soon as we input 'exit', we exit the while loop and the program ends.

Example 2

Below is a function that takes in a number (n) and adds all integer numbers from 1,2 .... N.

```
def add_numbers(n):
    n = int(n)
    total = 0
    counter = 1
    while counter <= n:
        total = total + counter
        counter = counter + 1
    return total

n = input("Please enter value of n: ")
print("Total sum is",add_numbers(n))
```

Counter is the current number being added, starting from 1. Total is the summation of the numbers so far. We increment counter by 1 every iteration to change the number being added, so counter goes 1,2,3... n. When the counter reaches n + 1 the while loop will break, and we return the total at the end.

Output for n = 3, 1 + 2 +3 = 6:

```
Please enter value of n: 3
Total sum is 6
```

Output for n = 7, 1 + 2 + 3 + 4 + 5 + 6 + 7 = 28:

```
Please enter value of n: 7
Total sum is 28
```

Exercise

1) Write a program which takes a number as an input and returns the sum of all odd numbers between 0 and that number

2) Write a program which takes a number and prints the first 10 multiples of that number (excluding the number). So, if we accept 6 as an input, we print:

   6 x 1 = 6

   6 x 2 = 12

   6 x 3 = 18

   6 x 4 = 24

   6 x 5 = 30

   6 x 6 = 36

   6 x 7 = 42

   6 x 8 = 48

   6 x 9 = 54

   6 x 10 = 60

3) Make a guessing game.

a) Create a variable 'guess' and set it to a random integer between 0 and 10 and create a variable 'lives' and initially set it to 3.
b) Take the user's guess as an input, decrement 'lives' by 1 for each wrong guess
c) If player's guess is +/- 2 from the correct answer, print "Hot" else print "Cold"
d) The player has 3 lives. i.e once variable 'lives' is equal to 0, the game is over and the user cannot guess any more

4) Print a *n* x *n* square where every odd row is filled with '#" and every even row filled with '#'

Arrays

An array is used to store multiple values together. Imagine you want to store the names of 5 cars, one way would be create10 different variables to store the values. The
variables could be ‘car1’ , ‘car2’ , ‘car3’,’car4’‘car5’. Now if you have to print all the names, you’d have to type the print statement 5 times for each car. Now imagine if instead of 5 cars, you are dealing with 100 cars. It will be really tedious.

An array helps us solve this problem. An array in Python is called a List. Below is the syntax for declaring an array:

```
carNames = [ 'Toyota' , 'Ford' , 'BMW' , 'Ferrari' , 'Porsche']
```

The square brackets tells Python that the variable is a list and is expected to store multiple values. Each value in a list is called an element, i.e. ‘Toyota’ is an element, ‘BMW’ is an element and so on. Each element in a list has an index, the first element in the list has an index 0. Note that it’s not 1, it starts from 0. The last element in our case has an index 4.

Suppose we want to access the element at index x, we use the following syntax carNames[x]

Not x has to be a valid index, i.e it can not be greater than the total number of elements in the list -1.

```
carNames = [ 'Toyota' , 'Ford' , 'BMW' , 'Ferrari' , 'Porsche']

print('Car number 1 is',carNames[0])
print('Car number 2 is ',carNames[1])
print('Car number 3 is ',carNames[2])
print('Car number 4 is ',carNames[3])
print('Car number 5 is ',carNames[4])
```

Notice how the index is 1 less than the actual position of the element in the list. Below is the output for the print statements.

```
Car number 1 is Toyota
Car number 2 is  Ford
Car number 3 is  BMW
Car number 4 is  Ferrari
Car number 5 is  Porsche
>>>
```

This still doesn't solve the problem of typing multiple print statements. Notice how the index always increments by one, we can use a for loop and set the index as a variable.

```
carNames = [ 'Toyota' , 'Ford' , 'BMW' , 'Ferrari' , 'Porsche']

for i in range(0,5):
    print("Car numebr " , i+1 , " is " , carNames[0])
```

Variable 'i' is initially 0 and the loop executes as long as 'i' is less than 5, i.e 'i' takes the values between 0 and 5 excluding 5.The output for the above code will be similar to the previous output. There is another way to access all the elements in the list using a for loop.

```
carNames = [ 'Toyota' , 'Ford' , 'BMW' , 'Ferrari' , 'Porsche']

for car in carNames:
    print("Car is " , car)
```

We use the 'in' keyword. The variable car iterates over the list and takes each element's value.

- During the first execution of the loop, car has the value 'Toyota'
- During the second execution of the loop, car has the value 'Ford'
- During the third execution of the loop, car has the value 'BMW'

and so on.

The loop keeps on executing as long as there are elements present in the list.

A list can have duplicate values and it can have string values , integer values, boolean values , float values or a mix.

```
list1 = [ 1 , 'test' , True , False , 9.1 , 1 ,'test']
for element in list1:
    print("The element is ",element)
```

In the above piece of code, list1 has a mix of different types of variables and duplicate values. Below is the output for the print statement

```
The element is  1
The element is  test
The element is  True
The element is  False
The element is  9.1
The element is  1
The element is  test
>>>
```

Python has many built-in functions for lists and below are a few

1) Length of the List

   The len(list) function returns the length of the list, i.e the number of elements in the list

2) Add element to end of List

   The list.append(value) function lets us add an element to the end of the list

3) Add element to specific index of List

The list.insert(index , value) function lets us add an element at a specific index within the list

4) Remove last element of the list

   The list.pop() function removes the last element of the list

5) Remove a specific value from the list

   The list.remove(value) function removes the first occurrence of the value in the list

6) Accessing multiple elements in the list

   We can access multiple elements in a list using the ':' operator.

   list[0] returns the first element

   list[0:4] returns the elements from index 0 to index 3, Note index 4 is not included

   list[0:] returns the elements from index 0 till the end of the list

   list[2:] return the elements from index 2 till the end of the list

   The index -1 refers to the last element of the list , -2 refers to the second last element and so on.

Below various list functions are used in the Python Shell

```
>>> list = [ 1 , 5 , 10 , 90 , 100 , 13 , 15 , 19 , 20 , 10]
>>> len(list)
10
>>> list.append("New Element")
>>> len(list)
11
>>> list
[1, 5, 10, 90, 100, 13, 15, 19, 20, 10, 'New Element']
>>> list.insert(2,"New Elemeent")
>>> len(list)
12
>>> list
[1, 5, 'New Elemeent', 10, 90, 100, 13, 15, 19, 20, 10, 'New Element']
>>> list.pop()
'New Element'
>>> len(list)
11
>>> list.remove(10)
>>> len(list)
10
>>> list
[1, 5, 'New Elemeent', 90, 100, 13, 15, 19, 20, 10]
>>> 
```

1) First, we declare a list with various integer values
2) We use the len function to get the length of the list, which is 10
3) Then we insert a new element to end with the value 'New Element' and print the length of the list. The length increase by 1 as expected and upon printing the length we can see that the new element got inserted to the end of the list

4) We use the .insert() function to insert another element at index 2 and upon printing the list and the length, we see it works as expected.
5) Then we try to remove the last element, i.e the element we inserted in step 3.
   The length of the list should be decreased by 1 and print the length and the list confirms that it works as expected.
6) The .remove() function removes the first occurrence of that element, therefore .remove(10) removes the first occurrence of 10 in the list, i.e index 3.

Now we try accessing multiple elements in the list

```
>>> list
[1, 5, 'New Elemeent', 90, 100, 13, 15, 19, 20, 10]
>>> list[0]
1
>>> list[0:]
[1, 5, 'New Elemeent', 90, 100, 13, 15, 19, 20, 10]
>>> list[:4]
[1, 5, 'New Elemeent', 90]
>>> list[2:4]
['New Elemeent', 90]
>>> list[-1]
10
```

1) list[0] prints the first element
2) list[0:] prints all the elements from index 0 till the end

3) list[:4] prints all the elements from index 0 till index 3
4) list[2:4] prints elements at index 2 and 3
5) list[-1] prints the last element

Example 1

We will write a program to take 5 numbers as input from the user and return the sum of all the return all the number incremented by 10

```
input_complete= False
inputs = []
while(not input_complete):
    num = input("Input the number? ")
    inputs.append(int(num) + 10)

    if len(inputs) == 5:
        input_complete = True

print(inputs[0:])
```

First, we create a boolean variable and set it to false. We also create an empty list to store the input values. The while loop runs if the variable 'input_complete' is False. We keep on taking input from the user, increment it by 10 and add it to the list. We perform a check and set 'input_complete' to False once the length of the list is 5, i.e the user has input 5 elements. We then print the list.

Below is an execution of the program

```
Input the number? 1
Input the number? 2
Input the number? 3
Input the number? 4
Input the number? 5
[11, 12, 13, 14, 15]
>>>
```

Example 2

We will write a program to takes in as many numbers as inputted and prints out their average.

```
input_complete = False
inputs = []
while(not input_complete):
    num = input("Please enter number(enter q to stop):")
    if num == 'q':
        input_complete = True
    else:
        inputs.append(int(num))

print("Input array is ",inputs)

total = 0
count = 0
for i in inputs:
    total = total + i
    count = count + 1

average = total / count
print("Average is: ",average)
```

Similar to the previous example, we create a boolean variable (*input_complete*) and an array(*inputs*) and use a while loop to get the inputs, but this time the while loop will stop when we enter the letter 'q'. After getting all the inputs, we declare a variable *total* to find the sum of all the inputs and count to track the number of total inputs. We do this by using a for loop and iterating through each element in the inputs array. Finally to get the average we just divide the total by count.

```
Please enter number(enter q to stop):2
Please enter number(enter q to stop):3
Please enter number(enter q to stop):5
Please enter number(enter q to stop):4
Please enter number(enter q to stop):q
Input array is  [2, 3, 5, 4]
Average is:  3.5
>>> |
```

Example 3

This time we will write a function which takes in an array and returns the maximum value in the array.

```
def find_max(inputs):
    max_value = inputs[0]
    for item in inputs:
        if item > max_value:
            max_value = item

    return max_value

maximum = find_max([1,3,9,200,6,-10])
print("Max in array is: ", maximum)
```

First we set max_value to the first element in the array. This is temporary. Next we iterate through each element in the array and check if that element is greater than the max we set, if so it will set that value as the new max. Once it has iterated through the entire array, max_value should contain the absolute max in the array.

For the given array [1, 3, 9, 200, 6, -10], output is:

```
Max in array is:  200
>>>
```

Exercise

1) Take a student's marks in 5 different subjects as input and print the average of all the marks. Also find the minimum and maximum subject mark.

2) Create a list that stores the months of the year. The user can input the number of the month and the function should link the number with the actual month using the array. Then print out the relevant month in the array.

3) Create a list of names and check if there are any 2 names that are the same. Return a boolean (True or False) depending on whether there is a same name or not.

Having Fun with Strings

A string is an array of characters, i.e. 'Hello' can be represented as ['H','e','l','l','o]. Therefore we can use all the previously discussed array functions on strings as well.

```
string = "Hello"

for character in string:
    print(character)
```

Below is the output

```
H
e
l
l
o
>>> |
```

Below are a few functions that are helpful while dealing with strings.

Split

The .split() function takes in a value and splits the string using the value as a seperator into an array of smaller strings.

```
>>> s = "Python is cool"
>>> s.split(' ')
['Python', 'is', 'cool']
>>> s = 'a,b,c,d,e,f,g'
>>> s.split(',')
['a', 'b', 'c', 'd', 'e', 'f', 'g']
>>> |
```

In the first instance, we split the string using space as a separator and in the second instance we split the string using a comma as a separator

Is functions

isalnum() - Returns True if all characters in the string are alphanumeric

isalpha() - Returns True if all characters in the string are in the alphabet

islower() - Returns True if all characters in the string are lower case

isnumeric() - Returns True if all characters in the string are numeric

isupper() - Returns True if all characters in the string are in upper case

```
>>> 'Hello'.isalnum()
True
>>> 'Hello!!!'.isalnum()
False
>>> 'Hello'.isalpha()
True
>>> 'Hello'.isnumeric()
False
>>> '12345'.isnumeric()
True
>>> 'H3110'.isnumeric()
False
>>> 'Hello'.islower()
False
>>> 'hello'.islower()
True
>>> 'HELLO'.isupper()
True
>>>
```

1) 'Hello' only contains alphabets therefore isalnum returns True
2) 'Hello!!' contains exclamation marks therefore isalnum returns False
3) 'Hello' contains only alphabets therefore isalpha returns True
4) 'Hello' contains alphabets and not digits, therefore isnumeric returns False
5) '12345' contains numbers therefore isnumeric returns True
6) 'H3ll0' contains alphabets therefore isnumeric returns False
7) 'Hello' contains an upper case character therefore islower returns False

8) 'Hello' contains all lower case characters therefore islower returns True
9) 'HELLO' contains all upper case characters therefore isupper returns True

Strip

lstrip() removes trailing spaces in the beginning of the string , rstrip() removes trailing spaces at the end of the string, strip() removes trailing spaces from the beginning and end of the string

```
>>> s = '       Hi       '
>>> len(s.lstrip())
9
>>> len(s.rstrip())
9
>>> len(s.strip())
2
>>> |
```

's' is a string variable with 7 spaces at the beginning and 7 at the end. Therefore the total length is 16.

1) lstrip() removes the first 7 space characters therefore length is 9
2) rstrip() removes the last 7 space characters therefore length is 9

3) strip() removes the first 7 and last 7 therefore the length is 2

Case change

upper() converts all characters to uppercase, lower() converts all characters to lowercase and swapcase converts lowercase characters to uppercase and uppercase characters to lowercase.

```
>>> 'HeLLo'.lower()
'hello'
>>> 'HeLLo'.upper()
'HELLO'
>>> 'HeLLo'.swapcase()
'hEllO'
>>> |
```

Concatenation

The + operator can be used to join strings.

```
>>> s1 = 'Hello'
>>> s2 = 'World'
>>> s1+s2
'HelloWorld'
>>> |
```

Only two strings can be concatenated, you cannot use the + operator to concatenate a string and an integer. You could however convert the integer to a string using str() and concatenate it to another string.

```
>>> 'Hi' + 2
Traceback (most recent call last):
  File "<pyshell#23>", line 1, in <module>
    'Hi' + 2
TypeError: can only concatenate str (not "int") to str
>>> 'Hi' + str(2)
'Hi2'
>>> |
```

As you can see 'Hi' + 2 gives us an error since 2 is an integer but using str(2) converter it to a string and the result is 'HI2'

Join

The join function is used to create a string from a list. It accepts a value which can be used as a separator and joins all the elements in the list to form a string. Make sure all elements in the list are of type string or converted to a string

```
>>> ''.join(['Test' , 'Join' , 'Function' , 'Hello' , 'Wordl'])
'TestJoinFunctionHelloWordl'
>>> ' '.join(['Test' , 'Join' , 'Function' , 'Hello' , 'Wordl'])
'Test Join Function Hello Wordl'
>>> ','.join(['Test' , 'Join' , 'Function' , 'Hello' , 'Wordl'])
'Test,Join,Function,Hello,Wordl'
>>> |
```

In the first case we do not pass any separator and it joins the strings without any spaces or a separator. In the second instance we pass a space as the separator and therefore the result has spaces between the words. In the thor instance we pass a comma and words have a comma between them.

Find

The find functions returns the index of the first occurrence of the word in a string. If the word is not found it returns -1.

```
>>> "Hello World".find("Hello")
0
>>> "Hello World".find("World")
6
>>> "Hello World".find("world")
-1
>>> "Hello World".find("Python")
-1
>>> |
```

In the first instance we try to find “Hello” in the string “Hello World” and it returns 0 since 0 is the start index where it finds the first occurrence of ‘Hello”. Similarly, in the second instance, it returns 6 since 6 is the start index. Note that Python is case sensitive and therefore when we try to search for ‘world’ it returns -1. It also returns -1 when we try to search for ‘Python’ since it is not present in ‘Hello World’

Replace

The replace function is used to replace a string with another string as can be seen in the example below

```
>>> "Hello World".replace("o" , "2")
'Hell2 W2rld'
>>> "Hello World".replace("Hello" ,"*")
'* World'
>>> |
```

In the first instance we replace all occurrence of letter 0 with "2" and in the second instance we replace "Hello" with "*"

Exercise

1) Write a program that finds how many times a particular string occurs within a bigger string that is input.
2) Write a program that takes in a string that includes a name and marks separated by commas. Split the string and calculate the average of the marks. The return value should be the name followed by the average.
3) Write a program that takes in a name and address and checks if the address contains the text 'Atlanta'. Have a counter that increments every time this happens; and at the end of the program print out the number of people from Atlanta.

Math Functions

The Math Library provides us access to some common math functions and constants in Python. To use the math library we need to import it by typing “import math” in our python file. To access any of its functions or constants, we need to precede them by ‘math.’

Constants

```
import math

print(math.pi)
print(math.e)
```

Math.pi returns the constant pi and math.e returns the value for constant e

```
3.141592653589793
2.718281828459045
>>>
```

exp() Function

The exp() function can be used to calculate the power of e.

```
>>> math.exp(10)
22026.465794806718
>>> math.exp(5)
148.4131591025766
>>> |
```

log() Function

This function returns the logarithm of the specified number. The natural logarithm is computed with respect to the base e. The following example demonstrates the usage of this function:

```
>>> math.log(10)
2.302585092994046
>>> math.log(1)
0.0
>>> |
```

It can also be used as log(x,y) where y is base.

```
>>> math.log(100,10)
2.0
>>> math.log(10,3)
2.095903274289385
>>> |
```

Arithmetic Functions

Arithmetic functions are used to perform mathematical operations. Some of the most common arithmetic functions are discussed below:

- ceil(a): returns the ceiling value of the specified number.
- fabs(a): returns the absolute value of the specified number.
- floor(a): returns the floor value of the specified number.
- gcd(a, b): returns the greatest common divisor of a and b.
- pow(a,b): returns result of first number raised to the second number

- sqrt(a): returns the square root of the specified number.

```
>>> import math
>>> math.ceil(3.5)
4
>>> math.floor(3.5)
3
>>> math.fabs(-3.5)
3.5
>>> math.gcd(10,20)
10
>>> math.pow(2,3)
8.0
>>> math.sqrt(9)
3.0
>>> |
```

Conclusion

Thank you for downloading this book. I hope you have enjoyed the content and applied everything that is included in this book. This is just a first step to get you started and enjoying programming.

There's a lot more to come. I will come out with books that are a little more advanced in the future.

If you'd like one-on-one training as well, you can contact me at abiprod.pty.ltd@gmail.com

In the meantime, if you're interested, you can check out these books below:

Python Crash Course by Eric Matthes

Learning Python by Mark Lutz

Python Programming by John Zelle

If you'd like a similar basic introduction to JavaScript, you can try out my book below:

Coding for Kids in JavaScript by Bob Mather

Book 4: Coding for Kids in Python

Introduction

In the 21 century there is nothing around us that works without computers. Computers are everywhere around us. Mobile phones, laptops, ATMs, you name it. They have computers inside them. In addition, there are other machines with embedded computers hidden inside them. These include items like washing machines, dryers, refrigerators, car, vehicles, air conditioners and elevators, which have some sort of computer chip inside them. How do we tell computers how to work? It is through programming!

A programming language is a language that a machine can understand and run to perform various tasks. It is how we communicate with machines to make them understand what we want to accomplish.

A program is a logical sequential statement that perform a task. A program can be in any programming language we want. It can even be in 1s and 0s which is only thing that a computer understands. Everything in a computer is in 1s and 0s. A high level programing language uses English like language so we can program computers easily. Ultimately, any program in any language is converted into 1s and 0s so that a machine can understand.

Technology is already everywhere in our daily lives and it is increasing at an unprecedented rate. All this technology needs to be invented, programed and maintained! It is only through understanding computers that we can do all of this and maintain and develop technologies to get further ahead.

There are hundreds of programming language around. Though many languages are no longer used, some remain very popular and used widely like Java, JavaScript, C#, C++, PHP, Python, Swift, SQL, Ruby.

No one knows all these languages and actually no one can learn all of them because they are so vast and many. The good news is that you don't need to learn them all. One good popular

language suffices. You can get started and code what you need using only one language. Once you start picking things up and learn enough, any other language will be easy and should take less time. The main concepts and fundamentals are similar in different programming languages.
In this book we will use the Python programming language. Python is a great and easy language to learn for beginners. There are so many libraries and ecosystems specific to Python.
This book focuses on learning by practice and experimentation. Programs and outputs are provided. You are advised to implement the actual program and compare it with the code in the book. After the program runs, you are encouraged to adapt the code for your own purpose.
There are exercises at the end of each chapter that help to solidify the learning of each concept and move forward. This is the best way to get the most out of this book.

Why Python is Great for Beginners

Python is a great programming language to learn. It's easy to learn and it is a good entry point into the world of programming. Python was invented by a person named Guido van Rossum, he was working on an educational project to build a language for new coders called ABC. As a result of this project he created the Python programming language. Guido made Python with four main goals in mind. These goals are to be intuitive, open source, easy to understand and to be versatile to allow for shorter development time. Python continues developing and maturing till today. Many enthusiasts and developers use it every day for a variety of tasks. Python is used for many tasks like web development, scripting, web scraping, data analysis and automation.
Here's why Python is great:

Shallow learning curve

Python takes little time to learn. This makes it a great language for beginners to start learning programing. That is why it used in many introductory computer science courses around the world.

Intuitive

The syntax of Python is very easy to read. In fact, it reads very similar to English and that is one reason for its intuitiveness. The language is consistent overall and is easy to read. You don't have to spend time understanding arcane symbols and syntax. Code is read much more often than it is written. That's why readability is a great advantage for language to have.

Very little boilerplate

The "Hello World" program is a common basic program that is just one line of code. Simple programs like that can be written with very little "starting code" or additional codes. Python comes with powerful data types already built-in. Python has Lists, Dicts, Tuples, Sets, strings.

These datatypes make it easy to start developing right away without having to implement those data structures from scratch. These data types (and many more) facilitate short development times and more flexible timelines.

Great Ecosystem

A programming language is of little value only by itself. What makes a programming language widely adopted and useful is the supporting community and libraries it has. There are lots of third-party libraries and people to help you.

Interpreted language

Python is a high-level scripting language (like PHP, Ruby, Perl, JavaScript, etc.). High level Languages of this type generally don’t require variables to be declared in advance. They allow variables types to change. This called dynamic typing. Python in an interpretive language meaning programs can run directly without having to be compiled before execution.

Versatility

Python has many applications, including data science, machine learning, web development, and game development.

Here are some examples of Python modules.

- Pandas is used for data wrangling and analysis.
- matplotlib, a plotting library useful for plotting graphs using many sorts of graphs.
- Pygame for developing games
- Django, a framework for web development

Python emphasize fundamentals, the core philosophy of the language is “The Zen of Python”. You can get them by typing on python “import this”. The Zen of Python are:

1. Beautiful is better than ugly.
2. Explicit is better than implicit.
3. Simple is better than complex.
4. Complex is better than complicated.
5. Flat is better than nested.
6. Sparse is better than dense.
7. Readability counts.

Setting up python workspace

There are many ways to have a python environment to begin coding. I will illustrate here 2 easy methods to set up a python workspace.

Method 1 – Anaconda

Anaconda is an environment that comes with python and many other preinstalled libraries. You get them all as on package that is installed once. Anaconda come with a tool named Jupyter Lab, Jupyter lab is a great way to run python interactively. It is also used extensively in data science and python learning because of its ease of use.

This book uses mainly jupyter lab to run python scripts interactively.

To install Anaconda, follow the guideline below.

1- Open up the link

https://www.anaconda.com/products/individual

Click the download ***button an***d choose the version that correspond to your system

After downloading follow the instructions of installer to install it.

After installation locate "Anaconda Prompt (anaconda3)" on your system.

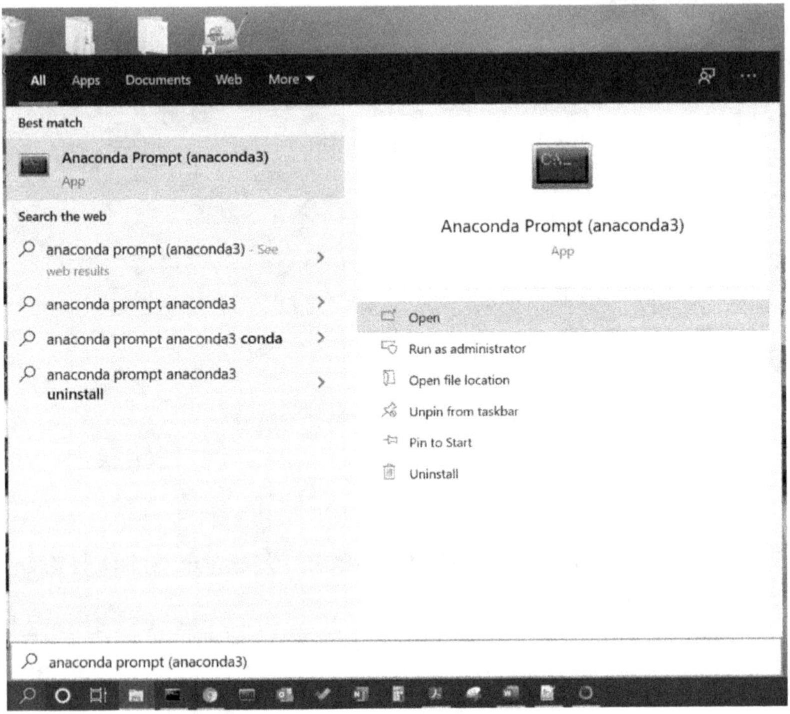

Click on "**Anaconda Prompt (anaconda3)**" to open it.

In the command prompt type "**jupyter notebook**" and press enter.

A browser page of jupyter lab should open

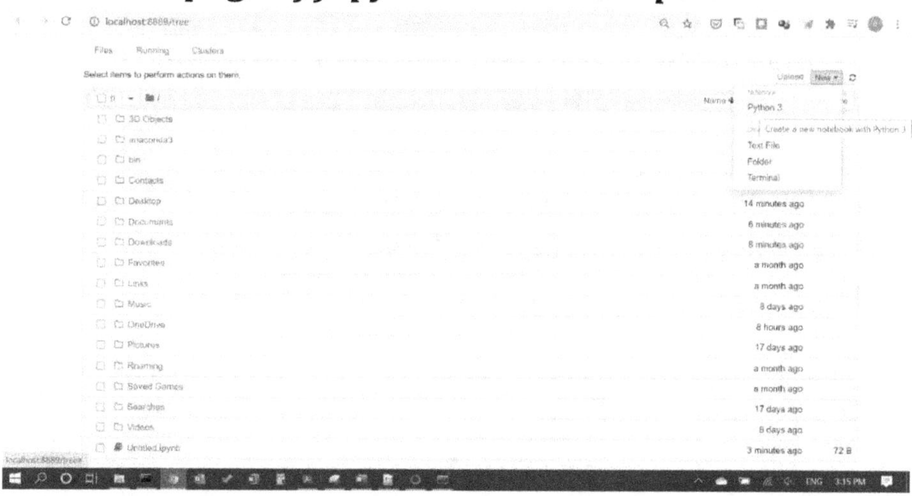

On the new box located on the top right corner click python 3.

Now you are ready to run python programs interactively.

To write a program type "**print("hello world")**" and click run or use shortcut shift + enter.

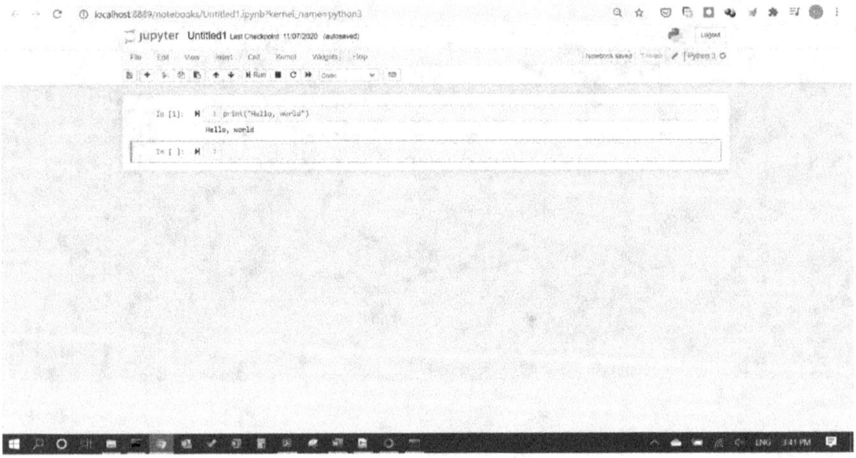

Congratulatons now you have your first program running

.

Alternatively, If you prefer working on the cloud, you can run jupyter lab online using jupyter website.

Open https://jupyter.org/try

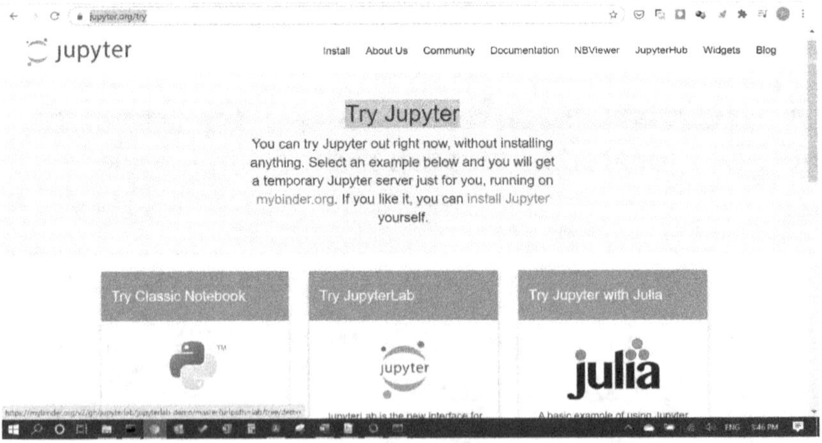

Click on **Try Jupyter lab**

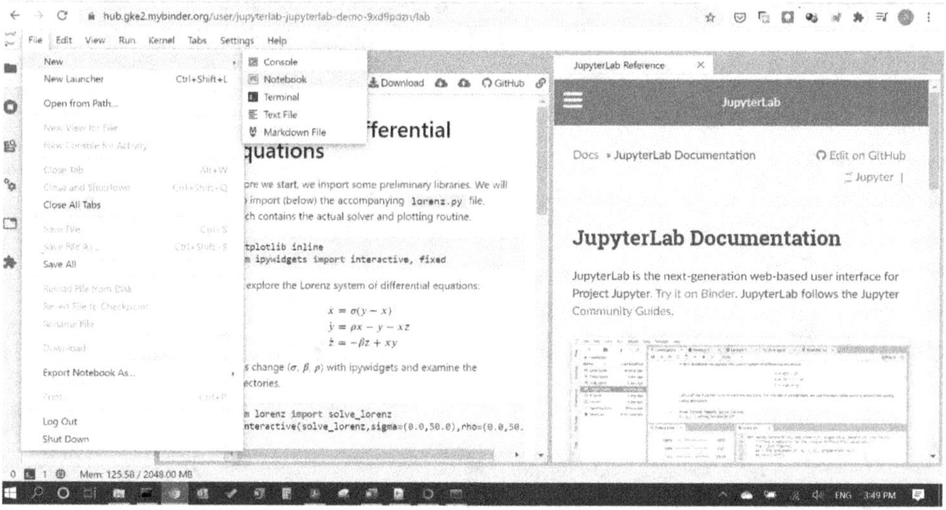

A page similar to the picture above should open, click on **File>New>Notebook.**

A prompt box will ask you about a kernel to choose, choose Python 3.

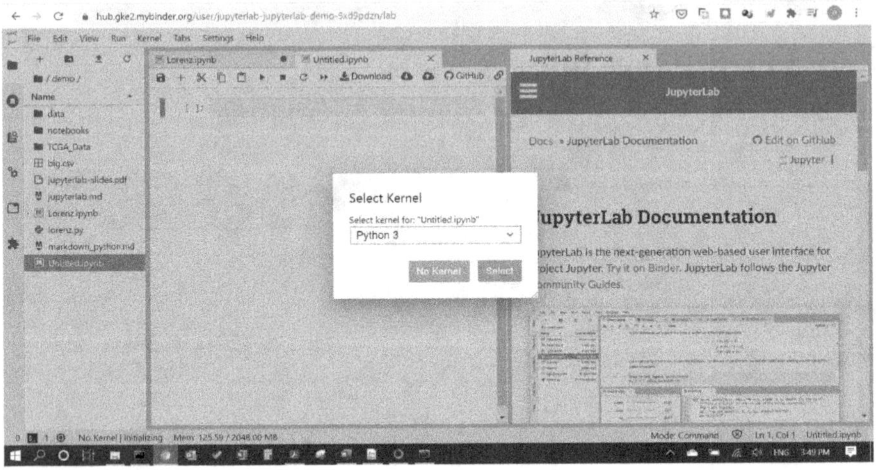

To write a program type **print("hello world")** and click run or use shortcut shift + enter.

Congratulatons now you have your first program running

.

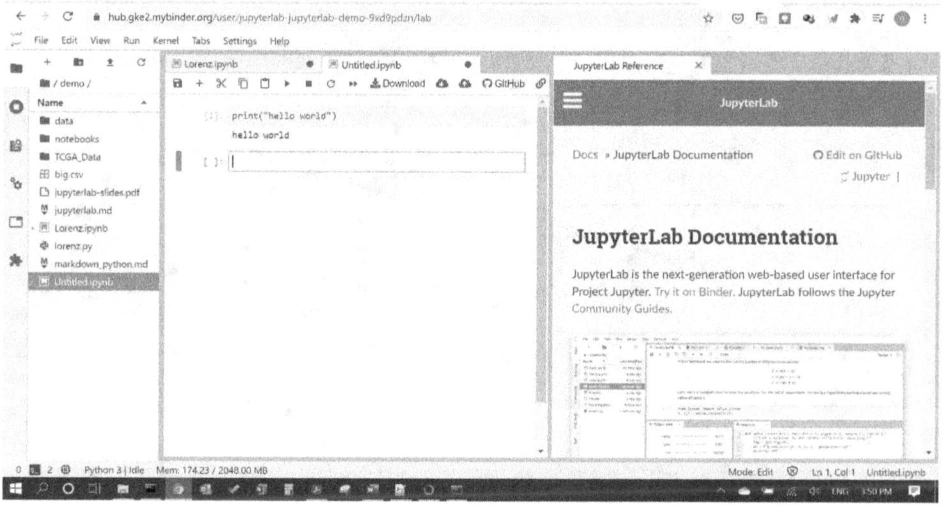

Method 2 – Installing python and a text editor

If you have large python programs it might be best to edit them using a text editor and the run them separately using python.

Step 1: install python

Open link https://www.python.org/downloads/ and download python.

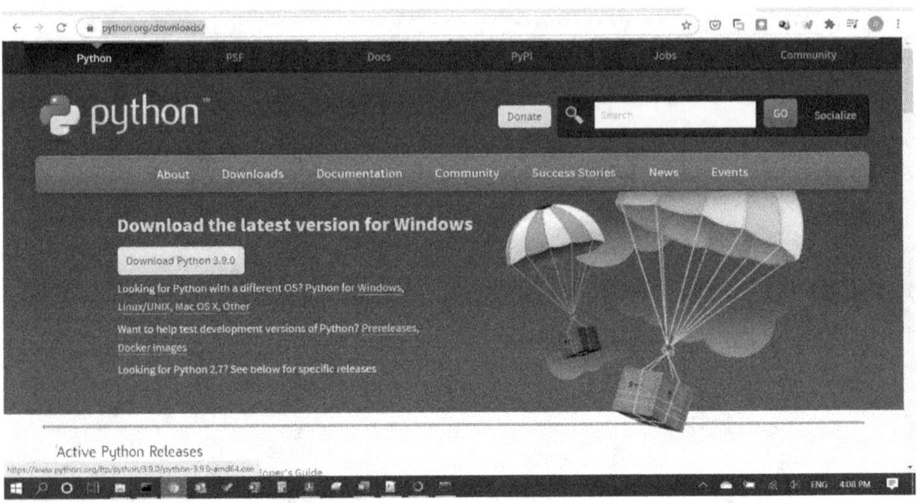

Open the installer package and install python .

Step 2: install Notepad ++

Notepad++ is an easy to use text editor for writing and editing codes .

Open URL: https://notepad-plus-plus.org/downloads/v7.9.1/

Download and install notepad++

Locate notepad++ on your system and open

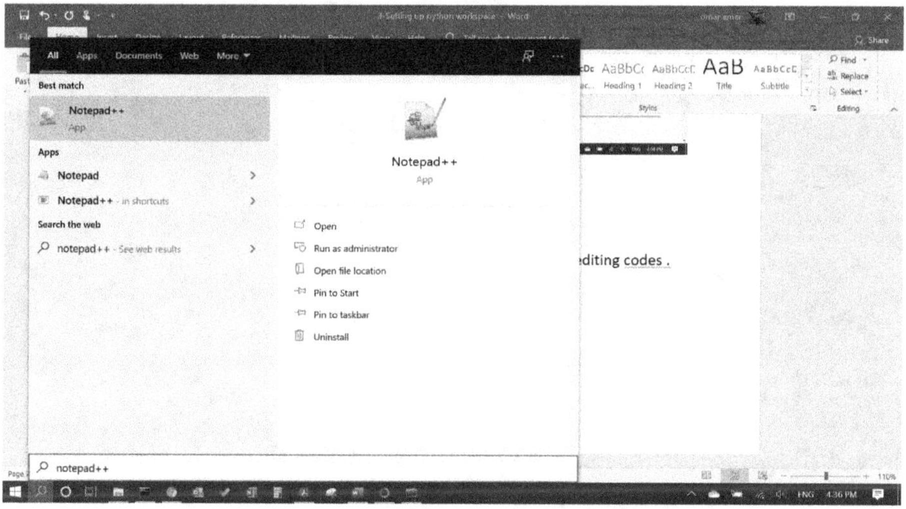

Write your first program **print("Hello, World")**

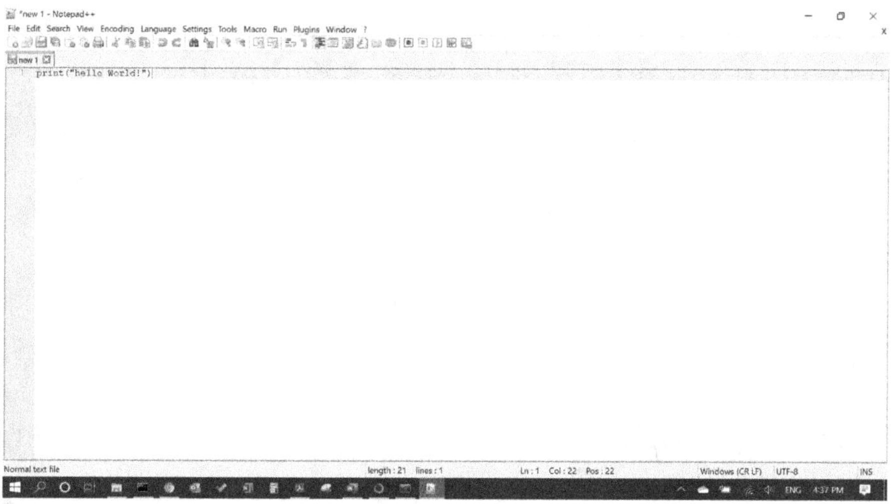

Save your program using File>Save As..

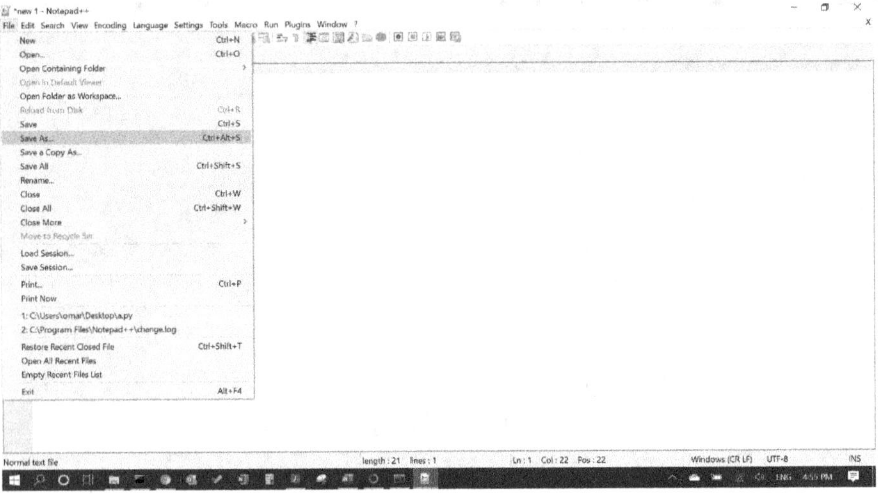

Name your program and save type as Python file

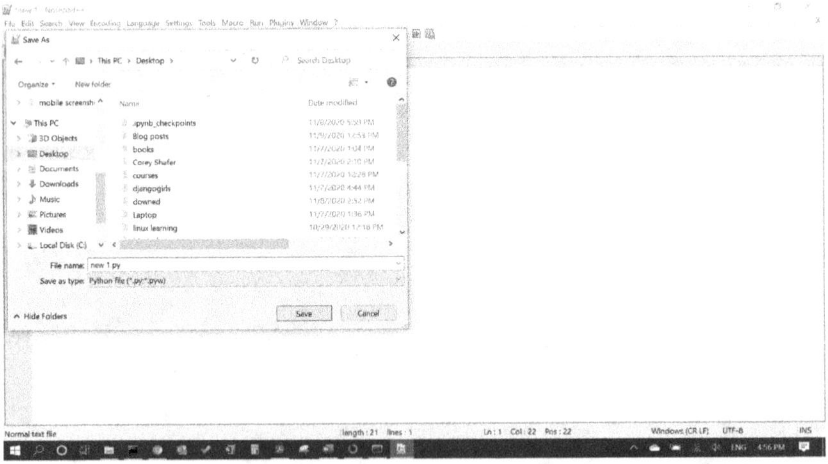

To run your program locate command Prompt on your system and open it.

Access the folder where your python file resides by typing cd "folder address" if your file is desktop then

type cd C:\Users\USER_NAME\Desktop

USER_NAME is specific to your user name on your Desktop and varies from computer to computer

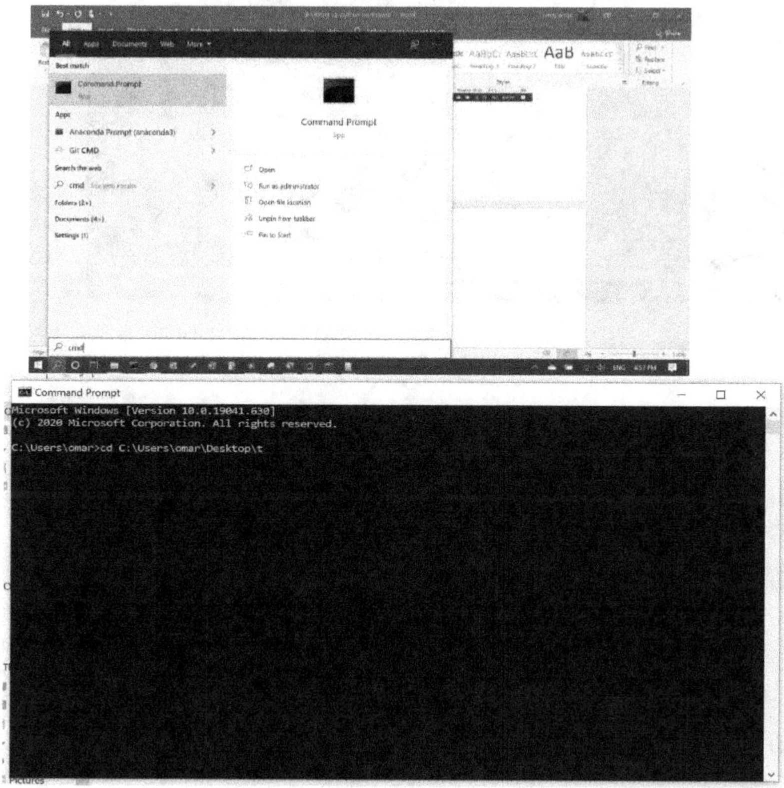

To run the program type

python “program_name”, for example if program name is run.py

then type **python “run.py”**

Congratulation now you have you first program working.

Variables

Introduction to variables

Think of a variable as a container used to hold some value. A variable is a location in memory holding some value. In static type programming language such as c and c++ variable type must be declared beforehand and variable type cannot change anytime later. That is why we first declare the variable where we assign the value type then we assign a value to the variable. Below is an example of variable declaration and assignment in a statically typed language.

int var; Variable declaration of type integer.
var = 8; Variable assignment to 8.

But since python is dynamically typed you don't have to declare variable type first, it will automatically work out the variable type for you. To define a variable, assign a value to variable name using equality sign. This is called assignment operator. The code below assigns three variables to a string, integer and a float.

```
# variables

lang = "python"
num1 = 2
num2 = 3.4

print(lang)
print(num1)
print(num2)
print('\n')

print(type(lang))
print(type(num1))
print(type(num2))
```

Output:

```
python
2
3.4


<class 'str'>
<class 'int'>
<class 'float'>
```

Observe that each variable has a type without being explicitly defined.
String variables are declared with either single quotes or double quotes.
we can define several variables on one line such as var1, var2, var3 = 1, 2, 3.

```
x, y, z = 1, 2, 3
print(x, y, z)
```

Output:

```
1 2 3
```

Variable Name Rules

In python variable names have few rules. The rules are

1. Variable name must start with a letter or "_" underscore.
2. Name of variables must be alphanumeric; no special characters are allowed.
3. Variable name is case sensitive A and a are different variables.

Example of different variable names.

```
num = 1
NUM = 2
_2num = 3
num2 = 4
num2_ = 5

print(num, NUM, _2num, num2, num2_)
```

```
1 2 3 4 5
```

Note that on the above snippet variables names were assigned a meaningful named. This is very important on programming as it makes reading programs easy to read.

Global and local Variables

Variables that are created outside functions are accessible to any function. They are called global functions. Global variables can be accessed by any function. Local variables are variables that are defined inside functions and cannot be accesses from outside function scopes.

In the code below “lang” variable is global so func() function can access it. When func() is called the output is python.

```
# this variable is global to this scope
lang = "Python"

def func():
    print(lang)

func()
```

```
Python
```

```
# this variable is global to this scope
lang = "Python"

def func():
    # this variable is local to this function
    lang = "C++"
    print(lang)

func()
print(lang)
```

```
C++
Python
```

Similarly, here “lang” variable is global, but we also have variable named lang that is equal to C++.When func() is called the output is C++ because the local variable inside func have precedence over global variable outside func. However, when we print variable lang we see that the global variable didn’t change. That is because even though we have lang variable inside func and outside, there scopes are separate and they do not interfere/override with each other.

Assignment Operators

Assignments operators are used to assign values in python. They are also used to manipulate and update variable values. The table below shows assignment operators and their names. These operators are used as shorthand to their equivalents.

Operator	Name	Example	Equivalent
=	Assignment operator	j = 2	j = 2
+=	Addition assignment	j += 2	j= j + 2
-=	Subtraction assignment	j -= 2	j = j - 2
*=	Multiplication assignment	j *= 2	j = j * 2
/=	Division assignment	j /= 2	j = j / 2
%=	Modulus assignment	j %= 2	j = j % 2
**=	Exponential assignment	j **= 2	j = j**2

The script below, assign all variables a, b, c, d, e, f in line 1, to 1. Then it uses assignment operator to update variables values. Investigate the output to understand how operator assignment work.

```
1  a, b, c, d, e, f = 1, 1, 1, 1, 1, 1
2
3  a += 2
4
5  b -= 2
6
7  c *= 2
8
9  d /= 2
10
11 e %= 2
12
13 f **= 2
14
15 print("a is ", a)
16 print("b is ", b)
17 print("c is ", c)
18 print("d is ", d)
19 print("e is ", e)
20 print("f is ", f)
```

```
a is  3
b is  -1
c is  2
d is  0.5
e is  1
f is  1
```

String methods

One of the most powerful aspects of python, is that it provides powerful functions right out of the box without having to re-implement them. String methods in python are versatile and so powerful that it spares you the need to spend time implementing them from scratch. You can easily manipulate string with them. In this section we will learn some of python string methods.

Here is list of common python string methods.

String concatenation: to concatenate two strings together just use + operator.

A = "Hello"

B = "World"

A + B *returns* "Hello World"

Also multiplying a string by any number n repeats the string n times.

A = 5 * "hi"

A *returns* "hihihihihi"

len(str) - length function returns string characters length.

len("python is amazing") - returns 17. Note that len count spaces too!

str[index] - indexing operator, selects a single character from string. The number inside the brackets is called index, it is an integer value. Indexing in python starts at zero.

a = "Python"

a[0] value is "P"

a[5] value is "n"

You can also use negative index, where it will start indexing backward, starting at the last character.
a[-1] value is "n"

a[-2] value is "o"

str[starting_index: ending_index] - slicing operator, slices the string at starting index and ends at one character before ending index.
a = "Programming is amazing"

a[0:11] value is "Programming"

a[15:19] value is "amaz"

in - in operator returns True if character is in string.

lang = "language"

"a" in lang, returns True

str.split(char) – Split a string into a list of strings by character char langs = "Python,C++,C"

langs.split(",") *returns* ['Python', ' C++', 'C']

str.replace(oldval, newval) - replace phrase oldval with newval in string str.

A="Python is powerful"

a.replace("Python", "C++") *returns* 'C++ is powerful'

f-string – is an easy way to format strings and variables, they are easy to use and also faster.

n = 7

print("number is ", n) outputs "number is 7"

print(f"number is {n}") outputs "number is 7"

str.capitalize() - Capitalize first letter of string, if its already capitalized it returns the original string.

sent = "message was sent"

sent.capitalize() *returns* "Message was sent"

str.count(substring) - returns how many times substring occurs in str.

mess = "Life is beautiful"

mess.count('is'), returns 1.

str.isalnum() - returns true if a string is alphanumeric meaning it's a combination of alphabet or/and numbers.

a = 'door2'

b='door'

c='door#$'

a.isalnum() *return* True.

b.isalnum() *return* True.

c.isalnum() *return* False.

str.isalpha() – returns True if all string characters are letters.

a = 'door1'

a.isalpha() *returns* False

str.isdigit() - returns True if str contains digits only.

n = '324235'

m = 'd4ds'

n.isdigit(), *returns* True

m.isdigit(), *returns* False

str.islower() - returns True if string characters are all lowercase.

s="People"

s.islower() *return* False

str.isupper() - returns True if string characters are all uppercase.

S = "ALL"

s.isupper() *returns* True.

Python also offer string comparisons operators just as you can compare numbers using ==, >, < etc. You can also compare strings using the same operators.

Operator	name	Description	Example	Returns
==	Equality	Returns True if strings are equal else False.	"Python" == "c++"	False
!=	Not equal	Returns True if strings are not equal else False.	"Python" != "c++"	True
>	Greater than	Returns True if len(str1) > len(str2) else False	"Python" > "c++"	True
>=	Greater than or equal	Returns True if len(str1) => len(str2) else False	"Python" >= "Python"	True
<	Less than	Returns True if len(str1) < len(str2) else False	"Python" < "c++"	False
<=	Less than or equal	Returns True if len(str1) =< len(str2) else False	"Python" <= "c++"	False

Example 1: String methods

The script below uses the string methods we learnt to do interesting operations on strings. This program takes username via input function and do interesting string methods on user name. The code is commented. Read and investigate the code. After you have understood the code, try to tinker with it.

```

name = "Nick John"

n = len(name)
index0 = name[0]
indexneg = name[-1]
index0_4 = name[0:4]

# Using f-string to concatenate sentences
job = f"\'{name} is an Engineer\'"
print("using f-string output is", job)

#slicing and indexing
print(f"name length is: {n}")
print(f"name index 0 is {index0}")
print(f"name index -1 is {indexneg}")
print(f"name slice [0:4] is {index0_4}")

# in operation, split, replace, capitalize
is_in = "Nick" in name
print(f"\"Nick\" in name returns {is_in}")
splited = name.split()
print(f"name.split() returns {splited}")
name = name.replace("Nick", "Biden")
print(f"Nick John after repleacing with name.replace() is {name}")
print(f"james captalized is {'james'.capitalize()}")


# count, isalnum, isalpha, isdigit
name = "Obama Jame"
count = name.count("Nick")
print(f"Nick occurs {count} times in \'{name}\'")

non_alphanum = "eoe12#"
non_alpha = "23"
digit = '223'

print(f"{non_alphanum} is alphanumeric is {non_alphanum.isalnum()}")
print(f"{non_alpha} is alphabitical is {non_alpha.isalpha()}")
print(f"{digit} is only digits {digit.isdigit()}")




```

Output:

```
using f-string output is 'Nick John is an Engineer'
name length is: 9
name index 0 is N
name index -1 is n
name slice [0:4] is Nick
"Nick" in name returns True
name.split() returns ['Nick', 'John']
Nick John after repleacing with name.replace() is Biden John
james captalized is James
Nick occurs 0 times in 'Obama Jame'
eoe12# is alphanumeric is False
23 is alphabitical is False
223 is only digits True
```

Example 2 – Reversing name

In this program, we will input our name through input function and the function will print the name length and the reverse of your name. First, we loop through name characters and print each character. For the reverse part, we loop through 1 and up to string length and index the name string using negative i starting backward. For example, if word length is 10, we start with index -1 through -10.

Note: print(char, end='.') prints char and end with '.' Instead of usual newline.

```
name = input("Enter your name: ")

n = len(name)
print("The length of your name is ", n)
print()
for char in name :
    print(char,end='.')

print()
print("The reverse is")

for i in range(1, n+1):
    print(name[-i], end=".")
```

```
Enter your name: James Bond
The length of your name is  10

J.a.m.e.s. .B.o.n.d.
The reverse is
d.n.o.B. .s.e.m.a.J.
```

Example 3 – Vowels counter program

This program counts the vowels in a string. It starts by initializing count to zero, then converting all text characters to lowercase so we can use comparison between text characters and vowels characters in lowercase. Then we loop through characters in text and check if char in vowels, if true count gets incremented by one.

```
vowels = 'aeiou'

# returns the count of vowels in text
def count_vowels(text):
    count = 0
    # convert text to all lowercase so it compares correctly
    # to vowels
    text = text.lower()
    for char in text:
        if char in vowels:
            count += 1
    return count

text = "Learning programming is amazing tool to learn"
count = count_vowels(text)
print(f"There are {count} vowels in text.")
```

```
There are 15 vowels in text.
```

Example 4 – Remove negative words from a text

This program iterates through the words by splitting them first using str.split().

str.split() splits negative_words by space into words. For example “I like CS”.split() returns [“I”, “like”, “CS”].The block function loop through negative_words list and if any word is in the text, we replace the word with asterisk string that math negative word length .

```
# replace all instances negative words with stars matching the Legnth of these words

negative_words = "bad kill haters"

def block(text):
    # split words into list of words
    for negative in negative_words.split():
        if negative in text:
            text = text.replace(negative, len(negative)*'*')
    return text

text = "haters kill love"
blocked_text = block(text)

print(f"Original text : {text}")
print(f"Blocked text : {blocked_text}")
```

```
Original text : haters kill love
Blocked text : ****** **** love
```

Practice Problems

1. Palindrome is a word which reads the same forward as backward, such as Civic, Level, Mom, Noon and radar. Write a program that return true if the phrase is a palindrome.

2. Write a program that prints how many one-character repeats are there in a given text.

3. Write a program that generate random n length alphanumeric password.

4. Write a program to replace comma with dots in given string, such as “32,323,23” to “32.323.23”

5. Write a program that computes sum of digits in a string, such as “452” digits sum to 11.

Doing Math with Python

Python is a great programming language to perform and analyze data from users. We'll go over a few functions that help you get familiar with python.

Now, this section is not for everyone. It's for those who are interested in implementing a math in their programs, or like math and would like to see it implemented in Python. Some of the concepts are taught in high schools, so this section may not be good for younger students.

int/float

int – Takes string variable and return an integer or if passed with a float returns the integer part of float.

float – Takes string variable and converts it to float number.

Let's look at an example below.

In this example, we put 3 of the numbers through int and float and see the output.

Output:

```
xi = int(5.2)
yi = int(5)
zi = int("5")
xf = float("5.2")
yf = float(5.01)
zf = float(5)

print(f"xi is {xi} and it's type is {type(xi)}")
print(f"yi is {yi} and it's type is {type(yi)}")
print(f"zi is {zi} and it's type is {type(zi)}")
print(f"xf is {xf} and it's type is {type(xf)}")
print(f"yf is {yf} and it's type is {type(yf)}")
print(f"zf is {zf} and it's type is {type(zf)}")
```

We can see in the output the difference between int and float. We can see that passing a string int

```
xi is 5 and it's type is <class 'int'>
yi is 5 and it's type is <class 'int'>
zi is 5 and it's type is <class 'int'>
xf is 5.2 and it's type is <class 'float'>
yf is 5.01 and it's type is <class 'float'>
zf is 5.0 and it's type is <class 'float'>
```

i.e. “5” to int function returns int type. Similarly, for float function it takes string that is float i.e. “5.2” and return float number. Note that “5” and “5.2” are strings because they are in quotes. We cannot use them in any mathematical information without using int or float to convert them into numbers.

We also note that for all values int remove the decimal part and keeps integer part. It does not round up or down, just removes the decimal part. float retains decimal part. So, use float to convert decimal numbers in strings into actual float numbers.

Rounding numbers – math.ceil(), math.floor() and round()

Python has a built in library called math, it includes a variety of useful mathematical functions.

To access a library in python you must import it first so the main program can have access to a library function.

Next, let's talk about rounding numbers. We use the functions math.ceil(), math.floor() and math.round(). math.ceil() rounds to first integer more than the decimal number , math.floor() rounds to first integer less than the decimal number and round() to the nearest integer (whether it's more or less). Let's look at a sample program.

```
# import the Library
import math

xc = math.ceil(5.2)
yc = math.ceil(7.8)
zc = math.ceil(4.5)

xf = math.floor(5.2)
yf = math.floor(7.8)
zf = math.floor(4.5)

xr = round(5.2)
yr = round(7.8)
zr = round(4.5)

print(f"Example of math.ceil()")
print(f"xc is {xc}")
print(f"yc is {yc}")
print(f"zc is {zc}")
print()
print(f"Example of math.floor()")
print(f"xf is {xf}")
print(f"yf is {yf}")
print(f"zf is {zf}")
print()
print(f"Example of round()")
print(f"xr is {xr}")
print(f"yr is {yr}")
print(f"zr is {zr}")
```

Output:

```
Example of math.ceil()
xc is 6
yc is 8
zc is 5

Example of math.floor()
xf is 5
yf is 7
zf is 4

Example of round()
xr is 5
yr is 8
zr is 4
```

Add, subtract, multiply, divide

It might seem self-explanatory, but because of how vital it is to do any basic calculation, I will go over the 4 basic mathematical operations.

```
n1 = float(input('num1: '))
n2 = float(input('num2: '))

Sum = n1 + n2
difference = n1 - n2
product = n1 * n2
quotinet = n1/n2

print()
print(f"The sum is {Sum}")
print(f"The difference is {difference}")
print(f"The product is {product}")
print(f"The quotinet is {quotinet}")
```

In this code, we accept two numbers using a python input() function. The two numbers are assigned to two variables n1 and n2.
Then we calculate the sum, difference, product and quotient and assign them to 4 different variables. At the end, these 4 variables are printed out using print().

Output:

```
num1: 9
num2: 3

The sum is 12.0
The difference is 6.0
The product is 27.0
The quotinet is 3.0
```

Modulus operation

The modulus operation returns the remainder between two numbers. It looks like the percentage sign %. Here's an example below:

The above code takes in two numbers via an input and finds the remainder between the two; as shown in output below.

```
n1 = float(input('num1: '))
n2 = float(input('num2: '))

remainder = n1 % n2
print()
print(f"Remainder is {remainder}")
```

Output:

```
num1: 9
num2: 2

Remainder is 1.0
```

The remainder when 9 is divided be 2 is indeed 1.

math.random()

math.random() returns a random number between 0 and 1. If we want to get a random between 0 and 10, we multiply by 10 and round the answer (using math.round()). Let's look at a few examples.

```
import random

n1 = random.random()
n2 = round(random.random() * 50)
n3 = round(random.random() * 50)
n4 = round(random.random() * 1000)

print(f"Random number between 0 and 1 {n1}")
print(f"1st random number between 0 and 50 {n2}")
print(f"2nd random number between 0 and 50 {n3}")
print(f"Random number between 0 and 1000 {n4}")
```

In the above example, n1 is a random number between 0 and 1. n2 and n3 are two different random numbers between 0 and 50. You should probably see that n2 and n3 are different because both numbers are randomized.

n4 returns a random number between 0 and 1000.

We can see the results in the output below. As the numbers are randomized, we should get a different result each time we run the program.

math.random() is a fun function and we are going to be using it in quite a few games this book.

Output:

```
Random number between 0 and 1 0.2054234851201563
1st random number between 0 and 50 3
2nd random number between 0 and 50 37
Random number between 0 and 1000 57
```

Exponent and Logarithms

Exponents in python are done using the pow(b, n) or b**n function and logarithm using math.log(n, base). So natural logarithm is done using
math.log(number, math.e). If we want logarithm to the base10 we use math.log(n, 10). math.e is Euler constant.

```
import math

n1 = 6 ** 2
n2 = 7 ** 3
n3 = pow(7, 3)
n4 = math.log(100, math.e)
n5 = math.log(100, 10)

print(f"6 raised to the power 2 = {n1}")
print(f"7 raised to the power 3 = {n2}")
print(f"7 raised to the power 3 = {n3}")
print(f"The natural logarithm of 100 is {n4}")
print(f"Logarithm base 10 of 100 is {n5}")
```

In the code above, we have three examples of exponents using both ** operator and pow(a, b) function. Basically, x is raised to the power of y in those cases. n1, n2 and n3 give exponents. N4 shows a natural logarithm of 100 and n4 shows logarithm to base 10 of 100.

Output:

```
6 raised to the power 2 = 36
7 raised to the power 3 = 343
7 raised to the power 3 = 343
The natural logarithm of 100 is 4.605170185988092
Logarithm base 10 of 100 is 2.0
```

Square root

math.sqrt() is used the find square root and math.abs() is used to find the absolute value of a number.

Note: You can also use operator ** to find square root by raising number to power 0.5.

Here's a few examples:

```
import math

n1 = 36 ** 0.5
n2 = 75 ** 0.5
n3 = math.sqrt(75)
n4 = abs(13)
n5 = abs(-14)

print(f"The square root of 36 = {n1}")
print(f"The square root of 75 = {n2}")
print(f"The square root of 75 = {n3}")
print(f"The absolute value of 13 = {n4}")
print(f"The absolute value of -14 = {n5}")

```

In the above code, n1, n2 and n3 are examples of the square root function; while n4 and n5 are examples of the absolute function.
If you haven't heard of the absolute value function, it basically returns a

positive value whether the number is +ve or -ve. So, 13 and -13 would both return an absolute value of 13.

Output:

```
The square root of 36 = 6.0
The square root of 75 = 8.660254037844387
The square root of 75 = 8.660254037844387
The absolute value of 13 = 13
The absolute value of -18 = 14
```

Trigonometry

Yes, Python can be used to do trigonometric functions as well. Here's a few of them. math.sin(x) returns the sine value of x radians. If we want to find the sine of x degrees, then we have to convert it to radians. So, we should change the function to math.sin(x*math.pi/180). Also, keep in mind that in python, we represent the value of π as math.pi We can also do cos and tan function using math.cos(x) and math.tan(x), where x is in radians. Let's look at an example program below:

```
import math

n1 = math.sin(5)
n2 = math.sin(5 * math.pi/180)
n3 = math.sin(90 * math.pi/180)
n4 = math.cos(10)
n5 = math.cos(10 * math.pi/180)
n6 = math.cos(0 * math.pi/180)
n7 = math.tan(30)
n8 = math.tan(30 * math.pi/180)
n9 = math.tan(45 * math.pi/180)

print(f"The sine of 5 radians = {n1}")
print(f"The sine of 5 degrees = {n2}")
print(f"The sine of 90 degrees = {n3}")
print(f"The cosine of 10 radians = {n4}")
print(f"The cosine of 10 degrees = {n5}")
print(f"The cosine of 0 degrees = {n6}")
print(f"The tan of 30 radians = {n7}")
print(f"The tan of 30 degrees = {n8}")
print(f"The tan of 45 degrees = {n9}")
```

In the above code, we show 3 examples of sine, cos and tan values. And we show the difference between calculating trigonometric values of degrees and radians. For example, for n1, we calculate the value of sin(5 radians) and in n2 we calculate the value of sin(5 degrees). In n2, we had to convert 5 degrees into radians by doing sin(5* π/180).

Output:

```
The sine of 5 radians = -0.9589242746631385
The sine of 5 degrees = 0.08715574274765817
The sine of 90 degrees = 1.0
The cosine of 10 radians = -0.8390715290764524
The cosine of 10 degrees = 0.984807753012208
The cosine of 0 degrees = 1.0
The tan of 30 radians = -6.405331196646276
The tan of 30 degrees = 0.5773502691896257
The tan of 45 degrees = 0.9999999999999999
```

Practice Problems

1. Write a program that calculate the salary of an employee. The program takes via input employee hourly rate and the total hours he worked in a month. Don't forget that input function outputs a string input and you need to parse the input to float. Use round function to round salary into 2 decimal numbers.
2. Write a calculator where you ask the user for 2 numbers and calculation operation symbol *, /,+,^,%,log, square root, trig functions. Note that

some of these operations require only one number so modify program behavior accordingly.

3. Create a program that calculates building height H given the distance D from building and the angle α to the tip of a building.

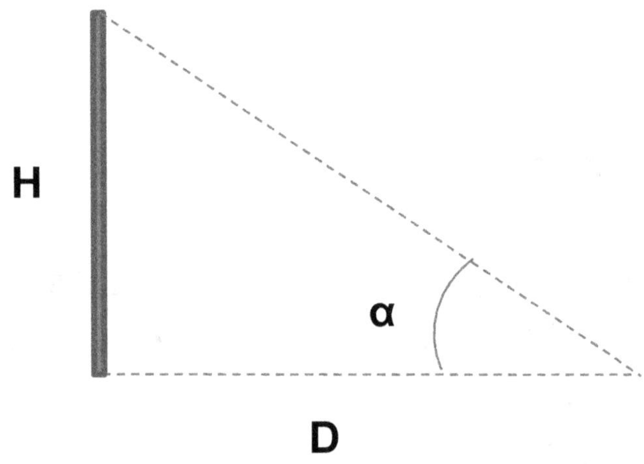

Conditionals and functions

Boolean values and expressions

Python has types int and float for numbers. Similarly, it has type bool for conditional values True and False. Bool is named after British mathematician George Boole who founded the mathematical discipline Boolean algebra, the basis of modern computer science.
Bool types are extremely important in Python because they are used to evaluate conditional statements. Conditional statements are statements that change behavior of program based on some condition.

```
print(type(True))
print(type(False))
print(type(true))
```

```
<class 'bool'>
<class 'bool'>

---------------------------------------------------------------------------
NameError                                 Traceback (most recent call last)
<ipython-input-34-5bfe175a5f35> in <module>
      1 print(type(True))
      2 print(type(False))
----> 3 print(type(true))

NameError: name 'true' is not defined
```

In this snippet, we print out type of True and False. Note that True is not the same as true as the code outputs an error when trying print the type of true instead of True. Boolean expressions are expressions evaluated to either True or False. We write Boolean expression using comparisons operators.

Comparisons operators

Comparison operators are used to compare value in python. Their output is always of type bool either True or False.

Operator	name	Description	Example	Returns
==	Equality	Returns True if numbers are equal else False.	5 == 9	False
!=	Not equal	Returns True if numbers are not equal else False.	5 != 9	True
>	Greater than	Returns True if n1 > n2 else False	10 > 1	True
>=	Greater than or equal	Returns True if n1 => n2 else False	10 >= 10	True
<	Less than	Returns True if n1 < n2 else False	5 < 10	False
<=	Less than or equal	Returns True if n1 =< n2 else False	1 <= 2	False

Logical operators

Python has three logical operators and, or and not. What each one does is similar to their intuitive meaning. The truth table below capture what they do exactly.

X	Y	not x	X or Y	X and Y
True	True	False	True	True
True	False	False	True	False
False	True	True	True	False
False	False	True	False	False

Example 1: Comparisons and logical operators

This snippet illustrates some examples using comparison and logical operators.

```
# comparison operators

x = 0
y = 10

# number comparisons
print("y == x is", y == x)
print("y >= x is", y >= x)
print("y < x is", y < x)
print("y <= x is", y <= x)

print()

# logical operators
print("(not True is)", not True)
print("(True and True) is", True and True)
print("(True and False) is", True and False)
print("(True or False) is", True or False)
print("(False or False) is", False or False)
```

```
y == x is False
y >= x is True
y < x is False
y <= x is False

(not True is) False
(True and True) is True
(True and False) is False
(True or False) is True
(False or False) is False
```

Conditional statements

If conditional

Conditional statement is what makes programs smart. A computer is able to make decisions that enable program to change its behavior according to some Boolean expression that evaluated to either True or False. if conditional in its simplest form is:

```
If expression:
      statement
```

Where it executes statement if expression evaluated to True only. Note that statements must be is indented below the if statement. The indented space is called block.

If else conditional

If else is very similar to if conditional except that we have else block that executes if expression is False.

```
If expression:
      statement1
else:
      statement2
```

Now we have 2 branches, first branch is statement 1 and second branch is statement 2. The program will execute the branch that correspond to logical expression evaluation. Think of branches as a road that forks into different roads.

if elif else conditional

What if want to have multiple branches instead of only two? if elif else conditional is also called chained conditionals. In chained conditional only one branch is executed. elif stand for else if. We can have any number of elif statements as the program logic needs.
First, if expression is evaluated, if it evaluates to false, then program proceed to evaluating

expresion2 belonging to first elif, the program keeps evaluating each expression until it evaluates to True and execute the corresponding statement/block. If all statements evaluate to False then it executes else block.

```
If expression:
      statement1
elif expression2:
      statement2
elif expression2:
      statement3
else:
      statement4
```

Nested Conditional

What if we want to create branches inside other branches? We can nest if conditional inside other if conditional. This is called nested conditional. Keep in mind that too many nested conditionals generally make the program difficult to read so use them only when you can't capture you program logic using combination of logical operators.

```
If expression:
      If expression1:
            statement1
      else:
            statement2
else:
      statement3
```

In this snippet, nested conditional was reduced into a flat if conditional using “and” logical operators. Observe that the second if conditional is easier to read.

```
x = -1
y = 5

# nested conditional
if x < 0 :
    if y < 10:
        print("nested conditional: x < 0 and y < 10")

print()
# Equivale version using and
if x < 0 and y < 10:
    print("and version conditional: x < 0 and y < 10")
```

```
nested conditional: x < 0 and y < 10

and version conditional: x < 0 and y < 10
```

Example 2: Conditionals:

In this program, we first check if x is a positive number using simple if conditional. Check if y is positive or negative number using if else conditional. Note that there is a corner case left unchecked when y is zero so we use if elif else to check if z is positive, negative or zero.

```
# simple if case
x = 5
y = -3
z = 0

# only check for positivity
if x > 0 :
    print("x is positive number !")

print()

# Check if number is positive or negative using if else
if y > 0 :
    print("y is positive number !")
else :
    print("y is positive number !")

print()

# Check if number is positive, negative or zero using if elif else
if z > 0 :
    print("z is positive number !")
elif z < 0 :
    print("z is positive number !")
else:
    print("z is zero !", z)
```

```
x is positive number !

y is positive number !

z is zero 0
```

Functions

A function is a block of reusable code that performs specific task when called. Think of them as a machine/black box which take inputs and transform them into outputs. This black box is run every time it's called. Functions help in breaking the code into simple easily maintainable reusable modules. In fact, you have been using function all the way through this book without noticing. For example, print() is a function that takes string input and display it on screen. Also, the string methods you learnt in the past chapter are function that operates on strings.

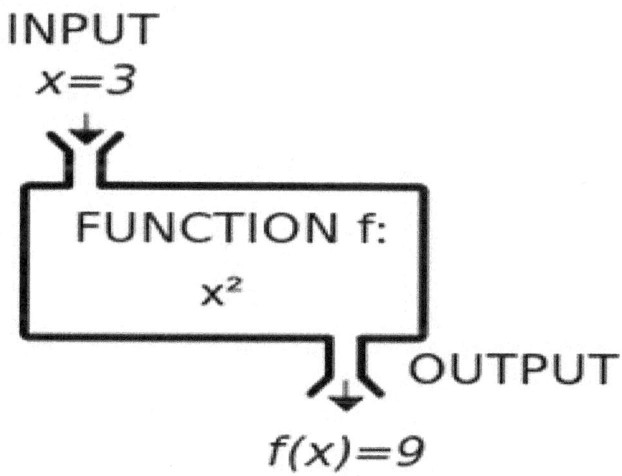

A black box representing square function

Functions definition

Functions are defined in python using def keyword.

```
def function_name(input_ parameters):
        statements
```

to call a function type the function name with inputs.

function_name(input_ parameters)

In the code below, we define a function that great a user by name. It takes one input a name and print hello to user name.

```
# function example
my_name = 'Jame'

# say hello to name
def hello(name):
    print("Hello !", name)

# function call
hello(my_name)
```

```
Hello ! Jame
```

return statement

In the previous script, we ran print function inside hello function, but what if we need to return just a value instead to the caller?

In this snippet, hello function returns a string. hello function is called first and the returned value is stored in the assigned variable.

```
# function example
my_name = 'Jame'

# return hello to name
def hello(name):
    return "Hello !" + name

# function call
retruned_name = hello(my_name)
print(retruned_name)
```

```
Hello !Jame
```

Empty return

When a function return statement is empty it terminates the function run and return None. In this example when func is called it only execute line 4 because it terminates when it reaches return statement at line 5. Also, note that it returns None value.

```
1  # None return
2
3  def func():
4      print("Before return nothing")
5      return
6      print("After return nothing")
7
8  m = func()
9  print()
10 print("func returned ", m)
```

```
before return nothing

func returned  None
```

Example 3: is divisible:

In this example, is_divisible function checks if a is divisible by b, if so, it prints a message and set div to true. If a is not divisible by b, else statement will handle this case where it prints message and set div to false.

```
# is divisible

# checks if a is divisible by b, print a massage
# return true if divisible else false

def is_divisible(a, b):

    div = None
    if a % b == 0 :
        print(f"{a} is divisible by {b}")
        div = True
    else:
        print(f"{a} is not divisible by {b}")
        div = False

    return div

n1 = is_divisible(8, 2)
n2 = is_divisible(8, 3)

print(n1)
print(n2)
```

```
8 is divisible by 2
8 is not divisible by 3
True
False
```

Practice Problems

1. Write a program that finds numbers divisible by 11 between 1 and 5000.

2. Write a function that test if a number is a prime number. Prime numbers are number divisible only by itself and 1.

3. Write a function that tests if number is odd.

Loops

Loops in coding are a sequence of instructions that are repeated a certain number of times. Think of a loop like repeating operation that keeps repeating until a condition is met. There are mainly 2 types of loops based on the conditions of execution. They are:

a. **FOR Loops:** FOR loops contain a sequence of instructions that are executed for a certain number of times. For example, a FOR loop from 1 to 10 executes the code inside the loop 10 times.
b. **WHILE Loops**: WHILE loops is a sequence of instructions that are executed till a certain condition is met.

Now, if we want to do a 1000 executions of execute function; we use a FOR loop. The FOR loop below starts at 0 and ends at 999, thus running execute function 1000 times.

```
for i in range(1000):
    Execute()
```

Finally, if we want to keep running execute() till 6 PM, we use a WHILE loop.

```
While (checktime!= 18:00):
    Execute();
```

These are simple examples of the loops to explain the concepts of loops. This concept is very important in coding.
Now, let's do some examples in python.

FOR LOOP Example 1

A simple example of a For Loop is a program that counts to 10.

```
for i in range(11):
    print(i)
```

The above code is probably the simplest example of a for loop. The loop runs from 0 to 10 so it runs 11 times each time printing i which is the loop iteration number.

Note: range(n) function makes the loop runs from 0 to n-1.

for i in range(11)

The line above means that the loop starts from 0 (i=0). It is increasing by 1 each time. The loop ends when i reaches 10.

Output:

```
0
1
2
3
4
5
6
7
8
9
10
```

You can see the numbers 0 to 10 printed on the screen.

FOR LOOP Example 2

Now, let’s do a slightly different version of this. In this example, we’re going to use an input that takes in a number for the loop. That means we can make the loop as long as we want.

```
loop_length = int(input("please enter the loop length: "))

for i in range(loop_length):
    print(i)
```

The input takes in a number input and stores in a variable called “loop_length”.
The loop prints all the numbers between 0 and “loop_length” variable. In the example below, we put 15 in input; and as we can see, it prints out numbers between 0 and 14. Note that loop stops right before n because python starts indexing at 0 and up to but not including “loop_length” .

```
Please enter the loop length: 15
0
1
2
3
4
5
6
7
8
9
10
11
12
13
14
```

FOR Loop Example 3 – Nested Loops

In this final example, we use FOR loops to create a star a half pyramid pattern. The program asks for a pyramid length and stores it in a variable called pyramid_height.

Then it runs 2 nested loops where the outer loop iterates for the pyramid 'levels' and the inner loop prints the stars at each level starting from zero. Each level contains j stars where j is the current level number.

So, for example, if you're going through the first loop for the 5th time, i=5. The second loop prints * from 0 to 4 (i.e. 5 times).

In the example, below, we print a half pyramid for a pyramid_height of 8.

```
pyramid_height = int(input("Please enter the pyramid height: "))


for i in range(pyramid_height):
    for j in range(i):
        print('*', end='')
    print()
```

```
Please enter the pyramid height: 8

*
**
***
****
*****
******
*******
```

WHILE LOOP EXAMPLE 1

A while loop runs while a certain condition is met. If the condition is no longer met, it breaks out of the loop. In the below example, the program executes a while loop that takes in a user input via the input function. The while loop keeps running and printing the user text. The loop stops when the user inputs the word ‘STOP’. Once the word is input, that’s the end of the while loops and the program stops.

```
text = ''

while(text != 'stop'):
    text = input("What do you want to do now ? ")
    print("Activity is :", text)
```

Output:

```
What do you want to do now ? Read
Activity is : Read
What do you want to do now ? play
Activity is : play
What do you want to do now ? study
Activity is : study
What do you want to do now ? stop
Activity is : stop
```

We can see while loop kept asking the user for an input until the user entered “stop”, the while loop condition was met and it ceased execution.

Practice Problems

1. Write a program that takes 2 inputs numbers a and b and return the remainder of a divided by b.

2. Write a program that outputs a number multiplication table up to 10.
For example, if 3 is entered it outputs:

3, 6, 9, 12, 15, 18, 21, 24, 27, 30

3. Write a program that find the length of given word using a for loop. Note: python already have len() function that return the length of a string, try to use both , a loop and len() .

4. Write a program that that counts the total number of digits in number. For example, “345abcd32” has 5 digits.

5. Write a program that keeps taking user input number until an even number is entered where it stops.

6. Write a program that takes two numbers a and b then it outputs all odd numbers between a and b inclusive.

7. Write a program that takes a user input pyramid height and outputs the following symmetrical pyramid pattern. For example, if the user inputs the number ‘5’ then the pattern is:

```
    *
   **
  ****
 ******
********
```

8. Write a program that sums all numbers from 1 up to n where n is a number that the user input. Note: First approach this problem using for loop then use the formula $1+2+\ldots+n = n(n+1)/2$.

Gaming Time - Loops

Now, it's time to design a few games based on what we've learned so far. There's no better way of learning concepts than applying them; and even better to apply them to something fun.

Game 1 – Guess Random Numbers

In this game, we're going to create a program that takes in a number via Input function. The number is between 0 and 10. Then we compare that number to a random number generated via random module (using random.randint). If it is the same, then the guessed number is correct. If not, then we give them the right number. See the code and output below.

```
1  import random
2  
3  print("You have only three tries to guesss number correctly")
4  
5  # generate random integer between 0 and 10
6  random_number = random.randint(0, 10)
7  
8  
9  won = False
10 for try_num in range(3):
11     print()
12     print(f"Try number {try_num+1}")
13     guessed_number = int(input("Guess a number between 0 and 10 inclusive: "))
14 
15     if(guessed_number == random_number):
16         won = True
17         print("Good job ! You won")
18         break
19     else:
20         print("Incorrect, try again !")
21 
22 if(won == False):
23     print()
24     print("You ran out of tries, Good luck next time")
25     print("The right number is ", random_number)
26 
```

random.randint(n, m) generates a random number between n and m inclusive this different from random. random() generates random real number anywhere in the range 0 and 1.

This is basically built around a for loop which runs 3 times giving the user 3 tries to guess the random number correctly. If the user guesses the random number correctly then, **if** block, at line 15 will set the **won** variable to **True** and break out of the loop. In python to break out of the loop we use “break”. The **if** block at line number 22 is used when the user has run out of his tries.

Output:

```
You have only three tries to guesss number correctly

Try number 1
Guess a number between 0 and 10 inclusive: 4
Incorrect, try again !

Try number 2
Guess a number between 0 and 10 inclusive: 4
Incorrect, try again !

Try number 3
Guess a number between 0 and 10 inclusive: 5
Incorrect, try again !

You ran out of tries, Good luck next time
The right number is  9
```

If the user wins here is a sample output:

```
You have only three tries to guesss number correctly

Try number 1
Guess a number between 0 and 10 inclusive: 5
Good job ! You won
```

This program is a good way to practice conditional loops and random number generators.

Game 2 – Math Quiz Game

This program prints out 5 simple math problems and takes in answers to these problems via input they are (user_ans1, user_ans2, user_ans3, user_ans4, user_ans5). The answers are stored in variables as (ans1, ans2, ans3, ans4, ans5). These answers are compared to the real answers using if conditional. A counter score is incremented by 1 each time the user gets a correct answer and finally the counter is printed to see how many correct answers the user gets.

```python
# Game 2 - Math Quiz Game

print("This is a game where you find basic mathmatical operations for 2 integer numbers n1 and n2 \n")
n1 = 8
n2 = 2

ans1 = n1 + n2
ans2 = n1 - n2
ans3 = n1 * n2
ans4 = n1 % n2

user_ans1 = int(input(f"{n1} + {n2} = "))
user_ans2 = int(input(f"{n1} - {n2} = "))
user_ans3 = int(input(f"{n1} * {n2} = "))
user_ans4 = int(input(f"{n1} % {n2} = "))
print()

score = 0

if ans1 == user_ans1:
    score += 1
if ans2 == user_ans2:
    score += 1
if ans3 == user_ans3:
    score += 1
if ans4 == user_ans4:
    score += 1

print(f'You have got {score} answers correct')
```

Output:

```
8 + 2 = [                              ]

This is a game where you find basic mathmatical operations for 2 integer numbers n1 and n2
```

The game keeps asking for input for the 4 questions here is the final output after all answers are entered.

```
This is a game where you find basic mathmatical operations for 2 integer numbers n1 and n2

8 + 2 = 10
8 - 2 = 6
8 * 2 = 16
8 % 2 = 0

You have got 4 answers correct
```

This is a great practice program. But you might be thinking that kids can use this program only once as we always use the same numbers. To fix this problem, we generate random numbers in the next game.

Game 3 – Math Quiz with Random Numbers

In this program below, there are 5 math questions generated by 10 random numbers. The 10 random numbers are variables **n1** through **n10**. The answers to the questions are calculated and are stored in variables **ans1** through **ans5**. These 15 variables are called global variables as they are outside any functions. This means that their values can be accessed anywhere in the program by any function. The function **print_ans()** uses the 5 variables **ans1** through **ans2** to write the quiz answers. These answers **(answer1-answer5)** are checked against user answers **(user_ans1-user_ans5)** using 5 different if conditionals in **check_ans** function. Each time there is a correct answer, a counter is incremented. Eventually, the counter is printed to show the number of correct answers. These questions are randomly generated which means that the user gets different questions each time.

Program

```
#Game 3 - Math Quiz with Random Numbers

import random

Max_int = 10

# Assign random integers between 1 and Max_int inclusive
n1 = random.randint(1, Max_int)
n2 = random.randint(1, Max_int)
n3 = random.randint(1, Max_int)
n4 = random.randint(1, Max_int)
n5 = random.randint(1, Max_int)
n6 = random.randint(1, Max_int)
n7 = random.randint(1, Max_int)
n8 = random.randint(1, Max_int)
n9 = random.randint(1, Max_int)
n10 = random.randint(1, Max_int)

ans1 = n1 + n2
ans2 = n3 - n4
ans3 = n5 * n6
ans4 = n7 * n8
ans5 = n9 % n10

user_ans1 = int(input(f"{n1} + {n2} = "))
user_ans2 = int(input(f"{n3} - {n4} = "))
user_ans3 = int(input(f"{n5} * {n6} = "))
user_ans4 = int(input(f"{n7} * {n8} = "))
user_ans5 = int(input(f"{n9} % {n10} = "))
print()
```

```
# check answers and find user score
def check_ans():
    score = 0
    if ans1 == user_ans1:
        score += 1
    if ans2 == user_ans2:
        score += 1
    if ans3 == user_ans3:
        score += 1
    if ans4 == user_ans4:
        score += 1
    if ans5 == user_ans5:
        score += 1
    return score

#print user answers
def print_ans():

    print("Answer 1 = ", ans1)
    print("Answer 2 = ", ans2)
    print("Answer 3 = ", ans3)
    print("Answer 4 = ", ans4)
    print("Answer 5 = ", ans5)


# find user score
score = check_ans()
print_ans()
print(f'\nYou have got {score} answers correct.')
```

Output:

```
7 + 6 = 13
7 - 10 = -3
2 * 1 = 2
6 * 2 = 12
2 % 7 = 0

Answer 1 =  13
Answer 2 =  -3
Answer 3 =  2
Answer 4 =  12
Answer 5 =  2

You have got 4 answers correct.
```

Practice Problems

1. Write a program that generates two random numbers between 0 and 10 inclusive. Then it outputs their sum, multiplication, remainder and exponentiation.

2. Write a random password generator, the program takes the password length n from user and it creates n digits long password.

3. Write a program that takes 3 side lengths of a triangle from user and then it finds out whether it is acute, right or obtuse angle triangle (Hint: Use Pythagoras theorem to check).

Lists, tuples and dictionaries

Introduction to data structure

Data structures are structures used to store and group data so they can easily access and manipulate data efficiently .Each type of data structure has its advantages and disadvantages .A specific data structure is selected based on what you want to optimize .There are different aspects to optimize, for example, access speed or storage size or data modification speed. Each of these aspects will require different types of data structure optimized for this aspect.

In this chapter, we will explore three fundamentals built in python data structures. Lists, tuples and dictionaries. These data structures are immensely useful. They make your program easier to write and more efficient and you didn't have to implement your own data structures from scratch. Note that these data structures are also called containers since they hold/contain other objects.

Lists

Lists are sequences that store collections of items. List is one of the containers most commonly used due to its versatility. Lists can hold different types of data. They are heterogeneous meaning they don't have to store similar data types. Lists are mutable so you cany modify a list after its creation.
To create a list, put comma separated value in square brackets.

```
my_list = []    or
my_list = list( )
```

The code below creates lists of numbers, strings and a heterogenous list of both numbers and strings.

```
# create list either by square brackets or list()
my_list = []
my_list = list()


# Define list l1, l2, l3
# list1 sequnce of numbers
list1 = [1, 2, 3]

# list2 sequence of strings
list2 = ["Nick", "Tom", "Jane"]

# list3 sequence of numbers and strings
list3 = ["Nick", 10, "Python", 50]

# list4 a list containg other lists
list4 = [l1, l2, l3]

print("list1 is:", l1)
print("list2 is:", l2)
print("list3 is:", l3)
print("list4 is:", l4)
```

```
list1 is: [1, 2, 3]
list2 is: ['Nick', 'Tom', 'Jane']
list3 is: ['a', 1, 'Python', 5]
list4 is: [[1, 2, 3], ['Nick', 'Tom', 'Jane'], ['a', 1, 'Python', 5]]
```

List ***methods***

Similar to the string methods discussed in earlier chapters. Lists comes with useful methods to use. We will study frequently used list methods here, to find out and learn more methods follow this python documentation link. https://docs.python.org/3/tutorial/datastructures.html

Basic list operations

This table summaries basic list operations.

Expression	Name	Output
len(['a', 'b', '1'])	Length	3
['a', 'b', 'c'] + ['d', 'e', 'f']	List concatenation	['a', 'b', 'c', 'd', 'e', 'f']
['hi'] * 4	Repetition	['Hi!', 'Hi!', 'Hi!', 'Hi!']
'a' in ['a', 'b', 'c']	Membership	True
for num in [1, 2, 3]: print(num)	List iteration	1 2 3
n = ['a', 'b', 'c'] n[0] = 'z' print(n)	List element assignment	['z', 'b', 'c']

list[index] – Indexing operator, selects a single value from a list. The number inside the brackets is called index, it is an integer value. Indexing in python starts at zero. Similar to strings you can also have negative index where it starts indexing backward.

list1 = ['Python', 'C++', 'C', 'Java Script']
list1[0] value is 'Python'
list1[2] value is 'C'
list1[-1] value is 'Java Script'
list1[-2] value is 'C'

list[starting_index: ending_index] - slicing operator, slices the list at starting index and ends at one element before ending index.

list1 = ['Python', 'C++', 'C', 'Java Script']

list1[0:2] = ['Python', 'C++']
list1[0:-1] = ['Python', 'C++', 'C']

list.append(elem) – *Append element to list.*

list1 = [1, 2, 3]

list1.append(4)

list1 value is *[1, 2, 3, 4]*

list.clear() – Clears list values .

list1 = [1,2,3]

list1.clear()

list1 value is *[]*

list.count(elem) – Count how many times element elem is on list .

list1 = [1,2,2,2,3,4]

list1.count(2) outputs 3

list.extend(list2) – Adds list2 elements to list .This method performs same job as lists concatenation using '+' operator .

list1 = [1, 2, 3]

list2 = [4, 5]

list1.extend(list2)

list1 is [1,2,3,4,5]

list.insert(elem_index , elem) – Insert element elem into list at index elem_index.

list1 = [1, 2, 3]

list1.insert(3, 4))

list1 is *[1,2,3,4]*

list.pop() – Removes list last element.

list1 = [1, 2, 3, 4]

list1.pop() removes 4

list1 is *[1,2,3]*

list.index(elem) **–** Returns index of first occurrence of elem.

list1 = [1, 2 , 3, 4]

list1.index(2) returns 3

Example 1: List basic operation

Here we have a comprehensive example to various list methods discussed above. Experiment with the code to understand it.

```
# List basic operations


# List iteration and indexing
even_nums = [0, 2, 4, 6, 8, 10]

# Length of even_nums List
print("Length of even_nums list is:", len(even_nums))
print('\n')

print("Even numbers are:")
for number in even_nums:
    print(number)

# print 2 new lines, new line symbol is \n
print('\n')

# Slicing
# print even number list less than 5
even_nums_less_5 = even_nums[0:3]
print("Even numbers less than 5 are: ", even_nums_less_5)
print('\n')

# Append additional even number
even_nums.append(12)
print("Even number list after appending is: ", even_nums)
print('\n')

# count how many times 12 is in List
count = even_nums.count(12)
print(f"12 occurs {count} times in even_nums list")
print('\n')
```

```
print('\n')


# clear list values
even_nums.clear()
print("Even number list after clearing is: ", even_nums)
print('\n')

# extend the empty list
even_nums.extend(['Tom', 1, 'python'])
print("Even number list after extending is: ", even_nums)
print('\n')

# insert new element at index 0
even_nums.insert(0, 'new')
print("Even number list after inserting at index 0 is: ", even_nums)
print('\n')

# pop list last element
even_nums.pop()
print("Even number list after popping is: ", even_nums)
print('\n')


# find the index of 'Tom' and change it to Nick
index_python = even_nums.index('Tom')
even_nums[index_python] = 'Nick'

print("Even number after replacing Tom is: ", even_nums)
```

Output:

```
Length of even_nums list is: 6

Even numbers are:
0
2
4
6
8
10

Even numbers less than 5 are:  [0, 2, 4]

Even number list after appending is:  [0, 2, 4, 6, 8, 10, 12]

12 occurs 1 times in even_nums list

Even number list after clearing is:  []

Even number list after extending is:  ['Tom', 1, 'python']

Even number list after inserting at index 0 is:  ['new', 'Tom', 1, 'python']

Even number list after popping is:  ['new', 'Tom', 1]

Even number after replacing Tom is:  ['new', 'Nick', 1]
```

Tuples

Tuples are similar to lists as they also store collection of items. In facts tuple can be considered immutable lists. Tuples are immutable, once assigned, they can’t change. This makes them more efficient and faster.

Tuples are defined using parentheses whereas lists are defines using square brackets.

To create a tuple, put comma separated value in parentheses.

my_tuple = (1,3,5)

For a single value tuple follow the value with a comma. Without a comma python considers it a number.

my_tuple = (1,)

In this snippet we create tuples and try to modify its value, however python throws type error because tuples are immutable.

```
# create a tuple

# single value tuple
tu1 = (1, )

print("Single value tuple: ", tu)
# Multi values tuple
tu2 = (1, 'a', 'python')
print("Multi value tuple: ", tu)
print("tuple type is ", type(tu2))

# try modifying tuple
tu[2] = 'C++'
```

```
Single value tuple:  (1, 'a', 'python')
Multi value tuple:  (1, 'a', 'python')
tuple type is  <class 'tuple'>

---------------------------------------------------------------------------
TypeError                                 Traceback (most recent call last)
<ipython-input-7-a5d65c274c9b> in <module>
     11
     12 # try modifying tuple
---> 13 tu[2] = 'C++'

TypeError: 'tuple' object does not support item assignment
```

Tuples methods

Similar to lists, tuples support basic methods like indexing, len, slicing and in membership operator. Tuple also support index and count method. Note that tuples don't have many methods as lists because they are immutable.

Example 2: *Tuple* methods

In this example, we perform basic methods on a tuple. Note that these methods are the same as in list methods.

```
# Basic tuple methods
tu = ('Tom', 'Jane', 'Python', 10, 'Tom')

# len()
print("Tuple length is :", len(tu))

# Element access
print("Last element of tuple is :",tu[-1])

# slicing
print("tu[0:3] is :",tu[0:3])

# index method
print("'Python' is at index:",tu.index('Python'))

# count method
print("'Tom' occurs:",tu.count('Tom'))
```

```
Tuple length is : 5
Last element of tuple is : Tom
tu[0:3] is : ('Tom', 'Jane', 'Python')
'Python' is at index: 2
'Tom' occurs: 2
```

Dictionaries

Dictionaries are key value pairs. While lists and tuples are accessed by a position index, dictionary values are accessed by their corresponding key. The keys must be immutable such as strings, numbers or even tuples but not a list as lists are mutable. Keys are also unique you can't have 2 values with the same key. Dictionaries are defined by comma separate Key: Value pairs in curly brackets.

To create empty dictionary:

```
my_dict = {}
```

or

```
my_list = dict()
```

To create a basic dictionary:

```
num_dict = {'one':1, 'two':2, 'three':3}
```

Basic dictionary methods

To access a dictionary value, use its key.

```
num_dict = {'one':1, 'two':2, 'three':3}
num_dict['one'] is 1
```

Membership is similar to tuple and lists except that it checks for key.

num_dict = {'one':1, 'two':2, 'three':3}

'one' in num_dict **returns** True

To add new key value pair use assignment operator.

num_dict = {'one':1, 'two':2, 'three':3}

num_dict['four'] = 4

num_dict **now is** {'one':1, 'two':2, 'three':3, 'four':4}

dict.clear – **clears the dictionary .**

num_dict = {'one':1, 'two':2, 'three':3}

num_dict.clear()

num_dict **now is {}**

dict.get(key) – **retrieve a dictionary value by a key and returns None if no such key exists.**

num_dict = {'one':1, 'two':2, 'three':3}

num_dict.get('one') **returns** 1

dict.pop(key) – **removes key:value pair corresponding to key.**

num_dict = {'one':1, 'two':2, 'three':3}

num_dict.pop('three') **removes** 3

num_dict now is {'one':1, 'two':2}

dict.items() – return a list of (key, value) tuples.

num_dict = {'one':1, 'two':2, 'three':3}

num_dict.items() returns [('one', 1), ('two', 2), ('three', 3)]

dict.keys() – returns dict_key object containing all dictionary keys.

num_dict = {'one':1, 'two':2, 'three':3}

num_dict.items() returns dict_key(['one', 'two', 'three'])

dict.values() – returns a list of dictionary values.

num_dict = {'one':1, 'two':2, 'three':3}

num_dict.values() returns [1, 2, 3]

Example *3*: *Dictionary* methods

In example 3, We use and experiment with the dictionary method we learnt.

```
# create a dictionary of shopping items quantity

shopcart = {'chips':2, 'ink cartridge':1, 'paper':1}

# dictionary length counts key:value pairs
print('Shopcart is:', shopcart)
print('Your shopcart distinct items are ', len(shopcart))
print('\n')


# shope cart include a pens ?
pens_in = 'pens' in shopcart

# membership test
print("There is a pen in shopping car:", pens_in)
print('\n')

# accessing a value
print("The number of chips items is", shopcart['chips'])
print('\n')

# add a pair
shopcart['orange juice'] = 4
print(shopcart)
print('\n')


# get method
print("Quanattiy of orange juice is", shopcart.get('orange juice'))
print('\n')

# pop method removes element at a key
shopcart.pop('paper')
print(shopcart)
print('\n')

# get items, keys, values
items = shopcart.items()
keys = shopcart.keys()
values = shopcart.values()

print("Shopcart items are:", items)
print("Shopcart keys are:", keys)
print("Shopcart values are:", values)
```

```
Shopcart is: {'chips': 2, 'ink cartridge': 1, 'paper': 1}
Your shopcart distinct items are  3


There is a pen in shopping car False


The number of chips items is 2


{'chips': 2, 'ink cartridge': 1, 'paper': 1, 'orange juice': 4}


Quanattiy of orange juice is 4


{'chips': 2, 'ink cartridge': 1, 'orange juice': 4}


Shopcart items are: dict_items([('chips', 2), ('ink cartridge', 1), ('orange juice', 4)])
Shopcart keys are: dict_keys(['chips', 'ink cartridge', 'orange juice'])
Shopcart values are: dict_values([2, 1, 4])
```

Example 4 – Guess World Capitals

In this example we use both list and dictionary. A dictionary capital_dict is used to make country:capital key pairs. Then we get the dictionary keys using keys() method and store them in countries list. This is essential so we can use random.choice() function which takes a list and return a value from list randomly. Then inside an infinite while loop, user is asked for a capital using input function and the answer is compared to actual capitals.

```
# World capital game
import random

# World capitals dictionary
capital_dic={
    'spain':'madrid',
    'france':'paris',
    'germany':'berlin',
    'norway':'oslo',
    'india':'new delhi',
    'egypt':'cairo'
}

# get countries and convert it to list so we can use random function
countries = list(capital_dic.keys())
print ('Let\'s learn World Capitals. Enter quit to quit the game.')


while True:
    # pick a random country
    country = random.choice(countries)
    capital = capital_dic[country]

    guess = input(f'what is the capital of {country}.')
    # if user type quit, quit
    if guess.lower() == 'quit':
        break
    elif guess.lower() == capital:
        print(f'Correct !')
        break
    else:
        print(f'Incorrect. The capital of {country} is {capital}.')

```

Output:

```
what is the capital of india.

Let's learn World Capitals. Enter quit to quit the game.
```

Wrong answer is entered.

```
Let's learn World Capitals. Enter quit to quit the game.
what is the capital of india.cairo
Incorrect. The capital of india is new delhi.

what is the capital of norway.
```

Correct answer is entered.

```
Let's learn World Capitals. Enter quit to quit the game.
what is the capital of india.cairo
Incorrect. The capital of india is new delhi.
what is the capital of norway.oslo
Correct !
```

In above code, Cairo is entered as the capital of India. As the answer is incorrect, the program outputs 'Incorrect. The capital of india is new delhi'.

In the second part of the program, 'oslo' is entered as the correct capital of Norway, and the program outputs 'correct!'

Example 5 – Random quotes

This example generates random quote from a tuple of quotes using random.choice() function. While a list would also work, a tuple is used because we never intend to manipulate quotes, they remain immutable throughout the program. For large immutable object, tuple is more efficient and also secures since it guarantees that object can never change without having error. Preventing accidental manipulation.

```
# Random quote
import random

# since we dont intend to do any operation on quotes we use tuple instead of lists
quotes = (
    "Yesterday's the past, tomorrow's the future, but today is a gift.",
    "The best preparation for tomorrow is doing your best today.",
    "Change your life today.",
    "If you fell down yesterday, stand up today.",
    "Never give up. ",
    "Dream as if you'll live forever.",
    "The science of today is the technology of tomorrow.",
    "Did I offer peace today?",
)

rand_quotes = random.choice(quotes)
print("Todays quote is:", rand_quotes)

```

```
Todays quote is: Change your life today.
```

Example 6 – Guess a country name

In this example, we make a game similar to hangman where we ask the user to guess the name of the country. We have a tuple of various country names. The user is allowed to have guess a few times incorrectly before losing. We make a list of correctly guessed characters where correct guesses are appended to. The user wins when the guessed list length is equal to country name length.
Note that we used a list data structure for guessed characters since it is continuously updated while countries are in tuple since it is never mutated.

```
# guess a random country

import random

# List of countries
countries = ('france', 'usa', 'spain', 'india', 'brazil', 'norway', 'germany')

# Choose random country from countries
country = random.choice(countries)

# number of turns
turns = 4

# a list to store the guessed characters
guessed = []
while turns > 0:

    # print guessed characters
    for char in country:
        if char in guessed:
            print(char, end='')
        else:
            print('-', end='')

    print()
    print(f"You have {turns} left.")

    # user input
    guess = input("guess a character:")

    # make sure guess is lowercase
    guess.lower()
```

```

    # if guess already made
    if guess in guessed :
        print("You have already made this guess\n")

    # check input with the character in word
    if guess not in country:
        turns -= 1
    else:
        # character is in word , append character
        # the number of times it appear in word
        count = country.count(guess)
        for i in range(count):
            guessed.append(guess)

    # if guessed length match country length then user wins
    # else if ran out of turns user loses
    if len(guessed) == len(country):
        print("Congratulation you guessed correctly!!")
        break
    elif turns == 0 :
        print("Good luck next time")
```

Output:

```
Guess the characters
------
You have 4 left.
guess a character:n
n-----
You have 4 left.
guess a character:o
no----
You have 4 left.
guess a character:r
nor---
You have 4 left.
guess a character:w
norw--
You have 4 left.
guess a character:a
norwa-
You have 4 left.
guess a character:f
norwa-
You have 3 left.
guess a character:y
Congratulation you guessed correctly!!
```

Practice Problems

1. Write a program to append all dictionary values to a list.
2. Write a program to check if a given key exist in a dictionary.
3. Write a program to find highest numerical value in a dictionary.
4. Write a program that takes 2 equally sized lists and convert them into a dictionary where list 1 contains the keys and list 2 contains the values.
5. Create a program that picks and prints a random joke from list or tuple of jokes .

Objects

Objects

An object is a collection of instances of data structures that belong to a class. These instances can have different data types. Think of a class as a factory that produce objects.

Example 1: Object Shape

In this example. We create a class shape, the class assigns name, color, size and position to object. Then we create object my_shape by calling the class at line 8.
At line 9 through 12, we access object values by using dot '.' notation. For example, my_shape.name is circle.

Then we change object values by reassigning them to different values.

```
# create class
class shape:
    name = 'circle'
    color = 'red'
    size = 5
    position = (0,0)

my_shape = shape()
print("name is: ", my_shape.name)
print("color is: ", my_shape.color)
print("size is: ", my_shape.size)
print("position is: ", my_shape.position)

my_shape.name = 'triangle'
my_shape.color = 'black'
my_shape.size = 10
my_shape.position = (10, 10)

print()
print("my_shape values after reassignment are:")
print()

print("name is: ", my_shape.name)
print("color is: ", my_shape.color)
print("size is: ", my_shape.size)
print("position is: ", my_shape.position)
```

```
name is:  circle
color is:  red
size is:  5
position is:  (0, 0)

my_shape values after reassignment are:

name is:  triangle
color is:  black
size is:  10
position is:  (10, 10)
```

Example 2: Dice Game

This is a game of dice between 2 players where dice is flipped 1000 times. If dice flip result in an even number player 1 wins one point, if it is odd player 2 wins 1 point. The dice flip is implemented using random number function

```
# dice game if it is even player 1 point
# odd player 2 gets 1 point
# import random library
import random

# create class player with score intialize to zero
class player:
    score = 0

# if number is even return True ese return False
def is_even(n):
    even = None
    if n % 2 == 0:
        even = True
    else:
        even = False

    return even

# create players
player1 = player()
player2 = player()


# run loop for 1000 times
for i in range(1000):
    # dice flip , return random number between 1 and 6 inclusive
    dice = random.randint(1, 6)

    if is_even(dice):
        player1.score += 1
    else:
        player2.score += 1

print("Player 1 score is: ", player1.score)
print("Player 2 score is: ", player2.score)
```

randint which generate numbers between 1 and 6 inclusive.

Class player creates player objects with score initialized to zero. Each time one player wins we access player.score and increment it by one.

```
Player 1 score is:  518
Player 2 score is:  482
```

We can see that players score are close, which is expected since each player win probability is

50% as the ration of odd:even of dice output is 1:1.

Practice Problems

1. Write a program that creates an object of vehicle. The vehicle properties are name, model, color, country of origin and owner.
2. Write a program that simulates a school course. Each course is an object and has variables for name, number of enrolling students, lecturer, hall, department. Create 5 arbitrary courses.

Drawing shapes using pygame

Introduction to pygame

Learning coding is interesting but it's even more interesting and engaging when you're actually making games. While coding a game, you will find yourself applying all the ideas you learnt in this book like loops, conditionals, variables, functions, lists, objects and even more.
For coding games, we will use python library **Pygame**. Pygame is a python library for making games. It was created by Pete Shiners and it enjoys a wide community support.

Installation

To install pygame library on your system follow these steps.

If you are using anaconda <u>Jupyter lab on desktop</u>

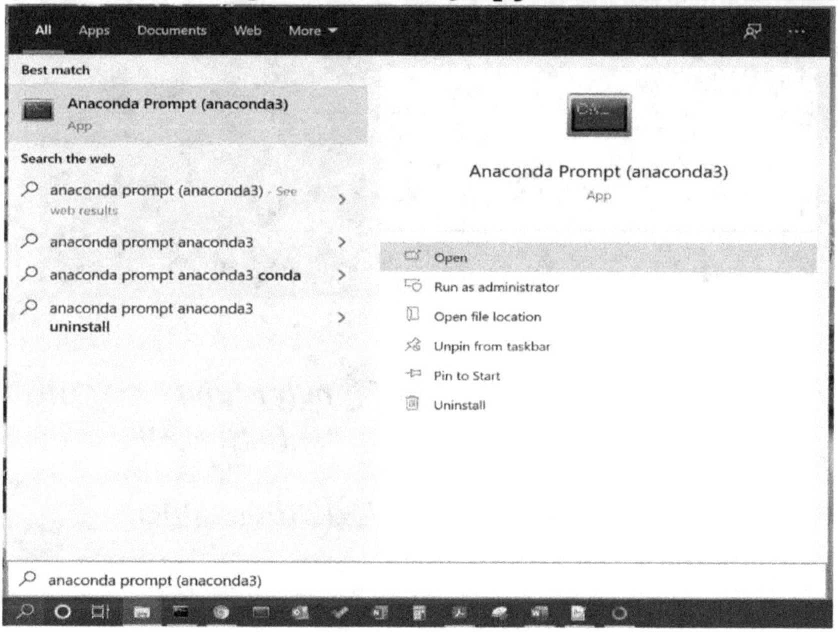

Locate "anaconda Prompt (anaconda3)" on your system.

Click on "anaconda Prompt (anaconda3)" to open it .

In the command prompt type "**pip install pygame**" and press Enter.If installed successful , it should display "**Successfully installed pygame**" massage .

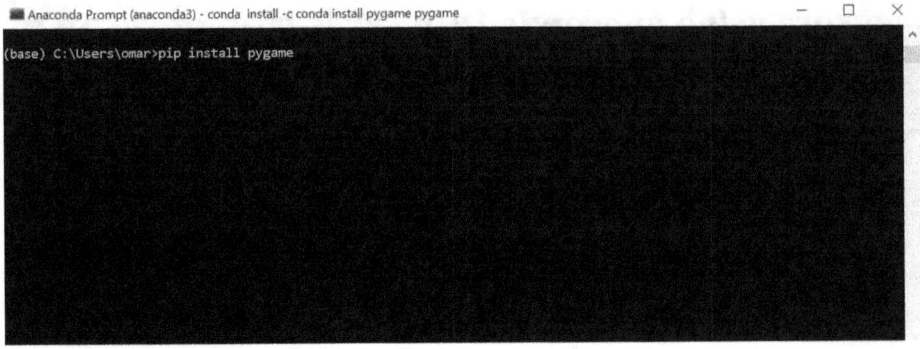

*If you are using the <u>online version of jupyter lab</u> , type "**pip install pygame**" inside the cell and execute the cell*

If you are using <u>notepad++ along with Python</u> , open command prompt

To run your program locate command Prompt on your system and open it.

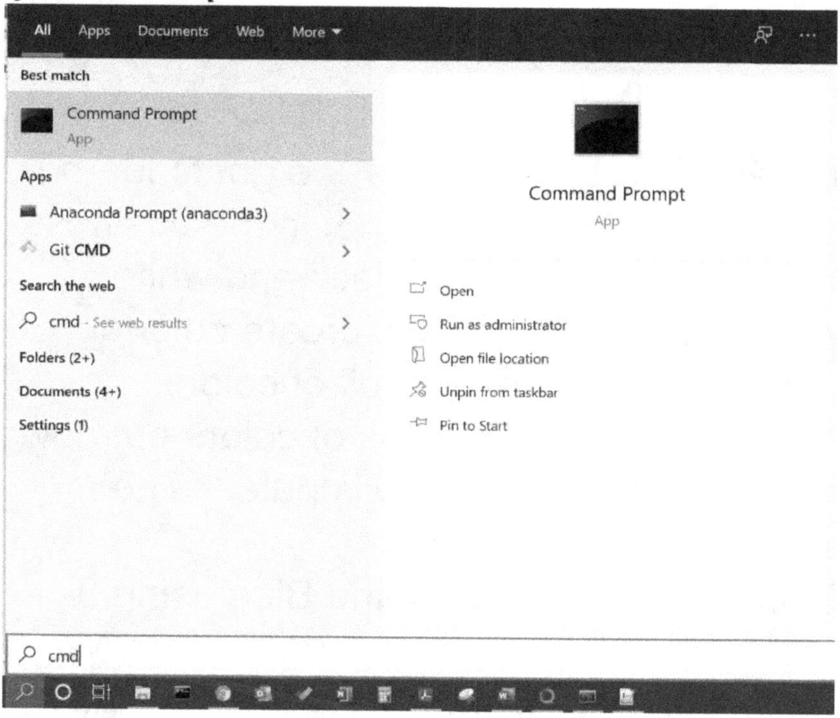

Type "**pip install pygame**" and Enter .

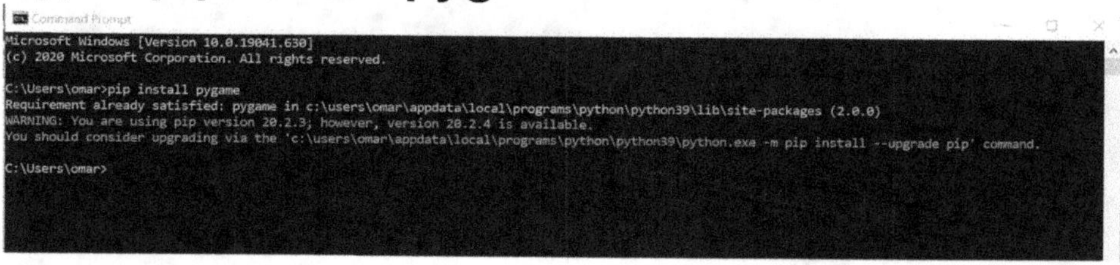

Now you are ready to start coding games !, let's start .

Colors basics – RGB color model

Before starting to code games, we got to learn about colors. After all we are not in the business of creating boring games in black and white shades! We should be able to create colorful interesting games full of life, full of colors.
There are millions and millions of colors but how can we determine color in a computer? The answer is RGB color model.
RGB stands for Red, Green and Blue using 3 corresponding numbers one for each color. We can create any color we want. Each color has a number ranging from 0 to 255 where 0 is null intensity and 255 is the maximum intensity of color. Here are some typical color values

(R, G, B)	Color name
(255, 255, 255)	White
(255, 0, 0)	Red
(0, 255, 0)	Green
(0, 0, 255)	Blue
(0, 0, 0)	Black

To further experiment with RGB, you can find free RGB calculator here https://www.w3schools.com/colors/colors_rgb.asp

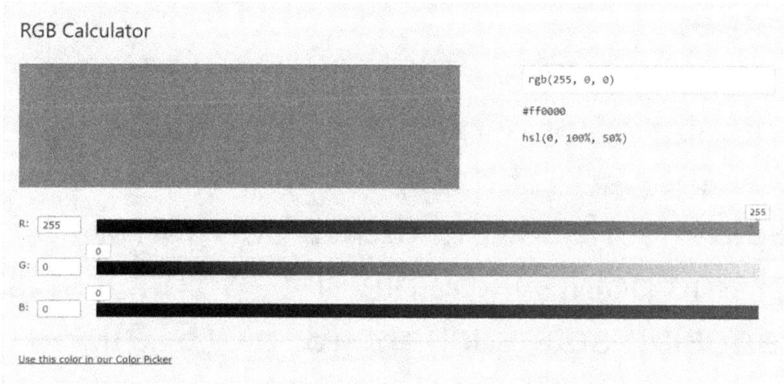

Source: RGB calculator in w3schools

Basic shape creation methods

Let's start learning basic methods to create shapes.

`pygame.init()` – Initialize pygame and give permissions. This line is essential to start pygame session.

`pygame.display.set_mode((X, Y))` – Creates a display window surface with dimension (x,y) where x is width and y is height .This acts as our background.

`pygame.display.set_caption('name')` – Sets display caption name.

`display_surface.fill(color)` – Fills display surface with a particular color. Color is a RGB tuple .

`pygame.draw.polygon(surface, color, points_list)` – Takes display_surface and draws polygon with color color and points in points_list . points_list is a list of cartesian sets such as [(3, 5), (5, 9)].

`pygame.draw.line(surface, color, start_point, end_point, thickness)` – Draws a line with color col , with starting point start_point and ending point end_point with optional thickness thickness.

pygame.draw.circle(surface, color, center, radius, thickness) -Draws a circle with color color , center center , radius radius and thickness thickness.

pygame.draw.ellipse(surface, color, bounding_rectangle, thickness) – Draws an ellipse bounded and centered by rectangle bounding_rectangle with optional thickness thickness. bounding__rectangle is given by (x, y, width , height) where x and y are upper left corner coordinate, width is rectangle width and height is rectangle height.

pygame.draw.rect(surface, col, (x, y, width, height), thickness) –
Draws a rectangle with color col and coordinates in rectangle_tuple and thickness thickness. (x, y, width, height) is same as bounding_rectangle discussed above.

To read and learn more methods use pygame documentation, Coders read much more than they write. They read others' codes,

documentations and manuals. This is a good practice in reading documentation.
https://www.pygame.org/docs/ref/draw.html

pygame coordinate system

pygame default coordinate system origin is centered at upper left (0,0) corner where positive x points rightward and negative y point downward.

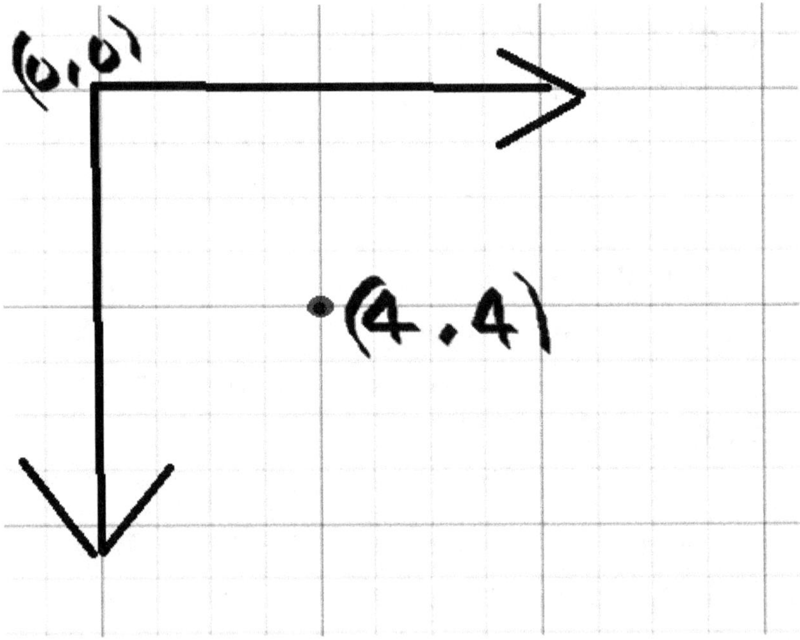

Example 1 Implementing basic drawing methods

In this example we implement the basic pygame drawing methods we discussed in this chapter. We create a circle, ellipse, polygon, square and lines. Each shape is created with its own color, position and size. Try to read and understand this program. It is well commented to facilitate easy reading.

```
# import pygame module
import pygame

# activate a pygame library inst .
pygame.init()

# define the RGB value some colors
white = (255, 255, 255)
black = (0, 0, 0)
yellow = (255, 255, 0)
red = (255, 0, 0)
green = (0, 255, 0)
random_color = (120, 30, 50)


# assigning width 600 , height 600 to background
dimensions = (600, 600)

# create the display surface object
# of specific dimension..e(X,Y).
display = pygame.display.set_mode(dimensions)

#pygame window name
pygame.display.set_caption('Basic shapes')

# Fill display surface with white
# with white colour
display.fill(white)

# draw a polygon using draw.polygon()
# pygame.draw.polygon(surface, color,  points_list)
pygame.draw.polygon(display, yellow,
                    [(446, 300), (591, 406),
                    (536, 577), (356, 577), (300, 406)])

# draw horizontal line
# pygame.draw.line(surface, color, start_point, end_point, thickness)
```

```
38 pygame.draw.line(display, random_color,
39                  (0, 300), (600, 300), 4)
40
41 # draw vertical line
42 pygame.draw.line(display, random_color,
43                  (300, 0), (300, 600), 4)
44
45 # draw a circle
46 # pygame.draw.circle(surface, color, center_point, radius, thickness)
47 pygame.draw.circle(display, red, (150, 150), 50, 0)
48
49 # draw a ellipse pygame.draw.ellipse(surface, color, bounding_rectangle, thickness)
50 pygame.draw.ellipse(display, green, (400, 100, 100, 150), 0)
51
52 # draw a rectangle
53 # pygame.draw.rect(surface, col, (x,y,width,height), thickness)
54 pygame.draw.rect(display, black, (100, 400, 100, 100))
55
56 # infinite loop to keep session on
57 while True :
58
59     # iterate over the list of Event objects
60     # that was returned by pygame.event.get() method.
61     for event in pygame.event.get() :
62
63         # if event object type is QUIT when corner exist button is clicked
64         # then quitting pygame and program
65         if event.type == pygame.QUIT :
66
67             # kill pygame session
68             pygame.quit()
69             # quit the program.
70             quit()
71
72         # Draws the objects screen.
73         pygame.display.update()
```

Infinite loop (game loop)

Why do we have infinite loop at line 57? Pygame library is used to create video games. Video is nothing but a continuous stream of pictures viewed in a short amount of time so human eyes can't detect the difference. The loop will keep updating the screen with any newly drawn shapes on it and keeps the session on. Without this infinite loop, Pygame will display the shapes momentarily and cease running. This infinite loop is called the game loop since it is the loop that contains the main logic of a game and is also responsible for updating the screen with any new status.

Output:

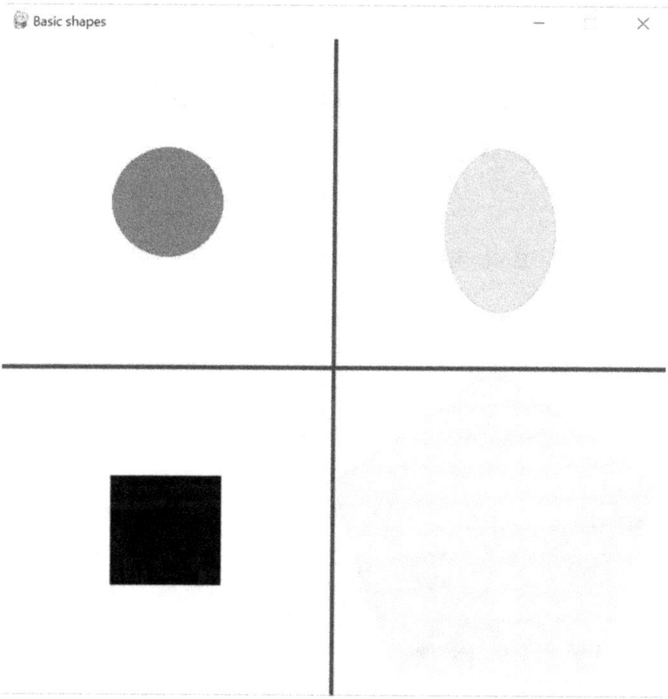

Output is a white background divided into four quadrants. Where a basic shape lives on each quadrant.

Example 2 Frowny face

In this script we create an angry frowny face. This program is very similar to the last example. Except that we draw different shapes. Frowny face basically consists of a 1 circle for face, 2 circles for eyes and an arc for mouth. To understand arc method, read **pygame** documentation. Try to understand how arc gets oriented, you will need it in the practice problems.

```
# import pygame module
import pygame
import math

# activate a pygame library inst .
pygame.init()

# define the RGB value some colors
white = (255, 255, 255)
yellow = (255, 255, 0)
red = (255, 0, 0)

# assigning width 600 , height 600 to background
dimensions = (300, 300)

# create the display surface object
display = pygame.display.set_mode(dimensions)

#pygame window name
pygame.display.set_caption("Frowny face !")

# Display color is white
display.fill(white)

# Draw face
pygame.draw.circle(display, yellow, (150, 150), 50, 0)

# Draw left eye
pygame.draw.circle(display, red, (130, 140), 10, 0)

# Draw right eye
pygame.draw.circle(display, red, (170, 140), 10, 0)

```

```
# Draw right eye
pygame.draw.circle(display, red, (170, 140), 10, 0)

# Draw mouth using arc
# arc(surface, color, bounding_rect, start_angle, stop_angle, width=1)
pygame.draw.arc(display, red, (135, 175,30,25), 0, math.pi, width=1)

# infinite loop to keep session on
while True :
    # iterate over the list of Event objects
    # that was returned by pygame.event.get() method.
    for event in pygame.event.get() :

        # if event object type is QUIT when corner exist button is clicked
        # then quitting pygame and program
        if event.type == pygame.QUIT :

            # kill pygame session
            pygame.quit()
            # quit the program.
            quit()

        # Draws the objects screen.
        pygame.display.update()
```

Output:

Practice Problems

1. Use frowny face program discussed earlier and turn it into smiley face instead.

2. Create a display of 800 by 800 and create 4 sides connected red boarders and a circle centered at center where it is circumscribed by the boarders.

3. Pick 4 of your favorite emojis and try to draw them using pygame.

4. Create a shape similar to Football pitch picture below.

Animations in Pygame

Animations are images manipulated to appear as moving pictures. To make an animation we create many continues pictures/shapes and view them continuously. The number of times we update the screen is called Frames per second (fps); fps is the number of frames/pictures showed in second. Greater fps numbers make the transitions in videos/games smoother thus increasing the quality. The game loop discussed in earlier chapter is responsible for updating the state of game at fps frame per second. This is how games are made, updating the screen continuously with pictures at a rate human eyes can't distinguish that pictures are in fact discrete. The figure below shows multiple frames of a running horse. Grouping these frames will result in a running horse video.

The famous horse in motion

Growing square

We make a square that grows in size until it fills the entire lower right screen quadrant. The logic is very similar to how we made various shapes in the previous example except for 2 main differences.

We make pygame clock instance `clock=pygame.time.Clock()` , this is a pygame method to keep track of time .We use it in the program to control how many frames per seconds (fps) we want using `clock.tick(fps)`.

Faster fps updates the shape more frequently which makes the square grows faster.
The second difference is that square side is not fixed anymore. Every loop iteration the square side is increased using line `side = 1.01 * side`, the screen is cleared (filled with white color) using `screen.fill(white)` and a new square with the new side size is drawn . Experiment with the value 1.01 , observe how increasing/decreasing this value affect the animation speed .

```python
# growing square
import pygame


# frames per second to control speed
fps = 50

# Define some colors
white = (255, 255, 255)
red = (255, 0, 0)

# A clock instance so we can control frames per second fps
clock = pygame.time.Clock()

# initialize display surface
screen = pygame.display.set_mode((500, 500))
pygame.display.set_caption("Growing square")

pygame.init()
# white background
screen.fill(white)

# intitial square side legnth
side = 50


# game infinite loop
loop = True
while loop:

    # if quit button press event quit
    for event in pygame.event.get():
        if event.type == pygame.QUIT:
            loop = 0

    pygame.draw.rect(screen, red, (250, 250, side, side))
    # update frame
    pygame.display.update()

    # update fps frames per second
    clock.tick(fps)

    side = 1.01 * side
    # clear screen
    screen.fill(white)



pygame.quit()
```

Output snapshots:

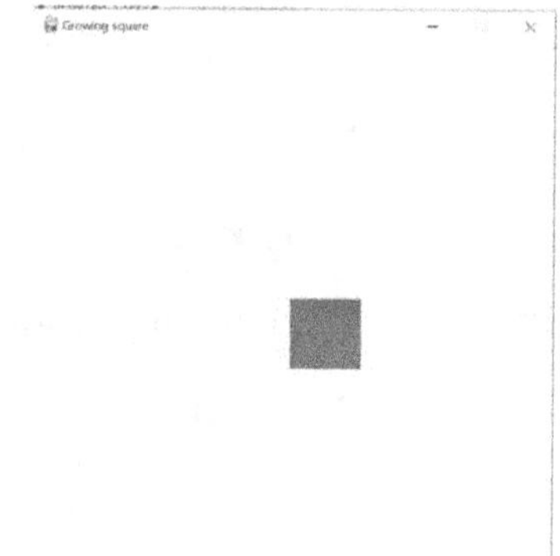
Growing square

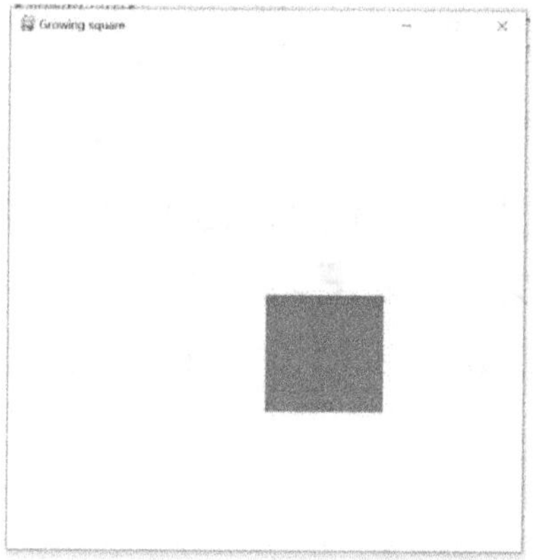
Growing square

Growing square

Growing square

Growing circle

This example is very similar to growing square example. Except that we draw a circle instead of square and increase the radius instead of side length.

```
# growing circle
import pygame


#  frames per second
fps = 50

# Define some colors
white = (255, 255, 255)
red = (255, 0, 0)

# A clock instance so we can control frames per second fps
clock = pygame.time.Clock()

# initialize display surface
screen = pygame.display.set_mode((500, 500))
pygame.display.set_caption("Growing circle")

pygame.init()
# white background
screen.fill(white)

# game infinite loop
loop = True

# intitial circle radius
rad = 50

while loop:

    # if quit button press event quit
    for event in pygame.event.get():
        if event.type == pygame.QUIT:
            loop = 0

    pygame.draw.circle(screen, red, (250, 250), rad)
    # update frame
    pygame.display.update()

    # update fps frames per second
    clock.tick(fps)

    rad = 1.01 * rad
    # clear screen
    screen.fill(white)

pygame.quit()
```

Output snapshots:

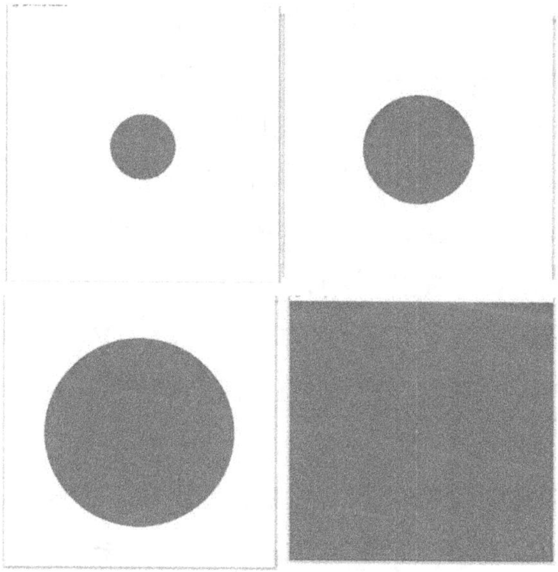

Moving a ball in different direction

In this example we move a ball in 4 different directions using move_right, move_left, move_up, and move_down functions.
The logic is similar to previous examples, instead of growing shape size every frame we 'grow' object position each time.
The ball starts in the center and keeps moving until it hits border where restarts from center again.
move_right() function works by updating the ball coordinates. The function does not take any inputs because it accesses x and y directly in the global scope because x and y are defined as a global variable.
With each function call the x coordinate is incremented by step size of 2 pixels. The step size determines how smooth the shape moves. The function makes sure the ball is near border by never incrementing x beyond 480. The background surface size is 500. If x > 480 the ball position is reset to center.

```
# global x and y so it have access to outer x and y
# right function
def move_right():
    global x,y

    # if ball is near border reset to center
    if x < 480:
        x = x + 2
    else:
        x = 250
        y = 250
```

Other function move_left, move_up, and move_down functions are implemented similarly but with changing whether x and y is incremented and detecting a different border. Read the code below carefully and try to understand it .

```
# moving ball
import pygame


#  frames per second
fps = 50

# Define some colors
white = (255, 255, 255)
red = (255, 0, 0)

# A clock instance so we can control frames per second fps
clock = pygame.time.Clock()

# initialize display surface
screen = pygame.display.set_mode((500, 500))
pygame.display.set_caption("moving ball")

pygame.init()
# white background
screen.fill(white)

# initial ball position at center
x = 250
y = 250


# global x and y so it have access to outer x and y
# right function
def move_right():
    global x,y

    # if ball is near border reset to center
    if x < 480:
        x = x + 2
    else:
        x = 250
        y = 250

```

```
# move left
def move_left():
    global x,y

    # if ball is near border reset to center
    if x > 20:
        x = x - 2
    else:
        x = 250
        y = 250

# move up
def move_up():
    global x,y

    # if ball is near border reset to center
    if y > 20:
        y = y - 2
    else:
        x = 250
        y = 250

# move down
def move_down():
    global x,y

    # if ball is near border reset to center
    if y < 480:
        y = y + 2
    else:
        x = 250
        y = 250


# game infinite loop
loop = True

```

```

while loop:

    # if quit button press event quit
    for event in pygame.event.get():
        if event.type == pygame.QUIT:
            loop = False

    pygame.draw.circle(screen, red, (x, y), 20)
    # update frame
    move_right()
    pygame.display.update()
    # update fps frames per second
    clock.tick(fps)

    # clear screen
    screen.fill(white)

pygame.quit()
```

Output snapshots:
Moving right

Example 4 Bouncing ball

In this program we create a ball that keep bouncing off borders.

What does it mean for a ball to bounce off border?

Earlier we kept moving the ball by incrementing/decrementing its x and y position by a unit step.

In moving the ball right, we incremented x by 1, while we decremented x by 1 to move it to left. So, to bounce the ball of a given border we need to detect which border it is hitting and increment or decrement the right coordinate x or y.

In bounce function,

```
stepx = -1 * stepx    , flip x direction if right or left borders touched
stepy = -1 * stepy    , flip y direction if top or bottom borders touched
```

These lines keep flipping the corresponding coordinate whenever a border is touched.

```
# bouncing ball
import pygame
import random


#  frames per second
fps = 50

# Define some colors
white = (255, 255, 255)
red = (255, 0, 0)

# A clock instance so we can control frames per second fps
clock = pygame.time.Clock()

# initialize display surface
screen = pygame.display.set_mode((500, 500))
pygame.display.set_caption("bouncing ball")

pygame.init()
# white background
screen.fill(white)

# initial ball position is random
x = random.randint(0, 500)
y = random.randint(0, 500)
stepx = 1
stepy = 1

# global x , y , stepx and stepy so it have access to outer variables
```

```
# bounce function
def bounce():
    global stepx, stepy, x, y

    # right border and left bounce then make horizontal step negative
    if x > 480 or x < 20:
        stepx = -1 * stepx

    # top border and bottom border bounce then make vertical step negativ
    if y > 480 or y < 20:
        stepy = -1 * stepy

    # update x and y
    x += stepx
    y += stepy


# game infinite loop
loop = True

while loop:

    # if quit button press event quit
    for event in pygame.event.get():
        if event.type == pygame.QUIT:
            loop = False

    pygame.draw.circle(screen, red, (x, y), 20)
    # update frame
    bounce()
    pygame.display.update()
    # update fps frames per second
    clock.tick(fps)

    # clear screen
    screen.fill(white)

pygame.quit()
```

Output snapshots:

Bouncing off the top border.

bouncing ball

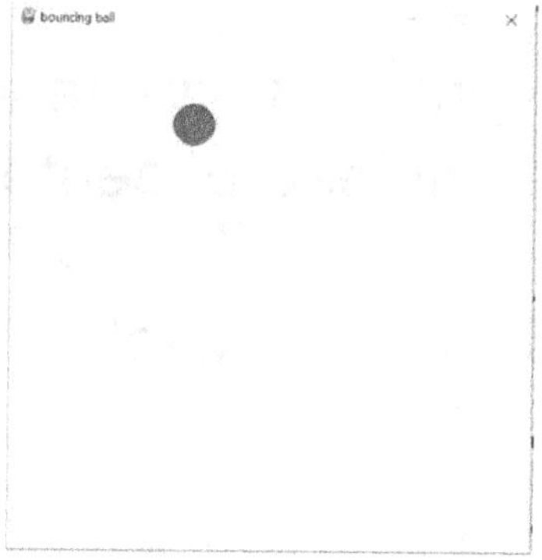
bouncing ball

Practice Problems

1. Modify the growing square so it grows form top left corner instead of center.

2. Make a blinking red circle at center that blinks every 2 seconds.

3. Create a shrinking circle, where it starts at radius equal to window size and shrinks to radius 10.

4. Create 2 bouncing balls where they bounce off borders and also bounce of each other if they collide. Hint: in bounce function check for the distance between balls, if close enough trigger a bounce.

Handling Keypress and Mouse Click events

Pygame deal with user inputs mainly using pygame.event module. pygame.event listens and register all events that comes from a keyboard or mouse.Every time event happen an event object is created to record it.
In fact, we have been using pygame.event several times in our programs.
In this snippet, in game loop we continuously check for any new events pygame.event.
`pygame.event.get()` returns a list of events that occurred since the last `pygame.event.get()` call.
When the quit button is pressed pygame.event registers this event as event with a type pygame.QUIT .
So we loop through all events and check if any of the events type is pygame.QUIT if so we set loop variable to false to quit the loop in next iteration.

```
# game infinite loop
loop = True
while loop:

    # if quit button press event quit
    for event in pygame.event.get():
        if event.type == pygame.QUIT:
            loop = False
```

To read more about pygame events refer to this link : http://man.hubwiz.com/docset/PyGame.docset/Contents/Resources/Documents/ref/event.html

This table show some of common pygame.event constant and their attributes.

Constant name	Attributes
QUIT	none
ACTIVEEVENT	gain, state
KEYDOWN	, key, mod
KEYUP	key, mod
MOUSEMOTION	pos, rel, buttons
MOUSEBUTTONUP	pos, button
MOUSEBUTTONDOWN	pos, button

Keyboard events

KEYUP and KEYDOWN events have attribute key constants representing keyboard keys.

Using capital k followed by underscore and key name ,

For example F1 is K_F1, w is K_w.

In this snippet, we check when a key is pressed down using pygame.KEYDOWN , we check what arrow key is pressed down and print a message for key name .

```
for event in pygame.event.get():
    if event.type == pygame.QUIT:
        pygame.quit()
    elif event.type == pygame.KEYDOWN:
        if event.key == pygame.K_UP:
            print("Player moved up!")
        elif event.key == pygame.K_LEFT:
            print("Player moved left!")
        elif event.key == pygame.K_DOWN:
            print("Player moved down!")
        elif event.key == pygame.K_RIGHT:
            print("Player moved right!")
```

To read all key binding, read pygame keys documentation on https://www.pygame.org/docs/ref/key.html

Mouse events

There are there types of mouse events in pygame .

MOUSEBUTTONDOWN, MOUSEBUTTONUP , and MOUSEMOTION.

MOUSEBUTTONUP , and MOUSEMOTION are received when user presses or moves a mouse.

They have attributes:

Button : 1 for left button , 2 for mouse wheel and 3 for right button .

Pos : Mouse absolute position of mouse (x,y) when button is pressed

MOUSEMOTION is received when user mouse moves, it has 3 attributes

Buttons : tuple of mouse button pressed or not (left, mouse wheel, right)

Pos : absolute cursor position (x,y) in pxels

Rel: position relative to previous position (relative_x, relative_y)

In this example we used to detect mouse using the three discusse mouse attributes .

```
# detect mouse actions

for event in pygame.event.get():
    if event.type == pygame.QUIT:
        pygame.quit()
    elif event.type == pygame.MOUSEMOTION:
        if event.rel[0] > 0:  # 'rel' is a tuple (x, y). 'rel[0]' is the x-value.
            print("Moving the mouse to the right")
        elif event.rel[1] > 0:  # pygame origin is at top left corner so higher y-val mean it further down.
            print("Moving the mouse down")
    elif event.type == pygame.MOUSEBUTTONDOWN:
        if event.button == 1:
            print("Left mouse button pressed")
        elif event.button == 3:
            print("Right mouse button pressed")
    elif event.type == pygame.MOUSEBUTTONUP:
        print("Mouse button released")
```

Example 1 : Moving Square

In this example we implement a moving square similar to past chapter but it moves by keyboard keys instead. We detect event of type pygame KEYDOWN then we check for event.

```
import pygame
import sys
pygame.init()
fps=30
fpsclock=pygame.time.Clock()
surface=pygame.display.set_mode((500, 500))
pygame.display.set_caption("Moving square")
White=(255,255,255)
x=10
y=10
step=5
while True:
    surface.fill(White)
    pygame.draw.rect(surface, (255,0,0), (x, y, 70, 65))
    for event in pygame.event.get():
        if event.type==pygame.QUIT:
            pygame.quit()
            sys.exit()
        elif event.type == pygame.KEYDOWN:
            if event.key == pygame.K_LEFT:
                x -= step
            elif event.key == pygame.K_UP:
                y -= step
            elif event.key == pygame.K_RIGHT:
                x += step
            elif event.key == pygame.K_DOWN:
                y += step

    pygame.display.update()
    fpsclock.tick(fps)
```

Moving

Example : Moving Square by Mouse .

In this example we let the square follow the mouse by updating the square position with the mouse cursor position.We access mouse cursor position pygame. MOUSEMOTION , mouse x position is event.pos[0] and y position is event.pos[y].We also change the color of square if mouse left button is clicked using pygame.MOUSEBUTTONUP.

```
import pygame
import sys
pygame.init()
fps=30
fpsclock=pygame.time.Clock()
surface=pygame.display.set_mode((500, 500))
pygame.display.set_caption("Moving square by mouse")
White=(255,255,255)
Black = (0, 0, 0)
red = (255, 0, 0)
x=10
y=10
step=5
color = red
while True:
    surface.fill(White)
    pygame.draw.rect(surface, color, (x, y, 70, 65))
    for event in pygame.event.get():
        if event.type==pygame.QUIT:
            pygame.quit()
            sys.exit()
        elif event.type == pygame.MOUSEMOTION:        # detect mouse motion
            # assign x,y to cursor positon
            x,y = event.pos[0], event.pos[1]          # move square to mouse location
        elif event.type == pygame.MOUSEBUTTONDOWN:
            if event.button == 1:                     # while left clicked square color is black else red
                color = Black
        elif event.type == pygame.MOUSEBUTTONUP:
            if event.button == 1:
                color = red


    pygame.display.update()
    fpsclock.tick(fps)
```

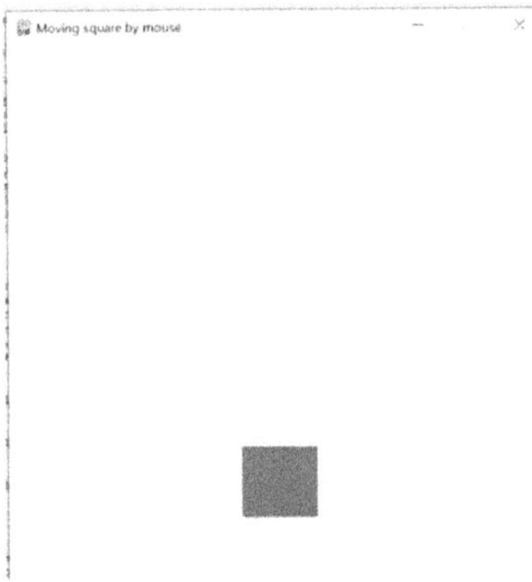

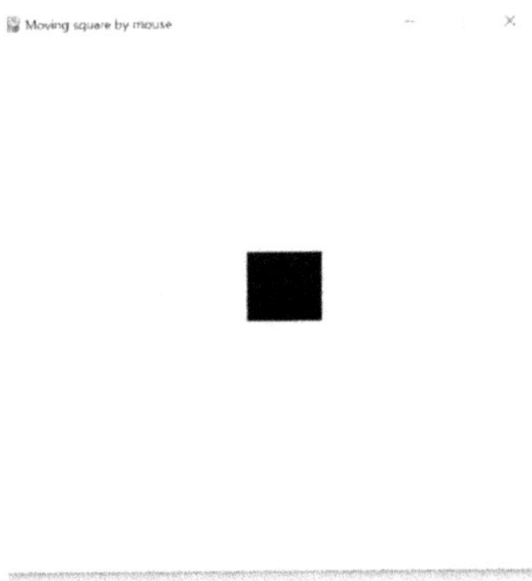

Practice Problems

1. Write a program of moving ball by following mouse cursor. When left mouse button is clicked the ball keeps growing. When right mouse button is clicked the ball shrinks.

2. Make hidden treasure seeker game, where once the mouse clicks at a specific hidden 10x10 square it change color to red and prints treasure found.

3. Make a signaling traffic light.

4. Implement a ball that bounces when space bar is clicked.

Pong game

This game builds on “Bouncing Ball” game discussed earlier. The game consists of a paddle moving horizontally on floor and a bouncing ball bouncing of the game window borders. Player moves the paddle so to bounce the ball up never letting it touch the ‘ground’. Player moves the paddle by pointing the mouse to intended direction. In the game loop, infinite loop, ball is moves using move_ball() function which updates the ball position .Then , we draw the ball at its new location and move the paddle to where the mouse pointer points. We update display at fps frame per second. Fps is set at 80 frame per second. We can make the game more challenging/faster by increasing this number.

It is always a good idea to read any game code in a top down approach, starting first at the main game loop getting high level idea about how the game operates. Then delving into functions definitions and understanding them one by on. The snippet below is our game loop.

Now that you have a high-level idea about the game you can read the complete program. The code is well commented for the ease of reading.

```
# pong game
import pygame
from random import choice

# Game frames per second to control game speed
fps = 80

# Define some colors
white = (255, 255, 255)
black = (0, 0, 0)
red = (255, 0, 0)
green = (0, 255, 0)

# initial ball coordinates
x_ball = 500
y_ball = 300

# direction to capture where the ball is heading
horizontal_direction = 'left'
vertical_direction = 'down'

# Eachtime ball is server, score is incremented
score = 0

# The step where ball postion is updated
step = 2

# A clock instance so we can control frames per second fps
clock = pygame.time.Clock()

# initialize display surface
screen = pygame.display.set_mode((500, 500))
pygame.display.set_caption("Pong game")

pygame.init()

```

```
while loop:
    # detect pressed keys
    keys = pygame.key.get_pressed()

    # if quit button press event quit
    for event in pygame.event.get():
        if event.type == pygame.QUIT:
            loop = 0
    # get mouse pointer coordinates
    x, y = pygame.mouse.get_pos()

    # move the ball by a step
    move_ball()
    # draw ball
    ball()
    # draw paddle at mouse x coordinate
    paddle(x,490)
    # is the ball served
    served()
    # update frame
    pygame.display.update()
    # white background
    screen.fill(white)
    # update fps frames per second
    clock.tick(fps)



pygame.quit()
```

```
        # if ball is near right border reflect left
        if x_ball > 480:
            horizontal_direction = "left"


# function to detect serving the ball by paddle
def served():
    global x_ball, y_ball # ball x and y
    global x, y           # paddle x, y
    global horizontal_direction, vertical_direction, step
    global score

    # detect if ball is heading to paddle
    if horizontal_direction == "left":
        if y_ball > 480:

            # ball is touching the paddle
            if x_ball >= x and  x_ball < x + 50:
                print("Good job")
                # increment score
                score += 1
                # flip direction
                vertical_direction = "up"
                step = 1

            # if ball missed reset ball coordinates and decrement score
            else:
                pygame.draw.circle(screen, black, (x_ball, y_ball), 10, 10)
                pygame.display.update()
                x_ball, y_ball = 500, 300
                score -= 1

        # print score in caption
        pygame.display.set_caption(f"Your score is: {score}")

```

Output:

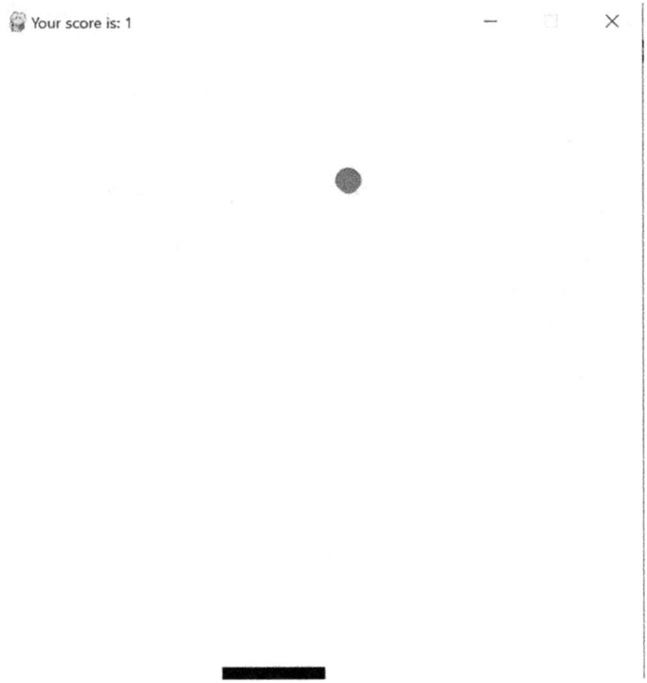

Practice Problems

1. After playing with pong game. You probably observed that when balls reset position, it always starts from the same position. Make a function that resets the ball at different random position each time it reset.

2.In Pong game, edit the code so you can use keyboard arrows to move the paddle.

3.In Pong game, implement a second player with a paddle on the top border. Each player must have his own score.

Conclusion

Congrats on getting through to the end of this book. You are definitely on the right track.

If you'd like a more beginner friendly version of this book, you can download my Coding for Kids and Beginners using Python.

If you're more interested in JavaScript, you can download my Coding for Kids Ages 9-15 and Coding for Kids Ages 10 and Up

Other Recommended Books for further reading:

Python Crash Course

Automate the Boring Stuff with Python

Learn Python Quickly

Free Gift

We do want you to succeed in coding. To ensure your success, we are giving you a free list of projects that you can work on once you are completed with this book.

https://coding.gr8.com/

www.ingramcontent.com/pod-product-compliance
Lightning Source LLC
LaVergne TN
LVHW052206200926
848481LV00001B/42
9781922659637